IMMIGRATION
LAW
AND PRACTICE

LAWRENCE GRANT LL.B.
Solicitor

IAN MARTIN
General Secretary
Joint Council for the Welfare of Immigrants

The Cobden Trust
LONDON: 1982

The Cobden Trust
21 Tabard Street
London SE1 4LA

Copyright © The Cobden Trust,
Lawrence Grant and
Ian Martin
1982

ISBN 0 900137 18 5 (paper)
0 900137 19 3 (cased)

PRINTED AND BOUND IN GREAT BRITAIN
at The Camelot Press Ltd, Southampton

Preface

The purpose of this book is to provide a practical guide for those advising in the field of immigration law. We hope that the book fills a gap in an area of law and practice in which a growing number of practitioners are attempting to respond to ever increasing difficulties and complexities. Our view of the causes of these difficulties are made clear in the final chapter.

The text of this book was already in preparation when changes in the immigration rules were proposed in November 1979 and brought into effect in March 1980. As it goes to press the British Nationality Act has been enacted, although it is still likely to be some time before consequential changes in the immigration rules are laid before Parliament and the Act brought into effect. There is no perfect moment to bring revision to an end. We have made the text as up-to-date as possible, and hope to be able to publish annual supplements. We would welcome criticism or suggestions for improvements.

We have tried to place emphasis on the practice of immigration control by including information which cannot be gleaned from a study of the Immigration Act or rules or appeal decisions. We have therefore, where it is known to us, set out current Home Office policy; this has been ascertained mainly from parliamentary answers and correspondence with the Home Office. There is a risk that policy may change without our being aware. Nevertheless, we regard the information as sufficiently valuable as to make the risk worthwhile.

This book has been a joint venture but one which could not have been achieved without the help and encouragement of many people. In particular we would like to thank the following for their valued criticism and advice: David Burgess, Maureen Connolly, Clement Richards JP, Richard Stewart and colleagues at the Joint Council for the Welfare of Immigrants. Any opinions expressed are however our own and any errors which appear in the text must be laid at our door. We are grateful for the assistance provided by Mr. P. G. Bailey, Secretary to the Immigration Appeal Tribunal, and by the staff at Thanet House, particularly Mrs Bridie O'Connor.

We would also like to express our gratitude to Caroline Holmes who has bravely tackled the manuscript and coped with our many last minute additions and deletions; to Geoff Wilkins who prepared the index; to Jonathan Harris and Charlotte Ritchie who have provided us with invaluable help in preparation of the footnotes; to Nina Dzaidel and Sue Mellors who typed and retyped the many drafts this book has been through in its long period of gestation; and to Charles Foster and Sarah Spencer of the Cobden Trust not only for their advice and assistance in bringing this book to fruition, but also for their patience.

We join the trustees of the Cobden Trust in thanking the Allen Lane Foundation for their financial contribution to the Trust, which enabled us to undertake the necessary research for this book.

The law stated is that in force on 30 June 1981 except as otherwise indicated.

London *Lawrence Grant*
November 1981 *Ian Martin*

Contents

PREFACE	v
TABLE OF CASES	
Reported	xiii
Unreported	xxiv
TABLE OF STATUTES	xxvii
TABLE OF STATUTORY INSTRUMENTS	xxxiii

1. **THE SCHEME OF IMMIGRATION CONTROL**
   - History of immigration control — 1
   - General scheme of the Immigration Act 1971 — 5
   - Immigration rules — 7
   - Instructions to immigration officials — 11
   - Appeal procedures — 12
   - Future changes — 13

2. **NATIONALITY AND PATRIALITY**
   - Introduction: patrials and the right of abode — 14
   - Nationality law background — 15
   - British Nationality Act 1948 — 16
   - Citizenship of the UK and Colonies — 16
     - *Acquisition of citizenship of UK and Colonies* — 17
     - *Loss of UK citizenship* — 23
     - *Resumption of UK citizenship* — 24
   - Citizens of the Republic of Ireland — 25
   - British subjects and Commonwealth citizens — 25
   - British protected persons — 27
   - Aliens — 27
   - Patriality — 28
   - Patrial citizens of UK and Colonies — 29
   - Patrial Commonwealth citizens — 32
   - Loss of patriality — 32
   - Patrials and the EEC — 33
   - Patrials and entry to the UK — 34
   - A note on the British Nationality Act 1981 — 37

3. SPECIAL PROVISIONS FOR NON-PATRIALS
   EEC nationals   41
      The Immigration Rules   43
   Citizens of the Republic of Ireland   44
   Non-patrial UK passport holders   44
      Special voucher scheme   44
   Representatives of overseas governments   48
   Military personnel   50
   Seamen and aircrew   51
   Commonwealth residents returning from Europe   51
4. THE COMMON TRAVEL AREA
   General principles   53
   Exclusion from provisions   55
   Restrictions on entry from Republic of Ireland   56
   Landing and embarkation cards   57
5. ENTERING THE UK
   General considerations   58
   Documents needed on entry   58
      Passport   58
      Landing card   59
      Entry clearance   59
      Failure to provide satisfactory clearance   62
      Work permit   65
   General grounds for refusing entry   67
   Powers and duties of immigration officers at port of entry   74
   Penalties for not co-operating   77
   Powers and duties of medical inspectors   77
   Examination: approach to be taken by immigration officers   78
   Decision: giving or refusing leave to enter   80
   Detention of passengers   82
      Release pending a decision   83
   Removal from the UK   84
   Right of appeal   85
   Responsibilities of shipping companies and airlines   86
   Advice to those assisting entrants   87
   Procedure for obtaining entry clearance   88
      Queue in the Indian sub-continent   88
      How to make an application   90
      Powers and duties of entry clearance officers   91
6. VISITORS AND STUDENTS
   Visitors   93

	Students	99
	Trainees	109
	Au pairs	110
7.	EMPLOYMENT AND BUSINESS	
	Taking employment	112
	Work permits	112
	Permit-free employment	118
	Commonwealth citizens with UK ancestry	121
	Working holidaymakers	121
	The old rules	122
	EEC nationals	122
	Businessmen and self-employed persons	122
	The old rules	125
	Writers and artists	127
	The old rules	128
	Persons of independent means	129
	The old rules	130
	Dependants of those admitted for work	131
	The old rules	132
	EEC nationals	132
	The immigration rules	136
8.	SETTLEMENT	
	Meaning of settlement	141
	Settlement in UK when Act came into force	142
	Qualifying for settlement under immigration rules	144
	Irrespective of nationality	144
	EEC nationals	145
	UK passport holders who are not patrial and dependants	145
	Refugees	145
	Freedom from internal control for those settled in UK	146
	Patriality and settlement	146
	Settlement of dependants	147
	General requirements for dependants of Commonwealth and non-EEC nationals	148
	Wives	148
	Children	155
	Parents and grandparents	164
	Other relatives	167
	The old rules	170
	Assistance by practitioners	171
	Settlement by marriage	173

		Husbands	173
		Fiancés	173
		Fiancées	177
		The old rules	178
	Returning residents		180
9.	REMAINING IN THE UK		
	Introduction		186
	General principles		187
	Permission to work after entry		190
	Refusal of extensions of stay: right of appeal		191
	Taking employment after leave has expired		193
	Successive applications		194
	Leaving the UK		195
		Leaving the UK while appeal pending	196
	Abandoning the application		198
	Remaining after application finally refused		199
	Advising those applying for extensions		202
	The old rules		204
	Registration with the police		205
	Travel documents		208
10.	CRIMINAL OFFENCES		
	Introduction		210
	Disregarding requirements of immigration control		211
	Powers of police and immigration officers		214
	Assisting illegal entry and harbouring		216
	Failing to co-operate with or misleading the immigration authorities		217
	Illegal entrants and the criminal law		220
11.	DEPORTATION		
	General rules		221
	Procedure on deportation		224
	Effect of deportation order		227
	Considerations in making a deportation order		228
		Breach of conditions	229
		Conducive to the public good	232
		Security cases	238
		Family deportation	240
		Recommendation by the court	243
	Signing of deportation order		248
	Revocation of deportation order		248
	Other forms of departure		250

	Exclusion and deportation of EEC nationals	252
	Appeals	255
	Repatriation	257
12.	REMOVAL OF ILLEGAL ENTRANTS	
	Illegal entry by deception	260
	Amnesties for illegal entrants	265
13.	DETENTION AND RELEASE	
	On seeking leave to enter	268
	Bail	270
	Temporary admission	274
	Illegal entrants	276
	Temporary release	276
	Habeas corpus	277
	Criminal offences	279
	Before sentence	279
	After sentence	280
	Following a decision to deport	283
	Following the making of a deportation order	284
	Seamen and Aircrew	285
14.	APPEALS	
	What decisions can be appealed against	286
	Limited right of appeal	286
	No right of appeal	287
	Appellate authorities	287
	Starting an appeal	288
	Limitations on right of appeal	289
	Appeals against exclusion	289
	Appeals against variation	291
	Appeals against deportation	292
	Time limit for appealing	292
	Notice of appeal	295
	Reasons for decision: explanatory statement	297
	Fixing a date for the appeal	298
	Objections by immigration authorities	299
	Determination of appeal without hearing	300
	Powers and duties of adjudicators	301
	Determination of appeals	301
	Reviewing the evidence	302
	Appeals to tribunals from adjudicators	305
	Right of appeal	305
	Powers of the tribunal	306

	Procedure on appeal	307
	References by the Home Secretary	310
	General rules of procedure: adjudicator and tribunal	310
	Procedure at the hearing	313
	Second identical appeals	315
	Withdrawal of appeals	316
	Hearing appeals in absence of parties	316
	General powers	316
	The decision	316
	Time limits	317
	Service of notices of documents	317
	Application for judicial review	317
	The European Court of Justice	319
	The European Commission of Human Rights and the European Court of Human Rights	320
15.	REFUGEE STATUS AND POLITICAL ASYLUM	
	Refugee status in international law	322
	Refugee status and political asylum	323
	Status of refugees under UK law	323
	Determining who is a refugee	325
	Applications for political asylum	327
	Appeals	330
	Granting of asylum	333
	Travel documents	334
	Transfer of asylum	335
	Loss of refugee status	336
	Stateless persons	337
16.	PREVENTION OF TERRORISM ACT	
	Exclusion orders	339
	Controls at the port of entry	343
17.	CONCLUSION	347
	APPENDICES	
	A note on 'recourse to public funds'	357
	Immigration certificates and endorsements on passports	362
	Detention under Immigration Act 1971	380
	Immigration appeals machinery	385
	Agencies advising immigrants	393
	Some useful addresses and telephone numbers	398
	INDEX	403

Table of Cases

REPORTED CASES

A (an infant), Re [1963] 1 All ER 531; [1963] 1 WLR 231   **2.10**
A (an infant) Re, Hanif v *Secretary of State for Home Affairs.* See Mohamed Arif (an infant) Re
Abdullah, Entry clearance officer, Lahore v [1973] Imm AR 57   **14.32, 14.34**
Aftab Miah v *Secretary of State for the Home Department* [1972] Imm AR 185   **8.35**
Afza Mussarat v *Secretary of State for the Home Department* [1972] Imm AR 45   **8.24**
Agee v *Rt Hon R. K. Murray* (1977) SLT (Notes) 54   **1.17**
Ahluwalia, ex parte, R v *Immigration Appeal Tribunal* [1979–80] Imm AR 1   **9.16, 11.7**
Ahmed v *Entry Clearance Officer, Islam* [1977] Imm AR 25   **14.58**
Akhtar Jan v *Entry Clearance Officer, Islamabad* [1977] Imm AR 107   **14.61**
Akhtar, ex parte, R v *Secretary of State for the Home Department* [1975] 3 All ER 1087; [1975] WLR 1717   **2.49**
Akhtar, ex parte, R v *Secretary of State for the Home Department* [1980] 2 All ER 735; [1980] 3 WLR 302, CA   **2.22, 12.6**
Ali v *Ali* [1908] P 564; [1966] 1 All ER 604; [1966] 2 WLR 620   **8.25**
Ali (Aisha Khatoon), ex parte, R v *Immigration Appeal Tribunal* [1979–80] Imm AR 195   **8.67**
Ali (DM) v *Immigration Appeal Tribunal* [1973] Imm AR 33, CA   **11.9, 11.13, 15.13**
Ali (MMH) v *Secretary of State for the Home Department* [1978] Imm AR 126   **11.12**
Al Abbas v *Secretary of State for the Home Department* [1979–80] Imm AR 189   **9.12**
Ally, Secretary of State for the Home Department v [1972] Imm AR 258   **7.35**
Altaf, Visa Officer, Islamabad v [1979–80] Imm AR 141   **14.33**
Al Tuwaidjii v *Chief Immigration Officer, London (Heathrow) Airport* [1974] Imm AR 34   **5.21**
Amer v *Secretary of State for the Home Department* [1979–80] Imm AR 87   **6.25**
Amin, ex parte, R v *Entry Clearance Officer, Bombay* [1980] 2 All ER 837; [1980] 1 WLR 1536   **3.12, 14.3**
Amusu, Entry Clearance Officer, Lagos v [1974] Imm AR 16   **6.22**
Anand v *Secretary of State for the Home Department* [1978] Imm AR 36   **11.33**
Ancharaz v *Immigration Officer, London (Heathrow) Airport* [1976] Imm AR 49   **14.59**
Andronicou v *Chief Immigration Officer, London (Heathrow) Airport* [1974] Imm AR 87   **5.9**
Apt v *Apt* [1948] P 83; [1947] 2 All ER 677, CA   **8.27**
Armstrong, ex parte, R v *Immigration Appeal Tribunal* [1977] Imm AR 80   **14.42**

TABLE OF CASES

Arshad v *Immigration Officer, London (Heathrow) Airport* [1977] Imm AR 19   **5.12, 8.20**
Ashraf, Visa Officer, Cairo v [1979–80] Imm AR 45   **14.34**
Awadallah, Visa Officer, Jerusalem v [1978] Imm AR 5   **5.21, 5.25**
Ayettey v *Secretary of State for the Home Department* [1972] Imm AR 261   **6.23**
Azam v *Secretary of State for the Home Department* [1974] AC 18; [1973] 2 WLR 1058; [1973] 2 All ER 765, HL   **8.4, 12.9**
 affirmed sub nom R v *Governor of Pentonville Prison, ex parte Azam* [1973] 2 WLR 949; [1973] 2 All ER 741   **13.7**
B (GA) (an infant), Re [1964] Ch 1; [1963] 3 All ER 125; [1963] 3 WLR 471   **8.36**
B (an infant), Re [1968] Ch 204; [1967] 3 All ER 629; [1967] 3 WLR 1438   **8.41**
Badaike, ex parte, R v *Secretary of State for the Home Department*, (1977) *Times* 4 May   **3.15, 5.41, 12.8**
Bahadur Singh, ex parte R v *Immigration Appeal Tribunal* [1976] Imm AR 143   **14.15**
Baidwan (IK), Entry Clearance Officer, New Delhi v [1975] Imm AR 126   **8.46, 8.50**
Baijal v *Secretary of State for the Home Department* [1976] Imm AR 34   **7.24**
Baker (GL) Ltd v *Medway Building Supplies Ltd* [1958] 2 All ER 532; [1958] 1 WLR 1216   **14.8**
Balbir Singh, ex parte, R v *Immigration Appeal Tribunal* [1978] Imm AR 641   **9.12**
Balbir Singh v *Secretary of State for the Home Department and Immigration Appeal Tribunal* [1978] Imm AR 204, CA   **14.12**
Bano v *Secretary of State for the Home Department* [1973] Imm AR 41   **8.45**
Bashir v *Immigration Officer, Dover* [1976] Imm AR 96   **8.66**
Bassoum, ex parte R v *Eastbourne J J* [1979] CLY, 488   **10.2**
Bater v *Bater* [1951] P35   **15.14**
Bernard v *Entry Clearance Officer, Hong Kong* [1976] Imm AR 7   **8.40**
Bhagat Singh v *Entry Clearance Officer, New Delhi*, [1978] Imm AR 134   **6.5**
Bhambra, Entry Clearance Officer, New Delhi v [1973] Imm AR 14   **6.5, 6.18, 14.36**
Bhanji, ex parte, R v *Immigration Appeal Adjudicator* [1977] Imm AR 89, CA   **14.12**
Bhatti, Immigration Officer, London (Heathrow) Airport v [1979–80] Imm AR 86   **5.21**
Bi (Alam), ex parte, R v *Immigration Appeal Tribunal* [1979–80] Imm AR 146, CA   **14.41**
Birdi v *Secretary of State for Home Affairs* (1975) *Times* 12 February; (1975) 119 Sol J 322; CA   **12.9**
Bonsignore: Case 67/74 [1975] 1 CMLR 472   **11.54**
Brown v *Entry Clearance Officer, Kingston, Jamaica* [1976] Imm AR 119   **5.55**
Brooks v *Waldren* (1963) *Times*, 4 October; [1963] Crim LR 864   **11.37**
Butt v *Secretary of State for the Home Department* [1979–80] Imm AR 82   **11.20**
C (an infant) v *Entry Clearance Officer, Hong Kong* [1976] Imm AR 165   **7.22**
Carltona Ltd v *Commissioners of Works* [1943] 2 All ER 560   **9.2**
Chagpar v *Secretary of State for the Home Department* [1972] Imm AR 137   **5.10**
Channo Bi, Visa Officer, Islamabad v [1978] Imm AR 182   **14.51**
Chetti v *Chetti* (1909) P 67; [1908–10] All ER 49   **8.23**
Chiew, ex parte, R v *Immigration Appeal Tribunal* (1981) *Times* 10 June   **7.40**
Chile, Two Citizens of, Secretary of State for the Home Department v [1977] Imm AR 36   **15.4, 15.14**
Choudary, ex parte, R v *Secretary of State for the Home Department* [1978] 3 All ER 790; [1978] 1 WLR 1177, CA   **12.3, 13.17**
Chulvi v *Secretary of State for the Home Department* [1976] Imm AR 133   **7.12**
Cicutti v *Suffolk CC* [1980] 3 All ER 689   **8.3**

TABLE OF CASES

Claveria v *Immigration Officer, London (Heathrow) Airport* [1978] Imm AR 176   **5.11**
Cooray, Immigration Officer, Ramsgate v [1974] Imm AR 38   **14.8, 14.32**
Costa v *Secretary of State for the Home Department* [1974] Imm AR 69   **8.70**
Csenyi v *Secretary of State for the Home Department* [1975] Imm AR 92   **11.45**
Derrick v *Secretary of State for the Home Department* [1972] Imm AR 109   **11.23**
Dervish v *Secretary of State for the Home Department* [1972] Imm AR 48   **11.44**
Dey v *Entry Clearance Officer, Dacca* [1975] Imm AR 142   **6.20**
Din v *Entry Clearance Officer, New Delhi* [1978] Imm AR 56   **6.8, 11.5**
Doeve, ex parte, R v *East Grinstead JJ* [1969] 1 QB 136; [1968] 2 All ER 666; [1969] 3 WLR 920   **11.48**
Emmanuel v *Secretary of State for the Home Department* [1972] Imm AR 69   **8.36**
Eugene v *Entry Clearance Officer, Bridgetown, Barbados* [1975] Imm AR 111   **8.36**
Farida Begum v *Immigration Officer, London (Heathrow) Airport* [1978] Imm AR 107   **5.11**
Fernandez v *Government of Singapore* [1971] 2 All ER 691; [1971] 1 WLR 987. HL   **15.14**
Fernandez ex parte, R v *Secretary of State for the Home Department* (1980) Times 21 November, CA   **11.39, 14.68**
Francis v *Secretary of State for the Home Department* [1972] Imm AR 162   **14.19**
Ghosh v *Entry Clearance Officer, Calcutta* [1976] Imm AR 60   **6.18, 6.20**
Giovanni v *Secretary of State for the Home Department* [1977] Imm AR 85   **7.57**
Glean, Secretary of State for the Home Department v (1972) Imm AR 84   **14.32**
Goffar v *Entry Clearance Officer, Dacca* [1975] Imm AR 142   **6.20**
Goodison v *Secretary of State for the Home Department* [1979–80] Imm AR 122   **8.67**
Grant v *Secretary of State for the Home Department* [1974] Imm AR 64   **7.24**
Greene, ex parte, R v *Secretary of State for the Home Department* [1974] 3 All ER 388   **13.15**
Grewal v *Secretary of State for the Home Department* [1979–80] Imm AR 119   **11.46**
Gunatilake v *Entry Clearance Officer, Colombo* [1975] Imm AR 23   **7.24**
Gupta v *Secretary of State for the Home Department* [1979–80] Imm AR 52   **3.14**
Gurdev Singh v *R* [1974] 1 All ER 26; [1973] 1 WLR 1444   **9.10, 10.5, 10.6**
HK (an infant), Re [1967] 2 QB 617; [1967] 1 All ER 226; [1967] 2 WLR 962   **5.38**
Halil v *Davidson* [1979–80] Imm AR 164, HL   **9.9, 9.16**
Haji v *Secretary of State for the Home Department* [1978] Imm AR 26   **7.35**
Hanks, Entry Clearance Officer, Colombo v [1976] Imm AR 74   **6.5**
Hardev Kaur v *Entry Clearance Officer, New Delhi* [1979–80] Imm AR 76   **8.54**
Harmail Singh v *Immigration Appeal Tribunal* [1978] Imm AR 140, CA   **8.52, 14.39**
Hasan (Bibi Musa) v *Entry Clearance Officer, Bombay* [1976] Imm AR 28   **8.45**
Hassan (Mohammed), Visa Officer, Karachi v [1978] Imm AR 168   **14.33**
Hazari, ex parte, R v *Chief Immigration Officer, London (Heathrow) Airport* (1975) Times 25 November; [1975] 120 Sol J 346, CA   **5.38**
Hessing v *Secretary of State for the Home Department* [1972] Imm AR 134   **8.28**
Holmes, Entry Clearance Officer, Jamaica v [1975] Imm AR 20   **8.38**
Home Office v *Commission for Racial Equality* [1981] 1 All ER 1042   **1.11**
Horne v *Gaygusuz* [1979] Crim LR 594   **10.5**
Hosenball, ex parte, R v *Secretary of State for the Home Department* [1977] 3 All ER 452; [1977] 1 WLR 776, CA   **1.16, 9.2, 11.28**
Howard v *Secretary of State for the Home Department* [1972] Imm AR 93   **8.38**
Huda v *Entry Clearance Officer, Dacca* [1976] Imm AR 109   **6.5, 14.34**
Hussain, ex parte, R v *Secretary of State* [1978] 2 All ER 427; [1978] 1 WLR 704, CA   **13.18**

Hussain (Shanaz), Visa Officer, Islamabad v [1978] Imm AR 103   **8.67**
Hyde v *Hyde and Woodmansee* 1866 LR1P and D 130; [1861–73] All ER 175   **8.23**
IRC v *Lysaght* [1928] AC 234; [1928] All ER 575, HL   **8.3, 8.69**
Ibrahim, ex parte, R v *Secretary of State for the Home Department* (1980) *Times* 29 March   **12.5**
Ibrahim v *Visa Officer, Islamabad* [1978] Imm AR 18   **8.33**
Immigration Appeal Tribunal v *Manek* [1978] Imm AR 131, CA   **8.20**
Insah Begum, ex parte, R v *Chief Immigration Officer, Manchester Airport* [1972] 1 All ER 594; [1973] 1 WLR 141   **5.41**
Iqbal Haque v *Entry Clearance Officer, Dacca* [1974] Imm AR 51   **8.35**
Ishiodu v *Entry Clearance Officer, Lagos* [1975] Imm AR 56   **8.24**
Jaspal Singh, ex parte, R v *Immigration Appeal Tribunal* [1977] Imm AR 105   **14.7**
Jeyaveerasingam, ex parte, R v *Immigration Appeal Tribunal* [1976] Imm AR 137   **14.37**
Joginder Kaur, Entry Clearance Officer, New Delhi v [1977] Imm AR 101   **8.48**
Jones, Secretary of State for the Home Department v [1978] Imm AR 161   **7.39**
Jordan v *Secretary of State for the Home Department* [1972] Imm AR 201   **11.15**
Joseph, Secretary of State for the Home Department v [1977] Imm AR 96   **7.35**
Joseph, ex parte, R v *Immigration Appeal Tribunal* [1977] Imm AR 70   **7.28, 7.31, 7.34**
Joshi, Entry Clearance Officer, Bombay v [1975] Imm AR 1   **8.69**
Juma v *Secretary of State for the Home Department* [1974] Imm AR 96   **6.25**
Kalsoom Begum, Visa Officer, Islamabad v [1978] Imm AR 206   **14.51**
Kassam v *Secretary of State for the Home Department* [1976] Imm AR 20   **14.55**
Kassam, ex parte, R v *Immigration Appeal Tribunal* [1980] 2 All ER 330; [1980] 1 WLR 1037, CA   **1.11**
Kelzani v *Secretary of State for the Home Department* [1978] Imm AR 193   **11.9**
Keshwani v *Secretary of State for the Home Department* [1975] Imm AR 38   **2.39**
Khan (Perween), ex parte, R v *Immigration Appeals Adjudicator* [1972] 3 All ER 297; [1972] 1 WLR 1058   **5.10, 6.17**
Khan (SGH), ex parte, R v *Immigration Appeal Tribunal* [1975] Imm AR 26   **6.19, 14.32**
Khan v *Secretary of State for the Home Department* [1977] 3 All ER 538; [1977] 1 WLR 1466, CA   **10.16, 12.5**
Khanom v *Entry Clearance Officer, Dacca* [1979–80] Imm AR 182   **8.22**
Kharrazi ex parte, R v *Chief Immigration Officer (Gatwick Airport)* [1980] 3 All ER 373, [1980] 1 WLR 1396, CA   **6.17, 6.25**
Kpoma v *Secretary of State for the Home Department* [1973] Imm AR 25   **6.25**
Kroohs v *Secretary of State for the Home Department* [1978] Imm AR 75   **11.9**
Kumar, Entry Clearance Officer, New Delhi v [1978] Imm AR 185   **6.7**
Lai, Entry Clearance Officer, Hong Kong v [1974] Imm AR 98   **6.7, 14.5**
Langridge v *Secretary of State for the Home Department* [1972] Imm AR 38   **5.25**
Levene v *IRC* [1928] AC 217; [1928] All ER 746, HL   **8.3**
Levy v *Entry Clearance Officer, Kingston, Jamaica* [1978] Imm AR 119   **8.49**
Liberto v *Immigration Officer, London (Heathrow) Airport* [1974] Imm AR 61   **5.25**
Lila ex parte, R v *Immigration Appeal Tribunal* [1978] Imm AR 50   **14.40**
Lubetkin v *Secretary of State for the Home Department* [1979–80] Imm AR 162   **9.10**
McBride v *Turnock* [1964] Crim LR 456   **10.15**
McGillivary v *Secretary of State for the Home Department* [1972] Imm AR 63   **8.36**
Malek, Visa Officer, Cairo v [1979–80] Imm AR 111   **6.9**
Malik v *Secretary of State for the Home Department* [1972] Imm AR 37   **8.42**

TABLE OF CASES xvii

Mangoo Khan, ex parte, R v *Secretary of State for the Home Department* [1980] 2 All ER 337; [1980] 1 WLR 549, CA **12.2**
Manmohan Singh v *Entry Clearance Officer, Bombay* [1975] Imm AR 118 **6.6**
Maqbool Hussain, ex parte, R v *Secretary of State for the Home Department* [1976] 1 WLR 97 **12.3**
Martin (SS), Entry Clearance Officer, Jamaica v [1978] Imm AR 100 **8.36**
Martin (JBS), ex parte, R v *Immigration Appeal Tribunal* [1972] Imm AR 275 **7.37**
Martin v *Secretary of State for the Home Department* [1972] Imm AR 69 **8.36**
Mathieu v *Entry Clearance Officer, Bridgetown* [1979–80] Imm AR 157 **8.31**
Mehmet, ex parte, R v *Immigration Appeal Tribunal* [1977] 2 All ER 602; [1977] 1 WLR 795 **11.6, 14.7, 14.8, 14.17**
Mehmet (AD) ex parte, R v *Secretary of State for the Home Department* [1977] Imm AR 68, CA **11.4**
Mehmet (Ekrem) (No. 2) ex parte, R v *Immigration Appeal Tribunal* [1978] Imm AR 46 **11.7, 11.30**
Mehta (BKD) v *Immigration Appeal Tribunal* [1979–80] Imm AR 16, CA **14.42**
Mehta (RP), ex parte, R v *Immigration Appeal Tribunal* [1975] 2 All ER 1084, [1975] 1 WLR 1087, CA **14.17**
Mehta (VM) ex parte, R v *Immigration Appeal Tribunal* [1976] Imm AR 174, CA **14.17**
Merchant v *Entry Clearance Officer, Bombay* [1975] Imm AR 49 **8.42**
Miah v *Secretary of State for the Home Department* [1972] Imm AR 185 **8.35**
Mohamed Arif (an infant), Re [1968] Ch 650; [1968] 2 WLR 1297 sub nom *Re A (an infant), Hanif* v *Secretary of State for Home Affairs* [1968] 2 All ER 149, CA **5.38**
Mohamed v *Knott* [1968] 2 All ER 503 **8.23**
Mohammed (AA) v *Secretary of State for the Home Department* [1979–80] Imm AR 103 **2.22**
Mohammed Zaman v *Entry Clearance Officer, Lahore* [1973] Imm AR 71 **8.45**
Moussa, Secretary of State for the Home Department v [1976] Imm AR 78 **9.21, 14.32**
Mughal, ex parte R v *Secretary of State for the Home Department* [1974] QB 313; [1973] 3 All ER 796; [1973] 3 WLR 647, CA **5.38, 8.7, 8.67**
Mukhopadyay v *Entry Clearance Officer, Calcutta* [1975] Imm AR 42 **8.49**
Munasinghe v *Secretary of State for the Home Department* [1975] Imm AR 79 **7.24**
Murgai v *Entry Clearance Officer, New Delhi* [1975] Imm AR 86 **6.21**
Musgrove v *Chun Teeong Toy* [1891] AC 272; **1.2**
Mustafa v *Secretary of State for the Home Department* [1979–80] Imm AR 32 **11.9**
Mustun v *Secretary of State for the Home Department* [1972] Imm AR 97 **5.10**
Muthulakshmi v *Secretary of State for the Home Department* [1972]K Imm AR 231 **14.19**
Myeen-ur-Rashid v *Entry Clearance Officer, Dacca* [1976] Imm AR 12 **6.17**
Nathwani, ex parte R v *Immigration Appeal Tribunal* [1979–80] Imm AR 9 **14.48**
Nazir Begum v *Entry Clearance Officer, Islamabad* [1976] Imm AR 31 **8.27**
Nicolaides v *Secretary of State for the Home Department* [1978] Imm AR 67 **9.21**
Nisa v *Secretary of State for the Home Department* [1979–80] Imm AR 20 **8.44**
Obavwana, ex parte R v *Inner London Crown Court* [1979] 69 Cr App R 125 **13.22**
Oberoi v *Secretary of State for the Home Department* [1979–80] Imm AR 175 **14.31**
Oh, Secretary of State for the Home Department v [1972] Imm AR 236 **6.18**
Osama v *Immigration Officer, (Gatwick Airport)* [1978] Imm AR 8 **5.27, 8.67**
Owusu v *Secretary of State for the Home Department* [1976] Imm AR 101 **6.9**
Ozter v *Secretary of State for the Home Department* [1978] Imm AR 137 **11.32**
Padmore v *Secretary of State for the Home Department* [1972] Imm AR 1 **14.55**

TABLE OF CASES

Paet v *Secretary of State for the Home Department* [1979–80] Imm AR 185   **9.20**
Palacio, ex parte, R v *Immigration Appeal Tribunal* [1979–80] Imm AR 178   **5.25**
Parekh v *Secretary of State for the Home Department* [1976] Imm AR 84   **7.31**
Parvez v *Immigration Officer, London (Heathrow) Airport* [1979–1980] Imm AR 84   **5.21**
Patel (AD), Secretary of State for the Home Department v [1975] Imm AR 95   **14.51**
Patel (MR) v *Entry Clearance Officer, Bombay* [1978] Imm AR 154   **6.8**
Patel (NN), Secretary of State for the Home Department v [1979–80] Imm AR 106   **8.67**
Pearson v *Immigration Appeal Tribunal* [1978] Imm AR 212, CA   **9.8, 14.3**
Peart, Entry Clearance Officer, Kingston, Jamaica v [1979–80] Imm AR 41   **8.70**
Peikazadi, ex parte, R v *Immigration Appeal Tribunal* [1979–80] Imm AR 191   **7.35**
Pereira (HRN) v *Immigration Officer, London (Heathrow) Airport* [1979–80] Imm AR 58   **5.39**
Pereira (J) v *Entry Clearance Officer, Bridgetown* [1979–80] Imm AR 79   **2.37**
Pereyra, Secretary of State for the Home Department v [1978] Imm AR 13   **9.21**
Phansopkhar, ex parte, R v *Secretary of State for the Home Department* [1976] QB 613; [1975] 3 All ER 502; [1975] 3 WLR 328   **2.49, 5.42**
Phillips v *Entry Clearance Officer, Kingston, Jamaica* [1973] Imm AR 47   **8.44**
Pinnock v *Entry Clearance Officer, Kingston, Jamaica* [1974] Imm AR 22   **8.32**
Ponticelli v *Ponticelli* [1958] 1 All ER 357; [1958] 2 WLR 439   **8.27**
Practice Direction [1974] 3 All ER 528   **14.65**
Pritpal Singh v *Secretary of State for the Home Department* [1972] Imm AR 154   **7.36**
Purnshothaman v *Secretary of State for the Home Department* [1972] Imm AR 176   **14.32**
Pusey, Secretary of State for the Home Department v [1972] Imm AR 240   **8.36**
Puttick, ex parte, R v *Secretary of State for the Home Department* [1981] 1 All ER 776; [1981] 2 WLR 440   **2.17**
Qurasha Begum v *Immigration Officer, London (Heathrow) Airport* [1978] Imm AR 158   **5.11**
Qureshi v *Immigration Officer, London (Heathrow) Airport* [1977] Imm AR 113   **5.11**
R (adoption) Re [1966] 3 All ER 613; [1967] 1 WLR 34   **2.10**
R v *Antypas* (1972) 57 Cr App R 207   **11.36**
R v *Bangoo* (1976) Times, 28 July; [1976] Crim LR 746, CA   **12.3**
R v *Barnet LBC, ex parte Shah* [1980] 3 All ER 679; [1981] 2 WLR 80   **8.3**
R v *Bello* [1978] Crim LR 551   **10.5**
R v *Bhagwan* [1970] 1 All ER 1129; [1970] 2 WLR 837, CA; affirmed *sub nom DPP* v *Bhagwan* [1972] AC 60; [1970] 3 All ER 97; [1970] 3 WLR 501, HL   **1.3**
R v *Bisset* [1973] Crim LR   **11.35**
R v *Bouchereau* [1978] QB 732; [1978] 2 WLR 251   **11.54, 14.67**
R v *Caird* (1970) 54 Cr App R 499   **11.37**
R v *Chief Immigration Officer, London (Heathrow) Airport* (1976) Times 21 July; 120 Sol J 605, CA   **5.38**
R v *Chief Immigration Officer (Gatwick Airport)* [1980] 3 All ER 373; [1980] 1 WLR 1396, CA   **6.17, 6.25**
R v *Chief Immigration Officer, London (Heathrow) Airport, ex parte Hazari* (1977) Times 25 November; [1975] 120 Sol J 46, CA   **5.38**
R v *Chief Immigration Officer, London (Heathrow) Airport, ex parte Salamat Bihi* [1976] 3 All ER 843; [1976] 1 WLR 979, CA   **1.16, 5.38**
R v *Chief Immigration Officer, Manchester Airport, ex parte Insah Begum* [1972] 1 All ER 594; [1973] 1 WLR 141   **5.41**
R v *Eastbourne JJ, ex parte Bassoum* [1979] CLY 488   **10.2**

TABLE OF CASES

R v *East Grinstead JJ, ex parte Doeve* [1969] 1 QB 136; [1968] 3 All ER 666; [1969] 3 WLR 290   **11.48**
R v *Edgehill* [1963] 1 QB 593; [1963] 1 All ER 181; [1963] 2 WLR 170   **11.36, 11.37**
R v *Entry Clearance Officer, Bombay, ex parte Amin* [1980] 2 All ER 837; [1980] 1 WLR 1536   **3.12, 14.3**
R v *Fennell* [1971] 1 QB 428; [1970] 3 All ER 215; [1970] 3 WLR 513   **10.15**
R v *Gill* [1976] 2 All ER 893, CA   **10.13**
R v *Governor of Brixton Prison, ex parte Soblen* [1963] 2 QB 283; [1962] 3 All ER 658; [1962] 3 WLR 1176, CA   **1.7, 11.18**
R v *Governor of Pentonville Prison, ex parte Azam. See Azam* v *Secretary of State for the Home Department*
R v *Immigration Appeal Adjudicator, ex parte Bhanji* [1977] Imm AR 89, CA   **14.12**
R v *Immigration Appeal Adjudicator, ex parte Khan (Perween)* [1972] 3 All ER 297; [1972] 1 WLR 1058   **5.10, 6.17**
R v *Immigration Appeal Tribunal. ex parte Ahluwalia* [1979–80] Imm AR 1   **9.16, 11.7**
R v *Immigration Appeal Tribunal, ex parte Alam Bi* [1979–80] Imm AR 146, CA   **14.41**
R v *Immigration Appeal Tribunal, ex parte Ali (Aisha Khatoon)* [1979/80] Imm AR 195   **8.67**
R v *Immigration Appeal Tribunal, ex parte Bahadur Singh* [1976] Imm AR 143   **14.15**
R v *Immigration Appeal Tribunal, ex parte Balbir Singh* [1978] Imm AR 64   **9.12**
R v *Immigration Appeal Tribunal, ex parte Chiew* (1981) *Times* 16 June   **7.40**
R v *Immigration Appeal Tribunal, ex parte Jaspal Singh* [1977] Imm AR 105   **14.7**
R v *Immigration Appeal Tribunal, ex parte Jeyaveerasingam* [1976] Imm AR 137   **14.37**
R v *Immigration Appeal Tribunal, ex parte Joseph* [1977] Imm AR 70   **7.28, 7.31, 7.34**
R v *Immigration Appeal Tribunal, ex parte Kassam* [1980] 2 All ER 330; [1980] 1 WLR 1037, CA   **1.11**
R v *Immigration Appeal Tribunal, ex parte Khan (SGH)* [1975] Imm AR 26   **6.19, 14.32**
R v *Immigration Appeal Tribunal, ex parte Lila* [1978] Imm AR 50   **14.40**
R v *Immigration Appeal Tribunal, ex parte Mehmet (Ekrem) (No. 2)* [1978] Imm AR 46   **11.7, 11.30**
R v *Immigration Appeal Tribunal, ex parte Mehmet* [1977] 2 All ER 602; [1977] 1 WLR 795   **11.6, 14.7, 14.8, 14.17**
R v *Immigration Appeal Tribunal, ex parte Mehta (RP)* [1975] 2 All ER 1084; [1975] 1 WLR 1087, CA   **14.17**
R v *Immigration Appeal Tribunal, ex parte Mehta (VM)* [1976] Imm AR 174, CA   **14.17**
R v *Immigration Appeal Tribunal, ex parte Nathwani,* [1979–80] Imm AR 9   **11.48**
R v *Immigration Appeal Tribunal, ex parte Palacio* [1979–80] Imm AR 178   **15.25**
R v *Immigration Appeal Tribunal, ex parte Peikazadi* [1979–80] Imm AR 191   **7.35**
R v *Immigration Appeal Tribunal, ex parte Rashid* [1978] Imm AR 71   **8.66, 14.33**
R v *Immigration Appeal Tribunal, ex parte Shaikh* (1981) *Times* 3 March   **9.12**
R v *Immigration Appeal Tribunal, ex parte Subramanim* [1977] QB 194; [1976] 3 All ER 604; [1976] 3 WLR 633, CA   **9.9, 9.17, 11.17, 14.12**
R v *Immigration Appeal Tribunal, ex parte Suleman* [1976] Imm AR 147   **14.42**
R v *Inner London Crown Court, ex parte Obajuwana* (1979) 69 Cr App R 125   **13.22**
R v *Inspector of Leman Street Police station, ex parte Venicoff* [1920] 3 KB 72; [1920] All ER 157, CA   **1.7**
R v *Kamara* [1973] QB 660; [1972] 3 All ER 999; [1973] 2 WLR 126   **11.37**
R v *Kruger* (1973) *Times* 22 November; [1973] Crim LR 133   **11.34**

xx   TABLE OF CASES

R v *McCartan* [1958] 3 All ER 140; [1958] 1 WLR 933   **11.48**
R v *Mehet* [1980] Crim LR 374   **10.12**
R v *Mistry; R* v *Asare* [1980] Crim LR 177   **10.12**
R v *Nazari* [1980] 3 All ER 880; [1980] 1 WLR 1366, CA   **11.36, 11.37**
R v *Peterkin Adjudicator, ex parte Soni* [1972] Imm AR 253   **14.32, 14.65**
R v *Pieck:* [1981] 3 All ER 46; [1981] 2 WLR 46, ECJ   **7.51, 11.55**
R v *Secchi* [1975] 1 CMLR 383   **7.46**
R v *Secretary of State for the Home Department, ex parte Akhtar* [1975] 3 All ER 1087; [1975] WLR 1717   **2.49**
R v *Secretary of State for the Home Department, ex parte Akhtar* [1980] 2 All ER 735; [1980] 3 WLR 302   **2.22, 12.6**
R v *Secretary of State for the Home Department, ex parte Badaike* (1977) Times 4 May   **3.15, 5.41, 12.8**
R v *Secretary of State for the Home Department, ex parte Choudary* [1978] 3 All ER 790; [1978] 1 WLR 1177, CA   **12.3, 13.17**
R v *Secretary of State for the Home Department, ex parte Fernandez* (1980) Times 21 November, CA   **11.39, 14.68**
R v *Secretary of State for the Home Department, ex parte Greene* [1974] 3 All ER 388   **13.15**
R v *Secretary of State for the Home Department, ex parte Hosenball* [1977] 3 All ER 452; [1977] 1 WLR 776, CA   **1.16, 9.2, 11.28**
R v *Secretary of State for the Home Department, ex parte Hussain* [1978] 2 All ER 427; [1978] 1 WLR 704, CA   **13.18**
R v *Secretary of State for the Home Department, ex parte Ibrahim* (1980) Times 29 March   **12.5**
R v *Secretary of State for the Home Department, ex parte Mangoo Khan* [1980] 2 All ER 337; [1980] 1 WLR 549, CA   **12.2**
R v *Secretary of State for the Home Department, ex parte Maqbool Hussain* [1976] 1 WLR 97   **12.3**
R v *Secretary of State for the Home Department, ex parte Mehmet (AD)* [1977] Imm AR 68, CA   **11.4**
R v *Secretary of State for the Home Department, ex parte Mughal* [1974] QB 313; [1973] 3 All ER 796; [1973] 3 WLR 647, CA   **5.38, 8.7, 8.67**
R v *Secretary of State for the Home Department, ex parte Phansopkhar* [1976] QB 613; [1975] 3 All ER 502; [1975] 3 WLR 328   **2.49, 5.42**
R v *Secretary of State for the Home Department, ex parte Puttick* [1981] 1 All ER 776; [1981] 2 WLR 440   **2.17**
R v *Secretary of State for the Home Department, ex parte Rai* [1976] Imm AR 140   **14.15**
R v *Secretary of State for the Home Department, ex parte Ram* [1979] 1 All ER 687; [1979] 1 WLR 148   **12.8, 13.19**
R v *Secretary of State for the Home Department, ex parte Safira Begum* (1978) Times 28 May; [1976] 120 Sol J 542   **5.38**
R v *Secretary of State for the Home Department, ex parte Santillo* [1981] 2 All ER 897   **11.37, 11.54, 11.58, 11.59**
R v *Secretary of State for the Home Department, ex parte Sultan Mahmood* [1980] 3 WLR 312, CA   **2.22, 12.6**
R v *Serry* (1980) Times 31 October, CA   **11.37**
R v *Singh* [1973] 1 All ER 122; [1972] 1 WLR 1100, CA   **10.11**
R v *Stewart* (1963) Times 9 April; [1963] Crim LR 446   **11.37**
R v *Sweeney* (1964) Times 12 November; [1964] Crim LR 37   **11.34**

TABLE OF CASES

R v *Tzanatos* (1978) CLY, 523, CA **10.5**
R v *Zaman* [1975] Crim LR 710, CA **10.13**
Rai, ex parte, R v *Secretary of State for the Home Department* [1976] Imm AR 140 **14.15**
Ram, ex parte, R v *Secretary of State for the Home Department* [1979] 1 All ER 687; [1979] 1 WLR 148 **12.8, 13.19**
Ramjane v *Chief Immigration Officer (Gatwick Airport)* [1973] Imm AR 84 **5.8**
Ramzan v *Visa Officer, Islam* [1978] Imm AR 111 **14.58**
Rashid ex parte, R v *Immigration Appeal Tribunal* [1978] Imm AR 71 **8.66, 14.33**
Raval v *Secretary of State for the Home Department* [1975] Imm AR 72 **7.41**
Rehman v *Secretary of State for the Home Department* [1978] Imm AR 80 **11.4**
Rennie v *Entry Clearance Officer, Kingston, Jamaica* [1979–80] Imm AR 117 **8.38**
Rhemtulla v *Immigration Appeal Tribunal* [1979–80] Imm AR 168 **11.6**
Roper v *Taylor Garages Ltd* [1951] 2 TLR 284 **10.5, 10.6**
Royer: Case 48/75 [1976] 2 CMLR 619; [1976] ECR 497 **11.55**
Rutili: Case 36/75 [1976] 1 CMLR 140 **11.53**
Sacha, Entry Clearance Officer, Bombay v [1973] Imm AR 5 **5.21, 8.49**
Sadiq, Immigration Officer, Birmingham v [1978] Imm AR 115 **6.8**
Sae-Heng v *Visa Officer, Bangkok* [1979–80] Imm AR 69 **6.12**
Safira Begum, ex parte, R v *Secretary of State for the Home Department* (1976) Times 28 May; [1976] 120 Sol J 542 **5.38**
Salamat Bibi, ex parte, R v *Chief Immigration Officer, London (Heathrow) Airport* [1976] 3 All ER 843; [1976] 1 WLR 979, CA **1.16, 5.38**
Saleh v *Secretary of State for the Home Department* [1975] Imm AR 154 **14.59**
Sampson v *Secretary of State for the Home Department* [1974] Imm AR 27 **14.41**
Santillo, ex parte R v *Secretary of State for the Home Department* [1981] 2 All ER 897 **11.37, 11.54, 11.58, 11.59**
Sanusi, Secretary of State for the Home Department [1975] Imm AR 114 **11.44**
Sarwar, Secretary of State for the Home Department v [1978] Imm AR 190 **9.21**
Scheele v *Immigration Officer, Harwich* [1976] Imm AR 1 **5.27**
Schmidt v *Secretary of State for Home Affairs* [1969] Ch 149; [1968] 3 All ER 795; [1969] 2 WLR 337; affirmed [1969] 2 Ch 160; [1969] 1 All ER 904; [1969] 2 WLR 346 **1.2**
Secretary of State for the Home Department v *Chile, Two citizens of* [1977] Imm AR 36 **15.4, 15.14**
Seedat, Entry Clearance Officer, Bombay v [1975] Imm AR 12 **8.45**
Seth, Entry Clearance Officer, Nairobi v [1979–80] Imm AR 63 **8.49**
Shah, ex parte, R v *Barnet LBC* [1980] 3 All ER 679; [1981] 2 WLR 80 **8.3**
Shahnaz v *Riswan* [1964] 2 All ER 993; [1965] 1 QB 390; [1964] 3 WLR 759 **8.23**
Shaikh, ex parte, R v *Immigration Appeal Tribunal* (1981) Times 3 March **9.12**
Shaikh, ex parte, R v *Chief Immigration Officer, London (Heathrow) Airport* (1976) Times 21 July; 120 Sol J 605, CA **5.38**
Shamonda, Entry Clearance Officer, Lagos v [1975] Imm AR 16 **6.9**
Sidique, Secretary of State for the Home Department v [1976] Imm AR 69 **9.4, 14.45**
Sindu, Visa Officer, Islamabad v [1978] Imm AR 147 **8.54**
Sloley v *Entry Clearance Officer, Kingston, Jamaica* [1973] Imm AR 54 **8.36**
Sobanjo, Entry Clearance Officer, Lagos v [1978] Imm AR 22 **6.12**
Soblen, ex parte, R v *Governor of Brixton Prison* [1963] 2 QB 283; [1962] 3 All ER 658; [1962] 3 WLR 1176, CA **1.7, 11.18**
Soni, ex parte, R v *Peterkin Adjudicator* [1972] Imm AR 253 **14.32, 14.65**

Stillwaggon, Secretary of State for the Home Department v [1975] Imm AR 132   **7.38, 9.21**
Strasburger v *Secretary of State for the Home Department* [1978] Imm AR 165   **6.24**
Subhash v *Secretary of State for the Home Department* [1979–80] Imm AR 97   **8.65**
Subramanim, ex parte, R v *Immigration Appeal Tribunal* [1977] QB 194; [1976] 3 All ER 604; [1976] 3 WLR 633, CA   **9.9, 9.17, 11.17, 14.12**
Sudhakaran v *Entry Clearance Officer, Madras* [1976] Imm AR 3   **5.21**
Suleman, ex parte, R v *Immigration Appeal Tribunal* [1976] Imm AR 147   **14.42**
Sultan Mahmood, ex parte, R v *Secretary of State for the Home Department*, (Note) [1980] 3 WLR 312, CA   **2.22, 12.6**
Surak Miah, Re (1976) *Times*, 4 February, CA   **7.9**
Suthendran v *Immigration Appeal Tribunal* [1977] AC 359; [1976] 3 All ER 611; [1976] 3 WLR 725, HL   **9.9, 9.17, 14.12**
Sylvester v *Secretary of State for the Home Department* [1972] Imm AR 104   **14.36**
Taj Bibi v *Entry Clearance Officer, Islamabad* [1977] Imm AR 25   **14.58**
Tally v *Secretary of State for the Home Department* [1975] Imm AR 83   **9.21**
Tambimuttu v *Secretary of State for the Home Department* [1979–80] Imm AR 91   **14.8**
Taneja v *Entry Clearance Officer, Chicago* [1977] Imm AR 9   **8.67**
Thabet, Visa Officer, Aden v [1977] Imm AR 75   **14.31**
Thaker v *Secretary of State for the Home Department* [1976] Imm AR 114   **9.4, 14.34**
Thakerar v *Entry Clearance Officer, Bombay* v [1974] Imm AR 60   **14.34**
Theori v *Secretary of State for the Home Department* [1979–80] Imm AR 126   **9.16**
Tilak Ram v *Entry Clearance Officer, New Delhi* [1978] Imm AR 123   **8.54**
Udoh, Secretary of State for the Home Department v [1972] Imm AR 89   **11.44**
Undy v *Undy* [1869] LR 1 Sc & Div 441, HL   **8.24**
Unger: Case 75/63 [1964] CMLR 319   **7.46**
Van Duyn v *Home Office* [1974] 3 All ER 178   **14.66**
Van Duyn v *Home Office (No 2)* [1975] Ch 358; [1975] 3 All ER 190, ECJ   **11.53**
Venicoff, ex parte, R v *Inspector of Leman Street Police Station* [1920] 3 KB 72; [1920] All ER 157, CA   **1.7**
Villone v *Secretary of State for the Home Department* [1979–80] Imm AR 23   **11.20**
Virdee, Secretary of State for the Home Department v [1972] Imm AR 215   **6.20**
Waddington v *Miah* [1974] 2 All ER 377; [1974] 1 WLR 692, HL   **10.1**
Wadia v *Secretary of State for the Home Department* [1977] Imm AR 92   **14.35**
Wajid Hassan, Re [1976] 2 All ER 123   **5.42, 13.16**
West Riding CC v *Wilson* [1941] 2 All ER 827   **9.2**
Williams v *Secretary of State for the Home Department* [1972] Imm AR 207   **8.36**
Winans v *AG* [1904] AC 287   **8.24**
X a Chilean Citizen, Secretary of State for the Home Department v [1978] Imm AR 73   **15.5**
X v *United Kingdom* [1981] 3 EHRR 63   **3.13**
Yeong Yoi Huen v *Secretary of State for the Home Department* [1977] Imm AR 34   **6.26**
Yosef v *Secretary of State for the Home Department* [1979–80] Imm AR 72   **14.34**
Yuskel, Secretary of State for the Home Department v [1977] Imm AR 91   **11.12**
Zahra v *Visa Officer, Islamabad* [1979–80] Imm AR 48   **8.28**
Zaman v *Entry Certificate Officer, Lahore* [1973] Imm AR 71   **8.45**
Zamir v *Secretary of State for the Home Department* [1980] 3 WLR 249; *sub nom R* v *Secretary of State for the Home Department, ex parte Zamir* [1980] QB 378; [1980] 2 All ER 768,

HL; affirming *sub nom* [1980] 1 All ER 1041; [1980] 2 WLR 357, CH; affirming *sub nom* [1979] QB 668; [1979] 2 All ER 849; [1979] 3 WLR 89; *sub nom R* v *Home Secretary, ex parte Zamir*   **5.12, 5.13, 5.32, 5.57, 12.2, 13.18, 13.19**

UNREPORTED CASES

All decisions are those of the Immigration Appeal Tribunal unless otherwise stated

Abeye-wardene 44202/79 (1765) **7.12**
Abiodun 42792/79 (1627) **11.41**
Acharya 2246/71 (60) **15.14**
Aftab 60901/80 (1777) **5.22**
Ahmad (SM) 50579 (1760) **6.17**
Ahmed Mustafaj 10039/75 **11.12**
Akhtar (Mr) 49631/79 (1602) **11.22, 11.23**
Akpall 955/72 (39) **11.14**
Ali (AM) 40054/79 (2011) **8.70**
Al Ghoben 25499/78 (1155) **11.24**
Altiparmak 35422/78 (1570) **11.41**
Attray 49510/79 (1856) **8.65**
Amat ul Mafiz 7139/7 (1180) **8.28**
Anayat Bibi 53725/79 (1994) **8.21**
Anseereeganoo 60126/80 (1973) **8.60**
Arif 22223/77 (1161) **11.24**
Asghar 57739/80 (1722) **11.21**
Avtar Singh 47710/79 **6.5**
Ayomano 2421/71 **8.27**
Ayoola 151/72 (16) **11.44**
Bahmanpour 45131/79 (1753) **14.29**
Bagas 9086/75 (1105) **8.44**
Bano 61659/80 (1949) **11.16**
Barbillar 20007/77 (1366) **8.28**
Bashir 1448/76 (1102) **8.52**
Baxt 39730/79 (1854) **7.38**
Bhagwant Singh 58441/80 (1941) **7.12**
Blair 35635/78 (1797) **6.5**
Bobitiya 2403/76 (822) **6.22**
Bosch 2722/71 **11.23**
Bruder 41024/79 (1545) **8.28**
Buckley 3814/76 (1011) **8.28**
Buike 43/72 (41) **8.49**
Butt 10750/76 (862) **11.5, 11.21**
Caleira 1327/73 (148) **11.22, 11.23**
Chadva 9947/76 (1030) **8.47**
Chand 49904/79 (1609) **11.23**
Chanda 75343/81 (2043) **14.9**
Chandarana 44332/79 (1841) **6.17**

Chauhan 31206/78 (1449) **8.65**
Chopra 11160/77 (1198) **6.7**
Chukuri 587/73 (329) **8.21**
Claveria (1979) 22 November 37, 38/79, DC **12.4**
Cooper 434/70 **8.38**
Curtis 1575/72 (7) **11.23**
Dalal 52067/79 (1669) **5.11**
Darwood Shah (1977) 5 October 284A/77, DC **12.3**
De Andrade 42 615/79 (1501) **5.11**
De Souza 10381/76 (989) **7.12**
Deva 62141/80 (1975) **14.35**
Diljar Begum 682/73 (461) **5.39, 8.22, 14.51**
Ditta (Allah) 32394/78 (1704) **6.7**
D'Souza 15022/77 (1659) **11.15**
Dutschke 381/70 **11.26**
Dutta (Rinda) 40028/79 (1455) **14.8**
Eckstein 2500/71 **11.23, 11.25**
El-Sayed 46012/79 (1687) **8.65**
El Wahab 11907/77 (981) **11.5, 11.21**
Esteve-Varea 4241/79 (1706) **9.16**
Facey 32001/78 (1638) **8.67**
Fazil 7523/76 (1027) **14.35**
Fernandez 35494/79 (1598) **6.21**
Gautam 52226/79 (1891) **7.40**
Ghazanfar Khan 3249/74 (394) **11.23**
Gokulsing 24987/78 (1632) **8.70**
Goma (1977) 1 November 345/77, DC **11.21**
Gowreesunker 4177/74 adjudicator's decision) **13.27**
Gurdev Kaur 567/72 (452) **8.54**
Hailu 3926/76 (923) **15.4**
Haijipaschali 57439/80 (1903) **4.9**
Haq 385/76 **8.24**
Harding 743/75 **6.17**
Helies 3539/76 (208) **11.25**
Heng 27726/78 (1575) **14.34**

TABLE OF CASES

Hettice 4310/76 (926) **6.27**
Hossenbux 2971/76 (1040) **8.62**
Hussain (SB) (1972) 19 September 226/72, DC **5.38, 8.22, 14.51**
Hussein 898/74 **15.5**
Ieong 38423/78 (1991) **8.31**
Jacques 10318/76 (1035) **7.41**
Jahanara Begum 12361–3/77 (1261) **8.28**
Jardine 36713/78 (1787) **6.7**
Jhureea 1065/75 (adjudicator's decision) **13.27**
Jorrisch 8363/76 (adjudicator's decision) **5.27**
K 34539/78 (1732) **15.4**
Karsan 55577/79 (1978) **8.48**
Kaur 1810/76 (968) **14.42**
Khalid Mehmud (1979) 26 July 90/79 DC **12.5**
Khaliq 5037/75 (459) **5.21**
Khamma Jan 11541/77 (1183) **14.41**
Khatun (Neharun Nessa) 54541/79 (adjudicator's decision) **14.50**
Kent-Tak Lok 68500/80 (1911) **14.9**
Khazrai 66628/80 (1904) **5.27**
Klein 34474/78 (1629) **Appendix A**
Kolb 1705/72 (67) **8.45**
Kupfer 4419/74 (adjudicator's decision) **5.27**
Kus 31628/78 (1470) **15.5, 15.14**
Lakhoo 1735/72 **8.38**
Lawyer 49561/79 (1755) **14.29**
Lazari 10147/76 (1017) **6.7, 11.41**
Leong 55181/79 (1846) **14.34**
Leper 1548/76 (944) **7.53**
Lindeman 4420/74 (adjudicator's decision) **5.27**
Lipien 46916/79 (1682) **8.60**
Long 1883/72 (37) **11.20, 11.23**
McIntosh 59267/80 (1782) **11.22**
Madanipoor 59550/80 (1969) **7.40**
Mahmoudi 69569/80 (2134) **9.6**
Majed 21065/77 (1108) **5.28**
Malik 615121/80 (2014) **8.41**
Mannah 3546/76 (1141) **14.54**
Manraj Begum 23765/78 (1502) **14.34**
Markhan Singh (1976) 4 December 20, 21/76, CA **11.6, 14.7**
Maru 31188/78 (1628) **6.3**
Mehta 2778/71 **6.18**

Mendez 55336/79 (1956) **6.7**
Moghal (Mohammed Munawar) (1980) 1 February 223/79, CA **12.10, 13.18**
Mohamedy 29097/78 (1435) **14.35**
Mohammed (Ejaz) v *Secretary of State for the Home Department* (1978) 21 December, CA **14.33**
Mohammed Anwar (1978) 19 January 448/77, DC **10.15, 12.3**
Mohd Ashraf 43998/79 (1714) **11.22**
Mohd Ibrahim 9994/76 (976) **8.32**
Mohd Iqbal 1870/71 (87) **8.22**
Mohinder Kaur 337-96/78 (1959) **8.70**
Mohsen 14412/77 (994) **11.5, 11.21**
Morgan 21884/77 (1527) **5.11**
Morgan 3502/74 (406) **6.17**
Morgan 46014/5/79 (1586) **14.16**
Munk-Hansen 88073 (210) **5.27, 11.22**
Murderris 43694/79 (1690) **11.16**
Mussa 20100/77 (1071) **5.27**
Najam Anwar 15563/77 (1173) **11.16**
Naqvi 47947/79 (1913) **7.40**
Narseen Akhtar 50229/79 (1786) **11.16**
Nasim Akhtar 43199/79 (1992) **8.28**
Neharun Nessa Khatun 54541/79 **14.50**
Ngen Chung Kwan 70577/80 (1929) **14.9**
Noel 704/71 **8.38**
Nessa 11420/77 (1037) **8.52**
Nuzrat Shah (1979) 22 November 467/79, DC **12.5**
Ogunrotimi 3584/73 **6.18**
Ojikutu 8110/76 (1029) **14.30**
Oni 5539/74 (395) **11.6**
Panesar 4001/79 (1643) **8.65**
Paratian 10903/76 (992) **6.25**
Patel (1977) 7 July, CA **2.49**
Patel (PR) 43141/79 (1766) **8.65**
Patel (SVBA) 63611/80 (1845) **11.21**
Pradeep Singh 1407/73 (345) **7.35, 7.36**
Rafique 12374/77 (1206) **14.55**
Rahman 17209/11177 (1203) **14.58**
Rampersand 1654/72 (102) **8.67**
Rhyek 6211/80 (1982) **8.40**
Sadiq Masih (1980) 5 March 513/79, DC **12.5**
Sassi 2581/73 (188) **11.23**
Satchithandum 44002/ (1552) **5.11**
Sathiasilan 1919/73 (190) **5.10**
Sattar 9837/76 (1107) **6.7**

TABLE OF CASES

Satwant Kaur (1977) 13 October 331/77, DC **12.3**
Shahid Ali 30807/78 (1553) **14.34**
Shamin Begum 23318/78 (1150) **8.28**
Shams 59327/80 (1977) **14.42**
Shamshad Begum 7426/76 (1026) **8.19**
Shahnaz Noreen (1980) 26 November 261/80 **12.8**
Sharma 1571/71 **6.20**
Shaw (1978) 19 January 288/71, DC **11.21**
Shazad 32163/78 (1626) **9.7, 12.7, 14.28**
Sherifali 2968/73 (245) **11.15**
Shing 2293/73 (169) **11.22**
Sijarn Kaur 58392/80 (1752) **11.21**
Sikayenah 20263/77 (1738) **14.28**
Sikka 3319/74 (587) **3.14**
Mukhar Singh (1976) 14 December 20, 21/76 **14.7**
S K Singh 31906/78 (1703) **8.57**
Sule 45494/6/79 (1593) **5.39**
Soon Lim Lee 32291/78 (1557) **6.22**
Spens 3903/73 (adjudicator's decision) **5.27**
Stofile 122/72 **11.23**

Sultana 8945/76 (988) **6.9**
Supersad 713/76 (842) **7.41**
Sweidan 2598/73 (183) **11.22**
Syal 441/72 (6) **8.45**
Tackie 3311/72 (194) **6.9**
Tagbo 13298/75 (971) **6.17**
Tareen 55850/79 (1745) **14.28**
Tasci 22307/77 (1170) **11.21**
Thomas 5086/76 (986) **8.40**
Tolentino 17206/77 (1036) **5.15**
Trinca 2996/72 (78) **11.22**
Trividic 4379/74 (adjudicator's decision) **5.27**
Veerabharda 1198/71 **5.21**
Vincent 68344/80 (1935) **5.27**
Virani 54382/79 (1780) **6.27**
Walid 37074/78 (1662) **5.5**
Walker 12842/75 (1066) **8.40**
White (Nethline) 242/74 (380) **8.40**
Wijesuriya 52961/79 (1685) **3.14**
Yusuf 2863/73 (adjudicator's decision) **13.27**
Zafar Iqbal and Arif Hussain (1980) 7 February 251/79, DC **12.3**
Zartoon Begum 21809/77 (1642) **8.28**
Zulfiqar (Ali) 30055/78 (1660) **7.9**

Table of Statutes

Adoption Act 1958		20	2.22; 12.6
s. 3 (1)	8.41	(3)	2.22
(2)	8.41	(7)	2.22
19	2.10	23	2.22
Adoption Act 1968		(1)	2.11
s. 4	2.37	24	2.11
(3)	8.31	32 (1)	2.24; 2.30
Aliens Act 1793	1.2	(2)	2.11; 2.37
Aliens Act 1905	1.2; 1.8	33 (1)	2.7
Aliens Registration Act 1816	1.2	33 (2)	2.7
Aliens Registration Act 1826	1.2	British Nationality Act 1958	2.4
Aliens Registration Act 1836	1.2	British Nationality Act 1964	2.4; 2.23
Aliens Restriction Act 1914	1.2; 1.8	s. 1 (1)	2.23
Aliens Restriction (Amendment) Act		(2)	2.23
1919	1.2; 1.8	(6)	2.23
Bail Act 1976	13.5; 13.23	British Nationality (No. 2) Act 1964	
s. 3 (5)	13.20		2.4; 2.18
British Nationality Act 1948	1.1; 2.4;	s. 1 (1)	2.18
	2.6	(3)	2.18
s. 1 (1)	2.6	2 (1)	2.9
(2)	2.6	(2)	2.9
2 (1)	2.24	Sch.	2.18
4	2.8; 2.9	British Nationality Act 1965	2.4
5	2.11; 2.42	s. 3	2.22
5A	2.15; 12.6	(3)	2.22
(3)	2.14	British Nationality Act 1981	2.4
(4)	2.14	s. 1	2.54
6 (1)	2.13	2	2.54
(2)	2.17	3	2.54
7	2.37	4	2.54
(1)	2.16	5	2.54
(2)	2.16	6	2.54
8 (2)	2.32; 2.37	7	2.54
12 (1) (a)	2.9	8	2.54
12 (2)	2.11	11	2.52
19 (1)	2.22	23	2.52

26	2.52	(7)	16.8
30	2.53	Diplomatic Privileges Act 1964	
31	2.53	s. 5 (2)	2.9
39	2.56; 2.57	Sch. 1	
50	2.54	art. 1	3.14
51	2.53	Family Law Reform Act 1969	
Sch. 1	2.54	s. 1 (3)	2.14
Sch. 2	2.56	9	11.34
British Nationality and Status of Aliens Act 1914	1.1	32 (9)	2.14
British Nationality and Status of Aliens Act 1918	1.1	Immigration Act 1971 s. 1	
		(1)	1.9; 2.46
British Nationality and Status of Aliens Act 1922	1.1	(2)	8.7; 8.67
		(3)	3.7; 4.1
British Nationality and Status of Aliens Act 1933	1.1	(4)	1.11; 1.17
		(5)	1.11; 8.8; 8.19
British Nationality and Status of Aliens Act 1943	1.1	2	1.9; 2.1
		(1) (a)	1.9; 2.35; 2.36; 2.38; 2.39; 8.42
Children and Young Persons Act 1933			
s. 107	13.1	(b) (1)	2.37
Children and Young Persons Act 1969		(c)	2.40; 3.12
Sch. 5	13.1	(d)	2.14; 2.42; 2.44
Childrens Act 1975		(2)	2.14; 2.38
s. 10 (2)	8.41	(a)	2.41
11 (2)	8.41	(b) (i)	2.41; 2.44
22	8.41	(ii)	2.41
Commonwealth Immigrants Act 1962		(3) (a)	2.37
	1.1; 1.8; 2.4; 2.6	(b)	2.35; 2.37
s. 2 (2)	8.8	(c)	2.41
6–11	1.6	(d)	2.42; 2.44; 8.2
7 (2)	11.34	(4)	2.37; 2.38
12	1.6; 2.13	(5)	2.4; 2.14
Sch. 1		(6)	1.9
para. 1 (2)	1.4	3	8.2
Commonwealth Immigrants Acts 1968		(1)	1.10; 8.2; 12.2
	1.4; 1.6; 1.8; 3.8; 3.13	(a)	1.10; 5.1
Consular Relations Act 1968		(b)	1.10; 5.1; 8.5; 9.1
s. 7	2.9	(c)	1.10; 5.1; 5.40; 8.5; 9.1; 9.11; 10.6; 15.13
Courts Act 1971			
s. 9 (2)	11.34	(2)	1.11; 1.12
13 (4)	13.21	(3)	12.2
Criminal Appeal Act 1968		(a)	9.1
s. 19	13.21	(b)	5.1; 9.1; 9.13
50 (1)	11.36	(4)	8.1; 9.13; 9.16
(2)	11.34	(5)	4.8; 11.1
Criminal Law Act 1977	13.21	(a)	9.17; 11.51; 13.25; 14.28
s. 28 (1)	16.8	(b)	9.17; 11.38; 13.25
(2)	10.11; 10.12	(c)	11.29; 11.51; 13.25

(6)	4.8; 11.1; 11.34; 11.51; 13.22	(2)	2.47; 3.12; 14.1
(7)	10.9; 14.3	(3)	2.47; 5.8; 13.4; 14.3; 14.9; 14.11; 14.12
(8)	2.46; 11.3	(4)	14.10
(9)	2.46	(5)	5.49; 14.9; 14.10
4	9.2	14	14.1
(1)	5.40; 9.1; 14.12	(1)	9.9; 11.46; 15.13
(3)	9.22; 10.3	(2)	3.14; 14.38
(a)	1.17	(3)	9.9; 11.57
(4)	1.17; 10.13	(4)	14.3; 14.12
5	11.1	15	11.1; 11.2
(1)	4.6; 11.11; 11.41	(1)	11.29
(2)	11.11	(a)	14.1
(4) (a)	11.29	(b)	14.1
(b)	11.29	(2)	11.30
(5)	11.9	(3)	11.2; 11.9; 11.26; 11.30; 11.42; 14.3
(6)	11.47; 11.51	(4)	11.2; 11.9; 14.3
6	11.1	(5)	11.2; 11.11; 11.57
(1)	4.8; 11.34	(6)	11.31
(2)	11.38	(7)	14.5
(3)	11.35	16	4.6; 10.16; 11.1; 11.9; 14.2
(a)	11.34	(1) (a)	11.11; 14.2
(b)	11.35	(b)	13.28; 14.2
(4)	11.35	(2)	11.11
(5) (a)	11.36	(3)	11.11
(6)	11.38; 12.23	17	11.1; 11.9; 14.2
7	8.16; 11.1	(1)	5.49
(1)	3.7; 8.16; 11.3	(b)	13.27
(2)	8.4; 11.4	(2)	5.49
(3)	11.4	(5)	5.49
(4)	11.4	18	14.6
(5)	8.2	(1)	10.7
8	10.7	19	14.4
(1)	3.19	(1) (a)	14.19
(2)	3.1; 14.38	(i)	14.30
(3)	3.14; 14.38	(ii)	14.30
(4)	3.18; 14.38	(b)	14.30
(5)	3.14; 8.2	(2)	9.2; 14.32
9	3.7; 4.1	(3)	14.30
(1)	13.22	20	14.4
(2)	4.5; 9.24	(1)	14.37; 14.40; 14.41
(3)	4.8	(2)	14.30; 14.41
(4)	4.5; 4.6	(3)	14.41
(5)	4.1; 4.5	21	14.4; 14.48
(6)	4.5	22 (4)	14.25
(7)	4.5	(5) (a)	14.38
11 (4)	4.2; 4.6	(b)	14.38
13 (1)	5.49; 13.4; 14.1; 14.11		

(6)		14.53			5.30; 5.47; 7.8; 8.4; 8.31;
24		10.1			8.68; 12.1
(1) (a)		10.2; 10.4	(2)		8.4
(b) (i)		4.8; 9.10; 9.17;	(5)		1.2
		10.2; 10.5	35 (2)		10.1
(ii)		10.6	(3)		10.1
(c)		4.6; 10.2; 10.7	36		4.4
(d)		10.8	Sch. 1		2.4; 2.14
(e)		10.8	para. 2		2.14
(f)		10.8	App. A		2.15
(g)		10.9	App. C		2.20
(2)		10.10; 10.14; 10.16; 13.13	Sch. 2		5.29; 10.13; 12.16
(3)		10.2	para. 1 (1)		10.13
(4)		10.16	(2)		5.36; 10.14
(a)		10.4	(3)		1.17; 5.29
(b)		10.4	(4)		5.30; 5.36; 5.50
25		10.1; 10.2	(5)		5.50
(1)		10.1; 10.11; 10.12	2		10.8
(2)		10.11; 10.12	(1)		5.31; 10.8; 10.13
(3)		10.1; 10.12; 10.14	(a)		2.50
(4)		10.1; 10.2; 10.12	(2)		5.36; 10.8; 10.14
(6)		10.1	(3)		5.31
(a)		10.11	3 (1)		10.13
(7)		10.1	4 (1)		5.32
(a)		10.11	(2)		5.32
(8)		10.1; 10.11	(a)		13.10
26		10.1	(3)		5.33
(1)		5.35	(4)		5.34; 13.10
(a)		5.22; 5.35; 5.36; 10.13;	5		10.13
		10.14	6 (1)		5.39
(b)		10.13	(2)		5.41
(c)		9.25; 10.2; 10.13	(3)		5.38
(d)		9.25; 10.2; 10.13	(4)		5.41
(e)		5.3; 10.13	7		5.41
(f)		9.25; 10.13; 10.14	8 (1) (a)		5.45
(g)		5.36; 10.13	(b)		5.45
(2)		10.2	(c)		5.45
27		5.50; 10.1	(2)		5.45
28		10.12	9		4.6; 10.16; 13.13
(1) (a)		10.2	10 (1) (a)		5.45
(b)		10.2	(b)		5.45
(c)		10.2	11		11.45
(2)		10.2	12		13.28
(3)		10.2	(1)		5.48
(4)		10.2	13		5.48; 13.28
29		11.62	14		5.48; 13.28
30		11.49	15		5.48; 13.28
33 (1)		2.37; 4.6; 5.4; 5.14; 5.15;			

TABLE OF STATUTES

16	5.31; 5.48; 10.16	
(1)	5.42; 13.1; 13.13	
(2)	5.42; 5.47; 5.48; 13.1; 13.13; 13.28	
(3)	5.42	
(4)	5.42; 5.48	
17	10.16	
(1)	5.42; 5.47; 5.48	
(2)	5.42	
18 (1)	5.47; 5.48; 13.1	
(2)	5.42	
(3)	5.42	
(4)	5.42	
19	5.50	
20	5.50	
21	10.8; 10.16; 13.14; 13.28	
(1)	5.44; 10.16; 13.11	
(2)	5.44; 13.10	
22	13.19	
(1)	5.39; 5.43	
(2)	5.43	
(3)	5.43	
23	13.9	
24	13.9	
25	13.9	
26 (1)	5.50	
(2)	5.50	
(3)	5.50	
27 (1)	5.50	
(a)	5.50	
(2)	5.50	
29 (1)	11.10; 13.4; 13.25; 13.26; 13.27	
(2)	13.4; 13.25	
(3)	13.4; 13.25	
(4)	13.4; 13.25	
(5)	13.4	
(6)	13.4	
30 (1)	13.27	
(2)	13.45	
31	13.4	
32	13.4	
Sch. 3	11.9	
para.		
2 (1)	11.10; 13.22; 13.23; 13.24	
(2)	11.10; 13.25; 13.26	
(3)	13.25; 13.27	
(4)	13.26; 13.27	
(5)	10.8; 11.10; 13.25; 13.26; 13.27	
3	13.25; 13.26	
Sch. 4		
para.		
1	4.4	
2	4.4	
3	4.4	
4	4.4	
Sch. 5	14.4	
Immigration Appeals Act 1969	1.7; 14.1	
Interpretation Act 1899		
s. 12 (3)	1.17	
18 (3)	2.7	
Ireland Act 1949		
s. 2 (1)	2.24	
Magistrates Courts Act 1980		
s. 44	10.6	
113	13.21	
127 (1)	10.2	
Matrimonial Causes Act 1973		
s. 11 (d)	8.24	
47 (4)	8.26	
Matrimonial Proceedings (Polygamous) (Marriages) Act 1972		
s. 4	8.24	
Mental Health Act 1959		
s. 26	11.49	
60	11.49	
90	11.49	
Mental Health (Scotland) Act 1960		
s. 82	11.49	
Naturalisation Act 1872	1.1	
Nullity of Marriages Act 1971	8.24	
Police (Scotland) Act 1967		
s. 9	16.13	
Prevention of Terrorism (Temporary Provisions) Act 1974	16.1	
Prevention of Terrorism (Temporary Provisions) Act 1976	2.1; 4.4; 8.17; 16.1	
s. 3 (1)	16.2	
(2)	16.4	
4 (1) (a)	16.3	
(b)	16.3	

(2)	**16.3**	(b)	**16.8**
(3) (a)	**16.5**	11	**16.11**
(b)	**16.5**	12 (1)	**16.8**
(c)	**16.5**	14 (1)	**16.3**
5 (2)	**16.3**	16 (1)	**16.1**
(3) (a)	**16.5**	17 (1)	**16.1**
(b)	**16.5**	Sch. 3	
(c)	**16.5**	para. 3	**16.8**
6 (2)	**16.3**	Race Relations Act 1976	**1.11**
7	**16.6**	Removal of Aliens Act 1848	**1.2**
(4)	**16.6**	Sex Discrimination Act 1975	**1.11**
8	**16.7**	Statute Law Revision Act 1875	**1.2**
9 (1)	**16.8**	Supplementary Benefits Act 1976	
(2) (a)	**16.8**	s. 3	**11.61**
(b)	**16.8**	Tanganyika Independence Act	
(3) (a)	**16.8**	1961	**2.26**

Table of Statutory Instruments

The following is a complete list of Statutory Instruments made under the Immigration Act 1971.

Immigration Act 1971 (Commencement) Order 1972, SI 1972 No. 1514
Immigration Appeals (Notices) Regulations 1972, SI 1972 No. 1683
Immigration Appeals (Procedure) Rules 1972, SI 1972 No. 1684
Immigration (Control of Entry through Republic of Ireland) Order 1972, SI 1972 No. 1610
Immigration (Control of Entry through Republic of Ireland) (Amendment) Order 1979, SI 1979 No. 730
Immigration (Control of Entry through Republic of Ireland) (Amendment) Order 1980, SI 1980 No. 1859
Immigration (Exemption from Control) Order 1972, SI 1972 No. 1613
Immigration (Exemption from Control) (Amendment) Order 1975, SI 1975 No. 617
Immigration (Exemption from Control) (Amendment) Order 1977, SI 1977 No. 693
Immigration (Revocation of Employment Restrictions) Order 1972, SI 1972 No. 1647
Immigration (Guernsey) Order 1972, SI 1972, No. 1719
Immigration (Hotel Records) Order 1972, SI 1972 No. 1689
Immigration (Isle of Man) Order 1972, SI 1972 No. 1720
Immigration (Jersey) Order 1972, SI 1972 No. 1813
Immigration (Landing and Embarkation Cards) 1975, SI 1975 No. 65
Immigration (Registration with the Police) Regulations 1972, SI 1972 No. 1758
Immigration (Registration with the Police) (Amendment) Regulations 1975, SI 1975 No. 999
Immigration (Registration with the Police) (Amendment) Regulations 1976, SI 1976 No. 2018
Immigration (Registration with the Police) (Amendment) Regulations 1978, SI 1978 No. 24
Immigration (Registration with the Police) (Amendment) Regulations 1981, SI 1981 No. 534
Immigration (Particulars of Passengers and Crew) Order 1972, SI 1972 No. 1667
Immigration (Particulars of Passengers and Crew) (Amendment) Order 1975, SI 1975 No. 980
Immigration (Ports of Entry) Order 1972, SI 1972 No. 1668
Immigration (Ports of Entry) (Amendment) Order 1975, SI 1975 No. 2221
Immigration (Ports of Entry) (Amendment) Order 1979, SI 1979 No. 1635
Immigration (Variation of Leave) Order 1976, SI 1976 No. 1572

ONE

The Scheme of Immigration Control

HISTORY OF IMMIGRATION CONTROL

1.1 The control and regulation of entry into the UK is not a new concept, although it was not until this century that a developed system of control of entry and removal emerged. Under common law those who owed allegiance to the Crown were subjects. They had a right to enter the UK free from control and to remain there for as long as they wished. Legislation in the nineteenth and twentieth centuries set out the methods of acquiring and losing this status,[1] and the British Nationality Act 1948 applied the term 'British subject' to all citizens of independent Commonwealth countries in addition to those who acquired the new status of 'citizens of the UK and Colonies'. All British subjects are Commonwealth citizens.[2] The 1948 Act did not affect the right of British subjects freely to enter and remain in the UK. The first restrictions were imposed on them in 1962.[3]

Aliens

1.2 Those who owed no allegiance to the Crown were known as aliens. There had been from time to time, usually in periods of emergency, statutory provisions restricting the admission and providing for the expulsion of aliens.[4] The common law position is however far from

---

[1] Naturalisation Act 1872; British Nationality and Status of Aliens Acts 1914, 1918, 1922, 1933 and 1943.
[2] See para. 2.25, post.
[3] Commonwealth Immigrants Act 1962; see para. 1.4, post.
[4] Aliens Act 1793, modified by the Aliens Registration Acts 1816, 1826 and 1836; Removal of Aliens Act 1848, repealed by the Statute Law Revision Act 1875.

certain: it would appear that there is a common law power vested in the Crown to refuse admission to aliens,[5] although this has been disputed.[6] The present law expressly preserves the Crown's prerogative powers but no reference is made as to what these powers are said to be.[7]

Control of aliens on a permanent basis arose out of the Aliens Act 1905 which gave power to immigration officers to refuse entry to, and deport, those considered to be 'undesirable aliens'. An 'undesirable' was considered to be a person who was unable to support and maintain himself, or was suffering from an illness or disability that endangered public funds or health, or had a criminal record. This legislation was reinforced at the outbreak of the First World War by the speedy enactment of the Aliens Restriction Act 1914 which gave the Government wide discretionary powers in the control of alien immigration. The Act was introduced as a temporary measure and similar assurances were given about the Aliens Restriction (Amendment) Act 1919 which maintained the strict controls and provided for an extension of the 1905 Act for a further period of one year. This legislation remained in force by annual renewals by Parliament under the Expiring Laws Continuance Act until the provisions relating to immigration control were repealed by the Immigration Act 1971.[8]

Commonwealth Immigration

1.3 The British Nationality Act 1948 was solely concerned with the question of citizenship and makes no reference to immigration to the UK, a subject which was not at issue at the time. All British subjects, whether they were citizens of the UK and Colonies or of independent Commonwealth countries, remained free from immigration controls: they did not require permission to enter or remain in the UK and they were not subject to deportation. British protected persons and citizens of the Republic of Ireland were treated in the same manner as British subjects.[9] From 1948 there was a steady flow of immigration to the UK of British subjects, first from the Caribbean and later from India and

[5] *Musgrove* v *Chun Teeong Toy* [1891] AC 272; *Schmidt* v *Secretary of State for Home Affairs* [1968] 3 All ER 795.

[6] See Thornberry (1963) 12 ICLQ 414, at 422–428.

[7] Immigration Act 1971, s. 33(5). 'This Act shall not be taken to supersede or impair any power exercisable by Her Majesty in relation to aliens by virtue of Her prerogative.'

[8] Detailed powers controlling alien immigration were made by Orders in Council. A number of Orders were made, the final being Aliens Order 1953, SI 1953, No. 1671, which continued until the Immigration Act 1971 came into force.

[9] *DPP* v *Bhagwan* [1970] 3 All ER 97, HL.

Pakistan. Many came as a result of encouragement by British Governments and industry which required labour to carry out post-war reconstruction.[10] A campaign to limit black Commonwealth immigration began to gather momentum after the 1959 general election and the Government eventually bowed to pressure by introducing legislation.[11]

1.4 On 1 July 1962, the Commonwealth Immigrants Act came into force, applying controls for the first time to British subjects. The Act imposed control on all British subjects, British protected persons and citizens of the Republic of Ireland, except for those who were (1) born in the UK; or (2) holders of UK passports, i.e. passports issued by the UK Government or by a UK Government representative overseas, usually a UK High Commissioner in an independent Commonwealth country, but not by the Government of a Colony; or (3) included in the passport of a person in one of the categories in (1) or (2), above.[12]

Although the concept of citizenship of the UK and Colonies remained, it no longer carried with it freedom from immigration control for most citizens of the UK and Colonies who had not been born in the UK. They, together with citizens of independent Commonwealth countries, now had no right of entry. Although the legislation affected many white people, particularly third generation Canadians, Australians and New Zealanders,[13] it was designed largely to limit black immigration and achieved its object.

1.5 An important group who escaped the new controls were those citizens of the UK and Colonies of Asian origin living in East Africa. In Tanganyika (now part of Tanzania), Uganda, Kenya and elsewhere not all UK citizens of Asian origin became citizens of the newly independent country on independence, and thus they retained their UK citizenship unless they chose to acquire the new citizenship and renounced their UK

[10] For a detailed examination of these developments see Rose *et al. Colour and Citizenship: a Report on British Race Relations.* Institute of Race Relations, 1969, pp. 43–81.

[11] The political history of this period is well researched in Paul Foot, *Immigration and Race in British Politics*, 1965 (Penguin). The effect of the legislation was to increase numbers in the period prior to the announcement of the legislation because people rightly thought that they would be excluded.

[12] Also exempted from control were diplomats, certain members of the home, Commonwealth or visiting forces and persons exempted by the Home Secretary. Others who escaped control were those Commonwealth citizens who landed in the UK and spent 24 hours (amended by the Commonwealth Immigrants Act 1968 to 28 days), without submitting to examination by an immigration officer. As to the last group see, Commonwealth Immigrants Act 1962, Sch. 1, para. 1(2); *DPP* v *Bhagwan*, cited in note 9, supra.

[13] See para. 2.42, post.

citizenship.[14] In Kenya most chose to remain citizens of the UK and Colonies. They had an entitlement to enter the UK as their passports had been issued by the British High Commission in Kenya, and in 1967 many began to do so because of the policy of 'Africanisation' under which the Kenya Government gave preference to its own citizens, particularly in the fields of employment and commerce.

1.6 Once again there were pressures to curtail immigration. The Commonwealth Immigrants Act 1968 was enacted and controls were placed for the first time on those holding UK and Colonies passports issued by the UK Government.[15] A citizen of the UK and Colonies was subject to control unless he could show that either he or at least one of his parents or grandparents was (1) born in the UK, or (2) acquired citizenship by adoption, registration or naturalisation in the UK.

These new restrictions affected a larger group of citizens than the Kenyan Asians alone. A special scheme was introduced by which a limited number of vouchers was allocated each year to UK passport holders seeking entry. These vouchers are issued mainly to those from East Africa, other countries having imposed similar restrictions on non-citizens.[16]

In addition to the imposition of controls, the 1962 Act had made provision for the first time for deportation of certain British subjects where they had been recommended by a court for deportation following conviction for a criminal offence.[17] Further hurdles were raised for those seeking UK citizenship by registration, by the amendment of the British Nationality Act 1948 so that the qualification of one year's residence in the UK prior to application was increased to five years.[18]

Appeals against Immigration Decisions

1.7 There was no comprehensive system of appeals against immigration decisions until the Immigration Appeals Act 1969.[19] There had been

---

[14] The provisions for the automatic acquisition of citizenship of the independent country vary, e.g. those born in Uganda, Kenya and Tanganyika with at least one parent born there became citizens on independence.
[15] For a history of the 1968 Act see David Steel, *No Entry*, 1969.
[16] The special voucher scheme is explained in para. 3.8, post.
[17] Commonwealth Immigrants Act 1962, ss. 6–11.
[18] Ibid. s. 12.
[19] The courts would not interfere with the Home Secretary's decision; e.g. see *R v Inspector of Leman Street Police Station, ex parte Venicoff* [1920] All ER 157, CA; *R v Governor of Brixton Prison, ex parte Soblen* [1962] 3 All ER 58, CA.

provision under the Aliens Act 1905 for appeals against decisions under the Act but this right was removed in 1914. The right was not restored at the end of the war although an advisory committee was set up following the 1919 legislation to recommend whether former enemy aliens should be exempted from deportation. Between the wars the Committee was not used regularly and it ceased to function after 1939. In 1956 a procedure was introduced to enable an alien against whom a deportation order had been made or was contemplated to make representations to the Chief Metropolitan Magistrate provided the alien had been resident lawfully in the UK for two years. The procedure, which could not be used where the court had made a recommendation for deportation or in national security cases, was introduced as an attempt to comply with the provisions of the European Convention on Human Rights relating to fair and public hearings. Although there has been no announcement that the procedure has been withdrawn, there is no evidence of it being used since 1969.

In 1966 a committee was set up to consider a system of immigration appeals. It reported in 1967.[20] The Immigration Appeals Act 1969 was enacted as a result of the report although not all the report's recommendations were accepted by the Government. The 1969 Act was repealed by the Immigration Act 1971 but the system and procedure for appeal were re-enacted in the 1971 Act almost unaltered.[1]

THE GENERAL SCHEME OF THE IMMIGRATION ACT 1971

1.8 The Act replaces all previous immigration legislation[2] and came into force on 1 January 1973,[3] with the exception of certain provisions relating to criminal offences, which came into force on 28 November 1971.[4] The Act provides for:

[20] Report of the Committee on Immigration Appeals (The Wilson Committee): Cmnd 3387.
[1] See para. 1.18, post; Chapter 14, post.
[2] The 1905, 1914, 1962 and 1968 Acts were repealed completely. The 1919 Act dealt mainly with restrictions on the employment of aliens and on their civil rights and these provisions are still retained. It is therefore no accident that it remains a criminal offence for an alien to promote or attempt to promote industrial unrest in any industry in which he has not been bona fide engaged for at least two years; see Aliens Restriction (Amendment) Act 1919, s. 3(2). For disabilities of aliens see *Halsbury's Laws* (4th Edn.), Vol. 4, paras, 948, *et seq.*
[3] Immigration Act 1971 (Commencement) Order 1972, SI 1972 No. 1514.
[4] For the offences, see Chapter 10, post.

(1) the regulation of entry into and stay in the UK[5] and in particular:
   (a) the limitation of free passage to those with a right of abode;
   (b) the establishment of a 'common travel area' comprising the UK, the Channel Islands, Isle of Man and the Republic of Ireland; and
   (c) the removal by deportation of those without a right of abode;
(2) the continuation of rights of appeal against certain immigration decisions;[6]
(3) the continuation and creation of criminal offences for breach of the immigration laws;[7] and
(4) a number of miscellaneous and supplementary matters.[8]

The Right of Abode

1.9 Those with a right of abode are known as patrials.[9] They may enter, remain and leave the UK without any restriction.[10] The status of patriality is limited to certain citizens of the UK and Colonies and of independent Commonwealth countries who have a connection with the UK either through birth, descent, settlement or because they acquired their citizenship in the UK.[11] Not all citizens of the UK and Colonies, and even fewer citizens of independent Commonwealth countries are patrial. A definition of patriality and a full description of that status is set out in Chapter 2.

1.10 A non-patrial[12] cannot enter the UK unless he has been given leave, i.e. permission to do so in accordance with the Immigration Act 1971.[13] Leave may be given for either a limited or an indefinite period,[14] and may be subject to restrictions.[15] If leave to enter is given for a limited period, leave to remain for further periods may be given at a later date and may again be subject to restrictions.[16] Whether a person qualifies to

---

[5] Immigration Act 1971, ss. 1–19.
[6] Ibid., ss. 12–23.
[7] Ibid., ss. 24–28.
[8] Ibid., ss. 29–37.
[9] Ibid., s. 2(6).
[10] Ibid., s. 1(1).
[11] Ibid., s. 2.
[12] I.e. one who does not qualify under one of the exempt categories, see para. 3.14, post.
[13] Ibid., s. 3(1)(a). For the requirements on entry see generally Chapter 5, post.
[14] Ibid., s. 3(1)(b).
[15] Ibid. s. 3(1)(c). I.e. on employment or occupation or requiring the entrant to register with the police.
[16] Ibid., s. 3(1). For the requirements for applicants for extensions of stay, see generally Chapter 9, post.

enter or remain in the UK will depend on whether he satisfies the requirements of the immigration rules made by the Home Secretary under the Act. But it should be remembered that although the rules lay down the practice to be followed in the administration of the Act, the Home Secretary is not prevented from authorising personally, or through his officials, a person to be admitted or allowed to remain even where the requirements under the rules have not been met.

THE IMMIGRATION RULES

1.11 The immigration rules set out the day-to-day immigration practice to be followed in the administration of the Act. Detailed knowledge of these rules is essential to a proper understanding of immigration control.

The Act requires the Home Secretary to make rules 'as to the practice to be followed in the administration of (the) Act for regulating the entry into and stay in the UK' of non-patrials 'including any rules as to the period for which leave is to be given and the conditions to be attached in different circumstances'.[17] He is specifically required to make rules concerning the entry and stay of visitors, students and workers and dependants, and is permitted to discriminate against particular groups.[18] The rules do not have to be uniform and 'account may be taken of citizenship or nationality'.[19] There is also a requirement that the rules are to be framed so that Commonwealth citizens settled here when the Act came into force, and their wives and children, are no less free to enter and leave the UK than if the Act had not been passed.[20]

1.12 The Home Secretary must lay a statement of the rules or any changes in the rules before Parliament. If no resolution disapproving them is made within 40 days, they become law. If they are disapproved, the Home Secretary has another 40 days to make any necessary alterations and lay before Parliament a further statement of the changes

---

[17] Ibid., s. 3(2).
[18] Ibid., s. 1(4).
[19] Ibid., s. 3(2). The Sex Discrimination Act 1975 does not apply to immigration matters as they are not a facility to the public within the meaning of the 1975 Act: *R v Immigration Appeal Tribunal, ex parte Kassam* [1980] 2 All ER 330, CA. In *Home Office v Commission for Racial Equality* [1981] 1 All ER 1042, the High Court held that an investigation into the control of immigration could be properly undertaken by the Commission of Racial Equality in carrying out its duty under the Race Relations Act 1976.
[20] Immigration Act 1971, s. 1(5).

of the rules.[1] When the Home Secretary introduced draft rules[2] in November 1972, Parliament rejected them following a campaign organised by some Conservatives and sections of the press to give special treatment to those from the 'old Commonwealth'. The draft rules were nevertheless the operative rules when the Act came into force on 1 January 1973 and remained so until 25 January 1973 when new rules were presented to Parliament.

The 1973 rules

1.13 The 1973 rules are contained in four basic statements:[3] these deal with control *on* entry and control *after* entry with separate sets of rules for Commonwealth citizens and foreign nationals.[4] These rules were significantly amended on two occasions, in both cases primarily to alter the rules for husbands and fiancés.[5] The rules were also amended when Pakistan left the Commonwealth to provide that from 16 October 1973 Pakistan citizens were to be treated in the same way as any other foreign national.[6]

The 1973 immigration rules and the main amendments still effective are set out in the table opposite. These rules remained operative until 1 March 1980 when they were replaced by the current rules.[7] The current rules apply to all decisions taken on or after 1 March 1980 except those to which the transitional provisions apply. These provisions provide that certain applications are dealt with under the old rules, and therefore a knowledge of the old rules remains necessary.

---

[1] Ibid. s. 3(2).

[2] Draft Immigration Rules: Control on Entry (Cmnd 4606); Draft Immigration Rules: Control after Entry (Cmnd 4792), revising an earlier draft (Cmnd 4610).

[3] HC (1972–1973) Nos. 79–82.

[4] The phrase 'foreign national' is used throughout the rules in place of 'alien'.

[5] On the first occasion the Home Secretary issued the amendments in the form of Command Papers: Changes in Immigration Rules: Control on Entry (Cmnd 5715–5718), and on the second occasion in the form of further House of Commons Papers: HC (1976–1977) Nos. 238–241. There is no significance in the different methods of releasing the rules, but House of Commons Papers cannot be laid while the House is not sitting.

[6] Statement of Change in Immigration Rules: Control on Entry, EEC and other non-Commonwealth nationals: HC (1972–1973) No. 437. The rules have been amended on a number of occasions when there have been changes in the list of foreign countries whose nationals require visas.

[7] Statement of Change in Immigration Rules: HC (1979–1980) No. 394. These rules have been amended to take into account the admission of Greece to the EEC: Statement of Change in Immigration Rules: HC (1980–1981) No. 84, see para. 3.3 note 10, post.

No.	Statement of Immigration Rules	Amended by	Paragraphs amended
HC 79	Control on Entry: Commonwealth citizens	Cmnd 5715	49 – fiancés entering UK temporarily to marry 60 – refusing entry for medical reasons
		HC 238	47 and 48 – admission of husbands and fiancés
HC 80	Control after Entry: Commonwealth citizens	HC 239	6, 25 and 26 – marriages to women settled in the UK
HC 81	Control on Entry: EEC and other non-Commonwealth nationals	Cmnd 5717	44 – fiancés entering UK temporarily to marry 53 – admission of families of EEC nationals 62 – refusing entry for medical reasons
		HC 240	42 and 43 – admission of husbands and fiancés
HC 82	Control after Entry: EEC and other non-Commonwealth nationals	Cmnd 5718	38 – families of EEC nationals
		HC 241	6, 23 and 24 – marriages to women settled in the UK

The 1980 Rules

1.14 These similarly deal with control *on* and *after* entry, but are now contained in one paper.[8]

It will be seen later that many of the rules are identical for both Commonwealth and non-EEC foreign nationals although there are a number of rules which are more favourable to Commonwealth citizens. There are special provisions for EEC nationals which are designed to comply with the UK's obligations under the EEC Treaty.[9] The rules set out the various categories under which a person may qualify to enter or remain in the UK, both on a temporary basis and indefinitely, and the

[8] Cited, see note 7, supra.
[9] There are, however, omissions in the rules. See para. 3.6, post.

requirements which must be met under these categories. The rules also specify the general grounds upon which entry and extensions of stay may be refused even if a person were to qualify under one of the categories, and the procedure to be adopted in deportation cases.

The Transitional Provisions

1.15 These provide that the current entry rules apply to all decisions taken on or after 1 March 1980 except that:
(1) an application made on or before 14 November 1979 for entry or an extension of stay in whatever capacity will be considered under the old rules, irrespective of the date of the decision;[10]
(2) an application in certain categories for an extension of stay for a further limited period will be considered under the old rules if the applicant:
  (i) had been given limited leave to remain in the UK before 1 March 1980,[11] or
  (ii) had been granted an entry clearance on the basis of an application made on or before 14 November 1979, or an application made and granted before 1 March 1980.[12]
  The categories relate to those who were admitted or obtained extensions on or for marriage, for approved employment (including employment as a trainee or student employee), for a working holiday, to set up as a businessman, as a self-employed person or a person of independent means. The application must be to remain in the same capacity;[13]
(3) an application for leave to remain for an indefinite period will be considered under the old rules where it is from an applicant in the circumstances set out in 2 (i) and (ii) above and he qualifies under one of the categories mentioned other than trainee, student employee or working holidaymaker.[14]

Status of the Rules

1.16 The status of the immigration rules has presented the Court of Appeal with some problems. In *R v Chief Immigration Officer Heathrow Airport, ex parte Salamat Bibi*,[15] the applicant sought an order of certiorari

[10] Ibid., paras. 157, 158.
[11] Ibid., para. 159.
[12] Ibid., para. 160.
[13] Ibid., paras. 159, 160.
[14] Ibid., paras. 161, 162.
[15] [1976] 3 All ER 843, CA.

to quash the decision of the immigration officer refusing her leave to enter. In the course of the argument, her counsel submitted that the immigration rules were not part of the law of the country but were departmental circulars laying down no more than good administrative practice. Roskill LJ was adamant that this was not so. 'These rules are just as much delegated legislation as any other form of rule making activity or delegated legislation which is empowered by Act of Parliament . . . they are just as much part of the law of England as the 1971 Act itself.'[16] But in *R v Secretary of State for the Home Department, ex parte Hosenball*,[17] a different approach was adopted. In that case counsel submitted that the Home Secretary had not complied with the 'statutory provision' of a particular immigration rule. Lord Denning MR believed that the statement in *Salamat Bibi* 'went too far'. The immigration rules were not rules of law but were:

'. . . rules of practice laid down for the guidance of immigration officers and Tribunals who are entrusted with the administration of the Act.'[18]

Although they were not 'rules in the nature of delegated legislation so as to amount to strict rules of law', the courts had to have regard to them because there were provisions in the Act showing that an appeal against an immigration decision must be allowed if the rules are not complied with. In addition, the rules are to be taken into account on an application for judicial review or habeas corpus where there is a question of whether the officers administering the Act have acted fairly.[19]

INSTRUCTIONS TO IMMIGRATION OFFICIALS

1.17 Immigration control is the responsibility of the Home Secretary. The Act refers to the powers of the 'Secretary of State'.[20] Although the powers may be exercised by any 'one of Her Majesty's Principal Secretaries of State'[1] the term 'Home Secretary' is used throughout the text as it reflects the true position in practice.[2]

---

[16] Ibid., at 848. [17] [1977] 3 All ER 452, CA.
[18] Ibid., at 459. [19] Ibid.
[20] Immigration Act 1971, s. 1(4), s. 4(3), (4).
[1] Interpretation Act 1899 s. 12 (3). This includes the Secretary of State for Scotland, *Agee v the Rt Hon. R. K. Murray* (1977) SLT (Notes) 54.
[2] Deportation orders have on occasions been signed by some other Secretary of State.

The Act is administered, in respect of those seeking entry, by immigration officers at the port of entry and by entry clearance officers at British Government posts overseas; in respect of those seeking extensions of stay the Act is administered by officials employed at the Home Office in Croydon.[3] Where a function is carried out by a particular official, for example, an entry clearance officer, he is specifically described as such in the text, but where the decision or action may be taken by any of the immigration officials mentioned or it is clear from the context which official is being referred to the term 'immigration authorities' is frequently used.[4] The Act states that in exercising their functions, immigration officers are to act in accordance with instructions given to them by the Home Secretary.[5] These instructions which are not published are required to be 'not inconsistent with the immigration rules'.[6] There is no reference in the Act to instructions to entry clearance officers and Home Office officials but there is no doubt that such instructions exist.

As a result of parliamentary questions and correspondence between immigrant organisations and pressure groups on the one hand and the Home Office on the other, some instructions have come to light, and where these are known they have been referred to in the text. It should be borne in mind that these instructions may change without anyone being aware that there has been a shift in policy.

APPEAL PROCEDURES

1.18 The Act provides for a two-tier system of appeal. An appeal is usually first made to an adjudicator with appeal lying to the Immigration Appeal Tribunal in limited circumstances. Certain deportation appeals are heard by the Tribunal at first instance. The procedure on appeal is set out in Chapter 14. A chart explaining the system of appeal can be found in Appendix 4. Selected decisions of the Immigration Appeal Tribunal are reported in the Immigration Appeal Reports. The text includes a large number of unreported decisions which can be obtained from the Secretary to the Tribunal, Thanet House, 231 Strand, London WC2, if they are required by practitioners in connection with proceedings before an adjudicator or the Tribunal.

[3] See para. 5.29 et seq., post, for a further explanation of their responsibilities.
[4] Where, under the Act, the Home Secretary does or is required to make a decision personally, this is stated in the text.
[5] Immigration Act 1971, Sch. 2, para. 1(3).   [6] Ibid.

FUTURE CHANGES

1.19 The British Nationality Act 1981 was enacted in October 1981. A note on its implications for immigration law and likely consequential changes in the rules is included at the end of Chapter 2. Changes in the immigration appeals system have been proposed by the Home Office.[7] Further legislation to implement the Conservative manifesto commitment to introduce a compulsory register of dependants appears unlikely.

---

[7] Review of Appeal under the Immigration Act 1971: a discussion document, Home Office, 1981.

TWO

Nationality and Patriality

INTRODUCTION: PATRIALS AND THE RIGHT OF ABODE

2.1 Those who are patrial have a right of abode in the UK and are not subject to immigration control. Those with a right of abode (1) may enter and remain in the UK; (2) are free from all restrictions, e.g. conditions prohibiting working, registering with the police; (3) are not liable to be deported.[1] The term 'patrial' is restricted to certain citizens of the UK and Colonies, and certain citizens of independent Commonwealth countries.[2] However not all citizens of these countries are patrials. The qualifications exclude most of those who were not born, adopted, registered or naturalised in the UK or do not have some close ancestral connection with the UK.

2.2 All others are non-patrials and have no right of abode. They can enter and remain in the UK only if they satisfy the requirements of the immigration laws. They are (1) citizens of the UK or Colonies and of Commonwealth countries who do not meet the patriality requirements; (2) aliens, i.e. citizens of foreign countries outside the Commonwealth or stateless persons; (3) British protected persons: they are neither citizens of the UK and Colonies nor of an independent Commonwealth country nor aliens.

2.3 The Act treats citizens of the Republic of Ireland as a special case. They are neither aliens nor Commonwealth citizens. Although not patrial, they have freedom of entry, but are liable to deportation.

---

[1] There are certain powers of removal and exclusion of patrials from parts of the UK under the Prevention of Terrorism (Temporary Provisions) Act 1976. See Chapter 16, post.

[2] Immigration Act, 1971, s. 2.

NATIONALITY LAW BACKGROUND[3]

2.4 It can be seen that patrial status is dependent on citizenship of the UK and Colonies or of an independent Commonwealth country. These terms must now be explained by referring to the British Nationality Act 1948, which created the distinction and sets out the qualifications for citizenship. The Act has been amended on a number of occasions by subsequent Acts.[4]

It is not possible to understand patriality without knowledge of the nationality laws. The subject is complex and at the time of publication of this text, the British Nationality Act 1981 has been enacted but no commencement date has been set (see Note at the end of this chapter). The last Government published a Green Paper in 1977[5] and the present Government published a White Paper in July 1980.[6] An explanation of the nationality law is given here only in outline.

2.5 The law has always distinguished between British subjects and aliens.[7] Until 1949 all subjects of the Crown throughout the Commonwealth and Empire had the common status of British subjects. The concept of a British subject was based on the principle of allegiance: all born within the territory owned or under the control of the King (including territories outside Britain) owed him allegiance and were his subjects. Others, e.g. those born to British subjects outside British territory and those who became naturalised, were also British subjects. Difficulties began to arise with the development of self-governing Dominions which were anxious to create their own nationality laws based on citizenship of their own particular countries. At the same time there was a desire to maintain links with the Crown, and the British Government was also anxious to retain a formal relationship with these countries. A new approach to British nationality recognising these aims therefore became necessary. As a result a conference was held in London

---

[3] See generally, *Halsbury's Laws* (4th Edn.) Vol. 4, paras. 901 et seq. There are no up-to-date text books on the subject but the standard work Parry, *Nationality and Citizenship Laws of the Commonwealth and the Republic of Ireland* (2 vols. 1957, 1960) sets out the law as at the beginning of 1960. Another useful work is Jones, *British Nationality Law* (1956).

[4] British Nationality Act 1958; Commonwealth Immigration Act 1962; British Nationality Act 1964; British Nationality (No. 2) Act 1964; British Nationality Act 1965; Immigration Act 1971, s. 2(5), Sch. 1.

[5] British Nationality Law – Discussion of possible changes: (Cmnd 6795).

[6] British Nationality Law – Outline of Proposed Legislation: (Cmnd 7987).

[7] For the pre-1949 history see Parry, op. cit., pp. 28 et seq.

in 1947 and agreement was reached that countries which became independent were free (1) to determine who were their citizens; (2) to declare those citizens to be British subjects; and (3) to recognise as British subjects citizens of other Commonwealth countries.

The effect of the agreement was that independent Commonwealth countries were able to enact legislation setting out qualifications for their own particular citizenship while at the same time enabling their citizens to retain their status of British subjects.

BRITISH NATIONALITY ACT 1948

2.6 The UK's contribution to this agreement was the passing by Parliament of the British Nationality Act 1948 which came into force on 1 January, 1949. Although the Act has been amended a number of times, it still remains the basis of our citizenship laws.

The Act created a new unit of citizenship, viz. citizenship of the UK and Colonies, broadly for those who were born in or had some other defined connection with either the UK or its colonies, and maintained the concept of British subject or Commonwealth citizen (the words are interchangeable), so that (1) a citizen of the UK and Colonies is a British subject and Commonwealth citizen,[8] and (2) all citizens of other independent Commonwealth countries, as defined by their own law, are British subjects and Commonwealth citizens under UK law.[9] The new category of citizenship did not change the position under the immigration law because at that time British subjects were free to enter the UK without restriction. It was not until 1962 that British subjects were made liable to immigration control.[10]

CITIZENSHIP OF THE UK AND COLONIES

2.7 The UK comprises Great Britain (England, Wales and Scotland), and Northern Ireland. The Channel Islands and the Isle of Man are technically not part of the UK and Colonies but are treated as part of the Colonies for the purposes of the nationality laws.[11] Colonies comprise those countries whose citizens owe allegiance to the Crown, excluding

[8] British Nationality Act 1948, s. 1(1).
[9] Ibid., s. 1(2).
[10] Commonwealth Immigrants Act 1962. See para. 1.4 ante.
[11] British Nationality Act 1948, s. 33(1). A UK citizen acquiring citizenship because of a connection with the Islands may if he wishes be known as 'a citizen of the UK Islands and Colonies': ibid., s. 33(2).

CITIZENSHIP OF THE UK AND COLONIES 17

independent Commonwealth countries, Protectorates and Trust territories.[12] The present Colonies are Anguilla, Bermuda, British Antarctic Territory, British Indian Ocean Territory, the Cayman Islands, the Falkland Islands and dependencies, Gibraltar, Hong Kong, Montserrat, the Pitcairn Islands Group, St. Helena and dependencies, Turks and Caicos Islands, and the Virgin Islands. In addition the Caribbean islands of St. Christopher and Nevis are an Associated State and those connected with the islands have citizenship of the UK and Colonies.[13]

Acquisition of Citizenship of UK and Colonies[14]

2.8 UK citizenship ('citizenship of the UK and Colonies') can be acquired (1) by birth within the UK and Colonies; (2) by adoption to a citizen of the UK and Colonies within the UK and Colonies; (3) in certain limited circumstances, by descent from the father of a UK citizen where the child is born outside British territory; (4) in the case of Commonwealth and Irish citizens, children, married women and certain stateless persons, by registration if certain qualifications are met; (5) in the case of aliens, by naturalisation if certain qualifications are met. These methods of acquisition of UK citizenship must now be examined in more detail.

Birth

2.9 Every person (irrespective of the nationality of his or her parents) born in the UK and Colonies after 1948 is a UK citizen by birth;[15] as is a person born before 1 January 1949 in a place which was part of the UK and Colonies on that date unless he has subsequently lost that citizenship.[16] There are only two exceptions: (1) children born to diplomats who are not UK citizens;[17] (2) children born in enemy occupied territory whose fathers are enemy aliens.[18] However, if this makes a child stateless and the mother is a UK citizen, a child born after

[12] Interpretation Act 1889, s. 18(3), as amended.
[13] West Indies Act 1967. Anguilla, Antigua, Dominica, Grenada, St. Lucia and St. Vincent have terminated their associate status.
[14] British Nationality Act 1948, ss. 4 et seq., as amended.
[15] Ibid., s. 4.
[16] Ibid., s. 12(1)(a).
[17] Ibid., s. 4; Diplomatic Privileges Act 1964 s. 5(2). See also Consular Relations Act 1968, s. 7.
[18] British Nationality Act, s. 4.

16 September 1964 will be a UK citizen.[19] If an infant is found abandoned within the UK and Colonies on or after 16 September 1964, he is deemed to have been born in the UK unless the contrary is shown, and will therefore be a UK citizen.[20]

Adoption

2.10 A child jointly adopted in the UK and who is not a UK citizen will become one from the date of the adoption order if the adopting father is a UK citizen; and similarly where the adoption is by a single parent only, if that parent is a UK citizen.[1] The courts, whose approval is required before an adoption order is made, are likely to refuse to make an order if the adopters are not genuinely taking the place of the original parents and the purpose of the adoption is to confer UK citizenship on the child, even if the order would be for the benefit of the child.[2] If, however, citizenship is only one benefit and the adopters intend to take the place of the original parents, an order may be made, although the courts can make it conditional on evidence being obtained from the Home Office that there is no objection to acquisition of citizenship.[3]

Descent

2.11 UK citizenship can be acquired by descent.[4] We have seen that those born within the UK and Colonies are UK citizens by birth. Those born outside the UK and Colonies (whether in an independent Commonwealth or a foreign country) may be UK citizens by descent if their father was a UK citizen at the time of the birth.[5] Citizenship by descent can only be acquired if the child is legitimate.[6] It can never be acquired through the mother.[7]

If the child was born before 1949, the child acquires UK citizenship irrespective of the method by which the father acquired UK citizenship.[8]

[19] British Nationality (No. 2) Act 1964, s. 2(1).   [20] Ibid., s. 2(2).

[1] Adoption Act 1958, s. 19.

[2] *Re A (an infant)* [1963] 1 All ER 531.

[3] *Re R (adoption)* [1966] 3 All ER 613. The question of obtaining entry for adopted children who are subject to control is considered below. See para. 8.41, post.

[4] British Nationality Act 1948, s. 5.

[5] Citizenship may also be acquired by descent where the father died before the birth, if he was a UK citizen at the time of his death. Ibid., s. 24.

[6] Ibid., s. 32(2). As to those legitimated by their parents' subsequent marriage, see ibid., s. 23(1).

[7] Except in connection with the registration of minors and stateless persons. See paras. 2.16 and 2.18, post.

[8] Ibid., s. 12(2).

For those born after 1948, citizenship by descent is limited if the father acquired his nationality by descent; then the child will be a UK citizen only if (1) he or she is born in a protectorate, protected state, mandated or trust territory or in any place where the Queen has jurisdiction over British subjects; or (2) he or she is born elsewhere in a foreign country and the birth is registered within a year at a British Consulate; or (3) the person's father is in Crown service at the time of the birth; or (4) the child is born in an independent Commonwealth country and does not become a citizen of that country on birth.

Registration

2.12 One method of acquiring UK citizenship, introduced in the British Nationality Act 1948, is by registration.[9] Registration can take place in the UK or elsewhere and is available to (1) citizens of the independent Commonwealth countries and of the Republic of Ireland; (2) children; (3) women who marry UK citizens; (4) certain stateless persons.

Registration: Commonwealth and Irish Citizens

2.13 Under the 1948 Act, any Commonwealth or Irish citizen over 21 was entitled to register as a UK citizen after one year's ordinary residence in the UK (or in Crown Service), by simply applying to the Home Office.[10] The Home Secretary was bound to register the applicant as a UK citizen. This right was restricted by the Commonwealth Immigrants Act 1962, which lengthened the qualifying period to five years' ordinary residence (or Crown Service) and which prevented a person under a deportation order from registering while the order was still in force.[11] Nevertheless, registration remained as of right once the qualifications were met.

2.14 The Immigration Act 1971 made registration more difficult.[12] In almost all circumstances it ceased to be a right and became a matter of the Home Secretary's discretion, and applicants had to meet additional qualifications. There are, however, two groups of people who retain an entitlement to register:

(a) Those Commonwealth and Irish citizens who were settled in the

---

[9] British Nationality Act 1948, ss. 6–9.
[10] Ibid., s. 6(1).
[11] Commonwealth Immigrants Act 1962, s. 12 (operative from 31 May 1962).
[12] Immigration Act 1971, s. 2(5); Sch. 1 and Appendices thereto, amending British Nationality Act 1948.

UK (ordinarily resident without restrictions on their stay) on 1 January 1973.[13]

They can still register as of right if they are of full age and capacity, but before doing so they must overcome a new hurdle: they must show that throughout the period since 1 January 1973 they have been settled in the UK.

(b) Patrial Commonwealth citizens. This group is described more fully in para. 2.42. In short, they are Commonwealth citizens whose mother was a UK citizen by birth, or who are women who have married a patrial.[14]

They will have to show: that they are of full age and capacity[15] and that for the five years before applying they have been either ordinarily resident in the UK or engaged in 'relevant employment', or a combination of both.[16] 'Relevant employment' includes Crown Service under an international organisation of which the UK is a member, or employment by a company established in the UK. The Home Secretary has power to shorten the qualification period, although he rarely does so.

2.15 Other non-patrial Commonwealth and Irish citizens of full age and capacity are eligible for registration if they satisfy the residential or employment qualifications but they must also show good character, sufficient knowledge of the English or Welsh language, an intention to reside in the UK or a colony or protectorate or to work in relevant employment. There is no obligation on the Home Secretary to register such an applicant even if the requirements are met, and he may refuse a registration without giving a reason.[17]

Registration: Children

2.16 A child whose parent is a UK citizen may be registered as a UK citizen,[18] and the Home Secretary may 'in special circumstances as he thinks fit' permit any child to be registered, irrespective of the

---

[13] Ibid., Sch. 1, para. 2. As to the meaning of 'ordinary residence' and 'settled' see paras. 8.1–8.4, post.

[14] Immigration Act 1971, ss. 2(1)(d); 2(2).

[15] Originally 21 but now 18: Family Law Reform Act 1969, s. 1(3). Full capacity means 'not of unsound mind'; ibid., s. 32(9).

[16] British Nationality Act 1948, as amended, s. 5A(3), (4).

[17] British Nationality Act 1948, s. 5A (as amended by the Immigration Act 1971, Sch. 1, Appendix A).

[18] British Nationality Act 1948, s. 7(1). Application is made by the parent or guardian.

nationality of the parents.[19] Such registration is always discretionary, and attention will be paid to (1) where the child's future is likely to be; and (2) the length of time that the child has been living in the UK. Until recently, applications had been refused if it appeared that the child was likely to live overseas or if, when the child was living in this country, the father had taken no steps to become a UK citizen. In a statement on 7 February 1979,[20] the Home Secretary said that registration will no longer be refused on those grounds. A woman born in the UK will normally be able to have her child registered, subject to there being no well-founded objection by the father, as there could be, e.g. if registration would deprive the child of his existing citizenship. It was made clear that this was an interim policy, pending the review of the whole question of transmission of citizenship in the female line in new nationality legislation.

Registration: Married Women

2.17 A woman, whatever her nationality, who has at any time been married to a UK citizen is entitled to register as a UK citizen as of right, irrespective of her age or capacity.[1] There is no similar right to UK citizenship where a man marries a UK citizen.

Registration: Stateless Persons

2.18 Certain stateless persons are entitled to citizenship on application.[2] An applicant must show that he is, and always has been, stateless and that (1) his mother was a citizen of the UK and Colonies at the time of his birth; or (2) he was born at a place which at the time of his application was within the UK and Colonies; or (3) he is otherwise qualified by parentage, or residence and parentage.[3] In the case of a minor, an application for registration may be made by his parent or guardian. He is entitled to make his own application on reaching the age of 16.[4]

[19] Ibid., s. 7(2).
[20] H. of C. 962 Official Report Written Answers, col. 203.
[1] Ibid., s. 6(2). If, however, the licence to marry was obtained by deception (e.g., by giving a false name to the Superintendent Registrar and signing the marriage register in that name) the Home Secretary is entitled to refuse the application, notwithstanding the marriage is valid. R v *Secretary of State for the Home Department, ex parte Puttick* [1981] 1 All ER 776.
[2] British Nationality (No. 2) Act 1964.
[3] Ibid., s. 1(1), and Sch. thereto.
[4] Ibid., s. 1(3).

Naturalisation

2.19 Aliens (including other stateless persons) and British protected persons can apply to the Home Secretary for naturalisation as UK citizens. Naturalisation can be effected in the UK or elsewhere. An alien must have been either ordinarily resident in the UK or in relevant employment continuously for the 12 months preceding the application and also have been resident in the UK, Colonies or other British territory *or* in relevant employment for a total of four out of the seven years immediately before that period. A British protected person must have been ordinarily resident in the UK or in relevant employment for the five years preceding the application. In either case the applicant must be of good character, have sufficient knowledge of English and show that he intends to reside in a British territory or to remain in relevant employment after naturalisation.

General Requirements for Registration and Naturalisation

2.20 No application for registration based on residence or naturalisation will be entertained from a person who has not become settled, and only legal residence can be counted towards the residence qualification. Applications at the Home Secretary's discretion will not normally be granted if a person's spouse lives abroad. There is no method of appealing against a refusal of registration[5] or naturalisation. The absence of a right of appeal has been criticised[6] and the possibility of its introduction is discussed in the Green Paper, but rejected in the White Paper.[7] There is nothing however to prevent further applications although an application is not likely to be successful if made immediately after a refusal. An oath of allegiance is required in the case of those who are not citizens of a country of which Her Majesty is Queen.[8] Representations by an MP may elicit some indication of the reasons for refusal and the earliest date at which a fresh application may be favourably considered is sometimes stated.

Multiple Nationality

2.21 British nationality law permits multiple nationality, i.e.

[5] Unless registration is as of right. If the Home Secretary were to refuse in such a case, an application for an order of *mandamus* could be sought in the Divisional Court of the High Court.

[6] See e.g., A. Dummett *Citizenship and Nationality* (1976) (Runnymede Trust), pp. 76–77.

[7] British Nationality Law – Discussion of possible changes: (Cmnd 6795) paras 59–60; British Nationality Law – Outlfne of Proposed Legislation: (Cmnd 7987) paras 83, 84.

[8] Immigration Act 1971, Sch. 1, App. C.

citizenship of the UK and Colonies and that of one or more other countries held simultaneously. However, citizenship laws of other countries may prohibit a person retaining citizenship if a new nationality is taken. Thus a US citizen marrying a man who is a UK citizen may register herself as a UK citizen; if she does so, in both US and UK law she will retain both citizenships. But, under Indian law, a citizen of India registering as a UK citizen will lose his Indian nationality on registration. Anyone intending to take UK citizenship will be well advised to consult their Embassy, or, preferably, a lawyer in their original country, to ascertain the effect under their own nationality and immigration laws of acquiring UK citizenship. On some occasions, the advantage of UK citizenship will be offset by the difficulties they will face should they wish to return to their country of origin.

Loss of UK Citizenship

2.22 There are three ways in which UK citizenship may be lost:

(a) when a colony becomes independent, a UK citizen connected with that country will usually lose citizenship and will become a citizen of the newly independent country. In some cases those with an ancestral connection with the UK will be permitted to retain their UK citizenship as well as acquiring the new citizenship.[9] They will therefore have dual nationality;

(b) where a person has dual nationality or is acquiring another nationality, he will lose his UK citizenship if he makes a declaration renouncing it.[10]

(c) where a person obtains citizenship by registration or naturalisation, the Home Secretary has the power to deprive him of it if satisfied that citizenship was obtained by fraud, false representation or concealment of material fact, or that it is not 'conducive to

---

[9] The position is complex and depends upon the independence legislation. See *Halsbury's Laws*, op. cit., paras. 936 et seq., for a more detailed explanation. In many cases the following groups were allowed to retain UK citizenship; (i) Those born or naturalised in the UK or Colonies or whose father or paternal grandfather so acquired UK citizenship; (ii) Those born in a protectorate or protected state, or whose father or paternal grandfather was so born and is or was a British subject, see, e.g. Barbados Independence Act 1966. An example of UK citizenship by registration being lost on independence can be found in *Mohammed (AA)* [1979–80] Imm AR 103.

[10] British Nationality Act 1948, s. 19(1). The method of doing so is set out in the British Nationality Regulations 1975, reg. 21.

the public good' to let him remain a UK citizen.[11] Before anyone is deprived of citizenship, he has a right to challenge the decision before a Committee of Inquiry.[12] However, this right is not open to those whom the Home Secretary has reasonable grounds to believe obtained citizenship by falsely representing their identity.

In *R v Secretary of State for the Home Department, ex parte Akhtar*[13] it was conceded that the Home Secretary had reasonable grounds in believing that the applicant was not the son of WA. The Court of Appeal held that the applicant had therefore not become a citizen of the UK and Colonies despite his purported registration as a minor. The Home Secretary was entitled to treat the applicant as an illegal entrant under the Immigration Act if he was not able to prove that he was the person described in the citizenship register. The Court followed an earlier decision in *R v Secretary of State for the Home Department, ex parte Sultan Mahmood*[14] where it was held that registration acquired by the fraudulent use of a passport which was not the applicant's was a nullity, but the Court in *Akhtar* did accept that the right to a Committee of Inquiry would arise if, for example, citizenship was obtained by falsely representing the period of residence required to qualify for registration.

Resumption of UK Citizenship

2.23 In practice there is only one set of circumstances in which UK citizenship may be resumed following renunciation of citizenship,[15] viz: where a person made a decision of renunciation and at the time of the declaration he was or was about to become a citizen of a Commonwealth country, if he can show to the Home Secretary, (1) he could not have remained or become such a citizen but for the declaration or had reasonable cause to believe that he would have been deprived of his

---

[11] British Nationality Act 1948, s. 20. See also British Nationality Act 1965, s. 3. The power to deprive naturalised persons of citizenship is wider than that for registered persons: ibid., s. 20(3)). For further details see *Halsbury's Laws*, op. cit., paras. 942 et seq.

[12] British Nationality Act 1948, s. 20(7); British Nationality Act 1965, s. 3(3).

[13] [1980] 2 All ER 735, CA.

[14] [1980] 3 WLR 312, CA.

[15] The circumstances arise from the British Nationality Act 1964 and are set out in the text. There are provisions in the British Nationality Act 1948 and the Cyprus Act 1960 for the resumption of citizenship by children who have lost their citizenship in certain circumstances which are not likely to occur in practice. See *Halsbury's Laws*, op. cit., para. 946.

citizenship of that country unless he made the declaration; and (2) he has a qualifying connection with the UK and Colonies or with a protectorate or protected state; or if a woman, had been married to a person who has or would if living have such a connection.[16] The qualifying connection with the UK and Colonies is that the applicant or his father or paternal grandfather was either born in the UK or one of the remaining colonies or obtained citizenship by registration or naturalisation, or became a British subject by reason of annexation of any territory included in the colony. The qualifying connection with a protectorate or protected state is that the applicant was born there, or his father or paternal grandfather was born there and is or at any time was a British subject.[17] There is a discretion for the Home Secretary to register an applicant who renounced but lacked the qualifying connection.

CITIZENS OF THE REPUBLIC OF IRELAND

2.24 The 26 counties of Southern Ireland became an independent country known as the Irish Free State in 1922 and later Eire in 1937. The country became a Republic in 1949. The Act places Irish citizens in a special position. Although they are not British subjects (Commonwealth citizens) they are not aliens.[18] Those who were British subjects before 1949 are able to choose so to remain merely by writing to the Home Secretary declaring that they have a connection with the UK, e.g. possession of a UK passport issued in the UK or Colonies, Crown Service or 'descent, residence or otherwise'.[19]

BRITISH SUBJECTS AND COMMONWEALTH CITIZENS

2.25 These terms have identical meanings and comprise three groups of people, (1) citizens of the United Kingdom and Colonies; (2) citizens of independent Commonwealth countries; (3) British subjects without citizenship.

Citizens of Independent Commonwealth Countries

2.26 As Commonwealth countries achieved their independence they

---

[16] British Nationality Act 1964, s. 1(1).
[17] Ibid., s. 1(2). Citizenship is effective from the date of registration; ibid., s. 1(6).
[18] British Nationality Act 1948 s. 32(1). See also, Ireland Act 1949, s. 2(1).
[19] British Nationality Act 1948, s. 2(1).

have made their own citizenship laws.[20] Most of these countries were formerly colonies but some were protectorates (e.g. Uganda).[1] Consequently amendments have been made to the British Nationality Act 1948 removing UK citizenship from those who acquired the new citizenship of the independent country unless they had ancestral connections with the UK or a remaining colony.[2]

Independent countries have not always given citizenship automatically to all those born within the country, e.g. when Kenya became independent those with neither parent born in Kenya were given a choice of retaining their UK citizenship or registering as Kenyan citizens.[3] Many, mostly of Asian origin, chose to retain UK citizenship because they were worried about their future in Kenya. A similar situation arose when Tanganyika and Uganda achieved independence.[4]

Loss of Commonwealth Status

2.27 If a person ceases to be a citizen of an independent Commonwealth country under the law of that country, e.g. by taking citizenship of another country, he will no longer be a British subject and Commonwealth citizen under UK law.

There have been two occasions when independent Commonwealth countries have left the Commonwealth, and the effect of withdrawal is that their citizens cease to be British subjects. In 1961 and 1972 respectively South Africa and Pakistan left the Commonwealth and legislation was passed to make their citizens aliens.[5] There were transitional provisions, much more generous in the case of South Africans, whereby for a limited period some could retain the right of British subjects and decide whether to apply for registration as UK citizens.[6]

---

[20] The Commonwealth countries are Antigua and Barbuda, Australia, the Bahamas, Bangladesh, Barbados, Belize, Botswana, Canada, Cyprus, Dominica, Fiji, the Gambia, Ghana, Guyana, India, Jamaica, Kenya, Kiribati, Lesotho, Malawi, Malaysia, Malta, Mauritius, Nauru, New Zealand, Nigeria, Papua New Guinea, St. Lucia, St. Vincent and the Grenadines, Seychelles, Sierra Leone, Singapore, Solomon Isles, Sri Lanka, Swaziland, Tanzania, Tonga, Trinidad and Tobago, Tuvalu, Uganda, Vanuata, Western Samoa, Zambia and Zimbabwe. South Africa left the Commonwealth in 1961 and Pakistan in 1972.

[1] There are now no existing protectorates or protected states.
[2] See para. 2.22, ante and note 9, ante.
[3] Kenya Independence Act 1963, s. 3.
[4] Tanganyika Independence Act 1961, s. 2. and Uganda Independence Act 1962, s. 2.
[5] South Africa Act 1962; Pakistan Act 1974.
[6] Pakistan citizens, although now foreign nationals, retain some of the benefits of Commonwealth citizens under the immigration laws. See para. 5.5 (entry clearance), post, and para. 11.15 (deportation), post.

British Subjects without Citizenship

2.28 These comprise a relatively small group of people born before 1949 whom the UK Government expected to become citizens of an independent Commonwealth country, mainly India and Pakistan. When these countries did not grant them citizenship, the UK refused to make these people UK citizens and they therefore remained British subjects without citizenship.[7]

BRITISH PROTECTED PERSONS[8]

2.29 At one time there were some 20 countries or territories which were under the control of the UK, but which were not colonies: they were British protectorates, British protected states or trust territories, most of which were former German colonies given to the UK to administer after the First World War, or territories in the Arabian Gulf. They have all now become independent countries or been incorporated into such countries. Most have remained within the Commonwealth. Those who had a connection with these territories (usually through birth, descent or registration) were known as British protected persons. Those who did not obtain citizenship when the former protectorates or trust territories became independent usually retain their status as British protected persons. The term is more or less meaningless because it confers no particular rights either under the nationality or immigration laws. British protected persons are not British subjects but are excluded from the definition of aliens under the British Nationality Act 1948. In practice their status is akin to that of aliens: e.g. they are able to apply for naturalisation in almost identical circumstances.

ALIENS

2.30 Under the nationality law an alien is a person who is not a British subject, a British protected person or a citizen of the Republic of Ireland.[9]

---

[7] See *Halsbury's Laws*, op. cit., paras. 925–927. The Government estimates that there are about 50,000 British subjects without citizenship. See British Nationality Law: Outline of Proposed Legislation. (Cmnd 7987), App. 13.

[8] See *Halsbury's Laws*, op. cit., para. 933, for a more detailed definition of British protected persons. The Government estimates that there are about 140,000 British protected persons (Cmnd 7987), App. 13.

[9] British Nationality Act 1948, s. 32(1).

PATRIALITY

2.31 We are now in a position to examine which citizens of the UK and Colonies and of Commonwealth countries qualify as patrials. The following summary may be useful in giving a general indication as to who are patrials and is followed by a more detailed explanation.

UK citizens (i.e. citizens of the UK and Colonies) are patrials if citizenship was acquired by:

(1) *birth* in the UK;
(2) *adoption* in the UK;
(3) *birth or adoption in the Colonies, or by descent,* but only if there is an ancestral connection with the UK (i.e. through a UK citizen parent who either:
   (i) acquired citizenship in the UK, or
   (ii) had a parent who acquired citizenship there);
(4) *registration* in the UK as a UK citizen by a Commonwealth citizen or by a child whose parent is a UK citizen or by a woman on the basis of marriage to a UK citizen prior to 28 October 1971;
(5) *naturalisation* in the UK by an alien or British protected person.

UK citizens who do not qualify under these categories may nevertheless be patrial (1) by having lived in the UK for five years and having become settled; (2) by being a woman who marries a patrial.

2.32 Citizens of an independent Commonwealth country are patrial (1) if they have close ancestral connections with the UK (i.e. a parent born in the UK); (2) by being a woman who marries a patrial. Commonwealth citizens who do not qualify under these categories may become patrial if UK citizenship is acquired by registration on grounds of residence in the UK.

2.33 Irish citizens are not patrials but may become patrials if (1) UK citizenship is acquired by registration on grounds of residence in the UK; (2) being a woman, she marries a patrial and registers as a UK citizen.

2.34 Aliens and British protected persons are not patrials but may become patrials if (1) UK citizenship is acquired by naturalisation in the UK; (2) being a woman, she marries a patrial and registers as a UK citizen.

Those who have dual nationality will be patrial if their UK citizenship is of the type which confers patriality.

PATRIAL CITIZENS OF UK AND COLONIES

Birth

2.35 UK citizens who are born in the UK are patrials.[10] Birth on a ship or aircraft registered in the UK, or one belonging to the UK Government is regarded as birth in the UK.[11]

Adoption

2.36 A child adopted in the UK who becomes a UK citizen on adoption is a patrial.[12]

Descent

2.37 UK citizens who acquire citizenship by birth or adoption in the colonies, or in independent Commonwealth and foreign countries (usually citizens by descent) will qualify as patrials if they show a link through a parent and grandparent with the UK as follows:

(a) one of the parents must be a UK citizen at the date of the child's birth or adoption;[13] and
(b) the UK citizen parent or that parent's mother or father must have become a UK citizen in the UK by birth, adoption, registration or naturalisation.[14]

If neither the parent nor the grandparent acquired citizenship in the UK there is no claim to patriality except in an extremely limited number of cases where the parent or grandparent acquired citizenship by registration overseas.[15] In the case of an illegitimate child, the link can be established through the mother.[16] This provision is only likely to be of

---

[10] Immigration Act 1971, s. 2(1)(a).
[11] Ibid., s. 2(3)(b).
[12] Ibid., s. 2(1)(a).
[13] The person must be 'legally adopted', ibid., s. 2(1)(b). This means 'adopted in pursuance of an order made by any court in the UK and Islands or by an adoption specified as an overseas adoption by order of the Secretary of State under section 4 of the Adoption Act 1968'; ibid., s. 33(1). See also *Pereira (J)* [1979–80] Imm AR 79.
[14] Ibid., s. 2(1)(b). Where the parent dies before the birth of the child, that parent must have been a UK citizen at the time of his death; ibid., s. 2(3).
[15] Ibid., s. 2(4), i.e. registration in an independent Commonwealth country by a UK High Commissioner (British Nationality Act 1948, s. 8(2)); and registration overseas of children before 28 October 1971; (ibid., s. 7).
[16] Immigration Act 1971, s. 2(3)(a).

benefit to those who acquired citizenship by birth in the Colonies, as an illegitimate child cannot acquire citizenship by descent.[17]

As there was no concept of UK citizenship before 1 January 1949, those who held British nationality before that date are to be regarded as UK citizens for this purpose.[18]

Registration

2.38 The effect of registration is to confer on the applicant UK citizenship. But not all those who acquire citizenship by registration qualify as patrials.

Registered UK citizens, formerly citizens of independent Commonwealth countries and the Republic of Ireland, will become patrial provided the registration (due to their residential or employment qualifications),[19] took place in the UK or was made in an independent Commonwealth country by a UK High Commissioner.[20]

Children who are registered as UK citizens (usually following their parents' registration or naturalisation) are patrial if registration took place in the UK at any time or if registration took place in an independent Commonwealth country at a British High Commission before the passing of the Act.[1]

Registration on the basis of marriage itself does not confer patriality on a woman unless (1) the registration took place before 28 October 1971; or (2) her marriage took place before that date and the registration was effected later. But a woman who registers as a UK citizen on marriage will be a patrial if her husband is a patrial UK citizen.[2] Registration may be effected in the UK or in an independent Commonwealth country by a UK High Commissioner.

Naturalisation

2.39 All those who are naturalised UK citizens are patrials provided the naturalisation was effected in the UK or Islands.[3]

A number of people, particularly those who were formerly British protected persons, have become naturalised by application in a Colony

---

[17] British Nationality Act 1948, s. 32(2).

[18] Immigration Act 1971, s. 2(3)(b); 'UK' in relation to a time before 31 March 1922 means Great Britain and Ireland; ibid.

[19] See para. 2.13, ante

[20] Immigration Act 1971, s. 2(1)(a), (4).

[1] I.e., 28 October 1971., ibid.

[2] Ibid., s. 2(2).

[3] Ibid., s. 2(1)(a).

or protectorate. They are not patrials. The Immigration Appeal Tribunal has rejected the argument that as all applications require the Home Secretary's approval, all naturalisations must take place in the UK and that the Governor of a territory is merely a delegate of the Home Secretary. In *Keshwani*,[4] the Tribunal held that the 1971 Act drew a distinction between naturalisation granted in the UK and Islands and naturalisation elsewhere. Thus UK citizenship conferred by the issue of a certificate of naturalisation in 1956 in the then protectorate of Uganda by the Governor was not 'citizenship by naturalisation in the UK' and the appellant did not qualify as a patrial.

Settlement

2.40 A UK citizen who does not otherwise qualify as a patrial will do so if at anytime (1) he has been ordinarily resident in the UK and Islands for at least five years; and (2) he was a UK citizen throughout that period; and (3) there were no conditions attached to his stay at the end of the period.[5] It should be noted that the qualifications do not require a person to have been settled here for five years. A person may have been ordinarily resident in the UK subject to conditions restricting the period of his stay or employment.[6] Once he has been ordinarily resident for five years and all conditions are removed, he will be settled in the UK and will become a patrial.

Married Women

2.41 A woman who is a UK citizen is a patrial if (1) she is married to a man who is a patrial, whether he is a citizen of the UK or some other Commonwealth country,[7] (2) she has at any time been the wife of a person who while they were married was a patrial:[8] this includes (a) marriage to a person who would have been a patrial (UK citizen by birth, adoption, descent, registration, or naturalisation in the UK) if such a concept had existed prior to 1973;[9] (b) marriage to a person who died before 1949, if, but for his death, he would have qualified as a patrial citizen of the UK and Colonies.[10]

[4] [1975] Imm AR 38.
[5] Immigration Act 1971, s. 2(1)(c).
[6] But there is increasing doubt as to whether a person is ordinarily resident in the UK while he is a student. See para. 8.3, post.
[7] Ibid., s. 2(2)(a).
[8] Ibid., s. 2(2)(b)(i).
[9] Ibid., s. 2(2)(b)(ii).
[10] Ibid., s. 2(3)(c).

PATRIAL COMMONWEALTH CITIZENS

Descent

2.42 Commonwealth citizens may qualify as patrials if they show a sufficiently close ancestral link with the UK, but the link must be closer than that for UK citizens. The Act[11] limits patriality to those having a parent who at the time of their birth or adoption was a UK citizen born in the UK or Islands. As those whose father was a UK citizen born in the UK would themselves be UK citizens under the British Nationality Act 1948,[12] those who qualify usually will be Commonwealth citizens whose mother was born in the UK and Islands.

Married Women

2.43 A woman who is a citizen of a Commonwealth country becomes a patrial on marriage to a patrial in the same circumstances as women who are UK citizens.[13]

LOSS OF PATRIALITY

2.44 A patrial citizen of the UK and Colonies may cease to be a patrial if he should lose his UK and Colonies citizenship. The circumstances in which citizenship may be lost have already been set out.[14] It should be particularly noted that when a colony becomes independent most citizens of the UK and Colonies will lose that citizenship and become citizens of the new country. If they were patrials, that status will normally be lost at the same time. The only circumstances in which patriality will be retained after loss of UK and Colonies citizenship are where a person becomes a citizen of an independent Commonwealth country and qualifies as a patrial either (1) because of close ancestral connection;[15] or (2) as a woman who has been married to a patrial.[16] A patrial Commonwealth citizen will cease to be a patrial on the loss of his or her Commonwealth citizenship.

---

[11] Ibid., s. 2(1)(d).
[12] British Nationality Act 1948, s. 5. See para. 2.11, ante.
[13] See para. 2.11, ante.
[14] See para. 2.22, ante
[15] Immigration Act 1971, s. 2(1)(d).
[16] Ibid., s. 2(2)(b). This may produce some odd results. Married women may thus retain their patriality when they become citizens of an independent country as a result of having been married to a citizen of the UK and Colonies who has lost that citizenship on independence.

PATRIALS AND THE EEC

2.45 The EEC Treaty provides for free movement within the Community for workers who are nationals of member states.[17] This caused particular problems for the UK Government when it joined the EEC on 1 January 1973,[18] the same date on which the Immigration Act 1971 came into force. As the status of 'UK national' does not exist in our law, the Government made a unilateral Declaration defining a UK national for the purposes of Community law, viz.[19]

'(a) persons who are citizens of the United Kingdom and Colonies or British subjects not possessing that citizenship or the citizenship of any other Commonwealth country or territory, who, in either case, have the right of abode in the UK, and are therefore exempt from UK immigration control;

(b) persons who are citizens of the UK and Colonies by birth or by registration or naturalisation in Gibraltar, or whose father was so born, registered or naturalised.'

It can be seen that this definition is in most respects narrower than that of patrial status. Although it includes UK citizens connected with Gibraltar, who may not be patrial, it excludes patrial citizens of independent Commonwealth countries.

The legal status of this unilateral Declaration is uncertain and it has been argued that it is illegal with regard to the basic requirements of Community law not to discriminate between nationals of member states.[20]

There are also special provisions for UK citizens connected with the Channel Islands and the Isle of Man. Not all provisions of the EEC Treaty apply to the Islands and those who acquired citizenship solely on the basis of their or their parents' or grandparents' birth, adoption, naturalisation or registration in the Islands are excluded from the EEC

---

[17] EEC Treaty, arts. 3, 48. The subject is considered more fully at para. 7.44, post.
[18] European Communities Act 1972.
[19] The Declaration is annexed to the EEC Treaty and the Treaty of Accession.
[20] W. R. Böhning, The scope of the EEC system of free movement of workers, (1973) *CMLRev.*, pp. 81–86. For further discussion of the definition, see: R. O. Plender, The right to free movement in the European Communities in J. W. Bridge, D. Lasak, R. O. Plender and D. L. Perrott (eds), *Fundamental Rights* (London 1973); G. S. Goodwin-Gill, *International Law and the Movement of Persons between States* (Oxford 1978), pp. 173–176.

laws on freedom of movement. Islanders whose citizenship or that of their parents or grandparents was acquired in the United Kingdom are free to move within the Community, as are those who have been ordinarily resident in the UK for five years.[1]

PATRIALS AND ENTRY TO THE UK

2.46 The Act states that patrials have the right to enter the UK 'without let or hindrance' provided they furnish proof of patriality, if required.[2] The burden of proof lies with the person claiming that he or she is a patrial.[3] The Act requires that a 'certificate of patriality' must be produced on entry by (1) UK citizens who acquired patriality by settling in the UK; (2) Commonwealth citizens with a UK-born parent; (3) women who are patrial by marriage to a person in one of the above groups.[4] A certificate can be issued by a 'British Government representative overseas' or by the Home Office.[5] A printed or stamped endorsement in a UK passport that the holder has right of abode in the UK is regarded as equivalent to a certificate of patriality.

2.47 There is a right of appeal to an immigration appeals adjudicator against a refusal to issue a certificate,[6] but this right will be of no immediate use to those who arrive at a port of entry without a certificate claiming that they are patrials under one of the three heads above. If they are refused entry, they cannot appeal on the ground that they are patrial, although they may have other grounds of appeal[7] and appeal against refusal of entry must be made from overseas unless the passenger holds an entry clearance or work permit. A UK citizen previously settled in the UK is unlikely to be refused if he has no certificate or endorsement since he will still re-qualify for admission under the immigration rules and may later pursue his patriality claim with the Home Office.[8]

2.48 Other patrial UK citizens do not need a certificate but must nevertheless prove they are patrial to the satisfaction of the immigration officer. In all cases the burden of proof is on the person claiming that he or she is a patrial. No problems will arise for those born in the UK

---

[1] Treaty of Accession, Cmnd 5179–1, Protocol No. 3, arts. 2, 6. Their freedom of movement within the UK and Islands is not affected by these provisions.
[2] Immigration Act 1971, s. 1(1).
[3] Ibid., s. 3(8).
[4] Ibid., s. 3(9).
[5] H C 394, para. 4.
[6] Immigration Act 1971, s. 13(2). As to appeals generally, see Chapter 14, post.
[7] Ibid., s. 13(3).
[8] HC 394, para. 5. See para. 8.67, post.

because their passports will show their place of birth. Moreover, the immigration rules provide that those holding UK passports issued in the UK, Islands or Irish Republic are 'to be admitted freely without proof of patriality' unless the passport is endorsed to show that the person is subject to immigration control.[9]

2.49 Difficulties have been particularly acute for wives abroad who wish to join their husbands in the UK. In India, Pakistan and Bangladesh there are delays of up to two years before wives are interviewed to establish their eligibility for entry.[10] Some wives are patrials but as a result of a rule of practice laid down by the immigration authorities they were informed that they had to obtain a certificate of patriality overseas and that a certificate would not be issued by the Home Office on arrival in the UK.

This practice was tested in *R v Secretary of State for the Home Department, ex parte Phansopkar*,[11] where a Commonwealth citizen arrived in the UK from India without entry clearance but claiming that she was patrial as a result of her marriage to a UK citizen who obtained citizenship by registration in the UK. She argued that she was therefore entitled to have a certificate issued to her by the Home Office. The Court of Appeal held that provided she could prove her right to a certificate such a right could not be taken away by arbitrarily refusing her a certificate or by delaying issue without good cause. The Court of Appeal rejected the Home Office argument that the application should be made overseas and be subject to the same delays as applications for entry clearance. She was entitled to have her application examined fairly and in a reasonable time. Lord Denning MR did however take the view[12] that if there was a separate queue overseas for applicants for certificates of patriality with little delay in considering applications, the Home Office could then reasonably refuse to entertain applications in London from persons arriving at the ports. Following *Phansopkar* the Foreign Office set up a separate queue overseas so that patrial wives are not subject to lengthy delays. It may now thus be possible to justify a refusal to consider an application made at the port of entry, but in practice Commonwealth patrial wives arriving without certificates are admitted.[13]

[9] H C 394, para. 5.   [10] See para. 5.52, post.   [11] [1975] 3 All ER 497.
[12] Ibid., at p. 507.
[13] In *Patel v Chief Immigration Officer (Heathrow) and Secretary of State for the Home Department* (1977) 7 July, CA (unreported) leave to move for *mandamus* requiring the Home Secretary to issue certificates of patriality was refused where the appellants had submitted themselves to immigration control and later, following refusal of leave to enter, claimed patriality.

This decision is only of help to those who can show they are patrial. The fact that an applicant is entitled to become a patrial will not enable him or her to enter the UK without entry clearance to take the necessary steps to qualify as patrial. Thus in *R v Secretary of State for the Home Department, ex parte Akhtar*,[14] a Pakistani (non-Commonwealth) woman sought to join her UK citizen husband who was patrial. She claimed that on entry she had the right to register as a UK citizen under the British Nationality Act 1948 and that on registration she would become patrial. The Court held that the immigration officer was entitled to refuse her entry because until she changed her status by registration she had no claim to a right of abode in the UK as a wife of a patrial.

Advice to Patrials Entering the UK

2.50 In view of the difficulties which can arise on entry, the following advice may assist.

(a) Patrial UK citizens who were born in the UK or who have passports stamped 'holder has the right of abode in the UK' should not experience problems about their entry. It should be borne in mind that an immigration officer has the power to examine any person for the purpose of determining whether he or she is patrial[15] but in almost all cases this will be evident from an examination of the passport. A more detailed examination will arise if the immigration officer suspects that citizenship was obtained by registration or naturalisation following an earlier illegal entry.[16]

(b) Patrial UK citizens who acquired their citizenship by registration or naturalisation may find it useful to keep their certificates of naturalisation or registration with their passports for production on entry: neither these certificates nor a certificate of patriality are strictly necessary and immigration officers should not be encouraged to demand them.

(c) Patrial UK citizens who acquired patriality by ancestral connections do not require a certificate of patriality, but it may be sensible to apply for one if there have been any difficulties in the past in gaining entry.

(d) Patrials from independent Commonwealth countries require a certificate of patriality on entry.

---

[14] [1975] 3 All ER 1087.
[15] Immigration Act 1971, Sch. 2, para. 2(1)(a), see para. 5.31, post.
[16] See, e.g. the situation which arose in *R v Secretary of State for the Home Department, ex parte Akhtar*, cited, note 14 ante.

(e) UK citizens who are patrials because their husbands are patrial and decide to enter the UK without obtaining a certificate of patriality should particularly ensure that they have sufficient documentation to prove they are married to a patrial. They should be always met at the airport.

(f) Patrial UK citizens whose passports do not show that they have a right of abode nor contain a certificate of patriality, should apply to the Home Office or when seeking a new passport to the Passport Office on Form P2 to have their passport endorsed to show they have a right of abode.

A NOTE ON THE BRITISH NATIONALITY ACT 1981

2.51 The Act will repeal almost the whole of the British Nationality Act 1948, as well as the British Nationality Acts of 1964 and 1965 and other amending legislation, including schedule 1 to the Immigration Act 1971. Although it was enacted on 30 October 1981, the necessary preparatory work is such that commencement is unlikely to be before 1 January 1983.

Change of Status at Commencement

2.52 Citizenship of the UK and Colonies will disappear, and those who hold it will acquire at commencement one or more of three new citizenships:

(1) British citizenship — acquired by all patrial citizens of the UK and Colonies except those registered under Section 1 of the British Nationality (No. 2) Act 1964 (stateless persons) whose mothers do not become British citizens.[17]
(2) British Dependent Territories citizenship — acquired by citizens of the UK and Colonies with a connection of birth, naturalisation, registration, descent or marriage with a dependent territory.[18]
(3) British Overseas citizenship — acquired by citizens of the UK and Colonies who do not acquire either British citizenship or

---

[17] British Nationality Act, s. 11.
[18] Ibid., s. 23.

British Dependent Territories citizenship.[19] British Overseas citizenship will thus be acquired by East African Asians who have not become patrial through settlement and residence in the UK, by other citizens of the UK and Colonies, e.g. in Malaysia who did not lose this citizenship under independence legislation, and by citizens of the UK and Colonies by descent and consular registration who are not patrial by virtue of having a UK born parent or grandparent.

2.53 The status of British protected persons will be unchanged. British subjects without citizenship will continue to be British subjects,[20] as will citizens of the Republic of Ireland who have made claims to remain British subjects; a citizen of the Republic who was a citizen of Eire and a British subject immediately before 1 January 1949 will continue to be able to make such a claim.[1] But Commonwealth citizens will no longer be British subjects, although where other legislation, e.g. Representation of the People Act 1949, refers to British subjects it will still be deemed to refer to Commonwealth citizens.[2]

Future Acquisition of British Citizenship

2.54 Substantial changes will be made in the provisions for future acquisition of citizenship.

(1) Birth – children born in the UK will no longer be citizens by birth alone. A child born in the UK will be a British citizen by birth if at the time of the birth the father or mother is (a) a British citizen, or (b) settled in the UK.[3] 'Settled' is defined as in the Immigration Act 1971 as being ordinarily resident without being subject under the immigration laws to any restriction on the period for which a person may remain.[4] A child born in the UK who does not become a British citizen at birth will be entitled to be registered at any time when a parent becomes a British citizen or settled, or at the age of 10 if he has not been outside the UK for more than 90 days in any of the first 10 years of his life.[5]

(2) Descent – a child born outside the UK will be a British citizen at birth if either the father or mother is a British citizen otherwise than by descent, or a British citizen by descent who was recruited in the UK for Crown service, service under an EEC institution or certain other designated service, e.g. employment by the British Council.[6] A child born

[19] Ibid., s. 26.
[20] Ibid., s. 30.
[1] Ibid., s. 31.
[2] Ibid., s. 51.
[3] Ibid., s. 1.
[4] Ibid., s. 50.
[5] Ibid., s. 1.
[6] Ibid., s. 2.

abroad to a British citizen by descent will be entitled to be registered as a British citizen by descent if application is made within 12 months of the birth and the parent (a) was born to a parent who was a British citizen otherwise than by descent and (b) has spent three years in the UK at any time prior to the birth.[7]

(3) Marriage – the entitlement to registration of women married to citizen husbands will be ended at commencement for widows and divorcees and five years after commencement for those whose marriages subsist.[8] Spouses of British citizens of either sex will be able to apply for naturalisation subject to the normal requirements except that the residence qualification will be reduced to three years and the language requirement will not apply.[9]

(4) Registration and naturalisation – the entitlement to registration of Commonwealth citizens settled in the UK before 1 January 1973 will be ended five years after commencement.[10] Citizens of the British Dependent Territories, British Overseas citizens, British subjects under the Act and British protected persons will have an entitlement to registration after five years residence.[11] In all other cases, acquisition by grant will be by naturalisation, subject to the same requirements as to good character, language and intentions to reside in the UK as under existing legislation.[12] The residence qualification will remain five years, but maximum periods of absence from the UK will be prescribed and the Home Secretary will be able to waive the language requirement on grounds of age or physical or mental condition.[13]

Dual or Multiple Nationality

2.55 UK law will continue to permit dual or multiple nationality.

Patriality and Certificates of Entitlement

2.56 The Immigration Act 1971 will be amended so that the term 'patrial' will disappear from UK law.[14] All British citizens will have the right of abode in the UK. Commonwealth citizens who at commence-

---

[7] Ibid., s. 3.
[8] Ibid., s. 8.
[9] Ibid., s. 6. Sch. 1.
[10] Ibid., s. 7. For those who are minors at the commencement the entitlement will continue for five years from their 18th birthday. The Home Secretary will have discretion to accept applications made after the five year periods have expired but within eight years.
[11] Ibid., s. 4. British Dependent Territories citizens from Gibraltar will have an absolute right to be registered without having lived in the UK: ibid., s. 5.
[12] Ibid., s. 6, Sch. 1.   [13] Ibid., Sch. 1.   [14] Ibid., s. 39, Sch. 4.

ment are patrial by virtue of having a UK-born parent or being the wife of a patrial will retain the right of abode for their lifetimes, but no one who is born or who marries a British citizen after commencement will have the right of abode without being or becoming a British citizen.

2.57 Those persons who now require a certificate of patriality will still require 'certificates of entitlement'.[15]

Implications for Immigration Law

2.58 The implications for immigration control are relatively easy to understand. No one without the right of abode under existing legislation will acquire it at commencement, since British citizenship will not be conferred on anyone who is not now a patrial citizen of the UK and Colonies. Almost all those who have the right of abode under existing legislation will retain it, the sole category excepted being those registered under the British Nationality (No. 2) Act 1964 (stateless persons) whose mothers do not become British citizens. All British citizens will have the right of abode, and for those born after commencement, the right of abode will be confined to British citizens alone.

2.59 The immigration rules will have to be amended where they refer to existing categories of citizenship. An undertaking has been given that UK passport holders previously settled here who become British Overseas citizens or who are British protected persons or British subjects without citizenship will continue to be freely readmitted.[16]

The Government has repeatedly stated that the special voucher scheme will be unaffected:[17] those who become British Overseas citizens will be eligible or ineligible according to the same criteria as are applied at present to non-patrial citizens of the UK and Colonies. New immigration rules will be necessary to cover the situation of children born in the UK who are not British citizens: the basic principle will be that a child born in the UK who is not a British citizen will be granted leave to remain such as to bring him into line with his parents. If the parents are here illegally, the child would not be an illegal entrant liable to removal but could be deported with the parents.[18] The Home Secretary has also stated that the immigration rules regarding husbands and fiancés will be reviewed after the Bill has been passed.

[15] Ibid., s. 39.
[16] Letters, Home Office to JCWI, 24 November 1980 and 21 May 1981.
[17] See for example the White Paper, British Nationality Law – Outline of Proposed Legislation. July 1980, Cmnd 7987, para. 105.
[18] H. of C. Official Report, Standing Committee F, 12 February 1981, col. 46.

THREE

Special Provisions for Non-Patrials

3.1 Not all non-patrials are subject to the same degree of immigration control. Under the Act and rules, special provisions are made for particular groups of people. In addition the Home Secretary is empowered under the Act to exempt from control either individuals or any class of person. The former may be exempted by the Home Secretary simply by signing an order;[1] the latter requires the introduction of a statutory instrument which is subject to annulment by resolution of either House of Parliament.[2]

The following groups are subject to control but receive special treatment: (1) EEC nationals; (2) citizens of the Republic of Ireland; (3) non-patrial United Kingdom passport holders.

The following groups are either partially or totally exempt from control: (1) representatives of overseas governments in the UK, and military personnel; (2) seamen and aircrew; (3) certain Commonwealth citizens resident in the UK returning from trips to Europe.

EEC NATIONALS

3.2 The effect of the Treaty of Rome[3] is that nationals of member states of the EEC have the right to work or seek work in the UK. There are

---

[1] H. of C. Official Report, Standing Committee B, 18 May 1971, col. 1006.

[2] Immigration Act 1971, s. 8(2). The only exempt classes are set out in the Immigration (Exemption from Control) Order 1972, SI 1972, No. 1613, as amended. See paras. 3.16–3.17, post.

[3] Act of Accession (Cmnd 5179-I); EEC Treaty (5179-II). The Treaty was incorporated into UK law by the European Communities Act 1972.

reciprocal rights for UK nationals who wish to work or seek work in other member states.[4]

There are three situations in which an EEC national is entitled to enter by virtue of the Treaty; (1) to take or seek employment;[5] (2) to engage in self-employed occupations and to set up and manage enterprises (i.e. businesses, companies and firms). This is referred to in the Treaty as the right of establishment;[6] (3) to provide and receive services,[7] i.e. 'services normally provided for remuneration'.[8] An EEC national thus has the right to enter not only to provide services but also for the purpose of receiving such services as private medical treatment, legal advice or private education. The scope of the Treaty is considered in more detail in Chapter 7.[9]

Member States

3.3 The member states are Belgium, Denmark, France, the Federal Republic of Germany, Greece, Ireland, Italy, Luxemburg, the Netherlands and the UK. Special provisions apply to Greece and to nationals of member states from overseas territories.[10]

French Nationals

3.4 Those from the French Overseas Departments of Martinique, Guadeloupe, Reunion and French Guiana receive the full benefit of EEC membership, but those whose nationality has been obtained from a connection with one of the French Overseas Dependent Territories (New Caledonia, Wallis and Futuna Islands, French Polynesia, St. Pierre and Miquelon and Mayotte) have more limited rights: they cannot enter to

---

[4] As to the definition of UK nationals for the purposes of EEC law, see para. 2.45, ante. Gibraltarians have been free to enter the UK without restrictions since 1968 following a statement by George Thomson, then Commonwealth Secretary, in the City Hall of Gibraltar on 23 May 1968.

[5] EEC Treaty, arts. 48–51 (freedom of movement of workers).

[6] Ibid., arts. 52–58.

[7] Ibid., arts. 59–66.

[8] Ibid., art. 60.

[9] See paras. 7.44 et seq., post.

[10] As to Greek nationals, they are not permitted until January 1988 to seek or take employment but the provisions for the right of establishment and the provision of services operate from 1 January 1981. As to the territories, they will be governed by agreements to be subsequently concluded. To date, no such agreements have been concluded. This latter subject is too complex to consider in detail in this book. For further information see T. C. Hartley *EEC Immigration Law*, Chapters 2 and 3, pp. 125 et seq.

take or seek employment but the provisions relating to the right of establishment and the provision and receipt of services apply to them.

Dutch Nationals

3.5 Those born in Surinam who have retained Dutch nationality (Surinam now being an independent country) receive the full benefit of EEC membership. The remaining Dutch overseas territory is the Caribbean Islands of Antilles (Curaçao, Bonaire, Aruba, St. Martin, St. Eustatius and Saba). Dutch nationals whose citizenship is obtained solely from birth in or other connection with Antilles benefit only from the provisions relating to the right of establishment and the provision and receipt of services.

The Immigration Rules

3.6 The rules only partly reflect the EEC requirements.[11] The full effect of the Treaty can only be understood by an examination of the relevant provisions of the Treaty and of the regulations and directives of the EEC Council.[12]

The right of entry applies, irrespective of nationality, to the spouse of the EEC national, their children under 21, any other dependent children and their dependent parents or grandparents.[13] Leave to enter may be refused if the national is personally unacceptable on the grounds of 'public policy, public security or public health'.[14]

Once in the UK the worker and his family have the right to remain, subject to certain limitations if the EEC national remains unemployed.[15] The effect is that in practice EEC nationals are generally free from the rigours of control although they are liable to deportation. There must however be reasons personal to the proposed deportee justifying the decision to deport.[16] The detailed provisions under the rules in respect of exclusion and deportation of EEC nationals are set out in Chapter 12.[17]

[11] HC 394, paras. 59–63, 132, as amended by HC 84, para. 2.
[12] A list of regulations and directives is set out at para. 7.45, post. The official texts are contained in 'Freedom of Movement for Workers within the Community' published by the Commission of the European Communities, obtainable through HMSO.
[13] HC 394, paras. 62, 63.
[14] EEC Treaty, art. 48(3). The same criteria operate before an EEC national may be excluded or removed but the rules make no reference to this. See paras. 11.51 et seq., post.
[15] See paras. 7.51 et seq., post.
[16] See note 14, supra.
[17] See paras. 11.51 et seq., post.

CITIZENS OF THE REPUBLIC OF IRELAND

3.7 Irish citizens are also EEC nationals and the same rules apply to them, despite the failure by the Home Office to refer to them as EEC nationals in the immigration rules. However, because of the existence of the common travel area[18] (allowing free movement within the area) all Irish citizens, including non-workers, have a greater degree of freedom of movement. We have seen that technically they are aliens[19] but because of the difficulty of administering a border in Ireland, the economic advantages of an Irish labour force and the number of Irish citizens already in the UK, the Act ensures that they are in effect free from controls.

Nevertheless, as non-patrials, they are liable to deportation, although the power to deport is limited in two respects: (1) if they qualify to remain in the UK because of the EEC provisions relating to freedom of movement, deportation can only take place if there are reasons personal to the proposed deportee which justify the Home Office taking the decision; (2) they cannot be deported if they were ordinarily resident in the UK on 1 January 1973 and have been resident for the five years preceding the decision to deport them.[20]

NON-PATRIAL UNITED KINGDOM PASSPORT HOLDERS

The Special Voucher Scheme

3.8 In 1968, after the Commonwealth Immigrants Act 1968 had made subject to immigration control citizens of the UK and Colonies who had no other citizenship but lacked an ancestral connection with the UK, the special voucher scheme on a quota basis was set up. The criteria by which the special voucher scheme is operated are not set out in the immigration rules, which provide only that a United Kingdom passport holder (UKPH) who presents a special voucher is to be admitted for settlement, as are his dependants if they have obtained entry clearances.[1] The scheme is intended only for those UKPH who have no other citizenship and are regarded as being under pressure to leave the country in which they have

---

[18] Immigration Act 1971, s. 1(3). See also ibid., s. 9, para. 4.5, post
[19] See para. 2.3, ante.
[20] Immigration Act 1971, s. 7. See para. 11.3, post.

[1] HC 394, para. 41. For some current problems regarding the operation of the special voucher scheme see *British Citizens Overseas*, JCWI, 1981.

been resident. Any citizen of the UK and Colonies who is a dual national is not considered eligible.

3.9 Originally, the scheme extended only to citizens of the UK and Colonies and not to other British passport holders: British protected persons and British subjects without citizenship did not qualify because they had been subject to immigration control since 1962.

An exception was subsequently made for British protected persons and British subjects without citizenship in East Africa on the grounds that the East African governments did not distinguish between them and those who held passports as citizens of the UK and Colonies. Those British protected persons and British subjects without citizenship who went to India from such East African countries are also permitted to apply, but no such exception is made in other countries.

3.10 Special vouchers are issued only to persons regarded as heads of household. This does not include married women whose marriages have not been terminated except where, e.g., it can be shown that the disability of the husband prevents him from being regarded as head of household. They can be issued to single persons of either sex over the age of 18. UKPH in Kenya, Tanzania, Zambia and Malawi appear to be regarded automatically as being under pressure to leave and applications in these countries are now normally granted promptly. This also applied to Uganda, from which remaining UKPH were expelled in 1972. UKPH who are now in India with a connection with these countries are also regarded as eligible. Citizens of the UK and Colonies elsewhere in the world who are not dual nationals or colonial citizens may apply for special vouchers, and occasional applications are granted from other countries where it is not held that UKPH are in general under any pressure to leave.

3.11 From 1968 until 1975, there were substantial delays before vouchers were allocated to eligible applicants in East Africa. The most recent change in the annual quota to 5,000 for 1975 and subsequent years led to the elimination of these queues. A limited allocation for UKPH in India was first made in 1972. Since 1977, less than half the announced overall quota has been taken up. Although it has been the practice of successive governments not to reveal the distribution of the quota, it is clear that substantial allocations are made to East Africa where the demand has been nearly exhausted, and unused vouchers have not been reallocated to India, where those issued with the vouchers in 1980 had waited for over five years from the date of application. Applications are accepted only in the country of 'normal residence'.

3.12 Where a UKPH head of household is issued with a special voucher, his eligible dependants may at the same time be issued with entry clearance. Although the rules limit dependent children to those under 18, it is Home Office practice to admit children who are unmarried and unemployed up to the age of 25. 'Sympathetic consideration' is given where it is clear that the child concerned has only taken occasional work or where an over-age child who forms part of the family unit is still dependent on his parents and would be isolated or suffer other hardship if left behind when the rest of the family comes to the UK.[2] Other dependent relatives have been admitted in the past where, e.g., the dependant is mentally handicapped. In the past it had been the practice of the Home Office to waive the accommodation and maintenance requirements under the rules,[3] but now entry clearance officers have instructions to defer the issue of clearance to any dependants where it is clear that the UKPH head of household 'will be unable to provide for himself and his dependants immediately on arrival in the UK'. Clearance will be delayed 'until such time as the voucher holder can meet the maintenance requirements of the rules'.[4] There is no right of appeal against the refusal by an entry clearance officer to issue a special voucher.[5]

A UKPH to whom a voucher has been issued will be given indefinite leave to remain (as will his dependants) on arrival in the UK. He is however subject to immigration control until he qualifies as a patrial, usually by remaining ordinarily resident in the UK for a period of five years.[6] He is still therefore liable to deportation until he obtains a right of abode, but in practice deportation cannot take place as it would not be possible to remove him to another country.[7]

There are a number of UKPH who are in the UK having entered without a special voucher for settlement. The general practice of the Home Office[8] is that if such a UKPH applies for settlement, he will be granted indefinite leave to remain outside the immigration rules if he has been lawfully here for at least four years. If he arrived as a student, he must also have completed his course and found employment. Where an

[2] Letter, Timothy Raison, Minister of State at Home Office to JCWI, 28 May 1980.
[3] HC 394, para. 42.
[4] Home Office letter, see note 2, supra.
[5] *R v Entry Clearance Officer Bombay, ex parte Amin* [1980] 2 All ER 837: Immigration Act 1971, s. 13(2) gives no right of appeal as a voucher is not an entry clearance.
[6] Ibid., s. 2(1)(c) See para. 2.40, ante.
[7] As to the problems of UKPHs who seek entry as visitors, see para. 6.8, post.
[8] The policy is set out in a Home Office letter to JCWI, 20 March 1981.

application is made before the four years are completed, the applicant may be granted an extension of stay. The Home Office has emphasised that it does not accept that settlement will be granted automatically after a fixed period and a person who has not complied with his conditions of entry or further stay or who is likely to be a charge on public funds would not normally be granted settlement at that stage.

3.13 On 14 December 1973, the European Commission of Human Rights adopted a report arising out of 31 applications lodged by East African Asians against the UK.[9] Most of the applicants were citizens of the UK and Colonies with no other nationality or citizenship and with no right of abode elsewhere. They complained that the Commonwealth Immigrants Act 1968 was discriminatory in its aims and its effect against citizens of the UK and Colonies of Asian origin. The Commission found as a fact that notwithstanding the neutrality of the language of the statute, it had racial motives and covered a racial group.[10] A majority of the Commission concluded that the Convention had been violated:

'the racial discrimination, to which the applicants have been publicly subjected by the application of the above immigration legislation, constitutes an interference with their human dignity which, in the special circumstances described above, amounted to "degrading treatment" in the sense of Art. 3 of the Convention'.[11]

The UK Government chose not to challenge the Commission's Report by referring the case to the European Court of Human Rights, but to have the matter dealt with by the Committee of Ministers. The Committee of Ministers was unable to form the two-thirds majority necessary for a decision and in October 1977 decided that no further action was called for, referring in its resolution to the fact that the quota had been increased.[12]

---

[9] See *X v United Kingdom* (1981) 3 EHRR 63. The Report has never been officially published. It was released in December 1979 by JCWI, and the Opinion of the Commission was published by JCWI, *The Unpublished Report: The European Commission of Human Rights and British Immigration Policy*; and subsequently in the First Report from the Home Affairs Committee 1979–80, Proposed New Immigration Rules and the European Convention on Human Rights, HC 434.

[10] Ibid., paras. 197–202, 207.

[11] Ibid., paras. 208–209.

[12] Resolution No. 77(2) of the Committee of Ministers, 21 October 1977.

REPRESENTATIVES OF OVERSEAS GOVERNMENTS

Diplomats

3.14 Section 8(3) of the Act exempts from control any person who is a member of a diplomatic mission[13] and members of their family who form part of their household.[14] The exemption lasts only so long as they are members of a mission. The group of people exempt is wide and comprises: (1) diplomatic 'agents', who are heads of the mission, and members of their diplomatic staff; (2) 'members of the service staff', e.g. drivers, cooks, cleaners, etc.[15] The effect of the exemption is that members of this group will be freely admitted to the UK and cannot be deported while they remain members of the mission. There are, of course, traditional methods of requiring diplomats to leave, but these are governed by practices outside the immigration laws.

Anyone who was initially subject to control, but after entry into the UK becomes a member of a mission, will become exempt and his passport will be endorsed accordingly. In the event of a person having limited leave becoming a member of a mission[16] and then ceasing to be a member during the period of the limited leave, the Act states that the limited leave is 'frozen' and that it will continue to operate after the exemption comes to an end provided it has not expired.[17]

The Act is silent about the position of others who cease to belong to a diplomatic mission or to the other exempted categories. Most will have

---

[13] The meaning of a 'diplomatic mission' is set out in the Diplomatic Privileges Act 1964, Sch. 1, art. 1.

[14] A sister may be a member of the family but each case will depend on its particular facts. The question is not whether the applicant and the diplomat are of the same family but whether the applicant is a member of the diplomat's family. The fact that the applicant has become part of the household will normally be sufficient to establish that the applicant has become a member of the family: *R v Secretary of State for Home Department, ex parte Gupta* [1979–80] Imm AR 52. A member of the family may cease to form part of a household and thus become subject to immigration control: see *Wijesuriya* 52961/79 (1685) (unreported). Similarly a visitor may become a member of a diplomat's family and thus there is no power to deport if at the date of the decision the applicant has acquired that status (*Gupta*).

[15] Diplomatic Privileges Act 1964, Sch. 1, art. 1. If, in any proceedings, any question arises as to whether or not any person is entitled to any privilege or immunity, a certificate issued by the Secretary of State stating any fact relating to that question is conclusive.

[16] Or a person qualifying for some other exempted category.

[17] Immigration Act 1971, s. 8(5).

either entered as diplomats or, if having entered with limited leave, their leave will have expired by the time their post comes to an end. It is the normal practice of the Home Office to treat both a person who originally entered as a diplomat and a person who entered with limited leave which has expired by the time he leaves the mission in the same way.[18] Limited leave to remain will be imposed, which the ex-diplomat can apply to extend if he can qualify under the immigration rules, and against the imposition of which he will have a right of appeal under section 14(2) of the Act. Where, however, a person had overstayed his leave before entering the employment of a mission, the Home Office does not consider that he would have any claim to further leave to remain on leaving such employment and contends that he can be dealt with like any other person who overstayed his leave.

It is clear that a person cannot be regarded as settled in the UK and Islands at any time during which he was entitled to an exemption in whatever capacity.[19] However, the Home Office accepts that ordinary residence, once established, is not interrupted by a period of exempt employment and that the exemption from deportation provisions do apply to Commonwealth citizens who have been in exempt employment for all or part of their stay here (originating before 1 January 1973) as they apply to any other Commonwealth citizen.[20]

3.15 If a person who ceases to be a member of a mission or other exempted category leaves the UK and returns, he will be eligible for entry only if he meets the requirements of the immigration rules. However, the immigration officer will not always be aware that the passenger has ceased to be exempt and may readmit him without imposing restrictions. If the passenger misled the immigration officer, he may find himself arrested as an illegal entrant and removed. In *R v Secretary of State for Home Affairs, ex parte Badaike*,[1] a successful application for *habeas corpus* was made by a Nigerian army officer. His first visit had been for six months and he was exempted from control as he was a member of a Commonwealth force training in the UK. He returned shortly afterwards and was arrested some 15 months later. The immigration officer could not recollect the case. As there was no evidence that he had misled the officer he was released, and presumably permitted to continue to remain in the UK indefinitely.

[18] Letter, Home Office to JCWI, 16 May 1979.
[19] Immigration Act 1971, s. 8(5). See also *Sikka* 3319/74(587) (unreported).
[20] Letter, Home Office, to JCWI cited, note 18, supra.
[1] (1977) *The Times*, 4 May.

As a person entering as a diplomat is exempt from control there is no need to endorse his passport on entry or departure. If an immigration officer does endorse the passport on entry, knowing that the entrant is a diplomat he will use a rectangular 'entry' stamp which sets out the date and port of arrival[2] but will make no other endorsement. This stamp is identical to that given to a person who has been given indefinite leave to remain in the UK and who re-enters as a returning resident. The endorsement given to the diplomat cannot however be interpreted as a grant of indefinite leave to remain: the diplomat is exempt from control and the question of granting leave to enter does not arise as only those subject to control require leave.

Consular Officials

3.16 Consular officers (other than honorary consuls) and consular employees of countries which have made consular agreements with the UK Government[3] are totally exempt from immigration control as are their families forming part of their household.[4]

Other Representatives

3.17 Members of foreign and Commonwealth governments visiting the UK on business for their governments (unless the Home Secretary directs otherwise) and others who under various statutes are entitled to diplomatic status (e.g. UN officials, members of the IMF) are exempt from all controls although they are liable for deportation. The full list of those entitled to exemption in this category is set out in the Immigration (Exemption from Control) Order 1972.[5]

MILITARY PERSONNEL

3.18 A more limited exemption is given to the military personnel of Commonwealth and friendly countries who are in the UK.[6] Broadly, the following are exempt from controls but are liable to deportation: (1) those non-patrials (usually Commonwealth citizens) who are members of the home forces and are subject to service law; (2) members of Com-

[2] The stamp is set out in Appendix 2.
[3] For the meaning of 'consular officer' see *Halsbury's Laws* (4th Edn.) Vol. 18, para. 1410.
[4] The Immigration (Exemption from Control) Order 1972 SI, 1972, No. 1613, art. 3.
[5] Ibid., art. 4.
[6] Immigration Act 1971, s. 8(4).

monwealth forces training in the UK with the home forces; (3) members of NATO and other 'friendly' forces posted to the UK.

SEAMEN AND AIRCREW

3.19 Seamen arriving in the UK for a short period during the course of their duties do not need leave to enter the UK provided they are under a contractual obligation to depart by the same ship on which they arrive. Members of an aircrew do not require leave if they depart by air within seven days on that or another plane as a member of its crew.[7] Similarly, seamen who are Commonwealth[8] or Irish citizens holding a British seamen's card do not normally require leave to enter if they are discharged from their engagement on a ship which has docked at any port in the common travel area.[9] In practice they are therefore exempt from immigration control, but an immigration officer can require them to submit to an examination. They will be refused entry if they are subject to a deportation order or if they have been previously refused leave to enter and have not subsequently been readmitted.[10]

COMMONWEALTH RESIDENTS RETURNING FROM EUROPE

3.20 Travelling in Europe now requires less formal documentation. In order to avoid difficulties at the ports of entry for patrials and others normally resident here, the following groups who have obtained documentation before they left the UK do not require leave to enter:[11] (1) a UK citizen holding a British visitor's passport issued in the UK; (2) a Commonwealth citizen travelling on a 'collective passport'[12] issued in

---

[7] Immigration Act 1971, s. 8(1). The exemption will also apply to a person who had limited leave to enter, who leaves the UK and returns within the period for which he had leave as a member of an aircraft crew, under an engagement requiring him to leave within seven days. Immigration (Exemption from Control) Order 1972, art. 5(1)(e).

[8] In this context this includes British protected persons; ibid., art. 5(3).

[9] Ibid., art. 5(1)(d).

[10] Immigration Act 1971, s. 8(1); Immigration (Exemption from Control) Order 1972, art. 5(2).

[11] Ibid., art. 5(1)(a)–(c).

[12] These are issued instead of individual passports in favour of approved parties of young people going overseas as a group with a leader. Eligibility for such a passport can be ascertained by enquiry of the Passport Office, Clive House, 70 Petty France, London SW 1.

the UK or Islands; (3) a Commonwealth or Irish citizen returning from an excursion to France, Belgium or the Netherlands[13] travelling on an identity card issued for that purpose. The exemptions do not apply if the person is subject to a deportation order or has previously been refused leave to enter.

[13] See also The Immigration (Exemption from Control) (Amendment) Order 1975, SI 1975, No. 617.

FOUR

The Common Travel Area

4.1 The Act creates the 'common travel area' comprising the UK, the Channel Islands, Isle of Man and the Republic of Ireland, the aim of which is to reduce internal immigration control.[1] The provisions are complex but the following summary may be useful.

GENERAL PRINCIPLES

4.2 The general rule is that there are no controls either on arrival or on departure from the UK on a local journey, i.e. one which begins and ends in the common travel area and at no stage goes outside it.[2] Non-patrials who have been examined at any port in the common travel area and who have been admitted are free to travel to any port within the area without having to present themselves to an immigration officer for examination.[3] Entry into the UK will be refused if an immigration officer has reason to believe that the passenger intends to go to another part of the common travel area where he is unacceptable to the immigration authorities there.[4]

4.3 There are similar provisions in the immigration laws of the Republic of Ireland which contain powers to refuse entry to those intending to travel to the UK.[5] These powers will presumably be used if the

---

[1] See generally Immigration Act 1971, ss. 1(3), 9. The Home Secretary may exclude any part of the common travel area, if e.g. legislation is passed in that territory which would conflict with UK immigration law, ibid. s. 9(5).

[2] Ibid., s. 11(4).

[3] HC 394, para. 8.

[4] Ibid.

[5] Aliens (Amendment) Order 1975 (SI 1975, No. 128) amending art. 5 of Aliens Order 1946 (SI 1946, No. 395).

Irish authorities know the passenger is unacceptable to the British authorities.

4.4 The provisions of the Immigration Act extend to the Channel Islands and the Isle of Man (which technically have their own immigration laws) subject to a number of 'exceptions, adaptions and modifications'.[6] In addition, the laws of the UK and Islands have been integrated so that, e.g., leave to enter and refusal of leave in any part of the UK and Islands operates in any other part.[7] There are similar provisions relating to deportation and illegal immigrants.[8]

Freedom of movement within the common travel area is also restricted by the Prevention of Terrorism (Temporary Provisions) Act 1976, which gives the Home Secretary power to exclude people from the whole or part of the UK.[9]

4.5 The Immigration Act prevents non-patrials using the common travel area as a device to enter the UK in a number of circumstances where had they sought leave to enter the UK without having first travelled to the Republic, leave would have been refused.[10] In addition the Home Secretary is given the power to make orders, (1) excluding the Islands and the Republic from the common travel area for any specified purpose;[11] (2) imposing restrictions on entry on certain people who arrive in the UK from elsewhere in the common travel area.[12] The Home Secretary has made an order affecting those coming to the UK from the Republic.[13] The Order is comprehensive and prevents most effectively the Republic of Ireland being used as a 'spring-board' for entry into the UK.

---

[6] Immigration Act 1971, s. 36 which provides that the Act may be extended to the Islands by Order in Council. The following Orders (containing 'exceptions adaptions and modifications') have been made: Immigration (Guernsey) Order 1972, SI 1972, No. 1719; Immigration (Isle of Man) Order 1972, SI 1972, No. 1720; Immigration (Jersey) Order 1972, SI 1972, No. 1813.

[7] Immigration Act 1971, Sch. 4, paras. 1, 2. See also Orders in Council, cited., note 6, supra.

[8] Ibid., Sch. 4, paras. 3, 4.

[9] See para. 16.2, post.

[10] Ibid., s. 9(4).

[11] Ibid., see s. 9(5)–s. 9(7).

[12] Ibid., s. 9(2).

[13] The Immigration (Control of Entry through Republic of Ireland) Order 1972, SI 1972, No. 1610 as amended by the Immigration (Control of Entry through Republic of Ireland) (Amendment) Order 1979, SI 1979, No. 730; the Immigration (Control of Entry though Republic of Ireland) (Amendment) Order 1980, SI 1980, No. 1859.

EXCLUSION FROM PROVISIONS

4.6 Certain non-patrials (including Irish citizens, unless otherwise stated) are excluded from the benefits of the common travel area arrangements. They therefore require leave to enter the UK and must present themselves to an immigration officer on arrival in the UK. Failure to do so is a criminal offence[14] and those who enter without permission are illegal entrants.[15] They comprise the following:

(1) anyone who arrives in the UK in a ship or aircraft which began its voyage from, or during its voyage called at, a place outside the common travel area;[16]

(2) anyone (other than an Irish citizen) who arrives in the UK by an aircraft which began its flight in the Republic, but where the passenger himself began his journey from outside the common travel area and was not given leave to land in the Republic[17] (e.g. a US citizen who flies from New York to Shannon and then transfers to an internal Dublin to London flight without being given leave to enter the Republic);

(3) anyone who arrives in the UK on a local journey[18] from the Republic by whatever method of transport,[19]
   (a) who is subject to a deportation order;[20]
   (b) who is refused entry after being given on arrival written notice that the Home Secretary has directed that his exclusion is conducive to the public good as being in the interest of national security;[1]
   (c) against whom directions have been given by the Home Secretary to refuse entry on the ground that his exclusion is conducive to the public good;[2]

---

[14] Immigration Act 1971, s. 24(1)(a). See para. 10.4, post.
[15] Ibid., s. 33(1). They can therefore be removed from the UK by order of the Home Secretary without right of appeal; ibid., Sch. 2, para. 9, and s. 16; see para. 13.13, post.
[16] Ibid., s. 11(4).
[17] The Immigration (Control of Entry through Republic of Ireland) Order 1972, art. 3(1)(a), 3(2).
[18] See para. 4.2, ante.
[19] I.e., to Northern Ireland by crossing the border on foot or by vehicle; or by aircraft to anywhere in the UK and Islands.
[20] Immigration Act 1971 s. 9(4). Entry will be refused if a deportation order is in force; ibid., s. 5(1).
[1] Ibid., s. 9(4)(a).
[2] Immigration (Control of Entry through Republic of Ireland) Order 1972, art.

(d) who has been refused leave to enter the UK and has not subsequently been given leave to enter or remain there;[3]
(e) who is a visa national and has no valid visa to enter the UK;[4]
(f) who entered the Republic unlawfully from a place outside the common travel area;[5]
(g) who originally entered the UK or Islands illegally or who overstayed, went to the Republic and returns where he has not subsequently been given leave to enter or remain.[6]

RESTRICTIONS ON ENTRY FROM REPUBLIC OF IRELAND

4.7 Non-patrials, who are not otherwise excluded, who arrive in the UK on a local journey from the Republic, after having entered the Republic on coming from a place outside the common travel area, or after leaving the UK while having limited leave to enter or remain, which has expired before their return, are entitled to enter the UK without reporting to an immigration officer.[7] But, unless they are Irish citizens, they are subject to a number of restrictions which are set out below.

Restrictions on those arriving on a local journey from the Republic, having entered the Republic from outside the common travel area

4.8 A visa national who has a visa containing the words 'short visit', (1) may not remain for more than one month from the date of entering the UK; (2) is not permitted to work; and (3) if over 16 must register with the police.[8] Any other non-patrial may remain for a period of three months but, unless an EEC national, is not permitted to work.[9] An

---

3(1)(b)(iv). Generally an immigration officer has the power to exclude on conducive grounds, (HC 394, para. 76) but not in this case.

[3] Immigration Act 1971 s.9(4)(b).

[4] Immigration (Control of Entry through Republic of Ireland) Order 1972, art. 3(b)(i). As to the meaning of visa nationals, see para. 5.4, post.

[5] Ibid., art. 3(1)(b)(ii).

[6] Ibid., art. 3(1)(b)(iii), as amended by the Immigration (Control of Entry through Republic of Ireland) (Amendment) Order 1979, SI 1979, No. 730.

[7] Ibid., art. 4(i).

[8] Ibid., art. 4(1)(a), 4(5), 4(6).

[9] Ibid., art. 4(1)(a), 4(3), 4(4). Nationals of Greece are to be treated as non-EEC nationals for this purpose: the Immigration (Control of Entry through Republic of Ireland) (Amendment) Order 1980, SI 1980, No. 1859.

application for an extension of stay can be made,[10] but if a person remains beyond the time limit without making an application or begins working, he is in breach of his conditions of entry[11] and is liable to be prosecuted and/or deported.[12]

Restrictions on those arriving on a local journey from the Republic having entered the Republic after leaving the UK while having a limited leave to enter or remain in the UK which has expired

4.9 Such a person (1) may remain for not more than seven days; (2) is not permitted to work unless an EEC national; (3) if a visa national over 16, must register with the police.[13] Provided they abide by these restrictions they are here lawfully. The same rules apply to extension of stay as are set out in para. 4.8.

LANDING AND EMBARKATION CARDS

4.10 Those travelling within the common travel area are not required to complete landing or embarkation cards[14] unless (1) in the case of non-patrials, they land from an aircraft coming from the Republic having begun their journey outside the common travel area and were refused leave to enter by the Irish authorities;[15] (2) in the case of both patrials and non-patrials, the immigration officer requires a card to be completed under the Prevention of Terrorism (Temporary Provisions) Act 1976.[16]

---

[10] See generally Chapter 9.
[11] Immigration Act 1971, s. 9(3).
[12] Ibid., 2. 24(1)(b), s. 3(6), s. 6 (prosecution and deportation); ibid., s. 3(5)(a) (deportation for 'overstaying'). An example of the operation of the Order may be found in *Hajipaschali* 57439/80 (1903) (unreported).
[13] Ibid., art. 4(1)(b), 4(7).
[14] See para. 5.3, post.
[15] Immigration (Landing and Embarkation Cards) Order 1975, art. 5.
[16] Prevention of Terrorism (Supplemental Temporary Provisions) Order 1976, SI 1976, No. 465, art. 8; Prevention of Terrorism (Supplemental Temporary Provisions) (Northern Ireland) Order 1976, SI 1976, No. 466, art. 8.

FIVE

Entering the UK

GENERAL CONSIDERATIONS

5.1 This chapter looks at the general requirements for admission to the UK. It explains the documents required on entry and the grounds upon which entry can be refused. The procedures at the port of entry, and on an application for entry clearance, are also examined.

A non-patrial cannot enter the UK unless given leave to do so in accordance with the Immigration Act.[1] If leave to enter the UK is given, it will be either for a limited or for an indefinite period.[2] If limited leave to enter is given, it may be subject to conditions restricting the entrant's employment or occupation, or requiring him to register with the police.[3] No other conditions may be imposed on entry.

DOCUMENTS NEEDED ON ENTRY

Passport

5.2 A person arriving in the UK must produce a valid national passport or some other document establishing his identity or nationality if requested to do so by an immigration officer.[4] EEC nationals may use national identity cards instead of passports.[5] Those from countries with which the UK has made specific arrangements may use national identity cards provided they also have a visitor's card.[6] It should be noted that

---

[1] Immigration Act 1971, s. 3(1)(a).
[2] Ibid., s. 3(1)(b)
[3] Ibid., s. 3(1)(c). The limitations on, and any conditions attached to, the leave may be imposed so that they will (unless superseded) apply to any subsequent leave obtained after leaving the UK and returning within the period granted in the original leave; ibid., 3(3)(b). See para. 9.13, post.
[4] HC 394, para. 3.
[5] Ibid., HC 394, para. 3 (note). HC 84, para 1.
[6] Ibid. The countries are Austria, Lichtenstein, Monaco and Switzerland.

DOCUMENTS NEEDED ON ENTRY

visitors' cards are only valid for six months and cannot be used by those coming for employment. A passenger may be refused entry simply because he fails to produce a passport or travel document or produces one which does not comply with international practice, or which was issued by a government which does not recognise the UK Government or which refuses to accept UK passports under its own immigration law.[7] A passenger may none the less be admitted without a recognised travel document. He will be issued with a special form on which the conditions of entry will be endorsed, and he will be required to surrender the form on departure.

Landing Card

5.3 All non-patrials aged 16 and over must, if required, complete and produce to an immigration officer a landing card.[8] The details to be completed are, (1) the passenger's full name; (2) date and place of birth; (3) nationality or citizenship; (4) occupation and the address at which he is staying in the UK. A similar (embarkation) card must be completed on departure.[9] Failure to complete the card is a criminal offence.[10] These requirements do not generally apply to those travelling within the common travel area.[11]

Entry Clearance

5.4 An entry clearance is a document which is to be taken as evidence that a non-patrial is eligible to enter the UK.[12] It is usually issued by a UK Government representative in the country of departure known as an 'entry clearance officer'.[13] There are three different types of document, (1) *visas*, issued (for the purposes for which entry is sought) to:
    (a) foreign nationals of the following countries:[14]

---

[7] Ibid., para. 6. The UK Government does not accept passports and travel documents from the following countries: Boputhatswana, North Korea, Taiwan, the Transkei and the Republic of Venda.

[8] Immigration (Landing and Embarkation Cards) Order 1975, SI 1975 No. 65. This requirement was dispensed with on 1 January 1980 for EEC nationals but may be reinstated in the event of a national emergency or crisis. Letter Home Office to JCWI 12 December 1980.

[9] Ibid.

[10] Immigration Act 1971, s. 26(1)(e).

[11] SI 1975 No. 65, art. 5. See also para. 4.10, ante.

[12] Immigration Act 1971, s. 33(1). It does not include a work permit, see para. 5.14, post.

[13] See generally para. 5.56, post.

[14] HC 394, para. 10 and Appendix.

in Europe: Albania, Bulgaria, Czechoslovakia, German Democratic Republic, Hungary, Poland, Romania, USSR;

in Asia: Pakistan (to those who seek entry to work or settle); all other countries except Bahrain, Israel, Japan, Kuwait, Maldive Islands, Republic of Korea, Qatar, Turkey and the United Arab Emirates;[15]

in Africa: all countries except Algeria, Ivory Coast, Morocco, Niger, Tunisia and the Republic of South Africa;

in America: Cuba;

(b) stateless persons and holders of non-national documents;

A visa is endorsed in the passport, and citizens of these countries are known as 'visa nationals'.

(2) *entry certificates* issued to Commonwealth citizens,[16] and endorsed in the passport;

(3) *Home Office letters of consent.*[17] These are separate documents issued to all other foreign nationals who are not visa nationals.

5.5 Certain categories of passengers must obtain entry clearance prior to departure and produce it at the port of entry. Failure to do so will result in refusal of entry.

Visa Nationals

5.6 They must always produce a passport or some other travel document endorsed with a current UK visa whatever the circumstances under which entry is sought. Entry is to be refused to a visa national who arrives without clearance (except for citizens of Pakistan entering for temporary purposes), although leave is to be given exceptionally outside the rules if there are strong grounds for so doing,[18] e.g. when the passenger has been misinformed by a UK official, including the police; when the passenger has genuinely mistaken a Home Office extension for a re-entry permit or believed that the grant of an extension removed the need for a re-entry permit during the currency of the authorised stay; where the journey is one of extreme urgency or where there are compassionate circumstances of a compelling nature. It is unlikely that the immigration officer would permit entry even where these grounds existed if the passenger had on a previous occasion been warned of the absence of a visa. The visa requirements are usually waived for air

---

[15] Iranian nationals have required visas since 12 May 1980.
[16] HC 394, para. 11.
[17] HC 394, para. 10.
[18] *Walid* 37074/78 (1662) (unreported).

passengers in transit provided they have entry facilities to their country of destination and transit visas for any other country en route which requires them. If a change of aircraft is involved they must depart within twenty-four hours. Heathrow, Gatwick and Stansted airports are regarded as one airport for the purpose of the waiver. The waiver will operate between other airports in most cases if a journey is necessary because of cancellation or diversion of flights.

The only exception to the general rule concerns the holders of refugee travel documents issued under the 1951 Convention relating to the Status of Refugees by countries which are signatories of the Council of Europe Agreement of 1959 on the Abolition of Visas for Refugees: they do not require visas if coming on visits of not more than three months.[19]

Commonwealth Citizens and Other Foreign Nationals except EEC Nationals

5.7 They must[20] produce an entry certificate or Home Office letter of consent if seeking admission in the following categories, (1) those seeking indefinite leave to remain because of UK ancestry, permit free employees (in certain cases), businessmen and self-employed persons, persons of independent means and writers and artists;[1] (2) the dependant of a work permit holder or a person in category (1);[2] (3) the wife, child or other dependant of a person settled in the UK who is being admitted for settlement;[3] (4) the husband or fiancé of a person settled in the UK.[4]

The immigration rules state that in all other cases a person 'who wishes to ascertain in advance whether he is eligible for admission' can apply for clearance. This is purported to be of particular value when 'the claim to admission depends on proof of facts entailing enquiries in this country or overseas'.[5] Yet applications for entry certificates (and also visas) can only be made through the British High Commission or Embassy overseas while those for Home Office letters of consent can be

---

[19] These documents are issued under the 1951 Convention relating to refugees. The signatories are the nine member states of the EEC, plus Iceland, Lichtenstein, Norway, Sweden and Switzerland.

[20] It has been the practice to waive the entry clearance requirement for non-visa foreign nationals if all the other requirements are met, but there is no certainty that this practice will continue.

[1] HC 394, paras. 29–41.
[2] Ibid., paras. 40, 41.
[3] Ibid., para. 43.
[4] Ibid., paras. 50, 52.
[5] Ibid., paras. 10, 11.

made either overseas or directly to the Home Office in the UK by a person acting on behalf of an applicant.[6]

The procedure for obtaining entry clearance is considered at para. 5.52.

Failure to provide Satisfactory Clearance

5.8 Holders of entry clearance are not automatically admitted and must still present themselves to an immigration officer for examination.

The immigration rules state that a person who holds an entry clearance which was duly issued to him and is still current is not to be refused entry unless an immigration officer is satisfied that, (1) false representations were employed or material facts were not disclosed either in writing or orally, whether or not to the holder's knowledge, for the purpose of obtaining a clearance; or (2) a change in circumstances since it was issued has removed the basis of the holder's claim for admission.[7] The immigration officer may also refuse leave to enter to an entry clearance holder on the grounds of restricted returnability, on medical grounds, on the ground that he has a criminal record, or because he is the subject of a deportation order or his exclusion would be conducive to the public good.[8]

Although the rules indicate that an examination should not be carried further than is necessary to decide these matters,[9] those with entry clearance are often likely to receive a rigorous interview on arrival. An immigration officer can act on reasonable inferences from the results of the interview and any other information available to him.[10] Information given to the immigration officer may be checked with any information given earlier to an entry clearance officer. Frequently telex enquiries are made to this end. If it arises that the passenger gave certain information to the entry clearance officer which was not communicated to the immigration officer or failed to give information to the entry clearance officer which was subsequently given to the immigration officer, the immigration officer may draw the inference that false representations were made.[11] There is however a right of appeal exercisable in the UK before departure for those refused entry who hold entry clearance.[12]

---

[6] Ibid.
[7] Ibid., para. 13(a), (b).
[8] Ibid., para. 13(c). See paras. 5.16 et seq., post.
[9] Ibid., para. 14.
[10] Ibid.
[11] See e.g. *Ramjane* [1973] Imm AR 84.
[12] Immigration Act 1971, s. 13(3). See para. 5.49, post.

The Validity of the Document

5.9 Entry will be refused if the immigration officer is not satisfied that the passenger is the person named in the clearance or if the document is not current. Any entry clearance specifies the date by which it must be used and therefore ceases to be 'current' after that date. Similarly, its validity is terminated on its presentation and it cannot be used on a second occasion to gain entry even if the date of expiry has not been reached.[13]

False Representations or Non-disclosure in obtaining Clearance

5.10 Entry may be refused on these grounds even if the holder of the clearance did not know that this has occurred,[14] e.g., where an application is made by a parent on behalf of a child who is ignorant of the details of the application. Particular care should be taken where applications are made by third parties, e.g. by a spouse, agent or other representative, on behalf of a person seeking entry, to ensure that the information given is correct and complete. Applications may be made on behalf of others either because of distance or illiteracy. The applicant nevertheless should be sure that he or she knows the exact nature and the contents of the application.

A person who has made false representations to an entry clearance officer or concealed material facts from him is not bound to be refused entry by an immigration officer although it is unlikely that the officer would permit a person to enter in such circumstances even if an entry clearance was not mandatory in the first place. There is, of course, a right of appeal and there have been occasions where the Tribunal has permitted a person to enter despite making false representations. In *Sathiasilan*,[15] the appellant had applied to enter the UK as a visitor but the true purpose of seeking admission was to qualify as a chartered accountant. Evidence was available that he had been accepted by a firm of accountants as an articled clerk and had sufficient funds and accommodation. However in other cases the Tribunal has not taken such an enlightened approach. In *Musotun*,[16] the Tribunal held that an immigration officer satisfied of false representations or concealment was entitled to look at the reasons for the passenger wishing to enter the UK. If he

[13] *Andronicou* [1974] Imm AR 87.
[14] HC 394, para. 13(a).
[15] 1919/73(190) (unreported).
[16] [1972] Imm AR 97. See also *Chagpar* [1972] Imm AR 137; *R v Immigration Appeals Adjudicator ex parte Perween Khan* [1972] 3 All ER 297.

were satisfied that the reason for the entry given to the entry clearance officer was not the true one (e.g. applying for a short visit when the true purpose was to seek work), the immigration officer was entitled to refuse admission. It is clear that entry will always be refused where the immigration officer believes the passenger is coming to work or settle when he does not qualify to do so.

5.11 Particular difficulty has arisen in deciding whether 'material facts' have been concealed. What facts are 'material'? A person who genuinely wishes to enter as a visitor but also intends, while in the UK, to see whether there are any courses of study open to him or discuss with friends the possibility of opening a business in the UK. Are these always material facts? If they are not disclosed and the facts emerge at the interview at the port, entry may be refused. If the entry clearance officer is informed, he may not believe the applicant to be a genuine visitor and refuse clearance, thereby involving a substantial delay while an appeal against refusal is made. The onus is on the immigration authorities to show that false representations have been made or material facts concealed.[17] Refusal of entry has held to be justified in the following circumstances, (1) application as a student and failure to mention two brothers resident in the UK;[18] (2) visitor's failure to disclose pregnancy and that child would be born during visit;[19] (3) widowhood deliberately concealed and false representations made designed to show that applicant would return to Pakistan after visit;[20] (4) visa obtained by husband falsely representing that his wife was lawfully settled in the UK when she was in fact an illegal entrant.[1] The Tribunal has however allowed appeals against refusal where a wife while disclosing that her husband was in the UK failed to disclose that he had applied for an extension of stay;[2] and similarly where a visitor failed to disclose that he had applied to a United States company for a job.[3] The conduct of close members of an applicant's family may be taken into account,[4] e.g. where they have entered illegally or have come here as visitors and overstayed.

[17] *Shawa* 21711/77 (1166) (unreported).
[18] *Qureshi* [1977] Imm AR 113.
[19] *Farida Begum* [1978] Imm AR 107.
[20] *Qurasha Begum* (1978) Imm AR 158.
[1] *Claveria* [1978] Imm AR 176.
[2] *Satchithandum* 44002/ (1552) (unreported). See also *De Andrade* 42615/79 (1501) (unreported).
[3] *Dalal* 52067/79 (1669) (unreported).
[4] *Morgan* 21884/77 (1527) (unreported).

Change of Circumstances since the Issue of Clearance

5.12 Although entry is to be refused if there has been a change in circumstances since the issue of clearance which has removed the basis for admission, the current rules provide an exception where the change amounts *solely* to a dependent child becoming over age between the issue of clearance and the date when admission is sought.[5] This resolves certain doubts which arose following the decision of the Divisional Court in *R v Secretary of State for the Home Department, ex parte Zamir*.[6] Examples of a change in circumstances justifying refusal can be found in *Arshad*,[7] where two children, who had been given clearance to join their parents in the UK, were refused entry because their mother had since returned to Pakistan, thereby removing the bases for their claim for admission under the rules, and in *Zamir*, where a dependent son had married since the issue of the clearance.

5.13 There is a duty to disclose information about change of circumstances to an immigration officer. In *Zamir v Secretary of State for the Home Department*,[8] the House of Lords held that the passenger 'owes a positive duty of candour on all material facts including those which denote a change of circumstances since the entry clearance'.[9] A change in circumstances discovered after entry may justify a refusal of an extension of stay or be a ground for holding a person as an illegal entrant on the basis of a deception on entry.[10]

Work Permit

5.14 Almost all non-patrials from outside the EEC who wish to enter the UK to work must produce a work permit on arrival.[11] This is a document issued by the Department of Employment for a specific post on an application by a specific employer.[12] As will be seen later, the work permit scheme has been designed to limit severely the number of overseas workers coming to the UK and to ensure that the non-patrial labour force is restricted only to those regarded by the Government as es-

---

[5] HC 394, para. 13(b). Similarly where the applicant became over age between the receipt of his application and the date of the decision HC 394, para. 12.
[6] [1979] 2 All ER 849.
[7] [1977] Imm AR 19.
[8] [1980] 2 All ER 768, see also para. 12.1, post.
[9] Per Wilberforce LJ, at 773.
[10] See para. 12.1, post.
[11] HC 394, paras. 27 et seq.
[12] Ibid., Immigration Act 1971, s. 33(1).

sential to the UK economy.[13] Some people are able to enter to work without a permit. They are:

(a) EEC nationals, including those seeking work;[14]
(b) certain non-patrials in 'permit free categories' e.g. ministers of religion, doctors, provided in some cases they have entry clearance for this purpose,[15]
(c) Commonwealth citizens with at least one grandparent born in the UK, including those seeking work, provided they have entry clearance for this purpose;[16]
(d) young Commonwealth citizens on working holidays;[17]
(e) businessmen and the self-employed[18] including writers and artists, provided they have entry clearance for this purpose;[19]
(f) wives and children of those allowed to work[20] and of students,[1] provided they have entry clearance for this purpose.

Anyone who does not qualify under these categories requires a work permit.[2] If he or she does not have one and is not otherwise eligible for admission to settle, leave to enter will be refused.[3]

5.15 A work permit is not an entry clearance.[4] The holder of a permit must therefore meet the entry clearance requirements; e.g. if he is a visa national, he must on arrival show that he has a current visa endorsed in his passport. In the case of other nationals there is no need to produce either an entry certificate or a Home Office letter of consent, although it may make entry easier if clearance has been obtained in advance. If the permit has been obtained by deceit, the immigration officer has no discretion and must refuse leave to enter.[5]

---

[13] See para. 7.2, post.
[14] HC 394 para. 59.
[15] Ibid., paras. 31–34.
[16] Ibid., para. 29.
[17] Ibid., para. 30.
[18] Ibid., paras. 35–37.
[19] Ibid., para. 39.
[20] Ibid., para. 40.
[1] Ibid., para. 25.
[2] But note *au pair* girls are not workers and do not require a work permit; ibid., para. 26.
[3] Ibid., para. 27.
[4] Immigration Act 1971, s. 33(1).
[5] *Tolentino* 17206/77 (1036) (unreported).

GENERAL GROUNDS FOR REFUSING ENTRY

5.16 An immigration officer can refuse entry (or an entry clearance officer can refuse clearance) if a non-patrial fails to meet the requirements of the specific immigration rule or rules under which entry is sought. In addition, there are two other hurdles to surmount. Firstly, there are a number of general grounds under which entry may be refused which are discussed below; and secondly, even where an applicant satisfies the requirements, this is not conclusive in his favour and he may be refused on the ground of his general immigration history.[6]

Travel Documents or Entry Clearance Unsatisfactory

5.17 The circumstances under which entry will be refused on this basis have already been discussed (see paras. 5.2 et seq., ante).

Restricted Returnability

5.18 This inelegant expression refers to a number of situations where a person may face difficulties in being admitted to another country after leaving the UK. The immigration rules state that a person who does not satisfy the immigration officer that he will be admitted to another country after a stay in the UK may be refused entry.[7] If he is permitted to enter another country by a particular date, the immigration officer is required to limit the length of stay so that it ends at least two months before that date. Some passports or travel documents will be endorsed with a restriction imposed by the Government issuing the document requiring the holder to return to the country by a particular date. This is often the practice of Eastern and Central European countries which grant their citizens 'exit visas'. In such cases, the immigration officer will limit the period of stay so as not to extend beyond the date of expiry of the exit visa.

5.19 In some cases the Home Office will issue non-patrials with travel documents,[8] and again leave to enter will not be given for a period beyond the validity of that document.[9] The following points should be borne in mind: (1) the rules relating to restricted returnability do not apply to those eligible for admission for settlement; (2) the rules will not

---

[6] HC 394, para. 67.
[7] HC 394, para. 15.
[8] See paras. 9.26 et seq., post. As to travel documents for refugees see paras. 15.20 et seq., post.
[9] HC 394, para. 15.

apply if the passenger qualifies for political asylum, i.e. he is not to be refused entry if the only country to which he can be removed is one to which he is unwilling to go owing to well-founded fear of being persecuted for reasons of race, religion, nationality, membership of a political or social group or political opinion;[10] (3) once a person is admitted to the UK on whatever basis, he may apply for an extension of stay.[11] While it is unlikely that an extension will be granted or that an appeal against refusal will be successful in circumstances of restricted returnability, the additional time available may be of assistance in finding the person an alternative country.

Medical Reasons

5.20 In a number of circumstances entry can be refused for medical reasons, except in the case of returning residents or the spouses and children under 18 of people settled in the UK. The following groups, other than EEC nationals, are to be referred to a medical inspector[12] for examination either at the port of entry or overseas before an entry certificate is granted:

(a) anyone intending to remain in the UK for more than six months will 'normally' be referred;
(b) anyone who mentioned health or medical treatment as the reason for visiting must be referred;
(c) anyone who 'appears to be mentally or physically abnormal' must be referred;
(d) in any other case a referral can be made at the discretion of the immigration officer (or entry clearance officer). This discretion 'should be exercised sparingly'.[13]

Refusal to submit to an examination is ground for refusal of entry.[14]

5.21 If the medical inspector advises that for medical reasons it is undesirable to admit the passenger the immigration officer must refuse permission to enter unless he considers admission is warranted by strong compassionate reasons.[15] He must, however, notify the passenger of the

[10] Ibid., para. 16.
[11] See generally Chapter 9, post.
[12] For the powers and duties of medical inspectors, see para. 5.36, post.
[13] HC 394, para. 70.
[14] Ibid., para. 71.
[15] Ibid.

contents of the medical inspector's advice. There is no method of challenging the medical inspector's decision. It is not possible, for example, to obtain a second medical opinion and submit it to an immigration officer for his consideration. If there are no compassionate reasons, entry must be refused and any appeal based on a challenge of the medical evidence must fail. This was the conclusion of the Tribunal in *Al-Tuwaidji*,[16] where it was held that a diagnosis of schizophrenia by the medical inspector was conclusive although the Tribunal had evidence from two psychiatrists who believed the appellant was merely suffering from depression. The medical inspector must however state in unequivocal terms that medical grounds make entry 'undesirable'. In *Sudhakaran*,[17] the Tribunal held that an entry clearance officer was wrong to refuse entry where the report stated: 'In view of the heart disease, candidate is medically unfit. Entry is not recommended.'

What will amount to 'strong compassionate reasons' enabling a person to enter despite the medical inspector's conclusion will clearly depend on the circumstances of each individual case. The Tribunal has however held that in the context of the immigration rules the reasons must be 'of a totally exceptional and compelling nature'.[18] In *Sacha*,[19] the Tribunal directed that permission to enter for settlement be granted where the applicant was mentally retarded, her cousin in India cared for her reluctantly and her half-brother in England with whom she was brought up was prepared and financially able to look after her. Again in *Parvez* compassionate circumstances were held to be sufficiently strong where facilities for treatment were available here, they were to be paid for privately by relatives and the applicant's fiancée had waited two years for his arrival.[20]

5.22 There are some situations where a medical inspector may diagnose illness but not consider that entry is necessarily undesirable. If

[16] [1974] Imm AR 34.
[17] [1976] Imm AR 3.
[18] See *Veerabharda* 1198/71 (unreported); *Khaliq* 5037/75 (459) (unreported), referred to in *Awadallah* [1978] Imm AR 5.
[19] [1973] Imm AR 5. Decided under earlier immigration rules which were similar to the present rules.
[20] [1979–80] Imm AR 84. An immigration officer will not grant entry solely on the ground that a passenger has claimed that he will undergo private medical treatment. The Tribunal allowed entry in *Bhatti* [1979–80] Imm AR 86 where the facts were similar to *Parvez* holding that *Parvez* 'carried to the limit what could properly be considered strong compassionate circumstances'. See also *Aftab* 60901/80 (1777) (unreported) where again the passenger was allowed to enter.

he advises that a passenger is suffering from a specified disease or condition which may interfere with his ability to support himself or his dependants, the immigration officer (or entry clearance officer) is required under the rules to take this into account along with other factors in deciding whether to admit.[1] If he refuses to admit, medical evidence may be given on appeal to rebut the medical inspector's opinion.

Although they cannot be refused entry on medical grounds, returning residents and the spouses and children under 18 of people settled here may still be required to submit to a medical examination. If, but for this status, a person would have been refused entry for medical reasons he will be given a notice requiring him to report to a Medical Officer of Environmental Health designated by the medical inspector with a view to further examination and any necessary treatment.[2] Notices will be similarly served on those admitted on compassionate grounds and in any other case if the medical inspector recommends.[3] Failure to comply with the notice is a criminal offence.[4]

5.23 EEC nationals are not to be referred to a medical inspector unless they show 'obvious signs of mental or physical ill health'.[5] They may only be refused if the medical inspector certifies that they are suffering from one of the diseases listed in the Annex to EEC Directive 64/221.[6] Members of the family of an EEC national, irrespective of their nationality, may only be refused on health grounds if they are suffering from such a disease.[7]

5.24 Other nationals may be declared medically undesirable if they have one of a number of diseases, including pulmonary tuberculosis, venereal disease, leprosy or trachoma; and in the case of those who are coming to work any disease, defect or deformity or fits which would prevent the entrant's supporting himself and his dependants.[8] The

[1] HC 394, para. 71. [2] Ibid., para. 72.
[3] Ibid.
[4] Immigration Act 1971, s. 26(1)(a).
[5] 'Home Office; Instructions to medical inspectors' set out in *The Medical Examination of Immigrants*: Report by the Chief Medical Officer, Sir Henry Yellowlees, released by the Home Office in December 1980. As to the powers and duties of medical inspectors see para. 5.36, post.
[6] These are diseases which might endanger public health (i.e. diseases subject to quarantine by the World Health Organisation, active tuberculosis, syphilis and other infectious or contagious parasitic diseases) or which might threaten public policy or public security (i.e. drug addiction, profound mental disturbance, etc.).
[7] See HC 394, para. 62.
[8] Home Office; Instructions to medical inspectors. See also *The Guardian*, 1979, 21 September 'Sexuality used to Ban Immigrants.'

medical inspector may also declare undesirable those suffering from mental disorder, senility or 'conduct disorder' which includes 'alcoholism, drug addictions and abnormal sexuality'.[9]

Criminal Convictions

5.25 Anyone, other than the wife or child under 18 of a person settled in the UK, who has been convicted in any country including the UK of a criminal offence included in the list of extradition crimes set out in the Extradition Act 1870 (as amended) or of an offence for which a person is returnable under the Fugitive Offenders Act 1967 must be refused admission unless there are 'strong compassionate reasons' justifying admission.[10]

The effect of this rule is that a conviction for a relatively minor offence may lead to exclusion, even where the offence was committed in the UK and the court did not recommend deportation. The Tribunal has held that it is not sufficient to show that considerable inconvenience or frustration will be caused by the refusal. In *Adwallah*,[11] it was said that refusal would cause 'considerable strain' to the applicant's married daughter if she had to travel with her young child to the continent on his visits there several times a year. Similarly in *Langridge*,[12] a marriage which the adjudicator accepted 'might well have been imminent' was not considered sufficiently compelling, nor in *Liberto*,[13] was the need to continue proceedings in the High Court for the recovery of two motor vehicles.

The Rehabilitation of Offenders Act 1974 applies to this rule and a person who has become a rehabilitated person and his conviction spent is not to be refused leave to enter on the basis of that conviction.

---

[9] There is no formal definition of 'abnormal sexuality' but the Home Office has given an assurance that 'homosexuality in itself is not regarded as a disqualification from gaining leave to enter the UK'. Letter, Private Secretary to the Home Secretary, William Whitelaw, to Robert Palmer, CHE Chairperson, 24 October 1979.

[10] HC 394 para. 74. In *R v Immigration Appeal Tribunal, ex parte Palacio* [1979–80] Imm AR 178 the Divisional Court held that 'strong compassionate circumstances' might be difficult to apply but the courts could give no more guidance than was provided by those 'perfectly plain and clear English words'. It held that the appellate authorities had misdirected themselves when seeking (1) to give particular emphasis to circumstances relating to wives and children; and (2) to redefine the words as meaning 'reasons of a totally compelling or exceptional nature'.

[11] [1978] Imm AR 5.
[12] [1972] Imm AR 38.
[13] [1975] Imm AR 61.

Subject to a Deportation Order

5.26 Anyone against whom a deportation order is still current must be refused leave to enter.[14] The immigration rules state that he will be told that the correct procedure is to return to his own country, and apply for a revocation of the order; if refused, he will have a right of appeal in most cases against the refusal to revoke. Revocation itself does not entitle a person to enter the UK; it merely makes him eligible for qualifying under the immigration rules.[15]

Exclusion Conducive to the Public Good

5.27 Any passenger except the wife or child under 18 of a person settled in the UK may be refused leave to enter on the ground that his or her exclusion is conducive to the public good if, (1) the Home Secretary has personally ordered it; or (2) it seems right from information available to the immigration officer e.g. in the light of the passenger's character, conduct or associations it is undesirable to give him leave to enter.[16]

In *Munk-Hansen*,[17] a Danish woman was refused leave to enter the UK with three men in whose vehicle was found a quantity of cannabis resin. She denied all knowledge of the drug and unlike the men was not charged. She had left her child and husband in Denmark and wished to continue an association with one of the men. She had been pursuing 'an informal life-style' in Morocco and survived after her money ran out by begging and scrounging. The adjudicator took the view that those convicted of criminal activity, or against whom there were doubts on political or security grounds, would be excluded under other sections of the immigration rules and asked 'what other class should be excluded for the public good? Primarily . . . those about whom strong and reasonable suspicion exists of criminal activities or associations or moral turpitude or both. The appellant in this case fits this description pretty well.' The Tribunal upheld the adjudicator's decision, rejecting the argument that it was necessary for the immigration officer to spell out what part of the public good he is safeguarding by the exclusion of a person.

In *Scheele*,[18] the Tribunal stated that the power to exclude on this

---

[14] HC 394, para. 75. Special consideration will however be given to a person made subject to a deportation order following a conviction for an offence which has become spent under the Rehabilitation of Offenders Act, but there is no guarantee that it will be revoked.

[15] Ibid., para. 155.

[16] Ibid., para. 76.

[17] TH/880/73 (210) (unreported).

[18] [1976] Imm AR 1. See also *Mussa* 20100/77 (1071) (unreported).

ground 'should not be lightly used and in trivial circumstances', but found exclusion of the appellant to be justified when herbal cannabis was found in his possession even though the amount was small and for his own use and where he was in transit to another country. The power has also been used to exclude a returning resident who contracted a marriage of convenience.[19]

In *Khazari*[20] the Tribunal rejected the argument that the principles relating to the making of deportation orders on conducive grounds, including the balancing of the public interest against any compassionate circumstances, are applicable to refusal of admission on such grounds:

'The effect of a refusal of admission is different from the effect of a deportation order, because a deportation order prohibits the subject of it from returning to this country, whereas a refusal of admission does not necessarily have this effect. If the principles relating to the making of a deportation order. . . . were intended to apply in cases of refusal of admission it is reasonable to assume that the rules would say so. They do not.'

It is difficult to imagine an immigration officer being able to come to a decision without balancing these interests. In practice they are two sides of the same coin in that the 'public' justification for exclusion can only be measured against the 'personal' circumstances of the passenger which would otherwise warrant admission. The Tribunal appears to accept this argument when it held in *Vincent*[1]

'Whilst (an immigration officer) is entitled in considering the conduct of the passenger to give appropriate weight to any relevant compassionate circumstances included in the information available to him, he is not, however, expected to, nor is he in a position to, anticipate compassionate pleas founded on subsequent hearings.'[2]

Visitors suspected of political activities which are undesirable in the view of the authorities can be excluded. Difficulties were experienced by a number of European visitors believed to be participating in an 'anti-

[19] *Osama* [1978] Imm AR 8.
[20] 66628/80 (1904) (unreported).
[1] 68344/80 (1935) (unreported).
[2] But if the appellate authority finds compassionate circumstances which existed at the time of the immigration officer's decision but were unbeknown to him, it is bound to give consideration to them in reaching its decision; see para. 14.33, post.

internment week' in Northern Ireland in the summers of 1974 and 1976 with varying results on appeal.[3]

General Immigration History

5.28 The rules enable an immigration officer to refuse entry if an entrant has a bad immigration record. In the past entry has been refused in such circumstances by excluding on 'conducive grounds'[4] but the present rules specifically state that leave may be refused,

'if, for example, the passenger has not observed the time limit or conditions imposed on any grant of leave to enter or remain; if, whether or not to the entrant's knowledge, false representations have been employed or material facts not disclosed orally or in writing for the purpose of obtaining entry clearance or if a previous leave to enter or remain has been obtained by deception'[5]

These instances are set out by way of example and there may be other circumstances relating to an entrant's immigration record which may be held to justify refusal.

POWERS AND DUTIES OF IMMIGRATION OFFICERS AT PORT OF ENTRY[6]

5.29 Entry is controlled at ports by immigration officers who are appointed by the Home Secretary. Customs and Excise officers may be employed as immigration officers by arrangement with the Home Secretary and Commissioners of Customs and Excise. The Act states that immigration officers are to exercise their functions in accordance with instructions given to them by the Home Secretary and that these instructions (which are not made public) are not to be inconsistent with the immigration rules.[7] The rules state that they will do so 'without regard to the race, colour or religion of people seeking to enter the UK'.[8]

---

[3] See *Trividic* 4379/74 (unreported); *Kupfer* 4419/74 (unreported); *Lindeman* 4420/74 (unreported); *Jorrisch* 8363/76 (unreported), (adjudicator's decisions). See also *Spens* 3903/73 (unreported), adjudicator's decision.

[4] See e.g. *Majed* 21065/77 (1108) (unreported).

[5] HC 394, para. 67.

[6] See generally Immigration Act 1971, Sch. 2.

[7] Ibid., para. 1(3).

[8] HC 394, para. 2. As to the nature of the immigration rules, see para. 1.16, ante.

Boarding Ships and Aircraft

5.30 An immigration officer may board any ship or aircraft for the purpose of carrying out his functions.[9] He may also search any ship or aircraft, anything on board or anything taken off it to see whether there is anyone he may wish to examine.[10] A ship includes every description of vessel used in navigation and an aircraft includes a hovercraft.[11]

Examining Passengers

5.31 An immigration officer may examine anyone arriving in the UK by ship or aircraft (including transit passengers,[12] members of the crew and even those not wishing to enter the UK) to decide, (1) whether any of them is or is not patrial; (2) whether, if he is not, he may or may not enter the UK without leave; (3) whether, if he may not, he should be given leave and for what period and on what conditions (if any), or should be refused leave.[13]

An immigration officer has the power to detain anyone who may be required to submit to examination and a person may be held pending his examination or pending a decision to give or refuse him entry; if he is refused leave to enter there are further powers to detain pending removal.[14] The extent of the powers of detention are discussed more fully at para. 13.1. If the immigration officer is not satisfied at the end of the examination, he can require the passenger to submit to a second examination.[15] This requirement must be made in writing and the passenger will be handed a form. Transit passengers and crew members cannot be prevented from leaving by their intended ship or aircraft.[16] An immigration officer has no power to examine other people connected with the passenger, e.g., relatives.

Demanding Information and Documents

5.32 The Act places a duty on anyone being examined to provide any

[9] Immigration Act 1971, Sch. 2, para. 1(4).
[10] Ibid.
[11] Ibid., s. 33(1).
[12] The immigration rules state that detailed examination of a passenger whose sole purpose is transit to a country outside the common travel area is unlikely to be required once he has satisfied the immigration officer that he has both the means and the intention of proceeding at once to another country and is assured of entry there. If the immigration officer is not satisfied leave to enter is to be refused.
[13] Immigration Act 1971, Sch. 2, para. 2(1); HC 394, para. 3.
[14] Immigration Act 1971, Sch. 2, para. 16.
[15] Ibid., para. 2(3).   [16] Ibid.

information in his possession which is required by the immigration officer in carrying out his functions.[17] If required, he must also produce a valid passport or some other satisfactory document establishing his identity and nationality, and declare whether he is holding or carrying any type of document described by the immigration officer.[18] If he is, he may be required to produce them.[19]

The House of Lords in *Zamir* v *Secretary of State for the Home Department*[20] rejected the argument that an entrant is under no duty to volunteer information. The court held that a person[1] seeking entry,

'owes a positive duty of candour on all material facts including those which denote a change of circumstances since the entry clearance. He is seeking a privilege; he alone is, as to most such matters, aware of the facts: the decision to allow him to enter, and he knows this, is based upon a broad appreciation by immigration officers of complex considerations, and this appreciation can only be made fairly and humanely if, on his side, the entrant acts with openness and frankness.'[2]

Searching

5.33 Once a passenger has been asked about the carrying of documents, he, and any luggage belonging to him or under his control, may be searched. The questions may be specific, e.g. 'Do you have any letters from the sister you intend to visit in the UK?', or more general, 'Have you anything in your possession relevant to your stay here?' Whatever the answer, a search is permitted after the question has been put to the passengers.[3] Women and girls must only be searched by women.[4]

Detaining Documents

5.34 An immigration officer is allowed to detain documents other than a passport for the purpose of examining them, but may only hold them for a maximum period of 7 days unless he believes that they may be

[17] Ibid., para. 4(1).
[18] Ibid., para. 4(2).
[19] Ibid.
[20] [1980] 2 All ER 768 HL.
[1] The word used was 'alien' but it is hardly conceivable that the courts would apply a different test to Commonwealth citizens.
[2] Per Wilberforce LJ, at 773.
[3] Ibid., Sch. 2, para. 4(3).
[4] Ibid.

needed for an immigration appeal or for a criminal prosecution.[5] In that case he may keep them until he is satisfied that they no longer will be needed.

There is no power to detain a passport.[6] The Home Office has issued a note reminding the Immigration Service that a passenger has to be given his passport back if he asks for it.[7]

PENALTIES FOR NOT CO-OPERATING

5.35 It is clear that failure to co-operate with or otherwise assist an immigration officer is likely to result in refusal of entry. There are a number of criminal offences which may be brought; (1) failing to submit to an examination; (2) failing to furnish or produce information or documents; (3) making or causing to be made false statements or representations; (4) obstructing an immigration officer.[8]

POWERS AND DUTIES OF MEDICAL INSPECTORS

5.36 Medical inspectors are fully qualified medical practitioners appointed by the Home Secretary and act in accordance with instructions given by him.[9] They have the same powers as immigration officers to board ships and aircraft,[10] and also to examine and further examine passengers.[11] Similarly, failure to co-operate is a criminal offence.[12] The circumstances under which passengers will be referred to a medical inspector have already been explained.[13]

5.37 On 2 February 1979 the Home Secretary acknowledged that 'in rare cases' internal vaginal examinations had been carried out on women passengers and stated that he had given instructions to immigration

---

[5] Ibid., para. 4(4). The prosecution need not be connected with immigration.

[6] See ibid., para. 4(4) which specifically limits the documents which may be detained to 'para. 4(2)(b)' documents.

[7] Letter, Home Office to JCWI 12 November 1980.

[8] See generally Immigration Act s. 26(1) and para. 10.14, post.

[9] Ibid., Sch. 2, para. 1(2). In Northern Ireland the appointment is made and instructions given by the Secretary of State for Northern Ireland.

[10] Ibid., Sch. 2, para. 1(4).

[11] Ibid., para. 2(2). The examination may be conducted by 'any qualified person carrying out a test or examination required by a medical inspector'.

[12] Ibid., s. 26(1)(a), (g).

[13] See para. 5.20, ante.

officers that they 'should not ask the medical inspector to examine passengers with a view to establishing whether they have borne children or had had sexual intercourse.'[14]

On 19 February 1979 the Home Secretary announced that he was instituting a review, in consultation with the Chief Medical Adviser to the DHSS and the Home Office, Sir Henry Yellowlees, of the objects and nature of medical examinations in the context of immigration control.[15] Interim instructions were given in October 1979 to entry clearance officers in the Indian sub-continent to the effect that they should not ask for bone X-ray examinations to help in the age assessment of adults[16] and presumably medical inspectors have been similarly instructed. Following the release of the Yellowlees Report by the Home Office in December 1980[17] the procedures for medical examination and instructions to medical officers are under review.

THE EXAMINATION: APPROACH TO BE TAKEN BY IMMIGRATION OFFICERS

5.38 The approach taken by immigration officers in reaching a decision has frequently been called into question and on a number of occasions the courts have been asked to release or to admit into the UK people being held at the ports. The courts have generally been reluctant to intervene and in consequence have interpreted narrowly the duties and responsibilities of immigration officers. The following emerges from their decisions:

(a) an immigration officer is not a judge. He does not therefore have to conduct a trial or obey a set of rules of procedure. He is an administrative officer engaged in an administrative enquiry and at the end of it has to be satisfied before he takes a particular decision;[18]
(b) an immigration officer does not have to be convinced of the passenger's case but the burden of proof is on the passenger to satisfy

[14] Statement by the Home Office, 2 February 1979.
[15] 963 H. of C. Official Report 19 February 1979, col. 219.
[16] 980 H. of C. Official Report 7 March 1980, Written Answers, col. 355.
[17] See para. 5.23 footnote 5, ante.
[18] R v *Secretary of State for Home Department, ex parte Mughal* [1973] 3 All ER 796, CA, per Denning MR at 803; per Scarman LJ at 807–8. See also Re *HK (an infant)* [1967] 1 All ER 226, per Parker LCJ at 231 and Re *A(an infant)* [1968] 2 All ER 144.

him on a balance of probabilities[19] that he is eligible for entry. He must act 'honestly and fairly' and natural justice requires that he should give the passenger a real opportunity of satisfying him. If he has done so, the courts will not interfere with his decision;[20]
(c) it is up to the passenger to show that he has established a basis for entry. There is no obligation on an immigration officer to suggest to the passenger that there are more solid or alternative grounds on which to base the application or more persuasive arguments to put forward; immigration officers are entitled to assume that the entrant is putting the best case forward on the grounds available and that he is answering questions truthfully.[1] There is also no obligation on an immigration officer to ascertain whether the passenger has disclosed all the information concerning the reasons for entry;[2]
(d) the courts will not look at events subsequent to a decision if satisfied that the immigration officer acted fairly; the matter must be looked at at the time when the immigration officer made his decision. If he acted unfairly, the courts can take into account anything subsequently discovered. Acting unfairly will include 'failing to take steps to ascertain what he plainly ought to have ascertained':[3] e.g. an immigration officer may be acting unfairly if he refuses to check a passenger's claim that he is visiting his brother and that the brother is at the port to meet him, particularly if the refusal is based on a belief that the passenger has no brother or that the brother had insufficient money to look after him for the visit. In other cases, the immigration officer might be expected to make some enquiries before making a decision but he cannot be expected to make extensive enquiries in every case;
(e) where a passenger has been refused entry but before he leaves additional information comes to light, an immigration officer has the power to reconsider his decision,[4] but there is no duty on him to do

[19] See *R v Secretary of State for the Home Department, ex parte S B Hussain* (1972) 19 September, DC, 226/72 (unreported) per Widgery LCJ: 'I can see no possible reason for requiring a higher standard of proof... it would be quite unreasonable to assume that (the immigration rules) contemplate proof beyond dispute or proof beyond reasonable doubt.' This passage is referred to in *Diljar Begum* 682/73 (461) (unreported).

[20] See *Mughal*, cited., note 18, supra.

[1] *R v Chief Immigration Officer, Heathrow Airport, ex parte Salamat Bibi* [1976] 3 All ER 843, per Geoffrey Lane LJ at 850.

[2] Ibid., see also *R v Secretary of State for Home Department, ex parte Safira Begum* (1976) *The Times*, 28 May, DC.

[3] *R v Chief Immigration Officer (Heathrow), ex parte Shaikh*, (1976) *The Times*, 21 July.

[4] Immigration Act 1971, Sch. 2, para. 6(3).

so merely because the passenger changes the grounds of his application.[5]

THE DECISION: GIVING OR REFUSING LEAVE TO ENTER

5.39 Once an immigration officer's examination is completed he has 12 hours in which to notify the passenger of his decision. In fact, people are detained for much longer periods because, as we have seen, if the immigration officer's enquiries are not complete, he can simply serve a notice on the passenger requiring him to submit to a further examination.[6] At the end of the further examination the 12 hour period will then begin again. In the event of 12 hours passing without the passenger receiving any notification, he is deemed to have been given indefinite leave and the immigration officer must put this in writing as soon as possible.[7] This is hardly ever likely to occur, particularly as the Tribunal has held that until the appellant is 'actually informed that the examination is concluded, such examination must be deemed to continue up to the (time of) service of the notice of refusal'.[8] It is submitted that this approach is wrong: the point at which an examination is concluded must be a question of fact in each particular case.

If the entrant thereby obtains indefinite leave to enter, the rules relating to returning residents are applicable to him in the same manner as any other person granted indefinite leave.[9] Although there is no effective time limit within which a decision must be made, it will usually be taken within seven days of the passenger's arrival in the UK. After this time he has a right to apply to an adjudicator for bail pending a decision.[10]

5.40 If the decision is to refuse leave to enter, an immigration officer cannot do so on his own authority; the approval of a chief immigration officer or an immigration inspector must always be obtained.[11] The decision must be given in writing whenever the passenger has a right of

---

[5] *R v Chief Immigration Officer (Heathrow), ex parte Hazari* (1975), *The Times*, 25 November, CA.

[6] Immigration Act 1971, Sch. 2, para. 6(1).

[7] Ibid.

[8] *Perera (HRN)* [1979–80] Imm AR 58. See also *Sule* 45494/6/79 (1593) (unreported).

[9] HC 394, paras. 56–58, see para. 8.66 et seq., post.

[10] Immigration Act 1971, Sch. 2, para. 22(1); HC 394, para. 79. See para. 13.4, post.

[11] Ibid., para. 69.

appeal (or would have had but for the ground on which the decision was taken) and served on the passenger 'as soon as is practicable'.[12]

5.41 A decision to grant entry must be given in writing[13] and is usually by way of an endorsement in the passenger's passport. As we have seen, leave to enter may be given subject to time limit or conditions, restricting the passenger's employment or occupation, or requiring him to report to the police.[14] Any restrictions will be endorsed in the passport together with a rectangular date stamp which also shows the port of arrival. If the passport is endorsed only with the stamp, the holder is deemed to have indefinite leave,[15] provided it was not obtained by deception.[16] An immigration officer can also require a person to whom he grants leave to enter to report on his arrival to a specified medical officer of health if a medical inspector believes this to be necessary in the interest of public health.[17] The passenger must receive written notification of any such requirement.

A decision, either refusing or granting leave to enter, may be reversed. If a passenger has been given leave to enter, cancellation of that leave and a refusal of leave to enter may be made within 12 hours of the conclusion of the examination, and must be in writing.[18] A refusal of leave to enter may be cancelled at any time by written notice.[19] If the passenger is then given leave to enter, it may be for a limited period and subject to conditions, but in the absence of a notice giving limited leave, the notice of cancellation is deemed to be a notice giving the passenger indefinite leave.[20] Notices will usually be served directly on the passenger, but will be valid if served on someone authorised by the entrant to receive it, e.g. a solicitor, or in the case of a member of a group, the person the immigration officer believes to be in charge of the group.[1]

[12] The Immigration Appeals (Notices) Regulations 1972, SI 1972 No. 1683, reg. 3.
[13] Immigration Act 1971, s. 4(1).
[14] Ibid., s. 3(1)(c). See para. 5.1, ante.
[15] See R v *Secretary of State for Home Affairs, ex parte Badaike* (1977). *The Times*, 4 May.
[16] As to what constitutes deception, see paras. 12.1 et seq., post. Those not subject to control may receive the same endorsement, but they do not obtain indefinite leave. See para. 3.15, ante.
[17] Immigration Act 1971, Sch. 2, para. 7, see para. 5.20, ante.
[18] Ibid., para. 6(2).
[19] Ibid., para. 6(2).
[20] Ibid.
[1] Ibid., para. 6(4). See also R v *Chief Immigration Officer Manchester Airport, ex parte Begum* [1973] 1 All ER 594 CA, decided under the previous law where notice held to be validly served on the entrant's solicitor, she being illiterate and incapable of understanding the notice.

DETENTION OF PASSENGERS

5.42 A person may be detained from the moment of his arrival and held while a decision is being made about him.[2] If the decision is that he is not to be admitted he can continue to be held until removed from the UK.[3] An immigration officer's power to hold a person arises as soon as the ship or aircraft arrives in the UK. He can remove anyone from a ship or aircraft, and conversely can require the captain to keep on board and hold in custody anyone refused entry.[4] Similarly he may place a person on board and require the captain to detain anyone refused entry.[5] Once off the ship, the passenger is still subject to the control of the immigration officer and anyone he authorises may detain the passenger. In practice this will be either a police or prison officer or a private security firm with whom the Home Office has a contract to hold immigrants. The only firm with which the Home Office has contracted is Securicor Ltd. Occasionally, a passenger may be entrusted to a private individual or organisation. Passengers awaiting a decision about entry or removal are normally kept at detention accommodation at the port of entry. If this is full or the delay is likely to be lengthy they may be removed to Harmondsworth Detention Centre, near Heathrow Airport, or to a prison or remand centre.[6]

The Act permits an immigration, prison or police officer and anyone else the Home Secretary authorises to 'take all such steps as may be reasonably necessary for photographing, measuring or otherwise identifying' a passenger.[7] He need not be kept in one place. He may be moved about for almost any purpose,[8] and while in detention or being removed he is in lawful custody.[9] The effect of this is that any application for *habeas corpus* is almost certain to fail, the onus being on the detainee to show that he is being held illegally.[10] Anyone liable to be detained can

[2] Immigration Act 1971, Sch. 2, para. 16(1).
[3] Ibid., para. 16(2).
[4] Ibid., para. 16(3).
[5] Ibid., para. 16(4).
[6] See para. 13.1, post.
[7] Ibid., Sch. 2, para. 18(2).
[8] Ibid., para. 18(3).
[9] Ibid., para. 18(4).
[10] See, e.g. observations of Denning MR in *R v Secretary of State for Home Department, ex parte Phansopkar* [1975] 3 All ER 497 at 508. If the return by the gaoler is valid on its face, the onus is on the applicant to establish a *prima facie* case to show that his detention was illegal. See *Wajid Hassan* [1976] 2 All ER 123, para. 13.16, post.

be arrested without a warrant by a police constable or by an immigration officer.[11] Magistrates can also grant warrants to police officers to search premises if there is reasonable suspicion that a person liable to be arrested is on the premises, the warrant being valid for a month and authorising the use of force if necessary to gain entry.[12]

Release Pending a Decision

Bail

5.43 In the unlikely event of no decision being made by the immigration authorities at the end of seven days from the date of the passenger's arrival, he can apply to an adjudicator for bail, and he must be notified in writing of this right.[13] To assist him in deciding whether to apply for bail he is to be given facilities to communicate with friends, relatives, a legal adviser, the UK Immigrants Advisory Service or his Consul or High Commission as he may wish.[14] Bail will not be granted automatically and may be opposed by the immigration authorities. If bail is granted it may be made subject to conditions;[15] e.g. reporting at regular intervals or at a specific time to the immigration authorities or the police, or residing at a particular address. Sureties may be required and if no one is available to act as surety, bail may be granted subject to sureties satisfactory to the police or immigration authorities coming forward later.[16]

The procedure adopted on applications for bail is discussed later when considering the other circumstances in which bail may be granted.[17]

Temporary Admission

5.44 A more common form of release is to admit the passenger on a temporary basis while a decision is being made.[18] The passenger is not granted leave to enter but is permitted physically to enter the UK subject to restrictions as to residence and as to reporting to the police or immigration authorities.[19] These restrictions must be notified to him in writing by the immigration officer. He can be re-detained at any time.[20]

[11] Immigration Act 1971, Sch. 2, para. 17(1).
[12] Ibid., para. 17(2).
[13] Ibid., para. 22(1).
[14] See HC 394, para. 79.
[15] Immigration Act 1971, Sch. 2, para. 22 (2).
[16] Ibid., para. 22(3).
[17] See paras. 13.4 et seq., post.
[18] Ibid., Sch. 2, para. 21(1).
[19] Ibid., para. 21(2).
[20] Ibid., para. 21(1).

A decision will subsequently be made and the passenger will either be given or refused leave to enter.

REMOVAL FROM THE UK

5.45 A passenger who is refused entry will be removed from the UK. The responsibility for his removal lies with the shipping company or airline which brought him and directions will be given to them by an immigration officer to ensure removal. If a decision to refuse entry is made speedily then the captain of the ship or aircraft on which the passenger arrived will be required to take him away on the return journey.[1] In other cases, the owners or agents of that line will be directed to remove him on one of their other ships or aircraft.[2] Alternatively the immigration officer may specify the country to which the passenger is to be removed (usually the country from where he set off or of which he is a citizen) and direct the line to make arrangements to take him to that country.[3]

An immigration officer can only give directions for removal for up to two months beginning with the date of refusal.[4] It is rare for decisions not to be made within that time, but where such circumstances do arise, the Home Secretary may still give directions for removal to any country he arranges, although the cost will be borne by the Home Office.[5] Similarly, the Home Secretary may remove anyone at Government expense if it is not practicable to ask the airline or shipping company to take responsibility or if the immigration officer's directions are not likely to be effective.[6] While most passengers refused entry leave peacefully, an immigration officer is authorised to place on board the ship or aircraft anyone against whom directions have been given. This means that to ensure departure force may be used if necessary.[7]

Consulting Friends and Others

5.46 The rules provide that before removal a passenger should be

[1] Ibid., para. 8(1)(a).
[2] Ibid., para. 8(1)(b).
[3] Ibid., para. 8(1)(c). The rules state that the power to refuse leave to enter should normally be exercised so as to secure the passenger's removal to the country in which he has boarded the ship or aircraft that brought him to the UK, HC 394, para. 77.
[4] Immigration Act 1971, Sch. 2, para. 8(2).
[5] Ibid., para. 10(1)(b).
[6] Ibid., para. 10(1)(a).
[7] Ibid., para. 11.

given the opportunity to telephone friends or relatives in this country or his consul, if he wishes to do so.[8] The immigration authorities often allow friends and relatives to see the passenger before departure but there is no obligation on them to do so.

Illegal Entrants

5.47 Illegal entrants are those who enter or try to enter the UK in breach of a deportation order or of the immigration laws.[9] If they are caught, whether at sea or after landing, they can be detained and removed under the same procedure as for those refused entry.[10] The subject is more fully considered in Chapter 12.

Seamen and Aircrew

5.48 We have already seen that seamen and aircrew between jobs will be admitted to the UK on a temporary basis without being subject to immigration control. The Act also permits members of crews to enter for the specific purpose of joining a ship or aircraft or for receiving hospital treatment.[11] Anyone overstaying the permitted time allowed can be detained and removed under a similar procedure as for those refused entry.[12]

THE RIGHT OF APPEAL

5.49 There is a right of appeal against a refusal of leave to enter[13] but unless the passenger holds a current entry clearance or a work permit issued to him, the appeal cannot be made until he has left the UK.[14] Where the appeal is exercisable in the UK, the passenger is to be given facilities to consult friends, relatives, a legal adviser, Consul or High Commission or the UK Immigrants Advisory Service.[15] In other cases it should be explained to the passenger that he can only exercise his right of appeal after leaving the UK.[16] There is no right of appeal against directions for removal to a particular destination unless the passenger is also

---

[8] HC 394, para. 78. There is no certainty that the immigration officer will not listen to the conversation on an extension.
[9] Immigration Act 1971, s. 33(1). See paras. 12.1 et seq., 13.3 et seq., post.
[10] Ibid., Sch. 2, paras. 9–11, 16(2), (4), 17, 18.
[11] Ibid., para. 12(1).
[12] Ibid., paras, 12–15, 16(2), (4) 17, 18. See para. 13.28, post.
[13] Ibid., s. 13 (1).
[14] Ibid., s. 13(5), see paras. 14.1, 14.9 et seq., post.
[15] HC 394, para. 79.
[16] Ibid., para. 82.

appealing against a decision, (1) that he requires leave to enter; or (2) refusing him leave to enter where he is holding an entry clearance or work permit.[17] There is no right of appeal against a refusal to give leave to enter where the Home Secretary personally decides that the passenger's exclusion is conducive to the public good.[18] Written notice of the right to appeal must be given by the immigration officer, usually in the notice refusing leave to enter.[19] The procedure on appeal is set out in Chapter 15.

RESPONSIBILITIES OF SHIPPING COMPANIES AND AIRLINES

5.50 It will have become apparent that the Act places considerable responsibilities on the shipping company and airlines to ensure that immigration control is carried out effectively. The requirements include; (1) landing only at ports of entry authorised by the Home Secretary;[20] (2) allowing immigration officers and medical inspectors on board, and permitting searches to check for non-patrials;[1] (3) preventing from disembarking and detaining anyone who an immigration officer requires holding;[2] (4) taking steps to prevent anyone from disembarking until cleared by the immigration authorities;[3] (5) complying with regulations made by the Home Secretary concerning the control areas at the ports where passengers may embark and disembark;[4] (6) providing information about members of the crew and the names and nationalities of the passengers;[5] (7) paying the cost of detaining and removing passengers refused entry.[6] Failure to satisfy any of these requirements is a criminal

[17] Immigration Act 1971, s. 17 (1), (2), (5).
[18] Ibid., s. 13(5).
[19] HC, 394, para. 80.
[20] Immigration Act 1971, Sch. 2, para. 26. The authorised ports are set out in the Immigration (Ports of Entry) Order 1972, SI 1972 No. 1668; as the Immigration (Ports of Entry) (Amendment) Order 1975, SI 1975 No. 2221; Immigration (Ports of Entry) (Amendment) Order 1979, SI 1979 No. 1635.
[1] Immigration Act 1971, Sch. 2, paras. 1(4), (5), 27.
[2] Ibid., para. 27(1) (a).
[3] Ibid.
[4] Ibid., para. 26(2), (3).
[5] Ibid., para. 27(2). The requirements are set out in the Immigration (Particulars of Passengers and Crew) Order 1972, SI 1972 No. 1667; Immigration (Particulars of Passengers and Crew) (Amendment) Order 1975, SI 1975, No. 980.
[6] Immigration Act 1971, Sch. 2, paras. 19, 20.

offence.[7] In some cases, the captain of the ship or aircraft will be liable to prosecution, in others liability falls on the owner or agent.

ADVICE TO THOSE ASSISTING ENTRANTS

5.51 Those advising would-be entrants to the UK and their friends and relatives should bear in mind,

(a) the necessity of obtaining entry clearance in certain cases and the advantages of obtaining it in others, but also of the delays and pitfalls if clearance is first applied for;[8]
(b) whenever possible, make sure the passenger has friends or relatives to meet him. They may themselves be questioned by immigration officers. It is important therefore to ensure that they will be accepted as of good character and that they do not have a bad immigration history. They should also be in a position to prove their own identity.
(c) if the time of the arrival is known in advance, you should be informed. The passenger or his relatives or friends can contact you from the port of entry in case of difficulties;
(d) if there is a delay in making a decision, discuss the matter with the immigration authorities. If the enquiries by the immigration officer are likely to be lengthy, try to secure temporary admission. In appropriate cases, try to delay the final decision until you have had an opportunity of interviewing your client and/or his relatives and friends. The Legal Advice Scheme is available for solicitors' visits to the port or detention centres.
(e) if removal is imminent, it may be justified to obtain the assistance of the MP of the passenger, or if he has none, that of his relatives or friends. If the MP is prepared to make representations, this will secure contact with the Minister's Private Office and will prevent immediate removal.
(f) if the MP is not available, it may be appropriate to ask for a delay of 24 hours in the removal of the passenger so that the MP can be contacted. It is Home Office policy not to remove for 24 hours after refusal if it is clear that the entrant's sponsor or representative intends to contact an MP. At weekends removal will not generally take

[7] Ibid., s. 27.
[8] See para. 5.52, post.

place before Monday afternoon if efforts to contact an MP in the first 24 hours have been unsuccessful.
(g) remember that there is only a right of appeal from within the UK in a limited number of cases. Be prepared for a hearing in these cases within two to three days;
(h) if an application is to be made to the High Court for *habeas corpus* or judicial review, removal will be deferred if the authorities are satisfied that proceedings are about to be brought. Notification of the application should be made to the immigration officer by the entrant's legal representative.

PROCEDURE FOR OBTAINING ENTRY CLEARANCE

Queue in the Indian Sub-Continent

5.52 The nature of entry clearance has already been explained.[9] The greatest problems concerning clearance have been experienced by those from the Indian sub-continent. Entry clearance for dependants of Commonwealth citizens in the UK was made mandatory in June 1969, and was justified on the ground that it would make matters easier for the families on arrival. There were a number of objections to this amendment to the legislation, and fears were expressed that the number of dependants joining those in the UK would be reduced and that the interviewing procedures would lead to injustice. The Home Office Minister responsible for introducing the system, Mr Merlyn Rees, poured scorn on these fears and told Parliament 'it is not the intention of the Amendment . . . to lead to a reduction of the number of dependants coming in'; and later '. . . there will be no question of extremely long examinations'.[10] In fact, extremely long delays have been a feature of the entry clearance system in the Indian sub-continent. There are now four categories treated separately in the queue. The table on page 89 indicates the length of the queue in years at the end of March 1981.

5.53 Special priority is given to the following categories:[11]

(a) wives, where neither partner has been married before and whose children, if any, are all under 10;
(b) children under 10 where neither parent has any older children;
(c) urgent compassionate cases;

[9] See para. 5.4, ante.
[10] 783 H. of C. Official Report, 15 May 1969, col. 1792.
[11] Letter, Foreign and Commonwealth Office to JCWI, 22 April 1980.

	March 1981
	Years
Main queue	
Bangladesh (Dacca)	$1\frac{1}{2}$
India (New Delhi)	$1\frac{1}{4}$
(Bombay)	$\frac{3}{4}$
Pakistan (Islamabad and Karachi)	$1\frac{1}{4}$
Priority queue	
Bangladesh (Dacca)	$\frac{1}{2}$
India (New Delhi and Bombay)	$\frac{1}{4}$
Pakistan (Islamabad and Karachi)	$\frac{1}{4}$
Husbands	
Bangladesh (Dacca)	$1\frac{1}{2}$
India (New Delhi)	$1\frac{1}{2}$
(Bombay)	$1\frac{1}{2}$
Pakistan (Islamabad and Karachi)	$1\frac{1}{4}$
Fiancés	
Bangladesh (Dacca)	$1\frac{1}{2}$
India (New Delhi)	$1\frac{1}{2}$
(Bombay)	$1\frac{1}{2}$
Pakistan (Islamabad and Karachi)	$1\frac{1}{4}$[12]

(d) returning residents;
(e) UK passport holders subject to immigration control;
(f) Commonwealth citizens applying for certificates of patriality;
(g) applicants for whom prior entry clearance is not mandatory.

Overseas posts have discretion to decide whether particular features justify priority in other cases: e.g. wives and children who have settled in the UK in the past but who have been back in the country of origin too long to qualify for readmission as returning residents; in Pakistan priority is given to dependent relatives over 70.

5.54 The main queue comprises other applications from wives and

[12] Lord Belstead 421 No. 99, H. of L. Official Report, 18 June 1981, Written Answers, col. 813.

children, parents and other relatives excluding husbands. Husbands and fiancés comprise two further separate queues.

By no means all applications are decided at first interview. Substantial further delays occur before an appeal against refusal can be heard: the time from receipt of appeal to dispatch of explanatory statement in settlement cases is usually three to six months.

How to make an Application

5.55 Care should be taken to ensure that an application for entry clearance has been properly made. Failure to do so may result in delays, or in some cases, a loss of eligibility to enter for settlement, e.g. if an application is not made for a child before he reaches 18. The application does not have to be in any particular form although there is a document which the immigration authorities encourage applicants to use. This is known as 'Form IM2'. Applicants should use this form wherever possible so that there can be no misunderstanding what has been applied for. If there is an urgency about the application it can be made by a simple letter or even verbally (if made verbally, it should be followed by a confirming letter). The Tribunal held in *Brown*,[13] that there must, however, be a request in unambiguous terms for clearance to be issued to a particular person. Provided this is done, it is not necessary to include all information required by 'Form IM2,' but clearly it would help to do so. An example of an 'ambiguous' request would be 'I want my children to join me in England. Please send me details.'

When an application is made, a date will be given for the person requiring the clearance to be interviewed: as we have seen this will often be many months later. (In Pakistan and Bangladesh the date may not be allocated at the time of application.) Make sure, wherever possible, that full documentary evidence is made available to the entry clearance officer. This may save further delay. The specific evidence which should be produced depends on the reason the certificate is required. The requirements and the problems arising (particularly where documents are not available or do not exist) are discussed under the relevant categories of entry, e.g. students, dependants, etc. Many posts, especially those in the Indian sub-continent, expect information about the sponsor to be provided in the form of a 'sponsorship declaration', signed and declared before a Commissioner for Oaths or Notary Public. This spon-

[13] [1976] Imm AR 119.

sorship form has no official status and a number of versions are available: specimen forms available from JCWI have been accepted by overseas posts as containing the necessary information.

Remember that entry may be refused on the grounds of false representation or concealment of material facts to the entry clearance officer, even if the holder of the clearance was ignorant about it. Again care should be taken if anyone is acting on behalf of an applicant.

Powers and Duties of Entry Clearance Officers

5.56 The powers and duties of entry clearance officers, unlike those of immigration officers, are not set out in the Act. Indeed the Act does not make any reference to such officials, nor did the former immigration rules. However, the present rules state that 'entry clearance may be granted at the appropriate British Mission abroad in accordance with the provisions in (the immigration rules) governing the grant or refusal of leave to enter and, where appropriate, the term "entry clearance officer" may be substituted for "immigration officer" accordingly'.[14] The approach an officer must take is therefore identical to that to be taken by immigration officers. There is no duty on entry clearance officers to inform an applicant of the most appropriate grounds on which to seek entry.[15]

Entry clearance officers do not have any of the powers of immigration officers, although they have the same discretion to refer applicants for medical examination.[16] They cannot compel anyone to be examined: any interview is voluntary and may therefore be terminated at any time by the applicant. Similarly officers have no power to demand information or documents, to search, or to detain documents. Of course, failure to co-operate will almost certainly result in the refusal of a clearance.

There is no criminal offence arising out of obstructing or giving of false or misleading information to entry clearance officers.[17]

---

[14] HC 394, para. 12. See also the references in the Immigration Appeals (Procedure) Rules 1972, SI 1972 No. 1684, r. 2, and the Immigration Appeals (Notice) Regulations 1972, SI 1972 No. 1683, reg. 2.

[15] See *R v Chief Immigration Officer Heathrow* (1976) *The Times* 18 June, where it was held that there was no duty on clearance officers to consider whether an applicant should be granted a special voucher as a non-patrial UK passport holder.

[16] And the same principles will apply when he decides whether or not to issue an entry clearance: HC 394, para. 73.

[17] An entry clearance officer is not an official 'acting in the execution of the Act.' See para. 10.14, post.

Change in Applicant's Circumstances

5.57 The rules now provide that applications are to be decided in the light of circumstances existing at the time of the decision, except that children to be admitted for settlement are not to be refused clearance solely on account of their becoming over age between the receipt of the application and the date of the decision on it.[18]

---

[18] HC 394, para. 12. The decision in *Zamir v Secretary of State for the Home Department* [1980] 2 All ER 768, HL has now been embodied in the new rules but its effect have been mitigated in respect of dependent children.

SIX

Visitors and Students

VISITORS

6.1 The immigration rules state that a person seeking to enter the UK as a visitor, including one coming to stay with relatives or friends, is to be admitted if he satisfies the immigration authorities that he is genuinely seeking entry for the period of the visit as stated by him; and for that period he will maintain and accommodate himself and any dependants or will with any dependants be maintained and accommodated adequately by relatives or friends, without working or recourse to public funds; and he can meet the cost of the return or onward journey.[1]

Special considerations apply to EEC nationals who seek entry as visitors. They are referred to later in this chapter.[2]

If the immigration authorities are satisfied that these requirements cannot be met or if there is reason to believe the passenger's real purpose is to take employment or that he may become a charge on public funds if admitted, leave to enter must be refused.[3]

Admission

6.2 Visitors and their dependants accompanying them are normally to be admitted for six months.[4] A longer period, not exceeding one year, may be given if the entrant satisfies the immigration authorities that he is able to maintain and accommodate himself and his dependants for the requisite period. The rules further provide that the period should not be restricted to less than six months 'unless this is justified by special

---

[1] HC 394, para. 17.
[2] See para. 6.10, post.
[3] Ibid.
[4] Visitors from the Indian sub-continent and other countries regarded by the Home Office as those from which there is pressure to emigrate are frequently admitted only for a much shorter period.

reasons': examples set out in the rules are cases of restricted returnability, or where the entrant is due to leave the UK on a particular charter service, or is in transit to another country, or 'if his case ought to be subject to early review by the Home Office'.[5]

Visitors are normally to be prohibited from taking employment.[6] They may, however, transact business.[7] Those wishing to establish themselves in business or self-employment require entry clearance granted for that purpose, and must comply with the other provisions of the rules in that category.[8]

Extension of Stay

6.3 This will now only be granted provided the total duration of the visit does not exceed one year.[9] It thus follows that an application will be refused if the visitor was initially granted entry for one year. He must also show that, (1) he has sufficient means to maintain himself and his dependants without working or becoming a charge on public funds for the remainder of the proposed stay; (2) he intends to leave at the end of his stay.[10] An application for an extension to remain in business and employment will be refused but extensions may be given to remain in some other temporary capacity, or on marriage.[11]

Medical Treatment

6.4 Visitors may be admitted for medical treatment. The visitor must show[12] (1) that the treatment is private and at his own expense. The immigration officer is to take into account the likely cost of the treatment in deciding whether the means are adequate; (2) that he meets the requirements of the rules relating to visitors as to means, support and the intention to leave at the end of the treatment; (3) if required, evidence that arrangements have been made for consultation or treatment; and (4) that where he is suffering from a communicable disease there is no danger to public health by his admission.[13]

---

[5] HC 394, para. 20.
[6] Ibid.
[7] Ibid., para. 19.
[8] Ibid., see paras. 7.27 et seq., post.
[9] HC 394, para. 94.
[10] Ibid.
[11] Ibid., para. 90. Problems may arise where an applicant seeks to remain in some other temporary capacity if he has given an undertaking on entry as to the duration and purpose of his stay. HC 394, para. 88, see para. 9.4, post.
[12] HC 394 para. 18.   [13] This is a decision for the medical inspector.

Extensions of stay may be granted on production of evidence (1) about the arrangements made for consultation and treatment, or the progress made with the treatment and its likely duration; (2) that he can meet the cost of the treatment and maintain himself and his dependants during his stay without recourse to public funds.[14] The rules state that an extension is to be refused if there is insufficient evidence of these matters or there is reason to believe that the treatment will be at public expense or that the applicant does not intend to leave the UK at the end of the treatment.[15]

Intention to Leave at the End of Stay

6.5 A frequent ground for refusal by both entry clearance and immigration officers is that there is a lack of incentive on the part of the applicant to return to his own country at the end of the stay. This claim is usually supported by inviting a comparison between the applicant's standard of living at home with the potential for him in the UK. The decision to refuse entry on this ground is often based on little more than suspicion in the mind of the official that the applicant is not a genuine visitor. It has been clearly established by the Tribunal that there must be evidence (as opposed to mere suspicion)[16] to lead to the conclusion that the applicant will not leave at the end of his stay.

The 'evidence', however, does not in practice appear to have to be substantial. In *Hanks*,[17] the Tribunal concluded that the entry clearance officer had rightly refused entry to one appellant who wished to visit his sister here. The evidence was solely that for four years he had not been in employment (or had taken only casual employment contributing negligibly to the family funds). This disclosed 'a strong incentive . . . to leave Sri Lanka and better himself in this country'. The presence of relatives in the home country is often taken as a guide to whether the applicant will return,[18] as is evidence that the applicant is or will be employed there.[19] In *Huda*, the Tribunal took into account that the applicant had good employment in a nationalised industry in

[14] HC 394, para. 95.
[15] Ibid.
[16] See *Bhambra* [1973] Imm AR 14.
[17] [1976] Imm AR 74.
[18] Although in *Hanks* the Tribunal did not accept that the presence of the appellant's mother provided an incentive. Cf., *Bhagat Singh* [1978] Imm AR 134, where the appeal was allowed because, inter alia, the appellant had three brothers and sisters living in his village.
[19] [1976] Imm AR 109.

Bangladesh, stating that it provided an incentive to return on the completion of his holidays here. Again, in *Selvapackian*,[20] it was accepted that the fact the appellant had a steady job which he had held for many years was an indication that he would leave the UK even though the salary was low by English standards.

The Tribunal in *Blair*[1] recently reaffirmed that lack of incentive to return is not in itself sufficient reason to refuse leave to enter, approving the observations of the adjudicator in *Avtar Singh*,[2]

'There is no authority for saying that while "lack of incentive" may be relevant when considering a person's intention, they should not in the absence of *mala fides* in the applicant, be equated with an intention to stay on in the United Kingdom indefinitely.'

6.6 The difficulties faced by those with limited means is illustrated by *Manmohan Singh*,[3] where the Tribunal stated that the immigration officer had to take into account the circumstances of the person seeking entry when considering whether the visitor was genuine. Recognising that a person might seek entry for unimportant or entirely frivolous reasons, the Tribunal held that,

'. . . a person of means and position in his own country might well be accepted as a genuine visitor even if his declared intention was only to visit the maze at Hampton Court. On the other hand when it is proposed that a considerable sum of money should be expended by a family with limited resources one is entitled to consider carefully the reasons for the expenditure.'

6.7 Previous unsuccessful application to enter the UK may be a relevant consideration in deciding whether a person will return. Failure to disclose this information will undoubtedly result in a refusal if this fact subsequently becomes known; full disclosure will, of course, leave the immigration authorities free to argue that the applicant's future is open to doubt. Nevertheless the Tribunal has accepted that an unsuccessful application for settlement does not necessarily indicate an intention to settle in the UK when an application to enter as a visitor was made four

---

[20] 931/76 (1103) (unreported).
[1] 35635/78 (1797) (unreported).
[2] 47710/79 (unreported).
[3] [1975] Imm AR 118.

years later.[4] Similarly a wish to settle in the UK is to be distinguished from an *intention* to do so and entry is not to be refused where all the visitor requirements are met, particularly where the applicant has made a full disclosure as to his wishes.[5] The intention of the sponsor is not itself a relevant factor to take into account. In *Allah Ditta*,[6] where the sponsors (sons) wanted the appellant to stay permanently in the UK, the appeal was allowed because the appellant intended to return at the end of his visit. If there are doubts about the applicant's intentions justifying refusal, these doubts cannot be resolved in his favour by accepting assurances from the applicant's sponsor.[7] The true test is: what is the intention of the applicant? Thus the sponsor's intention may be a relevant factor if it is likely to have a reaction on the applicant. In *Sattar*,[8] the visa officer's decision to refuse entry was reversed 'not on the basis of the accepted intentions of the (applicant's) father and representative, but upon the assessment of the (applicant's) own intention, that assessment being made after weighing the incentives of the (applicant) to stay on in the UK, such as the presence of all his near relatives in this country, and the incentives to depart such as the attitudes of his father (and others)'.[9]

6.8 A non-patrial UK passport holder should not be refused leave to enter by reason only of that passport. If the immigration authorities are satisfied that the applicant is a genuine visitor who will leave at the end of his stay, the fact that removal by deportation is unlikely, because of the passport, is not a relevant consideration.[10] It is, however, relevant in determining the intention of the applicant. In *Patel (MR)*,[11] the Tribunal accepted that while the appellant was not to blame for the fact that as a UKPH she probably could not be removed from the UK, it was a factor which the entry clearance officer had to take into account, and in the absence of an obvious incentive to return to India together with other facts, the officer was justified in refusing clearance.[12]

[4] *Chopra* 1160/77 (1198) (unreported).
[5] *Lai* [1974] Imm AR 98.
[6] 32394/78 (1704) (unreported).
[7] *Kumar* [1978] Imm AR 185, where the assurances took the form of an undertaking, a breach of which would greatly harm the sponsor's integrity.
[8] 9837/76 (1107) (unreported). See also *Mendez* 55336/79 (1956) (unreported).
[9] See also *Lazari* 10147/76 (1017) (unreported), where the applicant had previously left the UK following a recommendation for deportation. Entry allowed: influence of a sponsor in ensuring departure at the end of the visit was a relevant factor. Cf., *Jardine* 36713/78 (1787) (unreported).
[10] *Mohamed Din* [1978] Imm AR 56.
[11] [1978] Imm AR 154.
[12] See also *Maru* 31188/78 (1628) (unreported).

Finally, while the rules require evidence that the entrant can meet the cost of the return or outward journey, possession of sufficient funds and a return air ticket is not in itself conclusive evidence that the visitor is genuine.[13]

Purpose of the Visit

6.9 The present rules omit the phrase occurring in the old rules, that the immigration officer is to be satisfied that 'no more than a visit is intended'.[14] The officer now has to be satisfied that the applicant is 'genuinely seeking entry for the period of the visit as stated by him'.[15] While in most cases the new wording will make no practical difference to the admission or refusal of visitors, it will prevent the anomalous situation which arose in *Sultana*.[16] The applicant sought entry as a visitor to effect a reconciliation with her husband; if successful she wished to remain with him in the UK. It was held that refusal was justified as 'more than a visit was intended'. As there was no other rule under which entry could have been obtained, the Tribunal asked the Home Secretary to consider her case exceptionally.

The rules do not preclude a relative or friend coming to the UK for the purpose of assisting a parent in the care of his or her children in order to enable the parent to attend a course of study or training, although the position might be otherwise if the purpose was to relieve the parent of the care so that employment could be taken.[17] Those who intend to enter as visitors with a view to discovering whether there are any courses of study open to them may find themselves in difficulties. Failure to disclose the intention has been held to be a misrepresentation and an immigration officer may justify a refusal of an extension of stay although the applicant met all the formal requirements of the rules relating to students.[18] There are provisions for would-be students to be admitted for a short period to enable them to meet the formal requirements for students, but they must

[13] *Mohammed Sadiq* [1978] Imm AR 115.

[14] HC 79, para. 15; HC 81, para. 13. This paragraph does not confer a discretion to grant an application in the absence of satisfaction that the applicant is seeking entry only for the period as stated by him: *Malek* [1979–80] Imm AR 111.

[15] HC 394, para. 17.

[16] 8945/76 (988) (unreported).

[17] *Shamonda* [1976] Imm AR 16. See also *Tackie* 3311/72 (194) (unreported). The one-year limit on visitors remaining in the UK has, however, severely limited the advantage of these decisions.

[18] *Owusu* [1976] Imm AR 101.

satisfy the immigration officer that their intentions are 'genuine and realistic'.[19]

It is important, therefore, for those who wish to study to have made enquiries before departure, to make full disclosure to the entry clearance officer (if clearance is sought) and the immigration officer on arrival, and to be in a position to give the immigration officer as clear a picture as possible of their plans to study. Equally importantly, they must convince the officer that whatever the outcome of their application they will leave at the end of their stay.

EEC Nationals

6.10 Although the immigration rules do not distinguish between EEC nationals and others, in practice there is a distinction in the approach adopted by the immigration authorities. The EEC Treaty makes provision for freedom of movement only for those seeking or undertaking work, and thus those entering as visitors may fall outside the scope of the Treaty.[20] However, as an EEC national may enter as a visitor and seek work to support himself after arrival, an immigration officer may not be justified in refusing entry solely on the grounds that the entrant had insufficient means to support himself for the period of his stay. Accordingly the practice has arisen of refusing entry on the basis that if admitted the entrant is likely to become a charge on public funds.[1] An immigration officer may justify refusal on this ground, for example, where the entrant is only carrying a small amount of money, or has no return ticket or has a poor employment record, or has previously had recourse to public funds.

STUDENTS

6.11 Those who wish to come to study from overseas face a number of problems of which the need to comply with the requirements of the immigration rules is only one. For students planning further education in state institutions, the fees are several times higher than those for British students.[2] Others who use the private education sector particularly for

---

[19] HC 394, para. 24.

[20] See paras. 3.2 et seq., ante, and paras. 7.44 et seq., post.

[1] See Home Office evidence to the Select Committee on Race Relations and Immigration. Minutes of Evidence 26 April 1978 (HC 410–ii) p. 31.

[2] For up-to-date information on Department of Education and Science regulations concerning fees and awards, contact should be made with the United Kingdom Council for Overseas Student Affairs, 60 Westbourne Grove, London W2, which provides

the purpose of learning English or computer studies may discover that not only are they paying large fees but in some establishments the course offered is of little value and the certificates issued are worthless in the UK in educational terms. The result can often be that overseas students gain nothing from their course of study. Wherever possible potential students and those assisting them should be encouraged to examine carefully the reputation of the institutions the student proposes to attend, with a view to determining whether they satisfy the immigration rules and whether they offer the student adequate educational value.

Admission

6.12 The immigration rules make the following provisions relating to students: (1) entry clearance is not mandatory except for visa nationals[3] but it is often advisable for the student to obtain clearance. Admission will nevertheless be granted to an applicant without clearance if he can satisfy the immigration officer that he fulfils the requirements set out below; (2) entry clearance or admission will be granted if the applicant produces evidence satisfying the entry clearance or immigration officer that,

(a) he has been accepted for a course of study at university, a college of education or further education, an independent school or any *bona fide* private educational institution; and
(b) the course will occupy the whole or a substantial part of his time; and
(c) he can without working and without recourse to public funds meet the cost of the course and of his own maintenance and accommodation and that of any dependants during the course,[4] and
(d) he is able, and intends to follow a full-time course of study;[5] and
(e) he will leave the country on the completion of the course.[6]

advice and information for students and also produces a series of guidance leaflets on immigration, finance and welfare for those advising students. The National Union of Students, 3 Endsleigh Street, London WC1, also has had wide experience in advising overseas students.

[3] HC 394, para. 24.   [4] Ibid.
[5] If an immigration officer has doubts about the entrant's ability to follow the course, the practice is to invite the principal of the institution to send a member of his staff to make an assessment; if the principal is unable to do so the immigration officer will suggest a qualified person near the port, and if the principal is unwilling to avail himself of the services, the immigration officer will himself make arrangements.
[6] HC 394, para. 22. See also *Sobanjo* [1978] Imm AR 22.

In making an assessment the officer should consider such points as whether the applicant's qualifications are adequate for the course he proposes to follow, and whether there is any evidence of sponsorship by his home government or any other official body. As a general rule an entry clearance is not granted unless the applicant proposes to spend not less than fifteen hours a week in organised day time study of a single subject or of related subjects, and is not to be granted for the taking of a correspondence course.[7]

6.13 An applicant accepted for training as a nurse or midwife at a hospital is to be granted clearance or given entry as a student unless there is evidence that he or she had obtained acceptance by misrepresentation or does not intend to follow the course.[8] Doctors and dentists are admissible for full time postgraduate studies even though they also intend during their stay to seek employment in training posts related to their studies.[9]

6.14 Admission will be for an 'appropriate period' depending on the length of the course of study or the applicant's means. A condition restricting his freedom to take employment is imposed. The rules state that he should be advised to apply to the Home Office before the expiry of his leave to enter for any extension of stay that may be required.[10] An entrant who satisfies the immigration officer that he has 'genuine and realistic intentions' of studying in the UK, but who cannot satisfy the requirements relating to students may be admitted for a 'short period', within the limit of his means with a prohibition on the taking of employment, and should be advised to apply to the Home Office for further consideration of his case.[11] In all other circumstances, an entrant arriving without entry clearance who is seeking entry as a student is to be refused admission.[12]

6.15 The wife and children under 18 of a person admitted as a student are to be given leave to enter for the same period as the student, if they can be maintained and accommodated without recourse to public funds.

[7] HC 394, para. 22. If the appellate authority is satisfied that all the requirements were met at the time the clearance was refused but there is no evidence of whether a place is still available (or fees paid) the appeal should be allowed and directions given for an issue of clearance on production of documentation confirming enrolment: *Sae-Heng* [1979–80] Imm AR 69.
[8] Ibid., para. 23.
[9] Ibid.
[10] Ibid., para. 24.
[11] Ibid.
[12] Ibid.

They will not be restricted in taking employment unless the student is himself prohibited in which case the prohibition will also extend to them.[13]

The rules do not provide for the admission of a husband of a student wife. However, where he does not qualify in his own right, the immigration authorities may consider admitting him exceptionally on the same conditions as his wife if it can be shown there are compassionate circumstances, e.g. there are young children to care for or the husband is incapacitated requiring care and attention of the wife. The husband must also show that he will leave the UK with his wife at the end of her studies and he will be accommodated and supported throughout his stay without recourse to public funds.

The Nature of the Educational Institution

6.16 The immigration rules do not state what constitutes a *bona fide* institution and it is understood that there are certain institutions which describe themselves as 'educational' but which are not acceptable to the immigration authorities.

Leave to enter will be refused if admission is sought to a school wholly maintained by a local education authority unless it is a college of Further Education. If the entrant can show that he has genuine and realistic intentions of studying, can afford the fees for a private educational institution, and will enrol at such an institution, the immigration practice is to admit him for two months to allow him to make the necessary arrangements.

Intention to Leave

6.17 The rules require the student to leave at the end of the course for which he was admitted, or any further course for which he was given an extension of stay.[14] On many occasions on appeal, the Home Office will argue that the appellant's intention is to seek employment or to settle here and hence the application is not genuine. It is necessary to look not only at the immediate plans but also his intentions on the completion of his course. Often these plans will be vague, confused or arise out of mixed motives. In *R v Immigration Appeals Adjudicator, ex parte Perween*

---

[13] Ibid., para. 25.

[14] Ibid., para. 22. It is unusual, however, for a student nurse to be refused leave to enter solely because there are reasonable doubts about his or her intention to leave at the end of the course. Refusal usually only arises where there is definite evidence of a deliberate attempt to abuse the nursing facilities or to use it solely as a step to settlement.

Khan,[15] the Divisional Court held that the 'primary purpose' in coming to the country must be to study and 'that which is in the immigrant's mind in regard to conduct after the expiration of the course must be a factor in the determination of the purpose or purposes for which he was entering the country'. In *R v Chief Immigration Officer Gatwick Airport ex parte Kharrazi*[16] the Court of Appeal made it clear that an overseas student should not be refused entry to the UK simply because he intends to continue his education here after completing the full time course of study for which he has been accepted, provided his further arrangements are part of a coherent educational plan, capable of being carried out by him. However, an indication from the student that he wishes to remain in the UK at the end of his studies for some other purpose has frequently resulted in a refusal of the application.[17]

If the student is very young[18] or backward the intention of a financing sponsor will be relevant. But where the student is 'grown-up' it is necessary to examine his own intentions.[19] In *Myeen Ur Rashid*,[20] an eight year old who lived with his family in Bangladesh sought entry as a student. His uncle, a doctor here, agreed to be responsible for his education for at least 10 years. The Tribunal took the view that this was tantamount to settlement and that it was impossible to say that the mere fact that the appellant would be educated here brought him in any way within the provision of the immigration rules relating to students.

6.18 The Tribunal has accepted that intention is often difficult to assess. It is a question of fact and there is rarely direct evidence indicating the appellant's plans on the completion of his course. In many cases the circumstances surrounding an application will be sufficient to cast considerable doubt in the minds of the authorities about the genuineness of the applicant's intentions. Thus in *Oh*,[1] the appellant was refused permission to enter the UK because his wife was already here and he had in-

---

[15] [1972] Imm AR 28, DC. (Decided under earlier rules.)
[16] [1980] 3 All ER 373, CA.
[17] See *S M Ahmad* 50579/79 (1760) following *Harding* 743/75 and *Tagbo* 13298/75 (971) (unreported). This approach may now have to be modified following *R v Immigration Appeal Tribunal ex parte Shaikh* (1981), *The Times*, 3 March, para. 6.25, post.
[18] See *Myeen Ur Rashid* [1976] Imm AR 12.
[19] *Morgan* 3502/74 (406) (unreported) where the Tribunal was satisfied that the sponsor intended the 23-year-old appellant to return home after studying but was not satisfied about the appellant's intentions. See also similar decisions relating to visitors, para. 6.7, ante.
[20] Cited, note 18, supra. See also *Chandarana* 44332/79 (1841) (unreported).
[1] [1972] Imm AR 236.

dicated on his application form that two of his children would be accompanying him. The Tribunal commented tersely 'the facts . . . sustain the view that this is planned immigration'.

Nevertheless the Tribunal has held that there must be some evidence to support the intention that the appellant intends to remain here. Mere suspicion on the part of the immigration authorities[2] or doubts regarding incentive to return to the student's own country,[3] is not in itself sufficient. Yet the 'evidence' required for the Home Office to succeed may consist of no more than the fact that the costs of the course appear very high in relation to the sponsoring family's income and that opportunities for employment with the qualification gained appeared limited in the context of the appellant's country of origin.[4] In *Ghosh*,[5] the Tribunal held *inter alia* that where substantial sums of money were paid out for a short vocational course, the source of those funds (about which there was conflicting evidence) was 'clearly not an irrelevant matter and one to be disregarded'.

6.19 Frequent difficulties have arisen because of the insistence by entry clearance and immigration officers that the student's intentions are not 'realistic' – a word which does not appear in the present or old immigration rules. To some extent the issue has been resolved following the decision in *R* v *Immigration Appeal Tribunal, ex parte S. G. H. Khan*.[6] A Pakistani citizen applied to attend a short computer course. The entry clearance officer was satisfied that he had the necessary funds and a return ticket to Pakistan, but took the view that the sponsor who was financing the appellant was spending a large amount of money for such a short course, that the student's qualifications were on the arts rather than the science side and that the student had not made any enquiries about employment with companies in Pakistan who operated computers. He concluded that the student's intentions were not realistic, a decision upheld by the adjudicator. On an application for *certiorari*, the Divisional Court held that the officer had to be satisfied that the application was 'honest and genuine'. The officer's objections went to 'realism and thrift'. The two criteria were different and the latter were not proper considerations to be taken into account. The Court allowed the application holding that the officer had misapplied the rules and rejected the

[2] *Bhambra* [1973] Imm AR 14.
[3] *Ogunrotimi* 3584/73 (unreported) and see the references to 'incentive to return' in relation to visitors, para. 00, ante.
[4] *Mehta* 2778/71 (unreported).
[5] [1976] Imm AR 60. [6] [1975] Imm AR 26, DC.

adjudicator's view that the officer was suggesting obliquely that the student would not leave the UK on the completion of his studies.

6.20 Nevertheless, in a series of subsequent decisions on similar facts the Tribunal, while holding that 'realism is not a valid ground for refusal', has refused entry to students on the ground that the intention to study was not genuine because of the risk that the student would fail to leave at the end of his studies. Thus in *Dey*,[7] the student's appeal failed because it was held that his 'real intention was to see the UK and that he was only intending to undertake the course to enable him to have better prospects in the future although he had no intention of seeking employment in the computer field'.

'Realism' appears to have re-entered by the back door because any course of study which the immigration authorities consider unrealistic is now frequently objected to on the ground that the student will not eventually leave the UK and hence his application cannot be genuine. In *Ghosh*,[8] the Tribunal held that there was nothing objectionable in an entry clearance officer requesting an applicant wishing to take a 16 week course in computer programming to obtain written confirmation from his employers (who he claimed had given him leave of absence) that the qualification would be acceptable to them for employment in that field. His failure to produce such confirmation resulted in refusal on the ground that he would not leave on the completion of his studies. The effect of the decision, particularly in relation to short courses, is that the applicant may be in serious difficulties if he cannot show that he would obtain satisfactory employment at the end of his course. Yet the Tribunal has accepted (and under the earlier more rigorous rules) that an applicant is not required to show that he would 'obtain the maximum benefit from a course of higher education in the United Kingdom'.[9]

6.21 A UK passport holder is not to be refused entry as a student solely on the ground that it would be impossible to remove him at the end of his stay where the immigration authorities are satisfied that he fulfils the requirements of a student. The Tribunal so held in *Fernandez*,[10] where the applicant had applied for a special voucher for settlement but had provided evidence that his present intention was to go to the UK for the limited purpose of studying, and then depart until such time as the voucher was issued.

[7] [1975] Imm AR 142. See also *Goffar* [1975] Imm AR 142.
[8] [1976] Imm AR 60.
[9] *Sharma* 1571/71 (unreported), referred to in *Virdee* [1972] Imm AR 215.
[10] 35494/78 (1538) (unreported).

Finally, the background to any previous applications to enter the UK or any previous stay may have a material effect on any application to study here. In *Murgai*,[11] where it was established that the appellant had applied several years previously to enter as a visitor and had at the same time made enquiries about employment here, it was only with some reluctance that the Tribunal allowed his appeal, holding that '. . . a suspicion of intention, unsupported by evidence, is not sufficient to prevent a successful later application'.

Full-time Course

6.22 The rules state that 'as a general rule' an applicant must be attending a course which occupies him for a minimum of 15 hours daytime study per week.[12] An application for a course which occupies less than this number of hours will almost always be refused. The rules do, however, allow for some flexibility. In *Amusu*,[13] a Nigerian student satisfied the authorities that he had a genuine and keen interest in writing as a career. Consequently he had enrolled for a course in journalism which was primarily by correspondence but involved outside assignments where a student would be expected to work on his own. Supplementary tutorials were organised and it was estimated by the school that students utilising them would spend 15 hours per week at their studies and outside assignments. The Tribunal allowed the appeal because of the appellant's proven interest and because it was clear that in order to obtain the establishment's diploma a great deal of work and study were required.

The discretion to accept a smaller number of hours only arises where the applicant has complied with the mandatory requirement of showing that the course will occupy the whole or a substantial portion of the student's time, as in *Soon Lim Lee*,[14] where the Tribunal held that three hours organised study, two evenings a week together with some private study 'goes nowhere near . . . . to satisfying this requirement'.

Adequate Means

6.23 The question of adequate means for the purpose of carrying through studies is clearly one of fact, but it is worth pointing out that cases have been lost solely because of the absence of suitable documen-

[11] [1975] Imm AR 86.
[12] HC 394, para. 22.
[13] [1974] Imm AR 16.
[14] 32291/78 (1557) (unreported). See also *Bobitiya* 2403/76 (822) (unreported.)

tary evidence in circumstances where a proper presentation of the case would have shown adequate means. Attention should be paid to *Ayettey*,[15] where the Tribunal held that it was not sufficient to produce bare statements that the appellant was a man of substance and could afford to pay for his education. It is necessary to show that funds are available and, where appropriate, can be transferred to this country. An applicant may find himself in difficulty if his sponsor appears to have little or no connection with him, e.g. a distant relative or a not very close friend of the family. The rules provide for both the student's earnings (if he is given permission to work) and those of his wife to be taken into account in assessing the adequacy of means of support on an application for an extension of stay[16] but it appears that the wife's potential earnings on an application to enter are no longer to be considered.[17]

Working while a Student

6.24 Doctors, dentists and nurses admitted as postgraduate students are permitted to take full time employment associated with their studies.[18] Other students will have been given leave to enter with a restriction on their taking employment. Nevertheless a student may be permitted to take paid employment in his free time or during vacations with the consent of the Department of Employment.[19] Application is to the local Professional and Executive Recruitment Office, Jobcentre or Employment Office.[20] He will have to provide satisfactory (usually documentary) evidence from his college that employment will not interfere with the course of study. Permission will only be given 'where there is no suitable resident labour available to fill the post offered and the wages and other conditions of employment are not less favourable than those obtaining in the area for similar work'.[1] It is important for the student to emphasize that although working will supplement his income he is nevertheless not in need of the income in order to pay for his studies and maintain himself. Where an immigration officer has imposed a condition prohibiting employment on a person who later establishes satisfactorily that he is engaged in a full time course of study, the condition may be

[15] [1972] Imm AR 261.
[16] HC 394, para. 101.
[17] Cf., HC 79, para. 22; HC 81, para. 20, with HC 394, para. 25 where there is no reference to the wife's potential earnings.
[18] HC 394, para. 101.
[19] Ibid.
[20] Department of Employment leaflet 'OW5', para. 15.
[1] Ibid.

varied to one permitting him to take employment with the consent of the Department of Employment.[2] The rules state that except for the provisions set out above 'employment is inconsistent with student status'.[3] It is a criminal offence to work without permission. But in *Strasburger*,[4] the Tribunal held that it was unobjectionable for an art student to sell her art work provided she complied with the student requirements in the rules.

Extensions of Stay

6.25 Applications may be received from those who entered in some other capacity as well as those admitted as students.[5] Evidence must be produced that (1) the applicant is enrolled for a full time course of daytime study which meets the requirements for admission as a student; (2) where the application is from a student, he has given and is giving regular attendance;[6] and (3) he is able to maintain and accommodate himself and dependants without working or recourse to public funds. Enquiries may be made by the Home Office to establish that the student is registered on the course, and production of the receipt for fees will be required.

An extension is to be refused if there is reason to believe that the applicant does not intend to leave at the end of his studies.[7] In *R v Immigration Appeal Tribunal ex parte Shaikh*[8] the Divisional Court held that the mere fact that an applicant expresses a desire to remain in the United Kingdom if permitted to do so of itself will not disentitle him from the grant of an extension of stay. The Court acknowledged that different considerations would arise if the applicant were suspected of having some collateral purpose, and in particular an unlawful purpose, or had any intention of abusing, flouting or breaching the conditions of leave.[9]

[2] HC 394, para. 101.   [3] Ibid.
[4] [1978] Imm AR 165.   [5] HC 394, para. 98.
[6] As to regular attendance see *Juma* [1974] Imm AR 96 and *Paratian* 10903/76 (992) (unreported) where the Tribunal reviewed *Juma* and the unreported cases. The certificate of attendance is not conclusive in the student's favour: some establishments' certificates will be viewed with suspicion, see *Kpoma* [1973] Imm AR 25.
[7] HC 394, para. 98. As to the meaning of studies in this context, see *R v Chief Immigration Officer (Gatwick Airport) ex parte Kharazzi* [1980] 3 All ER 373, para. 00, ante.
[8] (1981) *The Times* 3 March.
[9] The Court also held that under the old immigration rules a student does not have to satisfy the immigration authorities at the time he applies for an extension that he intends to leave at the completion of his studies. The present rules, however, specifically empower the immigration authorities to refuse if there is reason to believe that the student does not intend to leave. HC 394, para. 98.

The rules now provide that extensions are not to be granted to students 'who appear to be moving from one course to another without any intention of bringing their studies to a close'. Again, a prolonged lack of success in examinations is a factor to be taken into account when considering an extension of stay.[10] Similarly an extension is normally to be refused if it would lead to more than four years being spent on short courses. A 'short course' under this rule is defined as 'one of less than two years but includes a longer course where this is broken off before being completed'.[11] Those on courses financed by governments (whether British or otherwise) or international agencies will not normally be eligible to remain for further studies once they have completed the course for which they received the award.[12] The rules emphasise that a student's leave to enter or remain may be curtailed if he fails to attend regularly his course of study.[13]

TRAINEES

6.26 A person may be admitted for training on the job provided he has a permit from the Department of Employment for this purpose.[14] He will be admitted for the period specified in the permit up to a maximum of twelve months. Extensions may be granted in order to continue or complete the training if the Department of Employment confirms that the training is continuing and the trainee is making satisfactory progress.[15] Visitors and students may be granted extension to stay as trainees if the Department of Employment considers the offer of training to be satisfactory and there are no doubts that the applicant will leave on the completion of training.[16] A person also may be admitted if he holds a

[10] *Ames* [1979–80] Imm AR 87.
[11] HC 394, para. 99.
[12] Ibid., para. 100.
[13] Ibid., para. 89.
[14] HC 394, para. 102, and Department of Employment leaflet 'OW 21'. As to the difference between trainees and students, see *Yeong Hoi Yuen* [1977] Imm AR 34. A person cannot be a student if he is not at an educational institution. This category is no longer restricted to Commonwealth citizens only. Cf. HC 80, para. 15 and no corresponding provision HC 82.
[15] HC 394, para. 102.
[16] Ibid., para. 105. The Department of Employment will, however, give approval for those who have qualified as chartered accountants to undertake employment (usually for two years to enable them to obtain a practice certificate). Reply to Parliamentary Question to Secretary of State for Employment. 980 H. of C. Official Report, 3 March 1980, col. 18.

Department of Employment permit for short term employment not leading to additional qualifications or skills but enabling him to widen his occupational experience and in some cases also to improve his knowledge of English.[17] He will be admitted for the period specified for a permit up to a maximum of 12 months, and subject to a condition restricting him to approved employment. Extensions to continue in approved employment will only be granted if, 'in exceptional circumstances,' the Department of Employment approve the proposed extension.[18]

Transfers from training or work experience to ordinary employment are not permitted. Work in these capacities does not constitute approved employment for the purposes of settlement.[19]

AU PAIRS

Admission[20]

6.27 'Au pair' is an arrangement restricted to an unmarried girl aged 17 to 27 inclusive and without dependants, who is a national of a western European country, including Malta, Cyprus and Turkey.[1] The purpose of the arrangement is for the girl to come to learn the English language and to live for a time as a member of an English-speaking family, that is, according to Home Office practice, one in which English is the normal means of communication between members of the family circle. It need not necessarily be the mother tongue.[2] A family includes a single parent family where the single parent is a woman.[3]

It is advisable for the 'au pair' to bring a letter from the family (preferably from the wife) describing the arrangement and in particular giving information about the household and family, including their number and relationships, what duties she will be expected to carry out,

---

[17] Ibid., para. 103, Department of Employment leaflet 'OW 21'.
[18] HC 394, para. 103.
[19] Ibid., para. 104. See also *Virani* 54382/79 (1790) (unreported).
[20] Ibid., para. 26.
[1] The full list of countries is Andorra, Austria, Cyprus, Finland, Greece, Iceland, Lichtenstein, Malta, Monaco, Norway, Portugal, San Marino, Spain, Sweden, Switzerland, Turkey, Yugoslavia and the EEC countries. Reply to Parliamentary Question to Home Secretary. 979 H. of C. Official Report, 26 February 1980, col. 497.
[2] Letter, Home Office to North Kirklees Community Relations Council 17 June 1980. There is no bar on the 'au pair' being related to the sponsor: *Hettice* 4310/76 (926) (unreported).
[3] Ibid.

what arrangements there will be for her to learn English, how much time she will have free for study and recreation and how much pocket money she will be paid.

A girl coming for full-time domestic employment or full-time employment requires a work permit. If the immigration officer is satisfied that the 'au pair' arrangement has been made, he may admit the entrant for a period of 12 months. A prohibition on her taking employment will be imposed. If she has previously spent time in the UK as an 'au pair' she may be admitted for a further period as an 'au pair' but the total aggregate period is not to exceed two years.

Young men may be given leave to enter as *visitors* if they fulfil the requirements relating to 'au pair' arrangements. It is Home Office practice not to object to their doing odd jobs about the house or garden; or, if staying on a farm, e.g. helping with the harvest.

Extensions[4]

6.28 An extension of stay may be given to a girl admitted as an 'au pair' provided the arrangement is satisfactory and the aggregate of her period of stay in the 'au pair' capacity does not exceed two years. Where an extension is granted she is to be told that two years is the maximum period permitted. An application for an extension as an 'au pair' from a girl admitted in some other capacity may be granted if she fulfils the 'au pair' requirements. A prohibition on her taking employment will be imposed. Although the rules state that 'au pairs' and others in a temporary capacity have no claim to remain here for any other purpose, applications may be granted to remain in some other temporary capacity if the relevant requirements of the rules are met.[5]

[4] HC 394, para. 106.
[5] Ibid., para. 90.

SEVEN

Employment and Business

TAKING EMPLOYMENT

7.1 The rules relating to the taking of employment are now so severe that there are few categories of entrant who can expect to be granted leave to enter without a condition on employment being imposed. The condition will either be a *prohibition* on working, by which the entrant is forbidden from entering or taking employment, paid or unpaid, or engaging in any business or profession in any circumstances (unless the condition is varied to permit work), or a *restriction* on working, by which the entrant is similarly forbidden from taking employment or engaging in a profession without the consent of the Home Secretary. There are severe restrictions on those who seek permission to work after entry. These are considered in Chapter 9.[1]

Those seeking to take employment will be required to produce on arrival at the port of entry a work permit issued by the Department of Employment unless they qualify for exemption under the following limited number of categories:[2] (1) as a person eligible to take permit-free employment; (2) as a person of UK ancestry; (3) as a working holiday-maker; (4) as an EEC national. The situation of those who are exempt will be considered later.[3]

Work Permits

7.2 The work permit scheme has been designed to limit severely the number of overseas workers coming into this country. If an entrant

---

[1] See para. 9.8, post.
[2] HC 394, para. 27.
[3] See paras. 7.22 et seq., post.

TAKING EMPLOYMENT 113

wishing to work does not have a work permit, leave to enter will be refused. There are strict limitations in the operation of the scheme which ensure that the non-resident labour force is restricted only to those who are regarded by the Government of the day as essential to the economic life of this country. The regulations relating to work permits are laid down by the Department of Employment. The present regulations[4] were introduced to come into effect from 1 January 1980. A summary of the work permit regulations and immigration rules follows.

Issuing of Permits

7.3 Permits are issued for employment in Great Britain by the Department of Employment, and for employment in Northern Ireland by the Department of Manpower Services.[5] A work permit will only be issued for a named overseas worker and for a specific job. The permit will be issued for an initial period not exceeding 12 months.

Basic Requirements

7.4 Only workers between 23 and 53 years of age are eligible for permits. A genuine vacancy must exist, generally in an occupation serviced by the Professional and Executive Recruitment (PER).[6] A permit will not be issued if, in the opinion of the Overseas Labour Section of the Department of Employment, after consultation with the Manpower Services Commission, suitable resident or EEC labour is available to fill the post offered, nor if the wages or other conditions of employment offered are less favourable than those obtaining in the area for similar work. The worker must also have an adequate command of the English language.

---

[4] See Leaflet 'OW5' issued by the Department of Employment. Additional information can be obtained from the Department's Overseas Labour section (for address, see Appendix 6).

[5] The arrangements described here apply in Great Britain. The same conditions apply in Northern Ireland but references to the 'Department of Employment' and the 'Manpower Services Commission' should be read as references to the 'Department of Manpower Services,' and to 'Professional and Executive Recruitment (PER)' as to 'Professional and Executive Personnel (PEP)'.

[6] As a general guide, those seeking employment in professional, managerial, administrative, executive, technical and scientific occupations who are qualified either academically or by experience are appropriate to Professional and Executive Recruitment. Advice about whether individual occupations fall within the scope of PER may be obtained from Jobcentres or PER offices.

Categories of Workers for whom Permits may be Issued

7.5 Not every type of job will qualify for the issue of a permit. There are eight categories, and a permit will only be issued for jobs requiring workers in these categories. Permits are no longer issued for resident domestics and the few other semi-skilled or unskilled workers permitted under the previous rules.[7] The eight categories are (1) those holding recognised professional qualifications; (2) administrative and executive staff; (3) highly qualified technicians having specialised experience; (4) other key workers with a high or scarce qualification in an industry or occupation requiring specific expert knowledge or skills; (5) highly-skilled and experienced workers for senior posts in hotel and catering establishments who have successfully completed appropriate full-time training courses of at least two years' duration at approved schools abroad or, exceptionally, have acquired other specialised or uncommon skills and experience relevant to the industry; (6) entertainers and sportsmen/women who meet the appropriate skills criteria (professional sportsmen/women taking part in competitions of international standing do not normally require permits); (7) people coming for a limited period of training on the job or work experience approved by the Department of Employment;[8] (8) other persons only if, in the opinion of the Secretary of State for Employment, their employment is in the national interest.

Exceptions to the Basic Requirements

7.6 Those in categories (5)–(8) above do not have to be in occupations serviced by the PER; the lower age limit does not apply to sportsmen; and the lower age limit is reduced to 18 years in respect of trainees.

Applications to Employ Overseas Workers: Procedure

7.7 Application to employ an overseas worker must be made by the employer on Form 'OW1'. These forms are available at PER Offices, Jobcentres and Employment Offices. When completed they should be returned to the PER Office nearest to the proposed place of work or, if more convenient, to the nearest Jobcentre or Employment Office. The Department of Employment states that an application should be made at

---

[7] Statement by Mr Patrick Mayhew, Parliamentary Under-Secretary of State for Employment, 976 H. of C. Official Report, 21 December 1979, col. 479.

[8] See Leaflet 'OW21' issued by the Department of Employment, and HC 394, paras. 102–105, para. 6.26, ante.

least eight weeks before the permit is required, and that failure to provide complete information may result in delay in processing the application.

The Department must be satisfied that the worker possesses the necessary qualifications, skills and experience and usually that these have been acquired outside the UK. Documentary evidence is required in all cases and should be submitted with the application. References must normally be original, on business headed paper, signed, dated and must bear the establishment's official stamp. The information given must show the type of employment and the precise dates of commencement and termination of each position held. As part of the requirements to satisfy the Department that there is no one available to fill the posts, and that the employer has made adequate efforts to find a worker from member states of the EEC, the employer is expected to notify details of the vacancy to the nearest PER Office, Jobcentre or Employment Office, and to allow four weeks for a suitable worker to be found.

The employer is further expected to (1) advertise the vacancy in the local and suitable national and EEC press and in any appropriate trade and professional journal(s); (2) send copies of any such advertisement(s) with the application for a permit, and give full details of the results of such advertising; (3) undertake to pay the travelling expenses for any worker resident in this country coming from a distance for a prearranged interview or to take up employment.

If a Work Permit is Granted: Entry into the UK

7.8 In the case of citizens of the Commonwealth and Pakistan the permit is sent to the relevant High Commission or Embassy in the employee's country and they notify the worker. At the same time the employer is informed. In the case of foreign nationals, the employer is sent the permit and he is responsible for forwarding it to the employee. A work permit is not an entry clearance[9] and it is therefore necessary for visa nationals to obtain clearance before arrival.

7.9 If the permit has been forwarded to the High Commission or Embassy, problems may arise. In *Ali Zulfiqar*,[10] a permit was confiscated by the entry clearance officer because he was not satisfied that the applicant was entitled to it. The Tribunal upheld the decision referring to the observations of Lord Denning in *Suruk Miah*,[11]

[9] Immigration Act 1971, s. 33(1).
[10] 3005 5/78 (1660) (unreported).
[11] (1976) *The Times*, 4 February, CA.

'It appears that the practice is for the High Commission there to hold the work permit and keep it whilst they make enquiries into the man's credentials, into his previous employment and into his suitability for this work. If those enquiries prove satisfactory they hand him the work permit; but if the enquiries prove unsatisfactory they will hold the work permit and not issue it to him.'

The Tribunal noted that the Court of Appeal had never objected to the procedure nor suggested it to be unlawful.

The holder of a permit will normally be admitted for the period specified in the permit, subject to a condition permitting him to take or change employment only with the permission of the Department of Employment.

7.10 It should be noted that in addition to the general grounds of refusal, an immigration officer has a wide discretion to refuse entry even if a person arrives with a current permit. Entry can be refused if 'examination reveals good reason for doing so'. The immigration rules give examples of when it would be proper to refuse entry:[12] where false representations have been employed or material facts were not disclosed either orally or in writing (whether or not to the holder's knowledge) for the purpose of obtaining the permit, or the holder's true age puts him outside the limits for employment, or he does not intend to take the employment specified or is incapable of doing so. This is clearly not an exclusive list and there may well be other circumstances where an immigration officer might conclude that there is 'good reason' for exclusion. Although it is necessary to hold a current permit, the rules provide that an immigration officer may nevertheless admit a person with an expired permit 'if satisfied that circumstances beyond his control prevented his arrival before the permit expired and the job is still open to him'.[13]

Change of Employment

7.11 A permit does not constitute a contract of employment between an employer and an overseas worker. It does not authorise an employer to retain the worker in employment if the worker does not wish to remain, nor does the employer require permission to terminate the employment. The worker will not be permanently restricted to the particular job for which the permit was issued, but will be expected to remain in the same occupation and will require the consent of the

[12] HC 394, para. 28.
[13] Ibid.

Department of Employment for any change of job. This consent is subject to the same conditions as the issue of the work permit.[14]

Changes of employment authorised by the Department of Employment will be recorded in a certificate of employment for a Commonwealth citizen, and in the police certificate of registration for a foreign national.[15]

Extensions of Stay[16]

7.12 Extension of stay may be granted by the Home Office to a permit holder who continues in approved employment. Where a permit is issued for a period of less than 12 months, an application for an extension of stay in the employment for which the permit was issued will be referred to the Department of Employment. Only if the Department is prepared to approve the continued employment will an appropriate extension of stay be granted. In cases where the permit was for 12 months, an extension may be granted if the applicant is still engaged, and the employer confirms that he wishes to continue to employ him, in the employment specified in the permit or other employment approved by the Department of Employment. The rules state that unless there are 'exceptional reasons to the contrary' the extension will be for a further three years, after which the applicant will be eligible for settlement,[17] although the practice is often to grant extensions of 12 months at a time. An application for removal of the time limit is to be considered 'in the light of all the relevant circumstances'.[18] It is now necessary to show that the employer is willing to employ the applicant not only at the time of the application but also at the time the application is considered.[19]

Those Admitted under the Old Work Permit Rules

7.13 Workers issued with permits before 1 January 1980 will not be

[14] It must be applied for on Form 'OW1' or, if the permit was issued under the conditions operative before 1 January 1980, on Form 'OW13'.

[15] Foreign nationals are required to register with the police if they are given leave to enter for employment lasting for more than three months: HC 394, paras. 65(a), 122; see para. 9.22, post.

[16] HC 394, para. 107.

[17] Ibid., para. 119; see para. 8.9, post.

[18] Ibid. As to the meaning of this phrase, see *Chulvi* [1976] Imm AR 133. Physical presence in the UK during this period is necessary. An applicant cannot qualify for settlement, if, e.g., he has for part of the period worked on a British ship overseas: *Abeye-Wardene* 44202/79 (1765) (unreported) following *de Souza* 10381/76 (989) (unreported). See also *Bhagwant Singh* 58441/80 (1941) (unreported).

[19] HC 394, para. 119.

subject to the present requirements as to categories of work and the conditions to be satisfied, but will be eligible for changes of employment under the arrangements applicable when the permit was issued.[20]

Permit-free Employment[1]

7.14 Those who qualify in one of the following categories do not need work permits. They will be admitted subject to the general grounds of refusal, provided they hold an entry clearance granted for the purpose. Admission initially will be for a maximum of 12 months.

Ministers of Religion

7.15 These include missionaries and members of religious orders, if they are coming to work full-time as such, and can maintain and accommodate themselves and their dependants without recourse to public funds. Members of religious orders engaged in teaching at establishments maintained by their order will not require work permits, but if they are otherwise engaged in teaching, permits will be required.[2] In order to establish a claim to entry, the immigration authorities normally expect the applicant to provide evidence of the 'formal qualifications (if any) which he holds, the extent of his priestly experience and the nature of his previous employment'.[3] Although the exact form of evidence will vary according to the particular case 'an applicant would normally also be expected to provide an invitation from the organisation which he was coming to join, explaining the precise nature of his duties (which should be full time) and the need which he would be coming to meet', and to provide information as to the terms of any contract which had been drawn up between the two parties. The immigration authorities would expect such a contract to make adequate provision for salary, maintenance and accommodation for the applicant and any dependants.

Representatives of Overseas Firms

7.16 They do not require a permit where there is no branch, subsidiary or other representative in the UK.[4]

---

[20] Leaflet 'OW 5', para. 16.

[1] See generally HC 394, paras. 31–34.

[2] Ibid., para. 31(a).

[3] Letter, Home Office to JCWI 16 April 1980, from which source the remainder of this information has been obtained.

[4] HC 394, para. 31(b).

Representatives of Overseas Newspapers

7.17 These include representatives of news agencies and broadcasting organisations on long-term assignment to the UK.[5]

Doctors and Dentists

7.18 This includes anyone coming to take up a professional appointment. Admission should be limited to six months where entry is sought by doctors eligible for hospital employment without undertaking the DHSS Attachment Scheme or dentists who are seeking employment in or practising their profession.[6] Doctors coming under arrangements approved by the DHSS with a view to their taking up attachment under the Scheme are also admitted for six months but do not require entry clearance.

Other Categories

7.19 There are a number of further categories where entry may be granted without a work permit. In these categories entrants have a choice of either obtaining entry clearance granted for the purpose, or producing some other form of documentary evidence to show that they do not require a permit. Again, subject to the general grounds of refusal, they will be admitted for a maximum period of 12 months. The categories are,

(a) private servants (aged 16 and over) of members of staffs of diplomatic or consular missions or of members of the family forming part of the household of such persons;
(b) persons coming for employment by an overseas Government or in the employment of the United Nations Organisation or other international organisation of which the UK is a member;
(c) teachers and language assistants coming to schools in the UK under exchange schemes approved by the Education Departments or administered by the Central Bureau for Educational Visits and Exchanges or the League for the Exchange of Commonwealth Teachers;
(d) seamen under contract to join a ship in British waters;
(e) operational staff (but not other staff) of overseas owned airlines;
(f) seasonal workers at agricultural camps under approved schemes.[7]

[5] Ibid., para. 31(c).
[6] Ibid., paras. 32, 34.
[7] Ibid., para. 33.

Extensions of Stay

7.20 Those admitted in a permit-free category, with the exception of crew members, may be granted extensions if they are still engaged in the category of employment for which they were admitted and the employer confirms that he wishes to continue the employment.[8] Extensions should be granted for three years 'unless there are special reasons to the contrary' except to, (1) teachers or language assistants under an exchange scheme, where the maximum period of stay is two years; and (2) seasonal workers at agricultural camps, where an extension is not to be granted beyond 30 November in any year.[9] The wife and children under 18 of the applicant are to be given corresponding extensions provided there is adequate support and accommodation for them.[10] At the end of the four year period in the UK those in permit-free categories will be eligible for settlement.[11]

7.21 The rules do not provide for the situation where a person in a permit-free category wishes to change to another job within that category. It is however to be expected that the Home Office would grant the application if the applicant meets all the requirements of the new permit-free employment.

A person given leave to enter in some other capacity will have no claim to remain for permit-free employment and applications to do so will be refused, except for doctors registered with the General Medical Council who may be granted extensions for up to three years.[12]

Those who have been given leave to enter to join a ship or aircraft as a member of its crew, or crew members who have been given leave to enter for hospital treatment, repatriation or transfer to another ship or aircraft will only be given extensions when this is necessary to fulfil the purpose for which they were given leave to enter, unless they qualify for an extension on the basis of marriage.[13]

---

[8] Ibid., para. 108.
[9] Ibid.
[10] Ibid., and para. 40.
[11] Ibid., para. 119, see para. 8.9, post.
[12] Ibid., para. 91.
[13] Ibid., para. 92.

COMMONWEALTH CITIZENS WITH UK ANCESTRY[14]

7.22 A Commonwealth citizen, who has one grandparent[15] born in the UK, who wishes to take or seek employment does not require a work permit. He will be admitted provided he has an entry clearance for that purpose and is not subject to any of the general grounds of refusal, and will be given indefinite leave to enter. His wife and children under 18 will similarly be admitted provided he can show adequate means of support and accommodation. There are no provisions in the 'after entry' rules for those with UK ancestry. However, it has been the Home Office's practice to grant applications by those who qualify in this category, but who obtained entry in some other capacity, e.g. visitor.

WORKING HOLIDAYMAKERS

Admission[16]

7.23 Young Commonwealth citizens aged between 17 and 27 inclusive, coming to the UK for an extended holiday 'before settling down in their own countries', will be permitted to take employment without a work permit. The employment must be 'incidental to their holiday'. They will have to satisfy the immigration officer that (1) they will not have recourse to public funds; and (2) they have the means to pay for their return journey. The maximum period of stay under this category is two years. Those who have previously spent time on a working holiday may still be admitted as working holidaymakers but the total aggregate period must not exceed two years.

Extensions

7.24 Applications to remain as a working holidaymaker may also be made by Commonwealth citizens in the UK in some other temporary capacity, provided they meet the requirements set out above. The rule requiring that employment should only be incidental to the holiday was at one time broadly interpreted by the Home Office but there has been a

---

[14] Ibid., para. 29.
[15] In *C (an infant)* [1976] Imm AR 165, the Tribunal held that on a true construction of the word, 'grandparents' under the old (identical) rules could not be taken to include paternal grandparents of an illegitimate child.
[16] HC 394, para. 30.

general tightening up. In *Baijal*[17] the Tribunal held on the particular facts of the case that freelance work taken in the textile industry by the appellant could not, because of her high earnings on commission, be accepted as employment incidental only to a holiday. A working holidaymaker cannot bring any dependants into the UK.

It is clear that few citizens from the new Commonwealth countries are admitted under this category. In *Grant*,[18] a 22 year old from the Bahamas was refused permission to remain here on a working holiday as he had no funds on his arrival and had been working for his sponsor more or less full time. The Tribunal found that his holiday was incidental to his work and that to be a genuine working holidaymaker the applicant must have some resources with which to finance the holiday, augmenting such resources from time to time by taking employment. If this approach was strictly followed in every case, only the children of the wealthy would be able to take advantage of the 'holiday' scheme.

The Old Rules

7.25 Those who were admitted under the old rules[19] may remain in the UK for a period of up to five years if they meet the qualifications set out in those rules, which for all practical purposes are identical to the present rules.

EEC NATIONALS

7.26 The position of EEC nationals taking employment is considered later.[20]

BUSINESSMEN AND SELF-EMPLOYED PERSONS

7.27 People wishing to transact business in the UK are classified as visitors and will be admitted provided they meet the requirements of the rules relating to visitors.[1] Those, other than EEC nationals,[2] who wish to establish themselves in business or self-employment or to take over or join an existing business, can only do so if they meet the extremely stringent requirements of the rules relating to businessmen and self-

[17] [1976] Imm AR 34.
[18] [1974] Imm AR 64. See also *Gunatilake* [1975] Imm AR 23 and *Munasinghe* [1975] Imm AR 79.
[19] HC 79, para. 28.
[20] See paras. 7.44 et seq., post.
[1] HC 394, para. 19.
[2] See para. 7.44, post.

employed persons.[3] These provisions apply to all forms of business and self-employment, whether on the applicant's own account or in partnership, with the exception of writers and artists who are treated as a separate category.[4]

Admission

7.28 The applicant must obtain a current entry clearance issued for this purpose. In order to obtain clearance he must satisfy the entry clearance officer that[5] (1) he will be bringing money of his own to put into the business; his level of financial investment will be proportional to his interest in the business; he will be able to bear his share of the liabilities; he will be occupied full time in the running of the business; and there is a genuine need for his services and employment. It is submitted that on a true construction of the wording of the rule all these requirements must be fulfilled and not merely some of them; (2) the amount to be invested by him is not less than £100,000. He must provide evidence that this amount or more is under his control and disposal in the UK; (3) he meets the additional requirements set out below relating to (a) those intending to take over or join as a partner an existing business; or (b) those wishing to establish a new business in the UK on their own account or to be self-employed.

Taking Over/Joining an Existing Business[6]

7.29 The applicant must (1) show that his share of the profits will be sufficient to maintain and accommodate himself and his dependants; (2) produce audited accounts of the business for previous years in order to establish the precise financial position; (3) provide a written statement of the terms on which he is to enter the business; (4) show that his services and investments will create new, paid full-time employment in the business for persons already settled here; (5) satisfy the entry clearance officer that (a) the proposed partnership or directorship does not amount to disguised employment; and (b) he can earn a living without supplementing his business activities by employment of any kind or by recourse to public funds.

---

[3] HC 394, paras. 35–37 (admission); paras. 109–111 (extensions).
[4] See ibid., paras, 39, 112. See para. 7.38, post.
[5] Ibid., para. 35. Cf., the wording of the old rules, HC 80, para. 21, and HC 82, para. 19. See also *R* v *Immigration Appeal Tribunal, ex parte Joseph* [1977] Imm AR 70, para. 7.38, post.
[6] Ibid., para. 36.

Establishing a New Business[7]

7.30 The applicant must show (1) that he will be bringing into the country sufficient funds of his own to establish the enterprise; (2) that he can realistically be expected to maintain and accommodate himself and any dependants without recourse to employment of any kind (other than his self-employment) or to public funds; (3) that the business will provide new, paid full-time employment in the business for persons settled here.

Interpretation of the Rules

7.31 An entrant admitted as a businessman or self-employed person will not obtain entry clearance if he fails to meet any of these requirements. If given leave to enter, he will be admitted for a period not exceeding 12 months, provided that there are no general grounds for justifying refusal. A condition restricting his freedom to take employment will be attached.

There will certainly be far fewer applications as a result of the financial requirements, and it remains to be seen how the new rules will be interpreted.[8] Decisions under the old rules will be of very little assistance but the following should nevertheless be borne in mind. The personality of the applicant may still be a relevant factor in deciding whether the enterprise is realistic and likely to succeed.[9] Failure to disclose how the applicant's funds come into his possession is likely to be a ground for refusal, as would be general lack of candour by the applicant about his financial affairs. Even if all the requirements are met an application may still be refused, where, for example there has been a deception of the immigration authorities.[10]

Extensions[11]

7.32 Applications for extensions will only be granted if the applicant continues to meet all the requirements which he had to meet in order to

---

[7] Ibid., para. 37.

[8] Following concern expressed by New York lawyers that the new rules would apply to foreign lawyers wishing to work in the UK and branch offices of their own firms, the Home Office have confirmed that the application of the £100,000 requirement would not be appropriate in the case of consultants and overseas lawyers. They will be admitted under terms similar to the old rules. *Law Society Gazette* (1980) 5 November.

[9] *R v Immigration Appeal Tribunal, ex parte Joseph* [1977] Imm AR 70.

[10] *Parekh* [1976] Imm AR 84. See generally HC 394, para. 13.

[11] HC 394, paras. 109, 110.

obtain entry.[12] Documentary evidence in support of the application will be needed, of the same nature as that of the original application. Extensions will be granted for a maximum period of 12 months with a condition restricting employment. On the completion of four years as a businessman or self-employed person, indefinite leave to remain may be obtained.[13] It is not now possible under the rules for those who entered in any other capacity to apply to remain as businessmen or self-employed persons.[14]

The Old Rules[15]

7.33 Where a person proposed to set up in business by joining an existing concern he had to produce evidence that (1) he was bringing money of his own into the business; (2) he would be able to bear his share of the liabilities of the business; (3) this share of the profits would be sufficient to support him and his dependants; (4) he would be actively concerned in the running of the business and there was a genuine need for his services and investment. Audited accounts of previous years had to be produced to show the exact financial position of the business. Permission would not be granted where the partnership or directorship amounted to little more than 'disguised employment', or where it appeared likely that the applicant would have to supplement his business activities by seeking employment for which a work permit was required.[16]

If the applicant wished to go into business on his own he would also have to show that he was bringing in sufficient funds to establish the venture and that he could 'realistically be expected' to support himself and any dependants without recourse to work permit employment.[17] There was no requirement, as under the present rules, about the amount of money to be invested, or that the investment must create employment for persons already settled here. Entry clearance was not mandatory for businessmen coming to the UK but where one was produced the holder was normally admitted to the UK for a period of 12 months. Extensions of stay of up to 12 months would normally be granted if the applicant

[12] Ibid., para. 110.
[13] Ibid., para. 119; see para. 8.9, post.
[14] Ibid., para. 109.
[15] HC 79, paras. 31–34; HC 81, paras. 27–30 (admission).
HC 80, paras. 21, 22; HC 82, paras. 19, 20 (extensions).
[16] HC 79, para. 33; HC 81, para. 29.
[17] HC 79, para. 34; HC 81, para. 30.

continued to fulfil the requirements. Indefinite leave was usually given after four years.[18]

7.34 Visitors were permitted to apply for a variation of their stay to set up their own, or join new or existing businesses.[19] The rules stated that any such application would be considered on its merits and that permission would depend on a number of factors including those set out above. In *R* v *Immigration Appeal Tribunal, ex parte Joseph*,[20] the Divisional Court held that the rules were intended to provide guidance as to the practice to be followed and were not to be construed too rigidly. The 'factors to be taken into account' were not pre-requisites, and failure to comply with any one of them would not necessarily be fatal to the application: the appellate authorities should look at cases 'in the round' after considering all relevant factors. The Court considered that it would be right to take into account the personality of the applicant as being a relevant factor to the success of the business.

'Assets of His Own'

7.35 A difficulty which has frequently occurred is the applicant being able to show that he has 'assets of his own' to bring into the business. The word 'assets' must not be given too narrow a meaning. In *R* v *Immigration Appeal Tribunal, ex parte Joseph*, the Divisional Court considered that it must nevertheless refer to assets having some economic value, i.e. assets in the sense of financial contribution or 'something of that kind' to the business itself. In *Ally*,[1] an application to remain in the UK as a businessman was rejected because a large part of the assets used to purchase a coffee bar and restaurant were given to him by his wife. The Tribunal allowed the appeal since he had 'unfettered control' of the assets. The Divisional Court in *R* v *Immigration Appeal Tribunal, ex parte Perkazadi*[2] accepted that monies in the form of a loan might be a person's own assets. Consideration had to be given as to how long-term was the loan because 'a man can acquire an asset by process of creating a liability to somebody else'. It was acquisition of degree and fact. The ease with which the assets are realisable will be an important factor. In *Joseph*,[3] the

---

[18] HC 80, para. 28; HC 82, para. 26.
[19] HC 80, para. 21; HC 82, para. 19.
[20] [1977] Imm AR 70.
[1] [1972] Imm AR 258.
[2] [1979-80] Imm AR 191. The Tribunal had previously adopted the approach that money borrowed by the applicant could not be 'assets of his own'; see, e.g. *Haji*: [1978] Imm AR 26.
[3] [1977] Imm AR 96.

Tribunal had some doubts as to the extent of the appellant's assets under the rules where the assets comprised life insurance policies, an interest in a house in Jamaica and one in this country.

Disguised Employment

7.36 It is imperative that the business operation must not be 'a disguised form of employment'. In *Pritpal Singh*,[4] the appellant was director and secretary of a private limited company selling sports goods of which he had considerable experience. He was paid a salary of £1,200 per year, held a 15 per cent shareholding and had loaned the company £4,600. The Tribunal dismissed the appeal as there was no evidence of the appellant's continuity in the company. In short he could be removed at any time by the majority shareholder. Moreover it appeared that no interest had been paid to him in respect of the loan and he had received no share of the profits. The Tribunal concluded that he was little more than a paid employee. In *Pradeep Singh*,[5] the appellant, who applied to change from a visitor to a businessman, as managing director of a shirt company in Northern Ireland, was allowed to remain where he held 4,500 fully paid up shares out of a 20,000 share capital. The firm was prosperous, it was important for it to continue effectively in Northern Ireland and he was in receipt of a good salary.

Adequate Income from the Business

7.37 The rules require the applicant to show that he will not have to supplement his income by employment for which a work permit is required. It is also essential that the appellant has a sufficient income from the business without recourse to unearned income. The Divisional Court so held in *R v Immigration Appeal Tribunal, ex parte Martin (JBS)*,[6] where a seamstress supplemented her income from monies received regularly from her father. The profits from the business were insufficient to support her and her application for certiorari to quash the Tribunal's decision was dismissed.

WRITERS AND ARTISTS

7.38 A writer or artist, other than an EEC national,[7] may come to the

[4] [1972] Imm AR 154.
[5] 1407/73 (345) (unreported).
[6] [1972] Imm AR 275. (The Tribunal's decision is at [1972] Imm AR 145.)
[7] For the position of EEC nationals, see para. 7.44, post.

UK to work provided he holds a current entry clearance issued for this purpose. Clearance will only be given if the applicant produces satisfactory evidence that (1) he does not intend to do work other than that related to his self-employment; and (2) he will be able to maintain and accommodate himself and his dependants from his own resources including the proceeds of that self-employment without recourse to public funds. Admission will be granted for a maximum period of 12 months and made subject to a condition restricting his freedom to take employment.[8] The Home Secretary has however given an assurance that consent will be given to engage in 'business which is part and parcel of an artist's and writer's profession such as the holding of an exhibition'.[9]

Extensions of stay will only be granted if the applicant can show that he is maintaining and accommodating himself and his dependants from the proceeds of his self-employment as a writer or artist without recourse to public funds and without having resorted to employment for which a work permit is required. Extensions will be granted for a maximum period of 12 months with a condition restricting employment.[10] On the completion of four years as a writer or artist, indefinite leave to remain may be obtained.[11] The rules make it clear that those who entered in some other capacity have no claim to remain as writers or artists and any such applications for extension will be refused.[12]

The definition of 'artist' was considered by the Tribunal under the old (but similarly worded) rules in *Stillwaggon*,[13] where it was held that the word was a reference to persons in the category of painter or sculptor rather than to singers. 'Artistes' are therefore required to apply for work permits.

The Old Rules[14]

7.39 An entry clearance was not mandatory except for visa nationals. Other than this change, in practice there is little difference between the rules. The old rules referred to 'self-employed persons, such as artists and

---

[8] HC 394, para. 39.

[9] Mr William Whitelaw 979 H. of C. Official Report, 20 February 1980, Written Answers, col. 189.

[10] Ibid., para. 112.

[11] Ibid., para. 119; para. 8.9, post.

[12] Ibid., para. 112.

[13] [1975] Imm AR 132. See also *Baxt* 39730/79 (1854) (unreported) where it was held that an actor is not an artist.

[14] HC 79. para. 36; HC 81, para. 22 (admission).
HC 80, para. 32; HC 82, para. 20 (extensions).

writers'[15] but there was no evidence to suggest that any other group of people were admitted in this category. Extensions of stay up to 12 months were to be granted if the applicant continued to fulfil the requirements and indefinite leave was to be given after four years. The rules required a person to support himself and his dependants 'without taking work for which a work permit is required'. Although no reference was made to obtaining funds from sources other than earnings as a writer or artist, the Tribunal held in *Jones*,[16] that the appellant did not meet the requirements of the rules where he had received no remuneration for his work as a playwright for one and a half years and was receiving money from his family abroad to cover his living expenses.

PERSONS OF INDEPENDENT MEANS

7.40 The immigration rules allow for the entry of 'persons of independent' means who hold a current entry clearance issued for that purpose. Clearance will only be granted if the applicant can show that[17] (1) he has under his control and disposal in the UK a sum of at least £100,000 or income of not less than £10,000 a year; (2) he is able and willing to maintain himself and support and accommodate any dependants indefinitely in the UK without working, with no assistance from any other persons and without recourse to public funds; (3) he has a close connection with the UK (including for example the presence of close relatives here or periods of previous residence) or his admission would be in the general interests of the UK. If these requirements are met, admission will be given initially for a maximum of 12 months with a prohibition on the taking of employment.[18] Extensions of stay will be given if the applicant is able to produce satisfactory evidence that he continues to meet the requirements.[19] On the completion of four years as a person of independent means indefinite leave to remain may be obtained.[20] The requirement that the applicant has funds 'under his control' was considered in *R v Immigration Appeal Tribunal, ex parte Chiew*[1] where the Divisional

[15] Ibid.
[16] [1978] Imm AR 161.
[17] HC 394, para. 38.
[18] Ibid.
[19] Ibid., para. 113.
[20] Ibid., para. 119, see para. 8.9, post.
[1] (1981) *The Times*, 16 June.

Court held that in establishing a claim to be a person of independent means the applicant must prove that he has a right to the supply of sufficient funds, legally enforceable against any person. It was not sufficient for him to prove the existence of family funds from which he might draw but which were under the control of the head of the family. The Court was considering the old rules which do not materially differ from the current rules. The decision confirms the approach of the Tribunal which has held that a husband's money was not under the control of the applicant even where the husband had been providing regularly and there was every reason to believe he would continue to do so;[2] and similarly guarantees to make regular payments were held to be inadequate, because the guarantor might cease sending money,[3] as has money in a joint account where either party can make withdrawals.[4]

The rules state that those who were given limited leave to enter in some other capacity have no claim to remain as persons of independent means and their applications will be refused.[5] The wife and children under 18 of a person of independent means will be permitted to enter and remain provided that there is satisfactory support and accommodation.[6]

The provisions in the present rules are far harsher than those in the old rules, and it is not anticipated that there will be a large number of successful applications in this category. Earlier decisions provide little assistance in interpreting the present rules.

The Old Rules[7]

7.41 There was no requirement, as under the present rules, about the amount of capital or income a person required to qualify under this category. Nor was an entry clearance mandatory except for visa nationals. The rules specified that applicants had to show that they would be able to support themselves and their dependants 'indefinitely' without working. To do so, they had to produce documents such as bank statements or letters of pension entitlement. Monies to be utilised in this way had to be under the applicant's own control and disposable in the UK. Moreover, they must be sufficient for the 'foreseeable future'. Extensions of stay up to 12 months may be granted if the applicant

[2] *Madanipoor* 59550/80 (1969) (unreported).
[3] *Gautam* 52226/79 (1891) (unreported).
[4] *Naqvi* 47947/79 (1913) (unreported).
[5] Ibid., para. 113.
[6] Ibid., para. 40. See para. 7.42, post.
[7] HC 79, para. 35, HC 81, para. 31.

continues to fulfil these requirements and indefinite leave may be granted after four years.[8]

It should be noted that while an applicant must show that he can support himself and his dependants, there is no requirement that he must also show that he *intends* to do so.[9] In *Jacques*,[10] the Tribunal stated that the applicant must be able to stand on his own feet financially without any form of subsidised accommodation or keep. Many of the cases involve old people on very small incomes who have claimed to qualify under the rules because of a relatively simple lifestyle and expectations. In *Raval*,[11] an Indian couple aged 62 and 59 had in 1974 an annual income of £885. It was said on their behalf that this was more than the current old age pension. Moreover they did not drink or smoke and were vegetarians. The couple were allowed to stay although their son provided them with accommodation. This factor was ignored by the Tribunal in its assessment that their income alone was sufficient to lead 'a frugal life'. However in recent years the Tribunal has been reluctant to accept that those on small incomes can live indefinitely on those incomes in times of increasing inflation.

DEPENDANTS OF THOSE ADMITTED FOR WORK[12]

7.42 A person admitted to the UK to take or seek employment, or as a businessman or self-employed person, writer or artist or a person of independent means, will be permitted to bring his wife and children under 18,[13] provided the sponsor is able and willing to maintain and accommodate them without recourse to public funds, in accommodation of his own which he occupies himself. He should give an undertaking in writing to this effect if requested.[14] They will require a current entry

---

[8] HC 80, para. 28; HC 82, para. 26.
[9] *Supersad* 713/76 (842) (unreported).
[10] 10318/76 (1035) (unreported).
[11] [1975] Imm AR 72.
[12] These provisions do not apply to EEC nationals. For the position of EEC nationals' families, see paras. 7.49 and 7.52, post.
[13] HC 394, para. 40.
[14] Ibid., para. 42.

clearance for this purpose.[15] There should be no restriction on their taking employment unless the sponsor is prohibited from taking employment in which case they will similarly be prohibited.[16] No other dependants will be eligible for admission before the sponsor is settled in the UK.[17]

The Old Rules[18]

7.43 The rules were similar, in that only a wife or children under 18 were to be admitted but there was no requirement that the accommodation provided was owned or occupied by the sponsor nor was there any requirement to give undertakings. The old rules, presumably inadvertently, did not provide for the admission of wives and children of writers or artists. The rules further stated that seasonal workers were not allowed to bring dependants.

EEC NATIONALS[19]

7.44 As we have seen, the EEC Treaty[20] makes provisions for the free movement of workers, businessmen and the self-employed, and those who provide and receive services.[1] The general principles are set out in EEC Treaty, arts. 48–51 (freedom of movement: workers), arts. 52–58 (freedom of establishment: non-wage earning activities), and arts. 59–66 (free movement of services). These principles have been put into effect by a number of regulations and directives of the EEC Council, the most important of which are contained in the table opposite.

7.45 The Regulations have general application and are binding in their entirety and directly applicable in all member states.[2] Directives are not directly applicable[3] but in practice may have direct effect and thus be

[15] Ibid., para. 43.
[16] Ibid., para. 40.
[17] Ibid.
[18] HC 79, para. 37: HC 81, para. 33.
[19] For a detailed examination of EEC immigration law, see T C Hartley *EEC Immigration Law*.
[20] Cmnd 5179 (I) and (II).
[1] See paras. 3.2 et seq., ante.
[2] EEC Treaty, art. 189.
[3] For the extent to which there are theoretical differences, see *Hartley* op. cit., pp. 13–17.

Regulations and Directives	Provision
(1) Directive 64/221:	specifies limitations on freedom of movement and residence on grounds of public policy, public security or public health
(2) Regulation 1612/68:	implements freedom of movement provisions of Articles 48 *et seq.*
(3) Directive 68/360:	sets out procedure for granting and withdrawing residence permits for workers
(4) Regulation 1251/70:	sets out rights of workers to remain in country of immigration after taking employment
(5) Directive 72/194:	extends to 1251/70 workers the provisions of Directive 64/221
(6) Directive 73/148:	sets out procedure for granting and withdrawing residence permits for those with right of establishment or providing/receiving services
(7) Directive 75/34:	sets out rights of the self-employed to remain in country of immigration after taking employment
(8) Directive 75/35:	extends to 75/34 self-employed the provisions of Directive 64/221
(9) Regulation 311/76:	provides for compilation of statistics on foreign workers
(10) Regulation 312/76:	amends the provisions relating to the trade union rights of workers contained in 1612/68

capable of giving rise to rights and obligations which national courts must observe.

The Treaty, and the secondary legislation made under it, are legally effective and binding in English law by virtue of the European Communities Act 1972, s. 2(1). Where there is conflict between English law and Community law, the latter is to prevail.[4] The requirements of EEC law are considered here only provided that special provisions have been made for EEC nationals under the rules. Other provisions under the rules are applicable to EEC nationals to the extent that they do not conflict with EEC law. They are not treated separately (except for certain aspects relating to public health, exclusion and deportation) as the provisions are at least as favourable as those required under EEC law.

Workers

7.46 Article 48 provides for (1) freedom of movement of workers

[4] The position is a little more complex than stated but in practice there are unlikely to be problems in the field of immigration on this point.

within the Community; (2) abolition of discrimination based on nationality between workers of member states, in the field of employment; and (3) the right to remain in the territory of a member state where they have been employed. This right is subject to certain limitations justified by public order, public safety or public health.[5]

'Worker' is not defined in the Treaty. The European Court has not however restricted the word solely to persons currently in employment. In *Unger*,[6] the Court held that the word included someone who had left one job and was capable of taking another. In this case the appellant had a contract of employment which had come to an end because she was expecting a child. As she was able to resume work at a later date she was clearly a worker. Moreover, it is generally accepted that a person looking for work is to be treated as a 'worker' under the Treaty, although there has been no direct decision of the European Court on this point. There are however limitations. In *R* v *Secchi*,[7] the Metropolitan Magistrate at Marylebone, declining to consider a definition, nevertheless took the view that 'not every (EEC) national who in the course of his life may at different times have done a few hours', a few days' or even a few weeks' work can be regarded as someone whose freedom of movement within member states is necessary for the fulfilment of the task of (the Community)'. In that case the magistrate held that a man of 20 who had abandoned his studies two years earlier without obtaining qualifications and had since lived the life of an itinerant vagrant wandering across Europe was not a worker. The only work that he had done was 'casual work of the washing-up-in-restaurants type'.

In short, workers may be defined as (1) those in employment; and (2) those out of work through circumstances beyond their control but who are willing and able to take work. To this group must be added, (3) those who have been employed in the country of immigration and have become permanently incapacitated through illness or injury; and (4) those similarly employed who are no longer working having reached the normal retirement age in that country.[8]

Businessmen and Self-Employed Persons

7.47 Article 52 provides for 'the right to engage in and carry on non-

---

[5] Article 48(3) and Directive 64/221. These limitations also apply to self-employed persons. See para 5.23, ante (public health), and paras. 11.5 et seq., post. (public safety and public order).

[6] Case 75/63: [1964] CMLR 319.

[7] [1975] 1 CMLR 383.

[8] See Regulation 1251/70.

wage earning activities, and also to set up and manage enterprises, and, in particular, companies . . .'. This is part of what is referred to in the Treaty as 'freedom of establishment', and it extends not only to persons who are established in the country of immigration but also to those who 'wish to establish themselves . . . in order to pursue activities as self-employed persons'. As in the case of workers, there are similar provisions for (including within the self-employed) those who have become incapacitated or retired.[9]

The Provision of Services

7.48 Article 59 provides for the progressive abolition of restrictions on the freedom of nationals of member states to provide services within the EEC. The freedom to provide services involves being established in one state while providing services in another, and it includes the right to perform activities on a temporary basis in another Community country.[10] 'Services' are 'services normally provided for remuneration' and include in particular activities of an industrial and commercial character, and activities of craftsmen and the professions.[11]

Restrictions on movement and residence are to be abolished not only in respect of those who wish to provide services, but also in respect of nationals of member states wishing to go to another member state as recipients of services.[12] Thus EEC legislation will apply in the granting of leave, for example, to a French citizen where the purpose of his entering it is to receive private medical treatment or private education. While there is no general obligation under the EEC Treaty not to discriminate on the grounds of nationality[13] the Treaty specifically states that until restrictions on freedom to provide services are abolished, the restrictions shall apply without distinction on the grounds of nationality or residence to all persons providing services.[14]

Families of EEC Nationals

7.49 Members of the family of an EEC national have the same rights as the EEC national. The family of a worker is defined as (1) the spouse and

[9] See Directive 75/34.
[10] EEC Treaty, art. 60.
[11] Ibid.
[12] Directive 73/148.
[13] EEC Treaty, art. 7.
[14] Ibid., art. 65.

their descendants who are under 21 years or are dependants; (2) dependent relatives in the ascending line of the worker and his spouse.[15]

Persons of Independent Means

7.50 There is no provision under EEC law for the free movement within the Community of those who have independent means of support. The EEC Commission has however drafted a proposal for a Council Directive 'on a right of residence for nationals of member states in the territory of another member state.'[16] This would require the UK to abolish restrictions on movement and residence of EEC nationals and their families[17] not actually covered by other provisions for free movement, subject to a right to require 'proof of sufficient resources to provide for their own needs and the dependent members of their family' which must not be greater than the minimum subsistence level as defined by UK law.

The Immigration Rules[18]

Admission

7.51 The rules provide that an EEC national (unless the holder of a residence permit or a returning resident) should normally be given leave to enter for six months.[19] No condition restricting employment or occupation is to be imposed.[20] If he wishes to enter the UK in order to take or seek employment, set up in business or work as a self-employed person he is to be admitted without a work permit or other prior consent.[1]

---

[15] Regulation 1612/68, art. 10. There is an almost identical definition in respect of families of the self-employed and providers and recipients of services, except that descendants other than children (e.g. grandchildren) must be dependent: see Directive 73/148. The immigration rules do not make the distinction (see para. 7.52, post.) and permit grandchildren (under 21) of the self-employed to be admitted although they are not dependent on the grandfather. Member states are to 'favour' the admission of other relatives living 'under the same roof' as the family in the country of origin.

[16] Submitted by the Commission to the Council on 31 July 1979.

[17] The definition of family is the same as that for other EEC Nationals with freedom of movement except dependent children must be under 18.

[18] HC 394, paras. 59–63 (admission); paras. 125–132 (extensions and settlement). The rules have been amended in regard to Greek nationals who are to be treated under the rules as EEC nationals for the purpose of setting up business or working as self-employed, but not for the purpose of taking or seeking employment: HC (1980–81) 84.

[19] Ibid., para. 60.

[20] Ibid.

[1] Ibid., para. 61.

The European Court in *R* v *Pieck*,[2] has held in terms that the imposition of the initial six months' time limit on an EEC national is inconsistent with the provisions of the Treaty. Council Directive (EEC) 68/360, art. 3(2), states that 'no entry visa or equivalent document' may be demanded for an EEC national. The Court held that this phrase covered 'any formality for the purpose of granting leave to enter which is coupled with a passport or identity card check at the frontier'. It rejected the British Government argument that 'entry visa' means exclusively a documentary clearance issued before the traveller arrives at the frontier in the form of an endorsement in a passport or other travel document. For the purpose of applying the Directive, the object of which is to abolish restrictions on movement, the time at which clearance is given is immaterial. The right to enter of an EEC national may not be made subject to the issue of a clearance to this effect. It now remains to be seen whether the immigration rules will be amended as a result of the Court's decision.

7.52 Members of the family of an EEC national accompanying him or joining him at a later date are to be given leave to enter on the same terms.[3] Members of the family are defined as (1) the EEC national's spouse; (2) their children under 21; (3) their children and grandchildren if still dependent; (4) their dependent parents and grandparents.[4] It will be seen that this definition is narrower than that under EEC law which includes great grandparents and great grandchildren.[5] In the unlikely event of such people seeking admission, they would have to be accepted.

Although an EEC national may be refused entry on the ground of criminal record or that his exclusion is conducive to the public good or for health reasons, special considerations apply. These aspects are discussed elsewhere.[6]

7.53 An EEC national who is seeking or taking employment, setting up in business or working as a self-employed person, may be refused entry if the immigration officer concludes that he is likely to be a charge on public funds. The basis for such refusal under the rules is the provision excluding an entrant on the ground that it is conducive to the public good,[7] although this is not normally set out on the formal refusal notice

[2] Case 157/79: [1981] 3 All ER 46.
[3] Ibid., paras. 62, 63.
[4] Ibid., para. 2. The provisions apply irrespective of the nationality of the member of the family. There is no requirement that the member must be an EEC national.
[5] See para. 7.49, ante.
[6] See para. 5.23, ante (health), and para. 11.51, post (criminal and conducive).
[7] HC 394, para. 76 (b).

which will simply state that the refusal is justified because the entrant is likely to be a charge on public funds if admitted. The circumstances in which a refusal may arise are where the entrant has insufficient funds to support himself until he has found employment or where his previous employment record is such that it is unlikely that he will take employment. An entrant who in the past has been a charge on public funds is also likely to be refused. In *Leper*,[8] where the appellant had previously been in receipt of supplementary benefit payments in the UK and was returning to seek employment, the Tribunal held that refusal was justified on this ground.[9]

Employment

7.54 Those admitted for six months who enter employment should be issued with a residence permit.[10] The permit should be for five years, unless the duration of the employment is expected to be less than 12 months, in which case the permit is to be limited to that period.[11] A permit is not normally to be granted to a person who has not found employment during the six month period or has at any time become a charge on public funds.[12] It may be appropriate in the case of a person who has been unemployed for more than 12 consecutive months during the previous five years to issue a residence permit for 12 months. The permit may be renewed.[13] Members of the family should on application be granted extensions of stay and issued with residence permits in the same terms as those relating to the EEC national at the time in question.[14]

Residence Permits

7.55 Council Directive 68/360, art. 4(2) states that 'as proof of the right of residence, a document entitled "Residence Permit for a National of a Member State of the EEC" shall be issued'. In *Pieck*,[15] the European Court confirmed that the issue of a residence permit has only declaratory effect. The document is not to be equated with a permission to remain, which may be granted to other non-patrials. Such permission is dis-

---

[8] 1548/76 (944) (unreported).
[9] The Tribunal also held that living on public funds was a ground of public policy which would be invoked under EEC Treaty, art. 48(3).
[10] HC 394, para. 127.
[11] Ibid.
[12] Ibid.
[13] Ibid., para. 130.
[14] Ibid., para. 131. Members of the family are defined; see paras. 7.49 and 7.52, ante.
[15] Case 157/79: [1981] 3 All ER 46.

cretionary whereas an EEC national is entitled to remain as of right. The Court further stated that a 'member state may not require from a person enjoying the protection of Community law that he should possess a general residence permit instead of the document provided for in Article 4(2) . . .'.

As has been seen, the immigration rules provide for residence permits to be issued to EEC nationals after they have remained in the UK for six months. From the judgment in the court in *Pieck*, it is clear that these permits are simply evidence that the holder is an EEC national who has a right under the Treaty to remain. There are therefore no grounds which would justify refusing the issue of a permit to an EEC national immediately on arrival or attaching conditions or otherwise restricting the permit other than for reasons specified by the Treaty, i.e. on grounds of public order, safety and health.[16] Although the immigration authorities may require a person to obtain a residence permit, the Court held that failure to obtain the permit must be regarded as a minor offence and cannot be punished by a recommendation for deportation or by measures which go as far as imprisonment.[17] The immigration rules relating to residence permits have therefore to be considered in the light of these EEC provisions.

Businessmen/Self-employment

7.56 A five year permit should be issued to a person admitted for six months who produces evidence by the end of that period that he has established himself in business or in a self-employed occupation.[18] A person who cannot show that he has established himself in business or self-employment may be refused a residence permit or may be granted a short extension of stay in order to complete arrangements for so establishing himself.[19]

7.57 The duration of the permit or of leave to enter or remain should be curtailed if it is evident that the holder is living on public funds although capable of maintaining himself.[20]

Settlement[1]

7.58 A person issued with a five year permit should have the time

[16] See paras. 5.23 and 11.51, post.
[17] See para. 11.55, post.
[18] Ibid., para. 128.
[19] Ibid.
[20] Ibid., para. 129; and see, e.g., *Giovanni* [1977] Imm AR 85.
[1] HC 394, para. 130.

limits removed after he has remained for four years in employment, business or self-employment unless (1) his conduct has been such that there are justifiable reasons under the rules[2] for not removing the time limit; or (2) he has been living off public funds although capable of maintaining himself.[3] Where a time limit is not removed, the case should be reviewed on the expiry of the residence permit.

7.59 In addition to the circumstance mentioned above, the time limit on the stay of the following groups is to be removed:

(a) a person who has been continuously resident in the UK for at least three years, has been in employment in the UK or any other member country of the EEC for the preceding 12 months and has reached the age of entitlement to a State retirement pension;
(b) a person who has ceased to be employed owing to a permanent incapacity for work arising out of an accident at work or an occupational disease entitling him to a State disability pension;
(c) a person who has been continuously resident in the UK for more than two years, and who has ceased to be employed owing to a permanent incapacity for work;
(d) any member of the family of a person in category (a), (b) or (c) above;
(e) any member of the family of a person who after residing continuously in the UK for at least two years, dies as a result of an accident at work or an occupational disease.[4]

Deportation

7.60 This may arise following a conviction for a criminal offence or where the Home Secretary deems it to be conducive to the public good. Special considerations apply to EEC nationals, which are discussed elsewhere.[5]

[2] Ibid., para. 88.
[3] Ibid., para. 129.
[4] Ibid., para. 132.
[5] See paras. 11.51 et seq., post.

EIGHT

Settlement

SETTLEMENT

8.1 Those who are 'settled' in the UK have been given permission by the immigration authorities to remain in the UK permanently. They do not have a right of abode and if they leave the common travel area they must present themselves to an immigration officer on their return and qualify afresh for entry.[1] Normally they will be admitted as returning residents provided they have not been away for more than two years.[2]

MEANING OF SETTLEMENT

8.2 Settlement has a special meaning under the Act: a person is settled in the UK and Islands if he is ordinarily resident there without being subject under the immigration laws to any restrictions on the period for which he may remain.[3]

Ordinarily Resident

8.3 Ordinary residence is not defined in the Act. It is a question of fact in each individual case: The courts have recently held[4] that the concept of ordinary residence embodies a number of different factors, such as time, intention and continuity, each of which might carry different weight according to the context in which, and the purpose for which it was used in a particular statute. Thus, in considering 'ordinary residence' in the context of awards under the Education Act 1962, the phrase was

---

[1] Immigration Act 1971, s. 3(4).
[2] HC 394, paras. 56–58, see para. 8.66, post.
[3] Immigration Act 1971, s. 2(3) (d), and note, ss. 8(5) and 33(1).
[4] R v *London Borough of Barnet, ex parte Shah* [1980] 3 All ER 679; *Cicutti* v *Suffolk County Council* [1980] 3 All ER 689. See also *Levene* v *IRC* [1928] AC 217, HL, *IRC* v *Lysaght* [1928] AC 234 HL.

used to distinguish those who were resident for general (or 'ordinary') purposes from those who were resident for a specific, special or limited purpose. The genuine intention to remain in the UK by a person who originally came for a limited purpose may be sufficient to make him ordinary resident. Similarly, the fact that a person may intend to return to his country of origin will not necessarily prevent him from being ordinarily resident in the UK. Absence abroad need not break ordinary residence although the length of absence and the purposes of the journey will be relevant factors.[5]

8.4 The Act makes it clear that generally 'a person is not to be treated for the purposes of . . . this Act as ordinarily resident in the UK or in any of the Islands at a time when he is in breach of the immigration laws'.[6] An illegal entrant or a person who has overstayed cannot therefore take any benefits conferred by the Act on those ordinarily resident in the UK.[7] There is a limited exception to this rule for some Commonwealth and Irish citizens ordinarily resident in the UK on 1 January 1973 who may face deportation.[8] A person who is not ordinarily resident under the Immigration Act may be so resident for other purposes, e.g. taxation.[9]

Without being Subject to 'Time' Restrictions

8.5 A person who has been given a limited leave to remain will have been admitted for a specific period of time. Conditions (i.e. a prohibition or restriction on working or a requirement to report to the police) may also have been attached to the stay.[10] If the restriction on time is lifted so are any conditions. A person whose time limit and conditions have been removed is said to have 'indefinite leave' to remain.

SETTLEMENT IN THE UK WHEN IMMIGRATION ACT CAME INTO FORCE

8.6 The Act makes two references to those resident permanently in the

---

[5] As to the factors which the Home Office regards as relevant in determining ordinary residence, etc., see para. 8.68, post.

[6] Ibid., s. 33(2).

[7] An illegal entrant under s. 33(1) cannot be settled here. He is in breach of the immigration laws and cannot therefore be 'ordinarily resident'. See *Azam* v *Secretary of State for the Home Department* [1973] 2 All ER 765.

[8] Immigration Act 1971, s. 7(2). See para. 11.3, post.

[9] Similarly a person may be ordinarily resident for immigration purposes while not for others.

[10] Ibid., s. 3(1) (b), (c).

UK when the Act came into force (1 January 1973): (1) indefinite leave to enter and remain is granted to those settled in the UK (whatever their nationality) when the Act came into force; (2) there are special provisions for Commonwealth citizens settled in the UK on 1 January 1973 and for their wives and children.

Indefinite Leave Granted to Those Settled in the UK on 1 January 1973

8.7 Section 1(2) of the Act states that non-patrials who were not already 'exempt . . . from the provisions relating to leave to enter and remain' are to be treated as having been given indefinite leave if they were in the UK and settled there when the Act came into force. The purpose of this provision is presumably to bring the terminology of the previous legislation into line with the new Act. No additional rights are conferred by this subsection. Its limited scope is indicated by *R v Secretary of State for the Home Department, ex parte Mughal*.[11] The applicant had lived in England for a number of years, left for Pakistan in November 1972 and returned in March 1973 when he was refused admission, the immigration officer claiming he had originally entered illegally. He claimed benefit of s. 1(2) but the Court of Appeal held that it applied only to those physically present in the UK on 1 January 1973, that indefinite leave did not confer automatic right of re-entry and the burden was on the immigrant to show that he was settled.

Special Provisions for Commonwealth Citizens Settled in the UK on 1 January 1973 and for their Wives and Children

8.8 Section 1(5) of the Act provides that the immigration rules shall be framed so that 'Commonwealth citizens settled in the UK at the coming into force of the Act and their wives and children are not, by virtue of anything in the rules, any less free to come into and go from the UK than if this Act had not been passed.' Until the Act, a Commonwealth citizen who was settled in the UK was entitled as of right to bring his wife and children under 16, although there were restrictions if the children were not accompanying or joining both parents.[12] The Government gave assurance that those who had been accepted for settlement before the Act came into force would not find themselves in any worse position because of the Act. The only benefits of this provision are (1) a husband will not have to show that he is able and willing to support and accommodate his

---

[11] [1973] 3 All ER 796, CA.
[12] Commonwealth Immigrants Act 1962, s. 2(2), as amended.

wife and children under 18 without recourse to public funds;[13] (2) if a returning resident satisfies an immigration officer that he was settled here on 1 January 1973 and is ordinarily resident in the UK or was so resident at any time during the two years prior to his return, he must be admitted for settlement; even if he received assistance from public funds towards the cost of leaving the UK.[14]

QUALIFYING FOR SETTLEMENT UNDER THE IMMIGRATION RULES

8.9 Under the immigration rules, certain groups are eligible for settlement on admission, or after they have been in the UK for a specific period.

Irrespective of Nationality

(a) Dependants of those settled here or who are on the same occasion admitted for settlement, i.e. wife, children under 18 and to an extremely limited extent, parents, grandparents and other relatives;[15]
(b) wives of those settled here marrying in the UK;[16]
(c) husbands of UK citizens (who were born or had a parent born in the UK) settled here or who are on the same occasion admitted for settlement; they are to be granted 12 months' stay, and thereafter, settlement;[17]
(d) fiancés of UK citizens (who were born or had a parent born in the UK) settled here: they are granted 12 months' stay after marriage, and thereafter, settlement;[18]
(e) fiancées of those settled here;[19]

---

[13] HC 394, para. 42.
[14] HC 394, para. 56, refers to the returning resident having been '*settled* here at any time during the two years preceding his return' (emphasis added) but it is submitted that this does not reflect the full extent of the protection offered by the Immigration Act 1971, s. 1(5). The wording of the Commonwealth Immigrants Act 1962, s. 2(2) (a), shows that to avail himself of this subsection the returning resident has simply to show ordinary residence within the two year period. This point was argued before the Tribunal in *Aisha Khatoon Ali* [1979–80] Imm AR 195, but the case was decided on a different point.
[15] Ibid., paras. 42–49. See paras. 8.20–8.55, post.
[16] Ibid., para. 115.
[17] Ibid., paras. 50, 51, 116. See para. 8.56, post.
[18] Ibid., paras. 52, 116. See para. 8.57, post.
[19] Ibid., para. 55. See para. 8.61 post.

(f) those admitted for approved employment may apply, after working for four years in the UK;[20]
(g) those admitted as businessmen, self-employed persons, writers or artists or persons of independent means may similarly apply after the same period.[1]

EEC Nationals

8.10 The following additional groups of EEC nationals[2] also qualify for settlement.

(a) those who have been continuously resident in the UK for at least three years; and (i) have been in employment in the UK or some other EEC country for the 12 months preceding the application; and (ii) have reached the age where they are entitled to a state retirement pension;
(b) those who have ceased to be employed because of incapacity for work arising out of an accident at work or an occupational disease entitling them to a state disability pension.
(c) those who have been continuously resident in the UK for two years and who have stopped work because they are permanently incapable of work;
(d) any member of a family (i.e. spouse, their children under 21, their other children and grandchildren if still dependent, and their dependent parents and grandparents) of any of the above categories;
(e) any member of the family or a person who dies as a result of an accident at work or an occupational disease *provided that* the deceased has resided in the UK continuously for at least two years.[3]

UK Passport Holders who are not Patrial and their Dependants

8.11 Certain UK passport holders who are not patrial may apply for a special voucher admitting them for settlement. This group has been considered in Chapter 3.[4]

Refugees

8.12 Those granted refugee status[5] may apply after remaining in the

---

[20] Ibid., paras. 119(a), (b). See para. 7.12, ante.
[1] Ibid., paras. 119(c)–(f). See para. 7.32, ante.
[2] See generally para. 7.58, ante.
[3] Ibid., para. 132.
[4] Ibid., para. 41. See para. 3.8, ante.
[5] See para. 15.15, post.

UK for four years. In some cases refugees may be given settlement from the outset, but this cannot be assured.

FREEDOM FROM INTERNAL CONTROL FOR THOSE SETTLED IN THE UK

8.13 We have already seen that those settled in the UK who leave the common travel area are subject to immigration control on their return. They are, however, generally not subject to controls while in the UK.

Freedom to Stay and to Work

8.14 As both the time limit and any conditions attached to the stay are removed, it is not necessary to apply to the Home Office for any further extensions of stay or to seek the approval of the Department of Employment to work.

Exemption from Registration with the Police

8.15 Most foreign nationals are required to register with the police on arrival.[6] This conditions lapses on settlement.[7]

No Exemption from Deportation Law in Most Cases

8.16 As those settled here are non-patrials, they are, however, still liable to deportation. The only exemption[8] is for certain Commonwealth and Irish citizens who must show they were (1) such citizens on the date of the decision to deport; (2) such citizens on 1 January 1973; (3) ordinarily resident in the UK on 1 January 1973; and (4) ordinarily resident there for the five years preceding the decision, or in the case of those recommended for deportation following conviction, for the five years prior to the conviction.

PATRIALITY AND SETTLEMENT

8.17 The difference between patrials and those who are settled in the UK is that the former are not subject to any control. Patrials therefore

---

[6] Ibid., para. 65. See also Immigration (Registration with Police) Regulations 1972, SI 1972, No. 1758 as amended. See para. 9.22, post. This condition will be reimposed if an extension of stay is granted: HC 394, para. 122.

[7] Ibid., para. 123.

[8] Immigration Act 1971, s. 7. See para. 11.3, post.

may, (1) leave the UK for any period of time and be re-admitted as of right if still patrial; and (2) are not liable to be deported from the UK in any circumstances.[9] Those settled here may in due course become eligible to apply for UK citizenship by registration (Commonwealth citizens) or by naturalisation (aliens and British protected persons). If they acquire citizenship in the UK they will become patrials.[10]

SETTLEMENT OF DEPENDANTS

8.18 The immigration rules[11] provide for the admission for settlement of certain people who are dependants of those settled in the UK, or who on the same occasion are given indefinite leave to enter. Those who are eligible for admission are (1) wives; (2) children; (3) parents, grandparents and other relatives. As will be seen, entry is greatly restricted by the rules and those who qualify are limited to a much smaller group of people than would appear at first glance.

Exceptions to the General Rule

8.19 The discussion of the rules which follows applies to the dependants of people irrespective of nationality with the exception of the following: (1) wives and children under 18 of patrials or of Commonwealth citizens settled in the UK before 1 January 1973; and (2) EEC nationals.

The wife or child under 18 of a patrial or of a Commonwealth citizen settled in the UK before 1 January 1973 (when the Act came into force) is to be admitted even if the person already settled is unable or unwilling to support or accommodate them without recourse to public funds.[12] They require entry clearance but unless they are subject to a current deportation order they cannot be refused entry.[13] Although citizens of Pakistan are now non-Commonwealth citizens, those who are dependants of a patrial UK citizen are entitled to enter under these provisions.[14]

---

[9] Under the Prevention of Terrorism (Temporary Provisions) Act 1976, patrial Commonwealth citizens may be excluded from the UK and UK citizens from either Britain or Northern Ireland, but not both. See para. 16.2, post.

[10] See paras. 2.38–2.39, ante.

[11] See generally HC 394, paras. 42–49; 131–132.

[12] HC 394, para. 42. See also Immigration Act 1971, s. 1(5).

[13] I.e. the general grounds of refusal (medical, criminal record and conducive to the public good) cannot be used to exclude; HC 394, para. 68.

[14] Immigration Act 1971, s. 1(5); *Shamshad Begum* 7426/76 (1026) (unreported).

'Members of the family' of an EEC national settled in the UK are also entitled to indefinite leave to remain.[15] They comprise the person's spouse, their children under 21, their other children and grandchildren if still dependent and their dependent parents and grandparents.[16]

GENERAL REQUIREMENTS FOR DEPENDANTS OF COMMONWEALTH AND NON-EEC NATIONALS

8.20 The sponsor must show that he is physically present[17] in the UK and settled here.[18] In *Immigration Appeal Tribunal* v *Manek*,[19] the Court of Appeal held that for dependants to qualify in these circumstances, their sponsor had not only to be settled in the UK but also be physically present when they applied for admission. He must further show that he is able and willing to maintain and accommodate his dependants without recourse to public funds in accommodation of his own or which he occupies himself.[20] He may be required to give an undertaking in writing to this effect.[1] The dependant must hold an entry clearance granted to him or her for the purpose of settlement.[2]

WIVES

8.21 The rules provide that 'the wife of a person who is settled in the UK or is on the same occasion being admitted for settlement is herself to be admitted for settlement', if the general requirements relating to

---

[15] As to the circumstances in which an EEC national is entitled to settlement see HC 394, para. 132. See para. 7.58, ante.

[16] HC 394, para. 131.

[17] Ibid., para. 42. This is an amendment to the old rules and confirms *Arshad* [1977] Imm AR 19.

[18] Ibid., para. 42.

[19] [1978] Imm AR 131, CA.

[20] The Home Office have stated that a sympathetic approach will be taken to plans made at the sponsor's expense for the reception of the family on arrival but the accommodation must be available for a long term and not the subject of short term arrangements made largely to secure the family's admission; nor must it be at the public expense. Letter, Home Office to North Kirklees Community Relations Council, 20 June 1980.

[1] HC 394, para. 42.

[2] Ibid., para. 43. It has been the practice to admit non-visa foreign nationals coming for settlement without clearance by giving them leave to enter for two or three months. They may then apply to the Home Office for indefinite leave to remain.

dependants are met.[3] A member of HM Forces based in the UK but serving overseas is regarded for this purpose as being in the UK.

Proof of Relationship

8.22 This difficulty applies particularly to those coming from the Indian sub-continent where documentation of status and differing traditions and customs can often leave room for doubt about the relationship. The applicant and children over 12 will initially be interviewed by an entry clearance officer in her own country and closely cross-examined. In some cases the application will be referred to the Home Office for the sponsor to be interviewed in the UK. If discrepancies arise between her statements, those of the children and the information provided by the sponsor, the application is likely to be refused. The most likely discrepancies are those relating to the family tree: the names and dates of birth of the children, whether the sponsor was with his wife at the date of conception and the names, ages and place of residence of other relatives. The applicant may be questioned about minor details concerning family possessions and about the marriage ceremony: when and where it took place, how it was conducted and who was present. Also relevant is whether and in what circumstances the sponsor has claimed tax relief for his wife and any children. In addition, the entry clearance officer may ask for further documentary evidence and in certain circumstances may require a medical examination.[4]

The standard proof of the relationship is that of the balance of probabilities.[5] Moreover the Tribunal has accepted that not all discrepancies need necessarily be explained,[6] although

'in many cases . . . (in) the absence of credible explanation for discrepancies in family matters and in the absence also of reliable documentary evidence of the claimed relationship it is inevitable that the entry cer-

---

[3] Ibid., para. 44. The wife must be coming *for settlement*. If she does not intend to remain in the UK, leave to enter under this category will be refused although admission as a visitor would normally be justified: *Anayat Bibi* 53725/79 (1994).

[4] See para. 5.56, ante.

[5] *R v Secretary of State for the Home Department, ex parte S B Hussain* (1972) 19 September 226/72 DC (unreported). Referred to in *Diljar Begum* 682/73(461) (unreported). See para. 14.45, post.

[6] See, e.g. *Diljar Begum*, cited supra. If there is evidence to show the applicant is the wife of the sponsor she is to be admitted notwithstanding that it is not possible to pinpoint the date of the claimed marriage. *Khanom* [1979–80] Imm AR 182.

tificate officer and the adjudicator should not be satisfied that an appellant has established his case'.[7]

Polygamous Marriages

8.23 A number of problems have arisen as a result of polygamous marriages. A marriage is polygamous if it is celebrated under a law which permits the husband to take more than one wife during the subsistence of the marriage.[8] Whether the marriage is monogamous or polygamous in character depends entirely on the law of the country where the marriage is celebrated: it is *polygamous* if that country permits polygamy and the marriage takes place in a polygamous form. Such a marriage is often referred to as *potentially polygamous*, if by the law of that country, a husband is entitled to marry more than one wife, even though he has not done so.[9] A marriage celebrated in the UK must be monogamous, whatever the form of the marriage.[10]

Admission for settlement may nevertheless be given to a wife who is a party to a polygamous or potentially polygamous marriage. Whether the wife must be accepted as a wife for the purpose of the immigration rules will depend on whether the English law recognises the marriage as valid. A polygamous marriage which is (1) in a form acceptable in the country where it is celebrated; (2) valid according to the law of the country where each party is domiciled will be recognised in English law as a valid marriage.[11]

8.24 The question of 'domicile' thus becomes an important issue particularly as a polygamous or potentially polygamous marriage is void under English law if entered into outside England at a time when either party is domiciled in England.[12] The law attributes to each person at birth a permanent home within a territory or country which has a legal system. This is known as a 'domicile of origin' which the person retains

---

[7] *Mohd Iqbal* 1870/71 (87) (unreported).
[8] See generally *Halsbury's Laws* (4th Edn.), Vol. 8, paras. 473 et seq.
[9] *Hyde v Hyde and Woodmansee* (1866) LR I P and D 130.
[10] *Chetti v Chetti* (1909) P 67.
[11] See *Shahnaz v Rizwan* [1964] 2 All ER 993; *Mohamed v Knott* [1968] 2 All ER 563.
[12] See Matrimonial Causes Act 1973, s. 11(d) in respect of marriages celebrated after 31 July 1971. A subsection similar to s. 11(d) was added to the Nullity of Marriage Act 1971 by the Matrimonial Proceedings (Polygamous Marriages) Act 1972, s. 4. This legislation was consolidated in the 1973 Act. It seems clear that the decision to make specific legislative provision was simply to express in statutory form what was thought already to be the common law. Thus in practice there is no significance in the 31 July 1971 date.

until he acquires a new domicile.[13] A person may change his domicile and thus acquire for himself a domicile of choice by residing in another country with the intention of residing there for an unlimited time, and with no intention of returning to the country where he was previously domiciled for anything more than temporary purposes.[14]

The issue of domicile has been considered in a number of appeals under the immigration rules, and while each case depends on its own facts, the following cases give some indication of the approach taken by the appellate authorities. In *Afza Mussarat*,[15] a man of Pakistani origin, resident in the UK for seven years, and a UK citizen, travelled back to Pakistan and contracted a second marriage, which was to the appellant. The marriage was lawful under Pakistani law. The application for an entry certificate was rejected since it was considered that the sponsor had acquired a domicile of choice in England and thus the second marriage would be invalid. On appeal, the application was allowed because it was held on the facts (the sponsor had given evidence that his first wife was to remain in Pakistan, he himself eventually wanted to open a business there, and that he would spend his last days in that country) that the sponsor had taken no steps to acquire a domicile in England since the acquisition of UK citizenship did not in itself indicate a change of domicile.

The husband in *Ishiodu*[16] entered into a second marriage in Nigeria by native custom. The marriage was potentially polygamous. He had resided in England for 12 years from 1961, the first six years as a student, and then as a businessman. He had lived with his first wife (married in Nigeria) and children until she died in 1970. He did not return to Nigeria in 1967 at the end of his studies because of the civil war there. He had prospered in the UK as a businessman, had properties in both countries, and had retained his Nigerian citizenship as well as a number of social links in Nigeria. It was held that the pattern of the sponsor's life did not show an 'intention of continuing to reside (in England) for an unlimited time' and accordingly the sponsor had retained his Nigerian domicile of origin. In *Haq*[17] the sponsor had contracted a second

---

[13] *Undy v Undy* [1869] LR I Sc and Div 441 HL. The subject of domicile is too vast to be dealt with here. For a full examination of the subject see Cheshire, *Private International Law*, 10th Edn., Ch. VII, and *Halsbury's Laws* (4th Edn.), Vol. 8, paras. 421 et seq.

[14] *Winans v AG* [1904] AC 287.

[15] [1972] Imm AR 45 (an adjudicator's decision).

[16] [1975] Imm AR 56.

[17] 385/70 (unreported).

marriage in Pakistan while the first was still subsisting. The applicant's second wife was refused admission under the rules. The factors which led the adjudicator to conclude that the husband had acquired a domicile of choice in England were (1) he had lived in England since coming from Pakistan in 1959; (2) he had married an English woman in 1962 and had established a family; (3) he had begun in employment but later established his own business; (4) he had purchased his own house in England; (5) he had registered as a UK citizen; and (6) he had declared in his divorce petition in 1974 that he was domiciled in England and Wales.

8.25 A potentially polygamous marriage may be converted into a monogamous marriage. The most frequent instance is where one party changes his or her domicile.[18] As particular hardship would be caused if the immigration authorities did not accept a woman who entered into a potentially polygamous marriage as a 'wife' under the immigration rules, it has been the Home Office practice to admit the wife of a man settled in the UK if the authorities are satisfied that the marriage although potentially polygamous was *de facto* monogamous.[19] The practice has not always been brought to the attention of the Tribunal. The Home Office has now given guidance to entry clearance officers that where the invalidity of a marriage is not relied on as a ground for refusal because the entry clearance officer is satisfied that the marriage is *de facto* monogamous, there is no reason for a reference to it to be included in the explanatory statement. An instruction on Home Office policy in this regard has also been issued to officers who are responsible for presenting the Home Office case to the appellate authorities.[20]

8.26 The following situations may arise where a man settled in the UK has contracted two polygamous marriages: (1) both are valid in English law because each of the parties had the capacity to contract the marriage under the law of his or her domicile and they were valid by the law of the countries in which they were celebrated: thus, in very rare cases two wives may qualify for entry under the immigration rules; (2) neither is valid in English law because the man was domiciled in England at the time of each marriage: neither wife would be able to satisfy the immigra-

---

[18] *Ali v Ali* [1966] 1 All ER 664. There are other events which may convert the marriage, e.g. a party changing his or her religion to a monogamous one or where the law under which the marriage is celebrated prohibits polygamy as a result of subsequent legislation.

[19] Letter, Home Office to JCWI, 10 October 1979, which also sets out the practice adopted by the authorities in the situations set out in para. 8.26, post.

[20] Letters, Home Office to JCWI, 12 December 1980; 3 January 1981.

tion authorities that her marriage was not *de facto* as well as potentially polygamous, but in such circumstances it would be open to one of the wives to seek entry as a fiancée with subsequent settlement once a valid marriage had taken place under English law; (3) the first is valid in English law, but the second is not valid in English law because the man became domiciled in England between the dates of the two marriages: There would be serious difficulties in satisfying an entry clearance officer that the second wife would be admissible as a partner to a *de facto* monogamous marriage on the basis of an assurance that the first wife would not exercise her right to come, although if satisfactory evidence could be provided of the death or divorce of the first wife, the second would then be eligible to apply for entry as a fiancée and contract a marriage valid in England after her arrival. Finally, it should be noted that English courts can now give matrimonial relief and make declarations concerning the validity of a polygamous marriage.[1]

Proxy Marriages

8.27 Marriage by proxy is recognised by English law if the law of the place of the celebration of the marriage permits the marriage to be celebrated by proxy.[2] The domicile of the parties is not a relevant factor.[3] Thus, although a marriage by proxy cannot be celebrated in England, a person domiciled in England and Wales who has signed the appropriate document conferring authority by the proxy may enter into a valid marriage in another country provided the ceremony was valid under that country's laws. These principles hold good even if the matrimonial home is to be England.[4]

Permanent Association

8.28 The rules specify that a woman living in permanent association with a man has no claim to enter, but may be admitted, as if she were his wife, 'due account being taken of any local tradition tending to establish

[1] Matrimonial Causes Act 1973, s. 47(4).
[2] *Apt* v *Apt* [1947] 2 All ER 677. See also *Nazir Begum* [1976] Imm AR 31.
[3] Unless the law of the country where the marriage is celebrated makes it a requirement that the parties should be domiciled in that country, e.g. Nigeria. See also *Chukuri* 587/73 (329) (unreported) and *Ayomano* 2421/71 (unreported).
[4] *Ponticelli* v *Ponticelli* [1958] 1 All ER 357.

the permanence of the association.'[5] A woman will not, however, be admitted (1) unless any previous marriage by either party has permanently broken down; (2) if the man has already been joined by his wife or another woman under this provision, whether or not the relationship subsists.[6]

The rule is designed to cover not only single persons co-habiting as man and wife, but also cases where one or other of the parties may already be married and unable to obtain a dissolution although the marriage has permanently broken down.[7] A woman whose marriage to the sponsor is not recognised in English law because of a subsisting marriage, and who therefore cannot enter as a wife, may be admitted under this rule. In *Amat ul Hafiz*,[8] the sponsor had purported to divorce his first wife and had two children by the appellant who was accepted as his wife by the people in her locality. The Tribunal found that although they had only lived together on his visits to Pakistan, they had had a 'permanent association' for some years. Second or other wives of polygamous marriages will not be able to gain admission by the use of this rule. The Tribunal so held in *Jahanara Begum*,[9] when it was stated that the rule,

'... was not intended to be used to enable men, coming from countries in which polygamy was lawful, to bring to this country for settlement more than one wife and her children. Indeed this paragraph makes this clear when referring to a woman being admitted "as if she were his wife".'

Although there may be some reluctance on the part of the appellate authorities to allow entry where the parties have a 'Western' cultural background, the phrase 'due account being taken of local tradition ...'

---

[5] HC 394, para. 45.
[6] Ibid.
[7] *Hessing* [1972] Imm AR 134.
[8] 7139/7 (1180) (unreported). But this provision could not be used to bring in the wife of a second marriage, the first still subsisting where the marriage was, in Pakistan according to Muslim rites: permanent association between a man and a woman outside marriage is foreign to the Islamic community: *Shamin Begum* 23318/78 (1150) (unreported).
[9] 12361–3/77 (1261) (unreported), but referred to and reaffirmed in *Zahara* [1979–80] Imm AR 48; see also *Zaitoon Begum* 21809/77 (1642) (unreported); *Nazim Akhtar* 43199/79 (1992) (unreported).

is not restricted to any particular part of the world. Finally, there must be evidence that the relationship is permanent and those who have lived together for a very short time are unlikely to succeed. A period of six to eight weeks is likely to be regarded as insufficient.[10]

CHILDREN

8.29 One of the most distressing aspects of the system of immigration control is that the rules have been framed strictly to limit the number of children who are able to join their parents settled here. The Tribunal has tended to give effect to this policy, which affects particularly those children from black Commonwealth countries, by consistently supporting a narrow interpretation of the rules.

The rules provide for the admission for settlement of children under the age of 18 as dependants if they meet a number of requirements;

(1) they enter in one of the following circumstances:
    (a) *both parents* are settled in the UK;
    (b) *both parents* are on the same occasion admitted for settlement;
    (c) *one parent* is settled in the UK and *the other* is on the same occasion admitted for settlement;
    (d) *one parent* is dead and *the other* is on the same occasion admitted for settlement;
    (e) *one parent* is settled in the UK or is on the same occasion admitted for settlement and has had the sole responsibility for the child's upbringing;
    (f) *one parent*, or a *relative* other than a parent, is settled or accepted for settlement in the UK and there are serious and compelling family or other considerations which make exclusion undesirable, for example, where the other parent is physically or mentally incapable of looking after the child, and suitable arrangements have been made for the child's care;[11]

---

[10] *Bruder* 41024/79 (1545) (unreported), where the Tribunal affirmed the adjudicator's decision. The adjudicator concluded that the rule was designed inter alia to deal with situations where there was a long term impediment which frustrated the parties' wish to marry, but not, as in this case where one of the parties was reluctant to enter into a marriage. See also *Barbillar* 20007/77 (1366) (unreported) and *Buckley* 3814/76 (1011)(unreported).

[11] HC 394, para. 46.

(2) those whom the child is joining are able and willing to support and accommodate the child without recourse to public funds, in accommodation of their own or which they occupy;[12]
(3) an entry clearance had been granted to the child for this purpose;[13]
(4) the child is unmarried at the date of entry.[14]

8.30 Children aged 18 or over must qualify for settlement in their own right.[15] The only exception is that 'special consideration may be given' to fully dependent and unmarried daughters who are over 18 and under 21 forming part of the family unit overseas, and have no other relatives in their own country to turn to. Any other children, whatever their age, will only qualify 'in the most exceptional compassionate circumstances', i.e. where they meet the requirements laid down for 'other relatives' described later.[16]

Definition of Parent

8.31 A 'parent' under the rules includes (1) the stepfather of a child whose father is dead; (2) the stepmother if the mother is dead; (3) the father as well as the mother of an illegitimate child; and (4) an adoptive parent if there has been a genuine transfer of parental responsibility because of the original parents' inability to care for the child, and the adoption has not been arranged merely to facilitate the child's admission.[17]

Both Parents Settled in the UK

8.32 If both parents are settled here but are separated, Home Office practice is to admit the child, although the Tribunal has held that on a proper construction of the rules, entry must be refused. In *Pinnock*,[18] the

[12] Ibid., para. 42.
[13] Ibid., para. 43.
[14] Ibid., para. 46.
[15] Ibid., para. 47.
[16] See para. 8.48, post.
[17] HC 394, para. 46. The adoptive parent must also show that the child qualifies for entry within the rules: *Ieong* 38423/78 (1991) (unreported). There is no requirement that the child be 'legally adopted' as defined in the Immigration Act 1971, s. 33(i), viz. that the adoption be 'specified as an "overseas adoption" by order of the Secretary of State under the Adoption Act 1968, s. 4 (3).' See *Mathieu* [1979–80] Imm AR 157. Adoption procedures are discussed at para. 8.41, post.
[18] [1974] Imm AR 22.

appellant was coming to join his mother in London. His father was presumed resident in Birmingham but had not seen the mother or child for more than 10 years. The Tribunal, in dismissing the appeal on the ground that there was no evidence to show the father was in this country, commented that even if it were proved that he were here, the appeal would have failed because the child was not coming to join both parents here.[19]

Same Occasion Admitted for Settlement

8.33 It is not sufficient that one parent accompanies the child to join the other parent settled here. The accompanying parent must also intend to settle in the UK. The Tribunal so held in *Ibrahim*,[20] where the sponsor's wife had no plans to settle but intended to return to Pakistan immediately after the child was admitted. Furthermore, the sponsor's declared intention to retire to Pakistan as soon as the child was settled was adjudged to be contrary to the purposes of the rule which was designed to reunite families. It is Home Office practice not to refuse entry to a child who has not travelled with his parent or parents where it is clear that this was because of booking difficulties and the parent is due to arrive very shortly.

Discrepancies

8.34 As in the cases involving wives, many decisions turn on the question of whether the child is that of the parents. The exact age of the child may be disputed to cast doubt that the father was in the country of origin at the time of conception, or to show that the child is too old to qualify under the rules or that he is not a child of the marriage. Difficulties may be considerable where the family comes from a country which does not keep public records as a matter of course.

Discrepancies may arise because the sponsor in the UK has in the past made false claims in respect of children for income tax allowance. There is a fear to tell the entry clearance officer the true position because of the risk of prosecution. The Policy Division of the Inland Revenue has stated,

'While it is not possible to give an absolute guarantee to cover every case . . . the Board do not normally prosecute in those cases where a complete and spontaneous confession to a false claim to personal allowances is

[19] See also *Mohd Ibrahim* 9994/76 (976) (unreported).
[20] [1978] Imm AR 18.

made. In such a case the Board is empowered to accept a monetary settlement. Similar treatment is usually accorded where there is a ready confession on challenge, and a monetary settlement has also been reached in many cases where there has not been an immediate confession on challenge, but where, before the investigation has gone too far, the claimant has sought advice and then confessed.'[1]

8.35 The Government's Chief Medical Officer in his report on the medical examination of immigrants endorsed the view that the use of X-rays of the limb bones of children provides 'a useful, fairly accurate and acceptably safe' way of estimating their age;[2] X-rays should not, however, be used for age estimates in adults aged 21 years or over, and entry clearance officers have been instructed accordingly. The accuracy as well as the ethics of this method of age estimation has, however, been powerfully challenged.[3]

Sole Responsibility

8.36 A large number of cases before the Tribunal involve single parents whose children wish to join them, where eligibility for entry depends on their showing that they have had the sole responsibility for the child's upbringing. The first case of significance was *McGillivary*,[4] an adjudicator's determination, but accepted as 'being broadly in line (with the Tribunal's approach) . . . providing a wide-ranging survey of the factors which are relevant when considering the practical application of the words "sole responsibility"'. The adjudicator held that mere demonstration of legal responsibility was not enough: 'an attitude of thoughtfulness and care' must be shown in addition to providing or ensuring the provision of material necessities. Moreover, the parent had to show responsibility for the child throughout its life. But 'sole responsibility' was not to be strictly interpreted so as to prevent an appeal

---

[1] Letter, Inland Revenue Policy Division to Tower Hamlets Law Centre, 21 September 1979.

[2] *The Medical Examination of Immigrants:* Report by the Chief Medical Officer, Sir Henry Yellowlees, published by the Home Office; especially Appendix 1. Examples of the use of X-rays in the past can be found in *Miah* [1972] Imm AR 185; *Iqbal Haque* [1974] Imm AR 51.

[3] See, for example, *The Guardian*, 26 November 1980, letter from N. Cameron, Institute of Child Health University of London. A critique is contained in a privately published report, 'The Use of X-rays for Age Determination in Immigration Control' by Edward White, research assistant to Lord Avebury.

[4] [1972] Imm AR 63.

succeeding if it were found another person had some responsibility for the child, otherwise every application under the rules would be bound to fail.[5] This was confirmed by the Tribunal in *Emmanuel*,[6]

'It appears plain to us that there must be in nearly all cases some form of responsibility of the relative or grandmother with whom the child lives. . . . We do not therefore think the literal or absolute sole responsibility of the parent in the UK could ever be established.'

The Tribunal added that the issue is not to be decided only between one parent and the other parent. The decision in each case will depend on its own particular facts and involve consideration, *inter alia*, of the sources and degree of financial support for the child and whether there is cogent evidence of genuine interest and affection for the child by the parent sponsoring the application. In *Emmanuel*, the parent was successful because the mother was able to show that she had retained 'a close interest in and affection for her daughter'. But in *Martin*,[7] the child's appeal failed, although it was accepted that the sponsor had the principal financial responsibility. There were other members of the family in the West Indies contributing to the child's support and it was found that before the mother had emigrated the child had at times been left in the care of the grandmother.

In *Sloley*,[8] the appellant was successful because of (1) the source and degree of financial support (the sponsor mother had provided sole support for nine years), and (2) she had demonstrated a continuing and positive concern for the child's welfare and upbringing. This case was distinguished in *Martin (SS)*,[9] where the sponsor mother had not been the sole financial support of the child, and while the mother had always been interested in her daughter's academic progress and general welfare, there was no evidence to show continuous consultation between her and the guardian overseas in which the guardian sought advice and approval regarding the child's upbringing and activities.[10]

---

[5] The adjudicator relied heavily on *Re B (GA)* (an infant) [1963] 3 All ER 125, to show that the words should not be construed in their most literal terms.

[6] [1972] Imm AR 69.

[7] [1972] Imm AR 69.

[8] [1973] Imm AR 54.

[9] [1978] Imm AR 100.

[10] For other examples of unsuccessful applications, see *Pusey* [1972] Imm AR 240; *Williams* [1972] Imm AR 207; *Eugene* [1975] Imm AR 111.

Family Considerations: Compassionate Grounds

8.37 Admission can be authorised for a child to join one parent (or relative) even where that person has not had sole responsibility, if it can be shown that there are *'serious and compelling* family or other considerations which make exclusion undesirable'.[11] The words emphasised have been added in the new rules; otherwise the wording is identical to the old rules. As the immigration and appellate authorities have always interpreted this rule narrowly, it is submitted that there has been no substantive change. Indeed, the example given in the rules of where exclusion would be undesirable '. . . where the other parent is physically or mentally incapable of looking after the child'[12] remains unaltered.

8.38 The Tribunal's approach can be ascertained from the decision in *Howard*.[13] There, a child of 15 applied to join her father in the UK. Her mother, who had played no role at all in her upbringing, gave her consent for the child to come here. The father, who had been settled here for several years, was particularly anxious that the appellant should join him as it was unlikely that he and his wife (he had since married in the UK) would be able to have children. The paternal grandmother with whom the child had been staying was now old and suffering from osteo-arthritis. The Tribunal in dismissing the appeal held that the family or other considerations which make exclusion undesirable must be applied to the country in which the appellant lives and not to those pertaining in the UK. In the particular case, there was 'no evidence before us that the child is unhappy or suffering from conditions which make her present life intolerable'. The effect of the decision is that argument about comparative facilities in the two countries is irrelevant. It cannot be put forward as a ground in itself that the child can be offered better education, housing or medical treatment in this country.

Howard was not, however, the first case to be decided by the Tribunal. In *Cooper*,[14] which was determined less than a month earlier, the Tribunal allowed an appeal by a 15-year-old Jamaican girl who was living in overcrowded conditions. There was, however, a report which stated that her welfare would suffer if she were not admitted. The more humane approach adopted in this case was abandoned in favour of the *Howard* 'formula,' probably because it was realised that many children, particularly in the West Indies from where many of the applications

[11] HC 394, para. 46.
[12] Ibid.
[13] [1972] Imm AR 93. See also *Rennie* [1979–80] Imm AR 117.
[14] 434/70 (unreported).

originated, lived in overcrowded conditions, and that it could be quite justifiably argued in a large number of cases that children would suffer hardships if they were not permitted to join an obviously caring parent here.

The Tribunal has amplified *Howard* in a number of subsequent decisions. It has held that lack of employment in the country of origin is not a proper consideration;[15] nor is the fact that the parent here would suffer hardship if the child were not admitted. Moreover it must be shown that the conditions establishing a claim to be admitted exist at the time the application is made; it is not sufficient that they are imminent.[16] It has been held, however, that the fact that there were far worse conditions elsewhere in the child's country was not relevant in deciding whether conditions were bad for the child as these conditions were not made better by the existence of even worse conditions.[17]

8.39 An example of a situation which the Tribunal accepted made exclusion undesirable can be found in *Holmes*,[18] where the facts were that the appellant was a girl of 12 living with her mother and five half-brothers aged nine to one and a half years in a single room in an overcrowded tenement where there were two beds (one single), a dresser and a cabinet all in a dilapidated condition; the kitchen and sanitary facilities were shared by five other families. The mother was receiving irregular payments from the father of the brothers and was going to join him in Canada. She was reluctant to take the appellant, who would be an outsider. Further, the appellant's maternal grandmother was too frail to look after her. In these circumstances she was allowed to join her father in London. It is current policy that children under 12 seeking to join a single parent settled in the UK should be regarded as within the definition of those whose exclusion would be undesirable, provided that, if the parent is the mother, she can provide adequate accommodation or, if the parent is the father, there is suitable accommodation and a female relative resident in the household willing to look after the child and capable of doing so.[19]

---

[15] *Williams* [1972] Imm AR 207, but not in *Lakhoo* 1735/72 (unreported), where the appellant was successful, since he could not obtain work because of a discriminatory policy against non-citizens in Kenya.
[16] *Noel* 704/71 (unreported).
[17] *Holmes* [1975] Imm AR 20.
[18] Ibid.
[19] Mr Timothy Raison, Minister of State at the Home Office 976 H. of C. Official Report, 19 December 1979. Written Answers, col. 220.

Children over 18

8.40 The rules emphasise that children over 18 must qualify in their own right, and now limit the circumstances where special consideration is to be given to *daughters* only who (1) are fully dependent; (2) are unmarried; (3) are between 18 and 21; (4) formed part of the family unit overseas; and (5) have no other close relatives to turn to.[20]

In *Rhyek*[1] the Tribunal held that the rules must be read in conjunction with the rules relating to children under 18; for example, a child of a one-parent family must show that the parent had sole responsibility or there were serious and compelling considerations making exclusion undesirable. It further held that the relevant date in testing these criteria is the date the family ceased living together overseas: there is nothing in the rules requiring the appellant to show that he remained a member of the family at the date of the application. The purpose of the rule is 'to enable family units which are broken up to be reunited'.

This and the cases referred to below were decided under the old rules which also applied to sons under 21. The rule has been tightened by imposing the additional requirement that the daughter must have no other close relatives to turn to.[2] Almost all the cases turn on the issue of whether the applicant forms part of the family unit. In *Bernard*,[3] the appellant was 19, an unmarried mother with a child of two. She lived with an aunt, received some financial support from her parents but more from the child's father with whom she was in some contact. Her application in 1973 to join her parents and five siblings was rejected. No cogent reasons had been disclosed why her parents had not attempted to regroup the family sooner (they had come to England in 1960 and 1964 and the rest of the children had come in 1973); the evidence showed a reasonably close association with the father of her child and it appeared she had already formed or was about to form her own family unit.[4] The rule '... is designed to enable family unity to be maintained in certain circumstances and to prevent the splitting up of a family who are accustomed to their mutual companionship and support'. The Tribunal so held in *Thomas*,[5] where the appeal was dismissed because the appellant

---

[20] HC 394, para. 47.

[1] 6211/80 (1982) (unreported).

[2] Cf., with HC 79 para. 44, and HC 81, para. 39, and see para. 8.47, post.

[3] [1976] Imm AR 7.

[4] See also *Nethline White* 242/74 (380) (unreported); referred to in *Bernard*.

[5] 5086/76 (986) (unreported) and similarly in *Walker* 12842/75 (1066) (unreported) where the parents had left the appellants when they were babies and had not seen them since, apart from a one month visit some years earlier.

had never seen his father at all, and had not seen his mother since he was four or five months old; he had therefore never formed part of a 'family unit' overseas.

Adoption

8.41 There is no provision in the immigration rules for a child to be brought to the UK for adoption.[6] The Home Secretary may, however, exercise his discretion, and exceptionally allow a child to be brought to the UK for adoption where he is satisfied that the intention to adopt under UK law is genuine and not merely a device for gaining entry; that the child's welfare in this country is assured; and that the court in the UK is likely to grant an adoption order.[7] Adoption cannot usually take place in English law unless the child is living in England[8] and is in the care and possession of the prospective adopters.[9] One of the adopters must be domiciled in the UK[10] and, if the child is under 16, they must give notice to the local authority of their intention to apply for an adoption order. An order cannot be made until at least three months has elapsed since the date on which the notice was given.[11] An application for an adoption order is made either to the High Court or to a county court, and an order cannot be made until the court is satisfied that all the necessary consents have been obtained, that the order will be for welfare of the child, and that the applicants have not received any payment or award in respect of the adoption.[12]

8.42 The procedure required by the Home Office is for the representatives of the intending adopters in the country where the child is living to apply to the nearest British Government representative for an entry clearance for the child to come to the UK. The entry clearance officer will ask to see (1) a written declaration from the child's parents that they

[6] See, e.g. *Malik* 61512/80 (2014) (unreported) which reaffirmed that the proposed parents cannot be regarded as adoptive parents under the old rule: HC 81, para. 38 (now HC 394, para. 46).

[7] The Home Office provides a document detailing the procedure for those considering adoption. The document should be consulted before any steps to adopt are taken. Details can be obtained by writing to the Home Office at Croydon.

[8] See *Re B (an infant)* [1967] 2 All ER 629. Where the child is or may be domiciled abroad or is a foreign national or was until recently resident abroad, the court should consider whether the order will be recognised elsewhere unless the making of the order is clearly for the child's welfare.

[9] Adoption Act 1958, s. 3(1).

[10] Childrens Act 1975 ss. 10(2) and 11(2).

[11] Adoption Act 1958 s. 3(2).

[12] Childrens Act 1975 s. 22.

understand what is involved and freely consent to the child going to the UK for adoption; and (2) a written declaration from the prospective adopters that they intend to initiate adoption proceedings after the arrival of the child and undertake to repatriate him if for some reason the adoption does not take place. The application is then referred to the Home Office with any other relevant details for further enquiries to be made on behalf of the Department of Health and Social Security, to make sure that the interests of the child would be fully safeguarded. If the outcome is satisfactory, an entry clearance is then authorised. When the child comes to the UK he will be admitted initially for a limited period, normally six months. If the adoption hearing is unlikely to be held before the end of that period, leave to remain for a further period will be granted on application. Once an adoption order has been made the child's passport should be forwarded to the Home Office for endorsement. The child will become a citizen of the UK and Colonies[13] in the case of a joint adoption, if the father is a UK citizen, and in the case of one person adopting alone, if that person is a UK citizen.[14] If the child does not become a UK citizen he will be granted indefinite leave to remain.

Difficulties can arise if the prospective adopters by-pass this procedure and effect an adoption overseas. Particular care must be taken to ensure that there has been a valid adoption in the country where the child is living. In *Malik*,[15] the Tribunal upheld the refusal of an entry clearance for a child alleged to have been adopted in Pakistan, as Pakistan had no adoption law, and an appeal failed in *Merchant*,[16] because the Tribunal found that the provisions for adoption under Indian law had not been complied with.

PARENTS AND GRANDPARENTS

8.43 The immigration rules severely limit the circumstances in which parents may join their children settled here. The following provisions apply equally to grandparents.[17] Those who may be admitted are

---

[13] He will also be patrial: Immigration Act 1971, s. 2(1) (a).

[14] See para. 2.10, ante.

[15] [1972] Imm AR 37. 'Close relatives' is not defined, but the Home Office consider them to be relatives to whom a person can reasonably be expected to turn: Letter, Home Office to North Kirklees Community Relations Council, 20 June 1980.

[16] [1975] Imm AR 49.

[17] HC 394, paras. 48, 49.

(1) widowed[18] mothers of whatever age; (2) fathers who are widowers aged 65 or over; (3) parents travelling together of whom one is 65 or over; provided,

(a) they are wholly or mainly dependent on their sons or daughters settled in the UK;
(b) those children have the means to support their parents and any other relatives who would be admissible as dependants of the parents[19] and are able and willing to do so without recourse to public funds;[20]
(c) those children have for the parent(s) adequate accommodation of their own or which they occupy;
(d) the parents are without close relatives in their own country to turn to;
(e) they obtain entry clearance granted for this purpose.[1]

Moreover, where a parent has remarried, admission will not be granted if he or she can look for support to the spouse or children of the second marriage. If support is not available, entry will still be refused unless the children here can show they have sufficient means and accommodation to support not only the parent and step-parent, but also any children of the second marriage who would be admissible as dependants.[2]

Finally, where they are under 65, a widowed father or grandfather and parents (or grandparents) travelling together will only be admitted where they are living alone 'in the most exceptional compassionate circumstances including having a standard of living substantially below that of (his) own country'.[3] The present rules differ from the old rules by the addition of the requirement that parents and grandparents must be without other close relatives in their country to turn to.[4]

Definitions

8.44 The rules do not permit unmarried mothers to enter under any of these even if it can be shown that the putative father is dead,[5] a situation

---

[18] Although the rules are silent on the point, it is the Home Office practice to treat divorced parents as widows or widowers.

[19] Ibid., para. 48.

[20] Ibid., para. 42.

[1] Ibid., para. 42.

[2] Ibid., para. 49.

[3] Ibid., para. 48. They must meet the qualifications for 'other relatives'. See para. 8.48, post.

[4] As to the old rules see HC 79, para. 45; HC 81, para. 40. See also para. 8.53, post.

[5] *Phillips* [1973] Imm AR 47, decided under earlier rules.

which severely affects those from the West Indies where there are a significant number of unmarried mothers whose children have settled here. Similarly a divorced mother cannot qualify.[6] 'Parent' excludes a step-parent.[7]

Dependency

8.45 There is no clear indication as to the standard of living of the parent which would justify the description that he is 'wholly or mainly' dependent on his children. The test is subjective. In *Syal*,[8] the Tribunal (in 1972) described as 'very meagre' a pension of £7.25 per month received in India by the appellant, a former teacher. The Tribunal found that he was 'mainly dependent' on his son and seemed to accept the argument that his standard of living was not to be compared with those in India in menial positions.

Dependency must arise out of necessity and not through the deliberate conduct of the parent. In *Zaman*,[9] an elderly farmer and his wife applied to join their son in the UK. The father owned two farms in his native Pakistan and the income from these was given away to three sons who were still resident in that country. This left the parents wholly dependent upon monies remitted to them from this country by their son. The adjudicator held that the word 'dependency' might not mean financial dependency alone, and that the term could also embrace physical and emotional elements. On appeal the Tribunal stated,

'In our view the purpose lying behind (the immigration rule) is to enable widowed mothers and elderly parents to join children in this country who have been supporting them because the resources of the parents are insufficient to meet their own needs. We agree with the view expressed by the adjudicator that such parents, to make a successful application must show that they are necessarily so dependent . . . there is (no) evidence to show that the appellants are to any extent physically or emotionally dependent on the sponsor.'

This approach was confirmed in *Hasan (Bibi Musa)*,[10] where the two younger brothers of the sponsor (aged 18 and 15) were held to be capable

[6] *Nisa* [1979–80] Imm AR 20, but see note 18, ante.
[7] *Bajas* 9086/75 (1105) (unreported).
[8] 441/72(6) (unreported).
[9] [1973] Imm AR 71.
[10] [1976] Imm AR 28.

of supplementing the mother's earnings. Moreover, it has to be shown that the applicant was mainly or wholly dependent at the time of the application. Thus in the case of *Kolb*,[11] a widowed father of 67 years of age applied to join his son. When interviewed he stated that he would be retiring in four or five months' time and that he would become destitute as he would not be in receipt of a pension from his employment. The Tribunal held that the rules were 'quite unambiguous' and did not allow for a dependency which was merely imminent.[12] If the dependency has arisen while the parent was in the UK for some other purpose, e.g. a visit, an application for settlement can now be made.[13]

Accommodation

8.46 The rules now require that the accommodation provided is either owned or occupied by the children. It will therefore no longer be sufficient for the children to show that accommodation belonging to others is available for the parents.[14]

No Other Close Relatives to Turn to

8.47 It is to be hoped that when interpreting this provision the Tribunal will follow its decision in *Chadva*.[15] In that case where the question of dependency was at issue, it was held that even though there were others overseas capable of supporting the parent, admission would be justified if she could not compel them to support her.

OTHER RELATIVES

8.48 The extent to which other relatives may be admitted is even more strictly limited by the present rules. Firstly, the only relatives who qualify are sons, daughters, sisters, brothers, uncles and aunts.[16] This differs from the old rules which allowed for the admission of more

[11] 1705/72 (67) (unreported). See also *Seedat* [1975] Imm AR 126.
[12] But there is nothing to prevent a further application once the dependency arises.
[13] HC 394, para. 119. The decision in *Bano* [1973] Imm AR 41, made under earlier rules, is no longer applicable. Care nevertheless should be taken in making such applications as an application may be refused if there has been a breach of an undertaking regarding the duration and purpose of stay. See HC 394, para. 88, para. 9.4, post.
[14] See the ruling under earlier rules in *Ind Kaur Baidwar* [1975] Imm AR 126, para. 8.50, post.
[15] 9947/76 (1030) (unreported).
[16] HC 394, para. 48. Parents and grandparents, under the age limits may also qualify.

distant relatives[17] in certain circumstances. Secondly, to qualify for entry relatives must show that[18] (1) they are living alone; (2) there are the most exceptional compassionate circumstances including their having a standard of living substantially below that of their own country; (3) they are mainly dependent on relatives settled in the UK;[19] (4) the sponsor is able and willing to maintain and accommodate them without recourse to public funds; (5) the accommodation provided is owned by the sponsor or is occupied by him,[20] (6) they have obtained entry clearance granted for this purpose.

There are no longer any limitations on the age of the applicant.[1]

Exceptional Compassionate Circumstances

8.49 In *Sacha*,[2] a mentally retarded woman was allowed to join her half-brother because she was in need of care and attention, her cousin in India was a not very willing custodian, and she would receive much better attention from her half-brother who had brought her up and whose affection for her was manifest. But in *Buike*,[3] the Tribunal, dismissing the appeal for other reasons, was not prepared to concede exceptional circumstances where a family had been through a very harrowing experience in Chittagong, had been displaced from their home and sought refuge in Pakistan.

The requirement regarding the standard of living means in effect that applicants from some countries appear to have to show a suffering from conditions little short of malnutrition. However, in *Mukhopadyay*,[4] where the appellant was from India, the Tribunal commented that 'if the lowest standard were to be taken as the correct criterion it seems to us that very few, if any, persons from the subcontinent could bring themselves within the provisions (of the relevant immigration rule)'. Although dismissing the appeal, the Tribunal accepted that regard must be had to the applicant's circumstances and to those of his family and the circle in which he moved in order to make realistic comparisons of their

---

[17] The old rules are set out in HC 79, para. 46; HC 81, para. 41. See para. 8.54, post.
[18] HC 394, para. 48.
[19] But if the relative can remain overseas and be equally as well supported, the application may fail: *Joginder Kaur* [1977] Imm AR 101, see also *Karsan* 55577/79 (1978) (unreported).
[20] Ibid., para. 42.
[1] The old rules required the relatives to be 65 or over.
[2] [1973] Imm AR 5.
[3] 43/72 (41) (unreported).
[4] [1975] Imm AR 42.

respective standards of living and to ascertain if the applicant's 'standard of living' had fallen 'substantially below' that of his relatives and friends. The Tribunal has, however, been unwilling to follow its own reasoning. In *Seth*,[5] the adjudicator had allowed the appeal of a recently widowed mother of 28 who was being cared for in Kenya by a cousin living there: both parents were dead and her nearest relatives were her sponsors, a brother and sister living in the UK. The adjudicator had 'no hesitation' in holding that she was a distressed relative within the rules, finding that:

'. . . she is an educated woman and the widow of a physician and her present standard of living, through no fault of her own, is pitifully low compared with her brother and sister who even by United Kingdom standards can only be described as affluent. The circumstances whereby this young woman has found herself isolated from relatives is exceptional in an Asian country where family units are large. Most right-thinking Asians would regard her position as being not only insecure but unsafe.'

The Tribunal conceded that there were 'compassionate circumstance' but rejected the adjudicator's decision without giving reasons, and simply stating:

'. . . there are other cases of young widows with a child or children to bring up and to find that this is a very rare or exceptional case is, in our judgement, simply not warranted by, or in accordance with the facts of this case.'

The Tribunal also indicated that it was contemplated under the rule relating to distressed relatives that account should be taken of whether or not the position of an applicant could be ameliorated by financial assistance from the sponsor or other relatives.

The meaning of 'own country' was considered in *Levy*,[6] where the appellant was a stateless person aged 84 who had lived most of her life in Libya, but had spent the last 12 years in Jamaica. Her argument that because she was stateless she could not be said to have her 'own country' was rejected, the Tribunal approving the adjudicator's ruling that 'common sense suggests . . . the reference in the rules to "his own country" means the country to which the applicant is currently resident, or if he is there only temporarily, the country in which he is normally resident.'

[5] [1979–80] Imm AR 63.   [6] [1978] Imm AR 119.

The Old Rules

Dependants Generally

8.50 An applicant might be admitted where the sponsor's own accommodation was inadequate, provided that the sponsor could show there was other accommodation available or that *bona fide* arrangements had been made for acquiring additional accommodation.[7] Such accommodation did not have to be owned or occupied by the sponsor, nor could any undertakings on accommodation be requested.[8]

Permanent Association

8.51 While it was unlikely that admission would be given if there were evidence of marriage involving either party which was subsisting and had not broken down, the rules did not preclude leave being given.[9] More importantly, it was possible for the woman to be admitted even where the man had already been joined by his wife, or another woman admitted under this provision.[10]

Children

8.52 It was not specified that children under 18 had to be single and it is thus submitted that marriage in itself was not an obstacle to the admission of a child who could be shown to be dependent.[11] Sons between 18 and 21 would qualify if unmarried and fully dependent. Daughters did not have to show that they were dependent on their parents,[12] but it was necessary to prove that the whole family were settled in the UK or were being admitted for settlement.[13] In theory children over 21 did not qualify as distressed relatives, but the Home Office gave an assurance that the provisions under this category would be borne in mind by entry clearance officers in considering applications by sons or daughters.[14]

---

[7] *Baidwan (I K)* [1975] Imm AR 126.
[8] Cf., the wording of HC 79, para. 39 and HC 81, para. 34, with HC 394, para. 42.
[9] Cf., HC 79, para. 42 and HC 81, para. 37, with HC 394, paras. 42, 45, para. 8.28, ante.
[10] Ibid.
[11] Cf., HC 79, para. 43, and HC 81, para. 38, with HC 394, para. 46, para. 8.29, ante. The Tribunal has, however, indicated that a married woman was not admissible as a dependant of her parents: *Nessa* 11420/77 (1037) (unreported).
[12] Cf., HC 79, para. 44, and HC 81, para. 39, with HC 394, para. 47, para. 8.40, ante.
[13] Ibid. See also *Harmail Singh* v *Immigration Appeal Tribunal* [1978] Imm AR 140, and *Stewart* [1978] Imm AR 32.
[14] *Bashir* 1448/76 (1102) (unreported).

Parents and Grandparents

8.53 The rule[15] relating to parents and grandparents was similar to the present rule but without the requirements that (1) the accommodation provided is owned or occupied by the children; and (2) that the parents have no close relatives in their own country to turn to.

Those who did not meet the requirements under this category had to satisfy the criteria under 'distressed relatives'.[16]

Distressed Relatives

8.54 The criteria were identical to those required under 'other relatives' in the new rules,[17] but it was not necessary to show that the relative was mainly dependent on the sponsor in the UK.

Although brothers, sisters, aunts and uncles had to be over 65, it was unusual for admission to be refused on the grounds of age alone. The new rules place no restriction in this regard.[18] Sons and daughters were not included but in practice were admitted.[19] The rules allowed for more distant relatives to be admitted 'in the most exceptional compassionate circumstances'.[20]

Assistance by Practitioners

8.55 (1) Those who are consulted by a husband in this country can assist him to obtain entry clearance for his wife by obtaining the following:

(a) Evidence that the husband is settled in the UK. This takes the form of a declaration giving the husband's full name, address, details of his employment and passport and the date of his entry into the UK. If the husband is a non-EEC foreign national or, if a Commonwealth citizen, is not patrial or was not settled in the UK until after 1 January 1973, he must state in the declaration that he will be

---

[15] HC 79, para. 45; HC 81, para. 40.
[16] Following the principle in *Bashir*, and note 14, supra.
[17] Cf., HC 79, para. 46; HC 81, para. 41, with HC 394, para. 48. See para. 8.48, ante. The relative had to show 'isolation' (living alone with no relatives in his own country to turn to) and 'distress' (having a standard of living substantially below that of his own country). See *Tilak Ram* [1978] Imm AR 123, and *Sindhu* [1978] Imm AR 147.
[18] See para. 8.48, ante.
[19] See para. 8.52, note 14.
[20] E.g. daughter-in-law; see *Gurdev Kaur*, 567/72 (452) (unreported), and possibly a widowed sister-in-law: *Hardev Kaur* [1979–80] Imm AR 76.

a sponsor and he must give evidence of ability to support the wife and any dependent children without recourse to public funds.
- (b) Recent correspondence in the husband's possession from the wife or their immediate families, relating to the wife's proposed settlement.
- (c) Attested photocopies of the husband's passport. A solicitor attesting these should declare them to be true copies of the originals.
- (d) Independent evidence (if necessary) that the husband can support and accommodate the wife, including evidence that he has been sending her money for her support, if that be the case. To show that the husband can accommodate the wife, it is not sufficient to confirm that he owns a house. Although no local authority department has any responsibility to verify this, the local environmental health or social services department may be willing to assist by preparing a short report stating the number of people the house can accommodate, and whether or not it is fit for habitation.
- (e) Evidence that the husband was indeed single when the marriage took place, if he returned home to marry after spending some time in the UK. Form P2, the employee's notice of his tax coding, for the three years preceding this marriage is the best evidence of this.

(2) Similar advice as in (1)(a)–(d) above applies in the case of children.

(3) In cases where the child wishes to be admitted because there are serious and compelling family or other considerations, ensure whenever possible that there are social reports of the child's circumstances in his own country. A report should also be obtained from the environmental health or social services department of the local authority to show that accommodation in this country is satisfactory. The Embassy or High Commission of the country where the child is resident may be able to assist. Also the International Social Service of Great Britain can assist in obtaining reports from most countries.[1]

(4) Remember that often the only information available at the hearing is the Home Office explanatory statement based on information supplied by entry clearance officers. Entry clearance officers rarely make any detailed enquiries about the home circumstances of the child and rely heavily on the impression created by the child and accompanying relatives on interview. Their reports are frequently prejudiced and often misleading.

[1] See Appendix 5, post.

SETTLEMENT BY MARRIAGE

Husbands

8.56 A husband who wishes to join his wife for settlement in the UK will only be admitted if he can show[2] that his wife (1) is settled in the UK, or is on the same occasion being admitted for settlement; and (2) is a citizen of the UK and Colonies; and (3) was born in the UK or one of her parents was born in the UK. He must also show that in relation to the circumstances of the marriage none of the following apply:

(a) the marriage was entered into primarily to obtain admission into the UK; or
(b) one of the parties no longer has any intention of living permanently with the other as his spouse; or
(c) the parties to the marriage have not met.

Entry clearance must have been granted to him to join his wife on the basis of his marriage and he must not be subject to the general grounds of refusal, although admission is not to be refused on grounds of restricted returnability or on medical grounds.

A husband who meets these requirements is to be admitted initially for 12 months. He will be permitted to work[3] and at the end of that period will be given indefinite leave to remain, unless the immigration authorities have reason to believe that any of the circumstances referred to earlier exist, or unless the marriage has been terminated or there are deportation proceedings pending against him.[4]

Fiancés[5]

8.57 A fiancé who wishes to enter the UK to marry and remain on a permanent basis will only be admitted if he can show[6] that his fiancée

---

[2] See HC 394, paras. 50, 51.
[3] The rules do not specifically provide for this, but since a person entering as a fiancé will be permitted to work if an extension is given after marriage (HC 394, para. 116) it is inconceivable that those who enter as husbands will be treated differently.
[4] HC 394, para. 117.
[5] A fiancé must be more than a 'suitor'. There must be a firm intention by both parties to marry, but the Tribunal rejected an adjudicator's ruling that there must be a certainty (barring an event supervening which is outside the control of either party) that the marriage will take place. See *S K Singh* 31906/78 (1703) (unreported).
[6] Ibid., para. 52.

(1) is settled in the UK; (2) is a citizen of the UK and Colonies and (3) was born in the UK or one of her parents was born in the UK. He must also show that in relation to the circumstances of the proposed marriage none of the following apply:

(a) the primary purpose of the proposed marriage is to obtain admission to the UK; or
(b) there is no intention that he and his fiancée should live together permanently as man and wife; or
(c) he and his fiancée have not met.

Entry clearance must have been granted to him to enter on the basis of his proposed marriage, the entry clearance officer having been satisfied that adequate maintenance and accommodation will be available until the date of his marriage without recourse to public funds. Further he must not be subject to any of the general grounds which would justify refusal.

A person meeting these requirements is to be admitted for three months with a prohibition on employment and will be advised to apply to the Home Office once the marriage has taken place.[7] If the marriage does not take place within this three month period an extension of stay will only be granted if 'good cause' can be shown for the delay and there is satisfactory evidence that the marriage will take place 'shortly thereafter'.[8] On application after the marriage, a 12 month extension of stay will be granted and the prohibition on employment removed unless the immigration authorities have reason to believe that any of the matters concerning the circumstances of the marriage referred to earlier apply or unless the marriage has been terminated or there are deportation proceedings pending against him.[9] At the end of the 12 months he will on application be given indefinite leave to remain unless again any of the circumstances previously mentioned arise.[10]

8.58 A man who has been admitted in a temporary capacity who marries will only be given an extension if he can show that[11] his wife (1) is settled in the UK; (2) is a citizen of the UK and Colonies and (3) was born in the UK or one of her parents was born in the UK. He must also show that in relation to the circumstances of the marriage, none of the following apply:

---

[7] Ibid., para. 53.
[8] Ibid., para. 116.
[9] Ibid.
[10] Ibid.　　[11] Ibid., para. 117.

(a) the marriage was entered into primarily to obtain settlement here; or
(b) the parties to the marriage have not met; or
(c) he has remained in breach of the immigration laws before the marriage; or
(d) the marriage has taken place after a decision has been made to deport him or recommendation for deportation or notice given that he is liable to a recommendation; or
(e) the marriage has been terminated; or
(f) one of the parties no longer has any intention of living permanently with the other as his or her spouse.

If he satisfies these requirements, the husband will on application be given a 12 months' stay without a prohibition on employment.[12] At the end of that period, he will be given settlement if the Home Office is satisfied that none of the circumstances mentioned above apply.[13]

8.59 These rules are much more severe than the old rules.[14] The Home Secretary has said, however, that there still remains scope for discretion outside the rules where the wife does not have the qualifications set out in the rules but 'her connection with the UK is substantial'; examples given were daughters born to parents in Crown Service overseas, and adopted daughters who arrived from abroad in infancy and have lived here since. It was indicated that discretion would be exercised in other (but not specified) cases which would be considered on their merits.[15] There is very strong evidence to suggest that the rules are in breach of the European Commission on Human Rights: the rules discriminate against women not born in the UK even where they are patrial citizens of the UK and Colonies; moreover, they discriminate against the genuine arranged marriage where the parties have not met. The provision that the parties must have met is meaningless as the requirement is satisfied if the parties meet at the marriage ceremony: only fiancés and husbands who have married by proxy will be affected by the provision.

The effect of these provisions in relation to those who marry after they

---

[12] Ibid.
[13] Ibid.
[14] See paras. 8.64–8.65, post.
[15] 980 H. of C. Official Report 10 March 1980, Written Answers, col. 1100. The Home Office might also be sympathetic to an application where all the immediate family members of the wife were settled in the UK.

have overstayed is that they have no claim to remain under the rules even where the wife has the necessary qualification. They must ask the Home Office to exercise a discretion outside the rules.

8.60 A husband who having at one time been settled in the UK goes to live abroad may have difficulties on his return if he does not qualify for entry under the rules relating to returning residents, although his wife may be patrial or entitled to return in her own right. If his wife has the 'qualifications' under the rules there should be no problems; if the wife does not so qualify the Home Office has said that it would be prepared to look at the case in the light of the wife's connection with the UK to decide if a discretion outside the rules should be exercised:

'If a woman, whose connection with this country is not strong enough to qualify her husband for entry, has established her residence abroad with him . . . it might be difficult to argue that she would suffer hardship in having to live abroad with him. It is likely therefore that it would only be in exceptional circumstances that long absence would not weaken the case for the admission of her husband.'[16]

The phrase 'no longer has any intention of living permanently with the other as his or her spouse' was considered by the Tribunal in *Lipien*,[17] in the context of the old rules where the word 'permanently' was omitted. The parties separated and the evidence of the wife was that she did not view the separation as permanent but was not ready to live with her husband; she regarded the reasons for the separation as fundamental but believed there was a chance of getting back together. The husband said that he wanted to live with his wife and that it was realistic to think that there could be a reconciliation. The Tribunal held that the word 'any' is important:

'Where the parties are separated it seems to the Tribunal that for refusal to be justified one of the parties must have abandoned all future intention of resuming cohabitation with the other and that it is not a sufficient ground of refusal if one of the parties has not made up his or her mind, one way or the other, provided of course that that party is giving serious consideration to rejoining his or her partner. The rule does not place an

---

[16] Letter, Home Office to JCWI 28 March 1980. The Home Office advises the husband in this position to apply for entry clearance, presenting the full facts of his and his wife's association with the UK.
[17] 46916/79 (1682) (unreported). See also *Anseereeganoo* 60126/80 (1973) (unreported).

onus on the parties that they intend to resume cohabitation – the onus is on the Secretary of State to be satisfied that one of them has decided not to live again with the other.'

Fiancées[18]

8.61 A woman who seeks admission to marry a man settled in the UK will be admitted if she satisfies the immigration officer that (1) the marriage will take place within a reasonable time; and (2) adequate accommodation will be available, without the need to have recourse to public funds either before or after marriage.[19] She will normally be admitted for three months and prohibited from taking employment. Entry clearance is not needed except for visa nationals.[20] If the marriage takes place within the three month period, she will, on application, be given indefinite leave to remain.[1] If the marriage does not take place within that period, she may be granted a further short extension but only if good cause is shown for the delay and there is satisfactory evidence that the marriage will take place at an early date.[2]

Wives Admitted Temporarily Seeking to Remain

8.62 A woman admitted in a temporary capacity who marries a man settled here will on application be given indefinite leave to remain.[3] This rule applies even though the couple have separated.[4]

Situations where Settlement will not Arise

8.63 A man seeking limited leave to enter the UK for marriage to a woman settled here may be admitted if the immigration officer is satisfied that (1) the marriage will take place within a reasonable time; (2) the entrant and his wife will leave the UK shortly after the marriage, and (3) the entrant meets the general requirements relating to visitors.[5] Admis-

---

[18] Wives have already been considered at paras. 8.21 et seq., ante.
[19] HC 394, para 55.
[20] Ibid.
[1] Ibid., para. 114.
[2] Ibid.
[3] Ibid., para. 115.
[4] *Hossenbux* 2971/76 (1040) (unreported).
[5] HC 394, para. 54.

sion will normally be for three months with a prohibition on employment. Entry clearance is not required except for visa nationals.

There are no corresponding rules for women seeking limited leave to enter the UK to marry a man settled here, but it is to be expected that she will need to meet the normal requirements for visitors entering the UK.[6]

A woman admitted in a temporary capacity marrying a person who has only limited leave to enter will, should this be necessary, on application have her conditions extended so that they coincide with his.[7]

The Old Rules

Husbands and Fiancés Seeking Admission[8]

8.64 The main difference was that admission was available to the husband or fiancé without the wife or fiancée having to meet requirements of nationality and birth. She had to be settled here or admitted for settlement on the same occasion, but there was no requirement that she must be a UK citizen or that she or one of her parents were born here. There was also no requirement that the parties have met.

Husbands and Fiancés Seeking to Remain[9]

8.65 Again there were no limitations on the citizenship or birth of the wife, nor need the parties have met. An extension was to be refused if the Home Secretary believed that 'the marriage is one of convenience entered into primarily to obtain settlement here, with no intention that the parties could live together permanently as man and wife', and settlement would not 'normally' be given if any of the following applied: (1) the husband had remained in breach of the immigration laws before marriage; (2) the marriage had taken place after deportation proceedings had been started; (3) the husband had been admitted as a fiancé and married a different person to the prospective spouse he named; (4) the marriage had been terminated; (5) the Home Secretary had reason to believe that one of the parties no longer had any intention of living with the other as his spouse.

There was nevertheless a discretion to grant settlement where any of

---

[6] Ibid., para. 17.

[7] Ibid., para. 115.

[8] HC 79, paras. 47, 48, as amended by HC 238: HC 81, paras. 42, 43, as amended by HC 240.

[9] HC 80, paras. 25–26A as amended by HC 239, paras. 23–24A, as amended by HC 241.

the above conditions applied. This discretion has been removed in the new rules. The Tribunal has been faced on a number of occasions with the issue of in what circumstances should the discretion be exercised in favour of the appellant, where one of the parties has no longer an intention of living with the other. In *Chauhan*,[10] it was accepted that the appellant had had a very raw deal: information given to the Home Office by his wife's family was a 'pack of lies': he had given in to pressure brought to bear by the family, had given up his studies in India to come to marry, and had spoiled his life. The husband's appeal was successful. This decision raised an important issue: to what extent is lack of blame for the breakdown of the marriage a factor which should be taken into account in deciding whether a husband should be allowed to stay?

A strong Tribunal in *Subhash*,[11] rejected the Home Office proposition that it was irrelevant that the husband was not responsible for the breakdown. The Tribunal held it was a factor to be taken into account with all the relevant facts and circumstances:

'It seems to the Tribunal that just as it is open to the Secretary of State to have regard to the behaviour of the parties after the marriage is reaching a conclusion as to the nature of the marriage, so too he may have regard to that behaviour in deciding whether he should exercise in favour of the husband the very limited discretion conferred on him to remove the time limit on the husband's stay, notwithstanding the fact that the parties are no longer cohabiting. There must be strong reasons for exercising the discretion in favour of the husband. In order to ascertain whether they exist it is necessary to look at all the relevant facts and while it does not follow, as night follows day, that a husband will be allowed to settle in this country if the fault for the failure of the marriage lies with his wife, it nonetheless forms part of the whole situation which has to be assessed.'

The Tribunal has further stated that although each case must be judged on its own facts, permitting an appellant to remain is an exceptional course and 'the position must be avoided of regarding so many circumstances as exceptional that permission to remain is normally given and only exceptionally refused'.[12]

The Home Office has given instructions to its officials always to

[10] 31206/78 (1449) (unreported). See also *Panesar* 40011/79 (1643) (unreported); *El-Sayed* 46012/79 (1687) (unreported).
[11] [1979–80] Imm AR 97. See also *Attray* 49510/79 (1856) (unreported).
[12] *P R Patel* 43141/79 (1766) (unreported).

consider whether the husband might qualify to remain under some other provision of the rules,[13] for example, if the Department of Employment are prepared to approve his employment. If there is no possibility of so qualifying the Home Office will consider any representations which may be made indicating that it would be an undue hardship to require the husband to leave the UK. A particularly sympathetic attitude will be taken in any case where the wife has died, and account will also be taken of any factors which might point to a reconciliation.

RETURNING RESIDENTS

8.66 Those who have been given indefinite leave to remain in the UK may find themselves in difficulties if they leave the country for a substantial period of time. There are important safeguards, however, in that although leave to enter is still required, the rules provide a special category of admission for returning residents.[14] The onus lies on the entrant to show that he is entitled to be admitted.[15]

The General Rules

8.67 The rules can be summarised as follows:

A Commonwealth citizen who was settled in the UK at the coming into force of the Act and was settled here at any time during the two years preceding his return is to be admitted for settlement whatever the circumstances of his departure unless there is a current deportation order against him.[16] An entry certificate is not mandatory. Entry cannot be refused because of a criminal record or because exclusion is deemed conducive to the public good or on medical grounds.[17] In *R v Secretary of State for the Home Department, ex parte Mughal*,[18] it was held that to qualify as a returning resident in this manner, the entrant had not only to be settled here at the coming into force of the Act, but on a proper con-

---

[13] Lord Harris, Minister of State at the Home Office, 383 H. of L. Official Report, 10 May 1977, col. 220.
[14] HC 394, paras. 56–58.
[15] *Bashir* [1976] Imm AR 96. New evidence not available to the immigration officer at the time of the refusal tendered to support the appellant's claimed status would be relevant and admissible on an appeal against refusal *R v Immigration Appeal Tribunal, ex parte Rashid* [1978] Imm AR 71.
[16] HC 394, paras. 56, 68(a); and see *Patel (W W)* [1979–80] Imm AR 106.
[17] Ibid.
[18] [1973] 3 All ER 796, CA.

struction of s. 1(2) he must also be physically present here on that date. If the Commonwealth citizen succeeds in gaining re-entry, his family (i.e. wife and children under 18) are to be admitted either at the time of entry or at a later date, irrespective of whether they have been previously resident here, provided they have current entry certificates issued for this purpose. No member of the family can be refused leave to enter unless he or she is currently subject to a deportation order.[19]

Other entrants, whether Commonwealth citizens or foreign nationals, are to be admitted for settlement as returning residents. But the entrant must show that[20] (1) he was settled here before he left; (2) he did not receive assistance from public funds towards the cost of leaving; (3) he has not been away longer than two years. Again an entry clearance is not mandatory. Entry may be refused if the immigrant has a criminal record for an extraditable offence[1] or is subject to a deportation order or his exclusion is conducive to the public good.[2] His family (i.e. wife and children under 18) are to be admitted for settlement if he is re-admitted provided they have entry clearance. A member of the family cannot be excluded unless he or she is subject to a deportation order.[3] Again neither the entrant nor his family can be refused on medical grounds.

There is no discretion to extend the two years period of absence.[4] If an entrant, whatever his nationality has been away for more than two years the rules provide the immigration officer with a discretion to admit. The circumstances in which the discretion should be exercised are not specified but the rules refer to admitting a person 'if, for example, he has lived here for most of his life.'[5]

An application to enter as a returning resident can be made on any number of occasions provided the requirements of the rules are met on each occasion. Where an entry clearance is granted, the period of its validity will be limited, usually for a period of six months (although it can be shorter). If it expires, the entrant can apply for another clearance and it must be granted if he were settled in the UK at any time within the two years prior to the new application.[6] The Divisional Court in *R v Immigration Appeal Tribunal, ex parte Aisha Khatoon Ali* held that the rules do

---

[19] See HC 394, para. 68(b).   [20] Ibid., para. 56.

[1] Ibid., para. 74.

[2] Ibid., para. 76. See, e.g. *Osama* [1978] Imm AR 8, where entry was refused on this ground because the entrant had entered into a marriage of convenience.

[3] HC 394, paras. 74, 76.

[4] *Taneja* [1977] Imm AR 9.

[5] HC 394, para. 57.

[6] *Rampersaud* 1654/72 (102) (unreported).

not provide for a person to claim that he is a returning resident on an application to vary leave: the claim may only be made when a person seeks admission to the UK as a person settled here.[7] Difficulties have arisen where an Immigration Officer doubts that a passenger is a returning resident but nevertheless admits him for a short period (usually as a visitor for six months) so that the Home Office may give consideration to the case. An application for indefinite leave to remain is then made and, in practice, such applications are given consideration. However, if the Home Office rejects the application, an appeal against the decision must now fail. Had the immigration officer refused leave to enter, the issue could of course have been considered on appeal.

A person whose stay here was subject to a time limit and who returns after a temporary absence abroad has no claim to admission as a returning resident. He may be admitted on the same time limit and conditions as his previous visit, but more likely he will be treated as a new arrival.[8] The rules do not apply to a UK passport holder, wherever issued, who has been previously admitted for settlement. They are to be freely admitted.[9] There is no requirement that the UKPH be ordinarily resident in the UK in order to qualify for admission in these circumstances.[10]

Particular Problems

8.68 It will be recalled that 'settlement' requires the applicant to be ordinarily resident here without any conditions attached to his stay.[11] If he is not ordinarily resident when he leaves the UK a person cannot qualify as a returning resident where he returns within the two year period. The test of whether a person is ordinarily resident is a question of fact and degree and has been discussed earlier. The matter, however, has taken on some importance in cases involving returning residents because of recent Home Office practice. According to the Home Office 'a relatively small but not insignificant number of people who had really severed their connection with the UK were seeking to preserve their "resident" status by

---

[7] [1979–80] Imm AR 195 confirming the Tribunal's approach in *Facey* 320001/78 (1638) (unreported) (cited at [1979–80] Imm AR 123) and *Goodison* [1979–80] Imm AR 122.

[8] HC 394, para. 58.

[9] HC 394, para. 5. See also *Shanaz Hussain* [1978] Imm AR 103 decided under the old but identical rules. In practice, British protected persons and British subjects without citizenship who have previously been admitted for settlement are similarly re-admitted although there is no reference to this in the rules.

[10] Letter, Home Office to JCWI, 21 May 1981.

[11] Immigration Act 1971, s. 33(1). See para. 8.2, ante.

judicially timed short visits every two years'.[12] The Home Office took the view that while a person may have qualified under the rules on his first return, he certainly would not so qualify on the second and subsequent returns if his stay on each occasion was relatively short, his 'ordinary residence' at the time of departure no longer being in the UK.

Instructions were given to immigration officers to curb this practice, but their effect was mitigated by the following provisions:

'Where on routine examination at the port of entry an immigration officer concludes that a former resident seeking re-admission in that capacity had not re-established his ordinary residence, limited leave for six months on conditions neither prohibiting nor restricting his taking employment is normally granted. Having been given entry the passenger is told that it is open to him to apply to the Home Office if he wishes to establish his claim to be settled here. If he does apply accordingly for removal of the time limit, the Immigration and Nationality Department of the Home Office examines the evidence submitted and, if necessary, calls for further evidence with a view to re-assessing in the light of the criteria set out (below) whether the applicant was ordinarily resident in this country when he was last here. A clear indication that the applicant has so arranged his affairs as to show that he intends to reside here permanently[13] is usually accepted as re-establishing ordinary residence. Only if there is reason to believe the applicant intends to make or retain his real home elsewhere is the application refused.'

The criteria which the Home Office use in satisfying themselves that 'ordinary residence' has been retained are,

'. . . ownership or current tenancy of property for personal residential use; permanent employment; length of previous stay; presence of close family; absence of negative evidence of an intention to make a "home" elsewhere'.[14]

8.69 The citing of individual cases is of little help in explaining 'ordinary residence' as each case will depend on its own facts. However,

---

[12] Letter, Mr Brynmor John, Minister of State at the Home Office, to Lord Avebury 26 February 1979.
[13] I.e. at the time the application was considered: see further letter, Mr Brynmor John to Lord Avebury, 9 July 1979.
[14] Ibid. The meaning of ordinary residence is also considered in para. 8.3, ante.

one case decided under earlier but similar rules may be of assistance in describing the approach to the problem. In *Joshi*,[15] the Tribunal were faced with the following facts. The applicant originally came here in 1955, his wife joined him two years later and his son was born here. They all returned to India in October 1958. The applicant was subsequently admitted unconditionally in 1964, entered employment with a British firm as an overseas sales representative and left for India on the firm's business in February 1965. He returned to the UK in 1966, and stayed for nearly three years, throughout almost the whole of this period there being no conditions attached to his stay. The reason for his departure in 1968 was to continue his job for the company. In early 1970 the firm went into liquidation and the following year he sought to return to the UK. The ECO submitted that he had never set up a permanent home here and had no property or business in the UK at the time of his application. The Tribunal were satisfied that at the time of his departure – the relevant date – he was ordinarily resident here and that in considering the question of residence, the ownership of 'house property' is relevant, but not a conclusive test.[16]

A person who has maintained close connections with the UK during his period abroad will, as a matter of immigration practice, be accepted as a returning resident even if his last stay in the UK was only for a short period.

Absence Longer than Two Years

8.70 Equally difficult problems have arisen where the immigrant has been away from the UK for more than two years. The rules merely state that he may nevertheless be admitted if 'for example, he has lived here for most of his life'.[17] The Tribunal accept in *Costa*,[18] that this example was given by way of guidance but that 'the underlying principle ... is that if a person cannot establish that he or she has not been away from this country for longer than two years that person must show strong connections with this country by a combination of length of residence and family or other ties.' In that case the Tribunal conceded that a Cypriot woman who had been ordinarily resident here from 1963 to 1966 had very strong family ties here and that these circumstances made her a

---

[15] [1975] Imm AR 1.
[16] The Tribunal relied heavily on *IRC* v *Lysaght* [1928] All ER 575, HL; per Viscount Sumner at p. 580.
[17] HC 394, para. 57.
[18] [1974] Imm AR 69.

'borderline' case. But the Tribunal upheld the refusal of admission because of her failure over an 18 month period to observe the time limits on her stay when she was admitted as a visitor in 1969. In *Gokulsing*,[19] the Tribunal accepted that mitigating circumstances to overcome the two year rule need not be limited to circumstances affecting a person in this country: '. . . there may be many good external factors also to be considered such as civil disturbance, personal accident or sickness which would prevent a person ordinarily resident in this country from returning within the two years laid down'.

In *Ali (AM)*[20] the appellant had been prevented from returning because of a court order requiring him to remain in Bangladesh until the completion of civil proceedings which took more than six years. He applied promptly for entry clearance at the end of the case. The Tribunal in permitting him to return approved the observation of the adjudicator that:

'the purpose of the (over two year) rule is . . . to avoid injustice or undue hardship which might arise from the inflexible non-discretionary provisions of the (two year) rule.'

Finally, the Tribunal held in *Peart*,[1] that where a person seeks entry on the basis that he has lived here most of his life, he must show as a mathematical calculation that he has so lived here for that period. It is not sufficient for him to show that he had been here most of his adult life. The decision is somewhat strange as the rule allows a general discretion to admit and it gives by way of example only the situation where a person has lived here most of his life. It can be said, however, that the Tribunal did not hear argument from the appellant's representative (who did not attend the hearing) and there were no other compassionate circumstances on the evidence which would have justified admission.

[19] 24987/78 (1632) (unreported).
[20] 40054/79 (2011) (unreported). Cf. *Mohinder Kaur* 33796/78 (1959) (unreported).
[1] [1979–80] Imm AR 41.

NINE

Remaining in the UK

INTRODUCTION

9.1 This chapter looks at the general requirements for remaining in the UK. It explains under what circumstances applications for extension will be refused, the problems facing those wishing to change the conditions to enable them to work, and the circumstances in which appeals against refusals can be brought.

Anyone who has been given limited leave to enter the UK may subsequently have the period of stay and any conditions altered.[1] A period of stay may be varied by restricting, enlarging or removing the time limit.[2] Conditions may be imposed, added to, varied or revoked.[3] However, once the time limit has been removed (and the applicant is thereby given indefinite leave), any conditions attached to the leave automatically come to an end.[4] A person whose stay is extended for a limited period may apply for further variations and the same principles apply. An indefinite leave to stay or remain cannot be restricted although a person with such leave is liable to deportation in certain circumstances.[5] Notice of any decision reached is to be given to the applicant in writing[6] and there is a right of appeal in most circumstances against an adverse decision.[7]

Officials Administering Control after Entry

9.2 The power to give leave to remain or to vary any leave is exercised

[1] Immigration Act 1971, s. 3(1)(b), (c).
[2] Ibid., s. 3(3)(a).
[3] Ibid., s. 3(3)(b).
[4] Ibid., s. 3(3)(a).
[5] See paras. 11.18 et seq., post.
[6] Ibid., s. 4(1). See also HC 394, para. 86. As to the nature of the notice, see para. 14.6, post.
[7] Ibid. See para. 14.1, post.

by the Home Secretary.[8] He will take very few decisions personally: most will be made by officials at the Immigration and Nationality Department of the Home Office at Croydon.[9] It is to this office that applications are to be sent. Advice on the making of applications is set out at the end of the chapter. The immigration rules[10] lay down the practice to be followed in regulating the stay of non-patrials. They set out in relation to the chief categories concerned, the principles to be followed in dealing with applications for a variation of leave to enter or remain.[11] A decision can be made outside the rules. However, an appeal will not succeed if its only ground is that an official refused to depart from the rules.[12]

GENERAL PRINCIPLES

Application for Variation of Leave

9.3 These considerations apply not only to an application for variation of leave or to remain but also 'in the absence of such an application, in deciding to vary leave'. They do not apply to EEC nationals exercising their rights of movement under the EEC Treaty where they are inconsistent with Community law.[13] The fact that an applicant meets the requirement of the specific immigration rule under which he seeks a variation does not necessarily mean that he will be permitted to remain in the UK. The rules state that 'account is to be taken of all the relevant facts'.[14]

---

[8] Immigration Act 1971, s. 4.

[9] The Minister is not required to act personally on every decision and may act through a duly authorised official in his Department: see *Cartolona Ltd* v *Commissioners of Works* [1943] 2 All ER 560, per Lord Greene at 563: *West Riding CC* v *Wilson* [1941] 2 All ER 827, per Viscount Caldecote CJ at 831. The Act clearly envisages immigration decisions being made by Home Office officials, since there are certain decisions which are not appealable (refusal of leave to enter; to curtail leave to enter or remain; and not to revoke a deportation order) if taken by the Home Secretary personally as distinct from a person acting under his authority: see para. 14.3, post. See also *R* v *Secretary of State for the Home Department, ex parte Hosenball* [1977] 3 All ER 452, at 458–459.

[10] HC 394, paras. 84, et seq.

[11] Ibid., para. 85; HC 82, para. 4. While the rules purport to cover the 'chief categories', it is somewhat uncertain what other categories are envisaged and the principles to be applied.

[12] Immigration Act 1971, s. 19(2). See para. 14.32, post.

[13] As to the immigration rules relating to extensions of stay for EEC nationals (HC 394, paras. 125–134), see paras. 7.54 et seq., ante.

[14] HC 394, para. 88.

9.4 Refusal is to be the normal course (1) if the applicant has made false representations in obtaining leave to enter 'including the giving of undertakings, express or implied, which he has not honoured, as to the duration and purpose of his stay'. This wording, which appears for the first time in the new immigration rules[15] is bound to lead to difficulties. For example, what kind of false representations will justify refusal? In what circumstances does a person give an implied undertaking, and how is it possible to dishonour one? (2) if the applicant has not observed the time limit or conditions subject to which he was admitted or given leave to remain;[16] (3) if in the light of the applicant's character, conduct or associations it is undesirable to permit him to remain;[17] (4) if the applicant represents a danger to national security;[18] (5) if the applicant might not be returnable to another country if allowed to remain for the period he wishes to stay.[19]

These circumstances are by way of example only.[20] Where they arise it is not necessary for the Home Office to consider any claim by the applicant that he satisfies the requirements of the specific immigration rule under which he is seeking a variation.

Refusal of an extension is to be justified where the applicant takes an 'unreasonable time' to produce any evidence required under the rules. Again, there are no guidelines as to what constitutes 'unreasonable time' in this new rule.[1] Curtailment of leave to enter or remain may arise where, for example, a person fails to comply with any condition attached to the leave, or if, given leave to enter or remain to follow a course of studies, the person fails to attend that course regularly.[2]

Application to Change Category

9.5 Visitors, students and au pair girls are admitted in a temporary

[15] Ibid., see also para. 9.7, post.

[16] Ibid. In *Sidique* [1976] Imm AR 69, the Tribunal held that the fact that the Home Office had given an initial extension despite the applicant's being in breach of his conditions, did not prevent the breach being considered on a later application. There was no doctrine of estoppel as the rules did not provide for the condonation, in the sense of full forgiveness, of past immigration offences.

[17] HC 394, para. 88.

[18] Ibid.

[19] Ibid.

[20] The Tribunal has emphasised that these considerations are to be taken into account in all cases and has rejected the argument that they are applicable only in extreme cases: *Thaker* [1976] Imm AR 114.

[1] HC 394, para. 88.

[2] Ibid., para. 89.

capacity.[3] The rules state that they have no claim to remain in any other capacity although in certain circumstances they may be able to obtain extensions as trainees.[4] There is, however, a contradiction in the rules as applications may be granted in the circumstances set out in para. 9.6 below. The rules emphasise that applications to remain for a purpose for which clearance is required are to be refused. The only exceptions are (1) women who marry men settled here are to be given indefinite leave on application;[5] (2) men who marry women settled here may be given an extension of stay and later indefinite leave but in much more limited circumstances,[6] (3) those admitted for some other purpose, but who nevertheless qualify for settlement as dependants of a person settled here, are to be given indefinite leave.[7]

9.6 Applications to change to another temporary capacity may be granted provided (1) the requirements of the rules relating to that new category are met; and (2) it does not appear to the Home Office that the applicant is attempting to remain permanently.[8] Applications from visitors and students to remain in employment are to be refused in almost all circumstances.[9]

Those who have been given limited leave to enter or remain in whatever capacity (including those admitted for work) are to be refused if they apply to remain here as businessmen or self-employed persons,[10] writers or artists[11] or persons of independent means.[12] Similarly, those who have been admitted as businessmen or self-employed persons, writers or artists, or persons of independent means are to be refused if they apply to remain here in another of these categories.[13]

---

[3] The rules refer to 'people admitted as visitors or students or for other temporary purposes:' (HC 394, para. 90). The only other group referred to in Part II of the rules (Passengers Coming for Temporary Purposes), are au pair girls. However, the wording of HC 394, para. 96, suggests that working holidaymakers are also so regarded.

[4] See HC 394, para. 105.

[5] Ibid., para. 115.

[6] Ibid., paras. 90, 117. But see *Mahmoudi* 69569/80 (2134) (unreported).

[7] Ibid., paras. 90, 119.

[8] Ibid., para. 90. Applicants must be prepared to deal with the allegation which may be made that they are in breach of an express or implied undertaking given on admission about the purpose and duration of their stay: HC 394, para. 88. See para. 9.4, ante.

[9] Ibid., para. 91.

[10] Ibid., para. 109.

[11] Ibid., para. 112.

[12] Ibid., para. 113.

[13] Ibid., paras. 109, 112, 113.

Deception of the Immigration Authorities as a Ground for Refusal

9.7 If it emerges during the course of an application for an extension of stay that the immigration authorities had been deceived at the time the applicant was given leave to enter (particularly as to the intentions of the applicant regarding his eventual departure from the UK) the Home Office may conclude that the applicant is an illegal entrant.[14] The Home Office has in the past agreed that not all forms of deception would justify this conclusion,[15] but if the application for an extension were refused on other grounds, there is no assurance that the appellate authorities or the courts would accept a Home Office submission that the applicant was not an illegal entrant. Indeed the appellate authorities have refused to hear appeals against refusals of extension of stay if they conclude that the appellant is an illegal entrant, on the ground that they have no jurisdiction.[16]

PERMISSION TO WORK AFTER ENTRY

9.8 A frequent wish of those admitted to the UK is to be permitted to work. As we have already seen, most non-patrials from outside the EEC will not be admitted unless they have a work permit obtained for them in advance from the Department of Employment by their employer. The immigration rules make it clear that generally it will not be possible to enter the work permit scheme by seeking a variation of conditions after being admitted in a temporary capacity. The position can be summarised as follows:

(1) Applications to remain in employment from persons admitted as visitors, students or au pairs are to be refused without reference to the Department of Employment unless the conditions on which entry was given left the applicant free to take employment without Department of Employment consent.[17]
(2) Where there was no prohibition or restriction on entry, there is still no claim to remain in employment, but if the Department of

---

[14] See generally paras. 12.1 et seq., post.
[15] See *Shazad* 32163/78 (1626) (unreported), para. 12.7, post.
[16] Ibid.
[17] HC 394, para. 91. This rule applies to all students, 'including those whose studies were financed by HM Government, an international scholarship agency or by their home government.'

Employment is prepared to approve the employment, it may be appropriate to grant an extension of stay.[18]
(3) There will be certain cases where it will be inappropriate to refer cases to the Department because of the applicant's immigration history, character, general undesirability or for reasons of national security. In such cases an extension should be refused.
(4) If the Department of Employment does not approve the employment, an extension should be refused.[19]
(5) These rules do not apply to doctors registered with the General Medical Council, nor to nurses or midwives offered employment at the completion of their training, provided their training was not financed by an international scholarship agency, or by their home government.[20]
(6) It is now established law that there is no right of appeal against the refusal of the Department of Employment to grant a work permit.[1]
(7) Doctors, dentists and nurses admitted as postgraduate students will be permitted to take full-time employment which is associated with their studies. Other students with the consent of the Department of Employment may work in their free time or vacations. If there was a condition imposed on entry prohibiting employment on a person who later becomes a student, the conditions may be varied to one permitting him to work with the consent of the Department. Students' wives may work without seeking permission and their earnings may be taken into account in assessing the adequacy of the arrangements for maintenance.[2]
(8) The position of those who work after their leave has expired is considered later in this chapter.[3]

REFUSALS OF EXTENSIONS OF STAY: RIGHT OF APPEAL

9.9 The Immigration Act provides a right of appeal against a refusal by the Home Secretary to vary the duration or conditions of a limited leave, and the appellant will not be required to leave the UK while the appeal is

[18] Ibid. The circumstances in which this situation arises are likely to be rare.
[19] Ibid.
[20] Ibid.
[1] *Pearson* v *Immigration Appeal Tribunal.* [1978] Imm AR 212, CA.
[2] Ibid., para. 101.
[3] See para. 9.11, post.

pending. There is also a right of appeal against a decision to vary, e.g. by imposing a prohibition on employment, and while the appeal is pending the variation will not take effect.[4] There is no appeal if the Home Secretary decides that departure is conducive to the public good as being in the interests of national security or of the relations between the UK and any other country or for other reasons of a political nature.[5]

Until the decision in *R v Immigration Appeal Tribunal, ex parte Subramaniam*,[6] in February 1976, it was generally accepted both by the Home Office and those representing immigrants that the Act gave a right of appeal even where the applicant had overstayed his original leave at the time he applied for an extension or at the time he lodged notice of appeal against refusal to grant an extension. It was believed that this was what Parliament had intended and that if there had been a lengthy period of overstaying, it was open to the appellate authorities to reject the appeal or for the Home Secretary to make a decision to deport or for the police to be informed so that a prosecution could be instituted. In *Subramaniam*, the Court of Appeal held that the right of appeal was limited to those who made their applications before the expiry of the limited leave which they were applying to extend.

Shortly afterwards, the immigration appeals system was thrown into chaos by the decision of the House of Lords in *R v Immigration Appeal Tribunal, ex parte Suthendran*,[7] where it was held that the applicant only retained a right of appeal if he lodged his appeal before the original leave expired. The effect was that the Home Office, if it so desired, could frustrate any appeal by not reaching a decision until the applicant's leave had expired; and probably more importantly, the right of appeal could be lost simply because of administrative delay. The difficulties arising from the *Suthendran* decision were remedied in part by the Immigration (Variation of Leave) Order 1976,[8] which automatically extended the leave of any person who applied in time for an extension until 28 days after his application had been determined. The order came into operation on 27 September 1976 and applies to applications made on or after that date.

9.10 Pressure was put on the government to 'restore' totally the right of appeal but this it was not prepared to do. Those who had applied in time and received a decision after their leave has expired, but before 27

[4] Immigration Act 1971, s. 14(1).
[5] Immigration Act 1971, s. 14(3).
[6] [1976] 3 All ER 604, CA.
[7] [1976] 3 All ER 611, HL; see also *Halil v Davidson* [1979–80] Imm AR 164, HL.
[8] SI 1976 No. 157.

September 1976, received some protection. The Tribunal and adjudicators agreed to hear their cases and give advisory opinions to the Home Office. Their opinions were not binding on the Home Secretary as they had no statutory force but the Home Secretary agreed to accept their decisions.[9] The appeal procedure for these reviews remained the same in most respects, and in appropriate cases, the Tribunal has reconsidered decisions of the adjudicator. Further, EEC nationals were entitled to a review by the Immigration Appeal Tribunal to meet the UK's obligation under EEC law.[10]

An application is in time if it is sent to the Home Office on or before the date of the expiry of leave and a right of appeal will therefore subsist even if the Home Office does not receive the application until after the date of expiry.[11] However, an applicant who applies late, even by one day, has now lost his right of appeal. Moreover the Home Office, under the present immigration rules, is no longer bound to consider applications which are late. An applicant is also liable to prosecution from the first date of his overstaying.[12] The Home Office will usually warn of the risk of prosecution in the notice of refusal.[13]

TAKING EMPLOYMENT AFTER LEAVE HAS EXPIRED

9.11 The position of those who enter into employment or business after their leave has expired is interesting. A prohibition or restriction on employment is a condition which is attached to a person's leave to enter or remain.[14] When the leave comes to an end, the condition attached to the leave ceases to apply. In the case of a person who has stayed beyond the period granted by the leave he may be prosecuted for 'overstaying' but he cannot be convicted of working in breach of his conditions as that offence merges with that of 'overstaying'.[15] Those who have applied for

---

[9] There is no provision for a review for non-EEC nationals who applied for an extension of stay after their leave had expired.
[10] Council Directive (EEC) No. 64/211.
[11] *Lubetkin* [1979–80] Imm AR 162.
[12] Immigration Act 1971, s. 24(1)(b)(i). See para. 10.5, post.
[13] 'From the date on which your limited leave expired you have remained in this country without authority. Knowingly remaining beyond the time limited by the leave is an offence punishable on conviction by a fine (maximum £200) or six months imprisonment or both and may result in proceedings for deportation. You should accordingly leave the United Kingdom without delay.'
[14] Ibid., s. 3(1)(c). See para. 5.1, ante.
[15] *Gurdev Singh* v *R* [1974] 1 All ER 26. See para. 10.5, post.

an extension of stay prior to their leave expiring and are awaiting a Home Office decision will, however, be committing an offence since the Immigration (Variation of Leave) Order 1976 extends the leave during this period[16] and for a further 28 days after the decision. However, once a decision has been made and the 28-day period has elapsed, no criminal offence is committed by working.[17]

A note of caution should, however, be sounded. Firstly, if the Home Office should discover an applicant to be working prior to making a decision, it will certainly have an adverse effect on that decision. Secondly, employers frequently require some form of proof that the Home Office or Department of Employment does not object to the employment: this is hardly likely to be forthcoming although the Home Office may be persuaded in some cases to confirm that no offence is being committed.[18] Finally, there will be a reluctance by the Department of Health and Social Security to provide a national insurance number in this situation. There is a long-standing arrangement whereby the DHSS check with the Immigration and Nationality Department the details of people born outside the UK who have recently arrived and who are applying for the first time for national insurance numbers.[19] There will, however, be circumstances where a person may have no alternative but to take employment. His mind can be put at rest that he is committing no offence; and in some circumstances the fact that he has taken work may be of benefit to his case; e.g., on an appeal in deportation proceedings where it is preferable to admit to taking employment than to confirm that the appellant has had recourse to public funds.

SUCCESSIVE APPLICATIONS

9.12 There is nothing to prevent a person who has been granted limited leave to enter the UK from applying for a number of variations over a period of time. Indeed, this may be necessary, e.g. in the case of a student who is undertaking a three-year course. He may initially be given leave to enter for one year and must apply for an extension of stay before that period expires. An extension may be given for a further year or longer when a similar application must be made again. The following

[16] See para. 9.9, ante.
[17] If an appeal against an adverse decision is lodged, the appellant will not be required to leave the UK by reason of the expiration of his leave while the appeal is pending: see para 9.14, post.
[18] As to the duties and obligations of employers, see para. 10.6, post.
[19] Letter, Home Office to Eric Deakins MP, 15 June 1981.

points should, however, be borne in mind. (1) Those who are admitted in a temporary capacity are expected to leave at the end of their stay. As has been shown there is limited scope for change into a different capacity, and while a person may be eligible for an extension of stay, the Home Office may suspect that the intention of the applicant is to remain in the UK permanently and consequently refuse the application, although the mere fact that he expresses a desire to remain in the UK if permitted to do so should not itself be a ground for refusing an applicant.[20] (2) It is now no longer possible to make successive applications whether on the same or different grounds after an initial application has been refused. Application from overstayers need not be considered at all and they have no right of appeal. Nor is there a right of appeal from the refusal of a further application made within the 28-day period granted under the Immigration (Variation of Leave) Order 1976[1] as the order specifically excludes such a right.[2] The only other possible gap was closed when in *R v Immigration Appeal Tribunal, ex parte Balbir Singh*,[3] the Divisional Court held the applicant had no right of appeal following the refusal by the Home Office to grant a further application made while an appeal was pending against an earlier refusal.

LEAVING THE UNITED KINGDOM

9.13 Once a person who has limited leave goes outside the common travel area, even for a short period, his leave to enter or remain in the UK lapses.[4] He has no claim to admission as a returning resident and the authorities have a discretion whether to readmit. The rules[5] specify that applications to re-enter should be dealt with in the light of all the relevant circumstances. A person who has been given a limited leave to enter or remain for three months or more and who is required to register with the police, or is given leave for 12 months or more without a police

---

[20] *R v Immigration Appeal Tribunal, ex parte Shaikh* (1981). *The Times*, 3 March.
[1] See para. 9.9, ante.
[2] The Order does not apply to an application if made at a time when by virtue of the previous operation of the Order an extension of the applicant's period of leave is taking effect: art. 3(2) and see *Al Abbas* [1979–80] Imm AR 189.
[3] [1978] Imm AR 64. The Court of Appeal subsequently dismissed a further appeal; see [1978] Imm AR 204.
[4] Immigration Act 1971, s. 3(4). There is a very limited category of people who may return to the UK without leave (seamen and aircrew, see para. 3.19, ante). Their leave will not lapse if they return within the period for which they were originally granted leave, but the terms of that leave will continue to apply: ibid., s. 3(4).
[5] HC 394, para. 58.

registration condition, should normally have little difficulty on his return from a temporary absence abroad, provided that the time limit has not expired and he can show the immigration officer that there has been no change in circumstances since the previous leave was granted. Such a person will usually have an endorsement placed in his passport immediately below the limited leave and conditions which state,

'This will apply, unless and until superseded, to any subsequent leave the holder may obtain after an absence from the United Kingdom within the period limited as above.'

If such an endorsement has not been made, an immigration officer may enter the endorsement on a subsequent admission within the period limited by the leave. It should be emphasised that a passenger whose passport is so endorsed nevertheless requires leave to enter. If leave is granted for the same period and under the same conditions as the original leave, the endorsement, 'Given leave to enter – section 3(3)(b)' will be placed in the passport.

An immigration officer may, however, decide to treat any passenger who has limited leave as a new arrival, in which case he must prove once again that he is eligible to enter. Thus, e.g. a visitor admitted for six months who leaves the UK after two months for a week's holiday in Europe will not necessarily be readmitted; and a student who goes abroad for a few days may find himself having to prove to the immigration officer that he is studying full-time at a *bona fide* institution and has sufficient means to continue to support himself. Those who leave the UK should always be prepared to prove afresh their eligibility for entry.

Visa nationals[6] who wish to travel overseas for a short period of time and then return will require a visa to produce to the immigration office on arrival. They should therefore apply for a re-entry visa at a UK Passport Office. Application is made on a form AV/UK. The applicant must produce his current passport (and previous passport if the most recent immigration stamp is in the passport) and if held, his Police Registration Certificate. Additionally work permit holders must submit a letter from their employers confirming that they have permission to leave their employment for a holiday abroad and will be resuming employment on their return. A small fee is payable for the visa.

Leaving the UK while appeal pending

9.14 A particular problem arises where a person wishes to leave the

[6] See para. 5.5, ante.

UK while an appeal is pending and return prior to the hearing. The Act has been deliberately drafted so that those waiting for their appeal to be heard are treated no differently than others leaving the UK, although they cannot be removed while the appeal is pending.[7] The Home Office has for some years been aware of these difficulties and has indicated,

'... in cases of this nature the immigration officer does not in any way attempt to assess the merits of the appeal: he has no knowledge of this in any detail. His duty is simply to examine the passenger and to decide, under the immigration rules, if he or she qualifies for entry'.[8]

As to the advice to be given to those who wish to leave, the Home Office suggests that they should be told that

'... although they cannot be required to leave pending the outcome of the appeal, if they choose to leave they will have no entitlement to re-enter solely because the appeal has not been determined; they should be prepared to satisfy the immigration officer that they qualify for entry under the immigration rules. They may also be advised, however, that leave to enter for a limited period will normally be given if the appeal is scheduled, and that provided that absence from the United Kingdom is not unduly prolonged leave will normally also be given if the immigration officer is satisfied that the passenger intends to pursue the appeal and that there are no factors entirely unconnected with the appeal which render his admission undesirable. The immigration officer will normally need to be satisfied that maintenance is assured.'[9]

9.15 This advice is sound and can be summarised as follows.

(1) The Home Office statement is not a guarantee that an appellant will be re-admitted in every case: e.g. there are bound to be difficulties if a person against whom a decision to deport has been made seeks re-admission.
(2) Advice on appeal should be sought and notice of appeal should be given before leaving.
(3) The appellant should take a letter from those representing him or her confirming that the appeal is pending, that they are acting for him or her and that the appellant is pursuing the appeal. If full instructions have not been taken, this fact should be emphasised if there is a genuine need to obtain further information from the appellant.

[7] Letter, Home Office to UKIAS, 24 June 1974.
[8] Ibid.   [9] Ibid.

(4) The appellant should not leave the UK for longer than is necessary even though the appeal may not be heard for a year or more. He should be in a position to justify his reason for leaving, e.g. visiting sick relative, and show that he can support himself until the appeal is heard.
(5) It is safer if the appellant does not leave at all; and if there is any doubt about re-admission his advisers should be informed of the exact date, time and place of arrival so that they can intervene with the authorities if necessary.

ABANDONING THE APPLICATION

9.16 An application may be expressly abandoned, and will by law be abandoned if the applicant leaves the UK.[10] If an applicant makes two inconsistent applications, the second application will be taken to have superseded the first. Where a person asks the Home Office for the return of a passport (submitted in support of an application) because the applicant is leaving the UK, the Home Office practice is to return the passport with a letter stating 'this request has been taken as superseding and therefore cancelling the previous application. . . .'[11] If the applicant has decided not to leave, he should inform the Home Office where appropriate that he wishes his application to be treated as continuing, and return the passport.

It was formerly the Home Office practice to send a letter to those applying for an extension authorising the applicant 'to remain in the UK pending a decision on your application to remain'. This phrase was held by the Divisional Court in *R* v *Immigration Appeal Tribunal, ex parte Ahluwalia*,[12] to be a grant of leave to remain, and not a mere indulgence. Although the letter has been withdrawn, it arose in *Esteve-Varea*,[13] where the Home Office gave the appellant such a letter in 1972 and having not heard from him for three years, noted on his file that it was assumed that he had left the country. In 1979 he was arrested and a decision to deport was made on the ground of overstaying. This appeal against the decision was allowed. The Tribunal held that no decision had been taken on his application and he had leave to remain as the authorisa-

[10] As the applicant's leave to enter or remain expires on departure: Immigration Act 1971, s. 3(4). See para. 9.13, ante.
[11] Form 'IMM 159'.
[12] [1979–80] Imm AR 1.
[13] 4241/79 (1706) (unreported).

tion was not withdrawn. It was implicitly accepted by the Tribunal that he had not abandoned his application.

In *R v Immigration Appeal Adjudicator, ex parte Bhanji*[14] the Court of Appeal considered the following words: 'for the purpose only of enabling you to make arrangements to leave this country your leave to enter is varied to permit you to remain in the UK until 18 June 1976. No further extension of stay will be granted.'

The Court held this to be only an indulgence to the applicant to 'pack his bags and make arrangements for his departure'. Again in *Theori*[15] the Tribunal came to the same conclusion when the words used were '[The Applicant] has no further claim to remain in the UK. However, in view of current medical treatment it has been decided that providing [she] leaves the UK on or before 30 September 1980 no action will be taken to enforce her departure.'

REMAINING AFTER THE APPLICATION HAS FINALLY BEEN REFUSED

9.17 Where a person has no right of appeal against a refusal of an extension of stay or he has exhausted his remedies under the appeals system, the Home Office will require the applicant to leave. There are two courses open to the authorities if a person does not leave: (1) to give notice of intention to deport under s. 3(5)(a) (for overstaying) or s. 3(5)(b) (deportation deemed conducive to the public good);[16] or (2) to bring a criminal prosecution for overstaying under s. 24(1)(b) of the Act.[17] Once a decision is made or a charge brought, there are provisions to detain in custody, but bail can be applied for.

9.18 Tougher measures have now been adopted in the case of those who have no right of appeal against refusal of an extension, i.e. those who have made an application after overstaying. The police are to be brought in to deal with these people at a much earlier stage. A Home Office circular details the new procedure.

---

[14] [1977] Imm AR 89, although Lord Russell in *Halil v Davidson* [1979–80] Imm AR 164, took the view that the words could be construed as a *de novo* grant of leave to remain.
[15] [1979–80] Imm AR 126.
[16] See paras. 11.14 et seq., post.
[17] See para. 10.5, post. Note that the authorities may be time-barred from bringing a prosecution. See para. 10.2, post.

'Home Office Circular No. 115/1979 3 July 1979
Immigration Act 1971: Service of refusal notice on overstayers
1. Home Office Circular 167/1976 sets out the implications of the judgments in the cases of *Subramaniam* and *Suthendran* which affected Home Office practice in regard to applications for extensions of stay and might therefore affect prosecutions under section 24(1)(b) of the Immigration Act 1971.

2. It has now been agreed, at the suggestion of the Association of Chief Police Officers, that the police should play a greater part in the service on overstayers of notices of refusal of their applications to the Home Office for extensions of stay. For the moment, this will only apply to those who have no right of appeal because they sought an extension of stay after their original leave to enter or remain had expired (i.e. persons affected by the *Subramaniam* judgement — see paragraph 2 of Home Office Circular 167/1976). In future, where applications from such persons to remain in the country are refused by the Home Office, the police will be asked to serve the notice of refusal in person on them.

3. A sample refusal notice, which has been agreed by the Association of Chief Police Officers, is attached. The notice states that, although the person on whom it is served is liable to deportation by administrative means (under section 3(5)(a) of the 1971 Act), the Secretary of State does not propose to initiate deportation proceedings against him for a period of 14 days from the date on which the notice is served on the person concerned. The notice of refusal, in triplicate, will be sent to the police, together with the person's passport, if available. The officer detailed to serve the notice should do so by reading it over to the overstayer and by leaving a copy of the original in his possession. The officer serving the notice should enter on all the copies the date on which it is served. The original notice, duly endorsed as to service, should be retained by the police until the overstayer has left the United Kingdom. A report, together with the original notice, should then be forwarded to the Home Office. The second copy may be retained by the police for their records.

4. The intention in granting a period of grace from administrative deportation is to allow the overstayer an opportunity to complete his arrangements before leaving the country. This policy is in line with a judgment by the Court of Appeal in the case of *Bhanji*, which contemplated the possibility of allowing an overstayer time to leave the United Kingdom without formally granting him a further leave to remain, leading to a further right of appeal. As the notice of refusal points out, however, the person refused may still be liable to arrest and prosecution for an offence under section 24 of the Immigration Act 1971.

This is a matter for the Chief Officer of Police concerned. The Association of Chief Police Officers has, however, agreed that the police should normally refrain from initiating a prosecution for the same period as the Secretary of State undertakes to refrain from deportation. It is recognised that there may be exceptional cases where the Chief Officer of Police will feel it desirable to initiate prosecution immediately. In exceptional cases where it becomes obvious from direct enquiries that the proper course of action is to initiate a prosecution the notice of refusal should not be served.'

9.19 The Home Office has accepted that there are a number of cases where service of notice of refusal by the police would be inappropriate. An applicant will therefore be served the notice by post in the following circumstances:

(a) where he is over 70 years old;
(b) where the Home Office considers him to be ill or infirm;
(c) where he is an unaccompanied child or a person whose stay is being considered separately from his parents;
(d) where he is already known to the Home Office to have left his last known address;
(e) where he is an overstayer and is time-barred from prosecution.[18]

Where the application for an extension of stay had been made by a representative, the passport will be returned to his representative unless either the representative or the applicant has asked that the passport be returned to the applicant. If the passport is returned to the representative, he will also receive a copy of the notice of refusal which the police have been asked to serve. There may be difficulties if representations are made to the Home Office following service of notice of refusal by the police. The Home Office has stated that it remains for the police to decide whether to prosecute should a person not leave on receipt of the notice, but there is no indication whether it makes recommendations to the police. The Home Office has, however, set up a special section 'to notify the police promptly of any development of which the police ought to be aware'. This is intended to cover the situation where representations are made from MPs, solicitors or other representatives. The police are said to have the telephone number in the Home Office which they can use to seek further information or guidance about a case. Even if the police prosecute while representations are being made, the Minister at the Home

[18] Letter, 18 June 1980. Home Office to JCWI.

Office will still be able to give full consideration to the representations before deciding on a person's future stay in this country.[19]

ADVISING THOSE APPLYING FOR EXTENSIONS

9.20

(1) Applications are made to the Home Office. Correspondence is to be addressed to the Under Secretary of State, Lunar House, Wellesley Road, Croydon CR9 2BY. There is also a public enquiry office at that address. Enquiries can also be made by telephone on 01-686 0688.

(2) Do not rely on advice given by the enquiry office or advice given over the telephone (great difficulty is experienced in getting through to the Home Office in Croydon by telephone). The Home Office staff are overworked and those on the counter are not experienced in all aspects of the immigration law. There have been occasions when the wrong advice has been given and it is extremely easy for there to be a misunderstanding on what advice has been given. Where assurances have been given in these circumstances, the Home Secretary will not normally be bound by such assurances.[20]

(3) Wherever possible applications should be in writing. Your client should be advised not to make personal applications at Croydon. Where he has been in correspondence with the Home Office, the applicant will have been given a Home Office reference number which can be found on the inside back cover of the passport if the Home Office has had it. The reference number will be in the form *A 123456*; the initial letter will correspond to the first letter of the surname. Always quote the number; it will save delays.

(4) Where the Home Office reference is not known, but it would appear that the applicant has had previous dealings with the Home Office, the full names, nationality and date of birth of the applicant should be provided. If the applicant is married, similar particulars of the spouse should be given, and in the case of an applicant under 18 years of age, similar particulars of the parents.

(5) Make sure the application is in before the date on which leave expires. If there is any doubt about the application arriving on time,

[19] Ibid.
[20] See *Paet* [1979–80] Imm AR 185.

deliver the letter personally or send a telegram or telex containing the following basic details: (i) name and address of applicant; (ii) Home Office reference number, where known; (iii) nature of application, e.g. 'require extension of stay as a student', and state in the telegram that a letter and documents will follow. A letter should be sent off the next day.

(6) Make sure the proper documentation is sent. Documentation which is required depends on the category under which the extension is sought under the immigration rules. If you do not have all the documents, it may be worthwhile getting the letter off and informing the Home Office that some or all the documents will follow in support shortly.

(7) Do not expect immediate replies to letters. A standard form of acknowledgement is usually sent quite quickly but there can be a delay of several months after that. If you do not receive an acknowledgement, write again. Better still, send your letters by recorded delivery.

(8) If it is necessary for your client to attend the Home Office for an interview, it may be better to attend with him or her. The Green Form can be used for this purpose. If you cannot attend advise your client to make a detailed note immediately after the interview of everything that has been said and to date and sign it. The statement may be useful in any appeal. The Home Office official will have made a note and you may be at a disadvantage if your client cannot remember particular details.

(9) If your client has overstayed and wishes to apply for an extension of stay (i) he or she should be advised never to make direct application or enquiry to the Home Office but only through a properly instructed representative; (ii) do not reveal his/her present address in any application; (iii) require the Home Office to inform you of the decision directly and insist that all documents are returned to you and not to your client, whatever the outcome of the application.

(10) In the event of a final refusal, in appropriate cases representations can be made directly to the Minister at the Home Office responsible for immigration. This requires involving your client's MP (or that of the relative or friend with whom he may be staying if he or she has no MP). Some MPs are more sympathetic than others. If the decision is to be reversed an MP may well have to do something more than simply pass on your letter to him with a covering note to the Minister. Try to get the MP to see the client and then send a

detailed letter to the Minister afterwards. There may be others who would also wish to make representations (e.g. community leaders, employers, etc.). Make sure they put their views in writing and that the MP reads them and forwards them to the Minister.

(11) Although prosecutions are a matter for the police, in practice prosecutions are rarely brought before representations are dealt with, and therefore representations can safely be made in meritorious cases.

(12) While an MP is involved no steps will be taken to enforce your client's departure until a decision has been made upon the representations and a reasonable time has elapsed to enable the Member to be notified. There have been occasions where the Minister has been willing to consider further representations if new facts have come to light or if it can be shown that the decision has been made on the basis of wrong or inaccurate information. Where further representations are made, the Minister may agree not to enforce departure until a further decision is made.

THE OLD RULES[1]

9.21 It is unlikely that the approach to applications under the old rules will differ to those under present rules, as many of the amendments were for 'tidying up' purposes and were already reflected in Home Office practice. The only difference of any practical consequence may arise in cases where a person prohibited from employment seeks a variation to take work. The old rules provided that such applications were 'normally' to be refused without reference to the Department.[2] If the Home Office were prepared to refer, they would not grant an extension unless the Department approved the employment. There was no way of compelling the Home Office to refer a case.

It is difficult to envisage circumstances which would be regarded as 'abnormal' in this context. In *Tally*,[3] the appellant sought to remain as a diesel fitter at British Rail, arguing that there was a shortage of skilled workers there. The Tribunal held that the fact that British Rail had vacancies did not constitute an abnormal situation which would warrant departure from the terms of the rule, and remarked that 'normally means

---

[1] See generally HC 80, 82 paras. 1–5.

[2] HC 80, 82 para. 5.

[3] [1975] Imm AR 83. See also *Moussa* [1976] Imm AR 78 and *Pereyra* [1978] Imm AR 13.

in the normal way or usually'. And in *Stillwagon*,[4] 'a singer of unique and extraordinary talent' was similarly refused. According to the Tribunal, 'there must be exceptional circumstances, such as strong personal and compassionate reasons or reasons involving an aspect of vital public interest'. The Tribunal did, however, hold in *Sarwar*,[5] that on the particular facts of the case the absence of religious instruction of Muslim girls in four English secondary schools could properly be regarded as a matter of vital public interest and that the Home Office were therefore wrong in refusing to refer an application by a qualified teacher who was to have been employed by an educational trust who ran the schools. In *Nicolaides*,[6] where the employer showed that he would be in difficulties without the applicant's services, the Tribunal took the view that the 'abnormality' should generally relate to the applicant's circumstances; those of the employer, if they are to be considered at all, were only of a minor consideration.

As most appeals of this nature are bound to fail, the applicant is only likely to succeed if he can persuade the Home Office at the outset to permit him to stay. Efforts should therefore be concentrated on providing the Home Office with sufficient information on the initial application to justify what in most cases will be a departure from the immigration rules. Consideration should also be given to the applicant leaving the UK and applying for a work permit from overseas. This may be the most sensible course of action if the employer can prove that he is unable to fill the job.

REGISTRATION WITH THE POLICE

9.22 A condition requiring registration with the police may be imposed on foreign nationals (including EEC nationals) but not on Commonwealth citizens.[7] A foreign national aged 16 or over who has *limited leave* to enter will normally be required to register if entry is for employment for longer than three months. This includes any person with a work permit and anyone in a permit-free category, except for ministers of religion, missionaries and members of religious orders;

[4] [1975] Imm AR 132.
[5] [1978] Imm AR 190.
[6] [1978] Imm AR 67.
[7] The Act empowers the Home Secretary to make regulations requiring any non-patrial to register with the police: s. 4(3); but the regulations, Immigration (Registration with the Police) Regulations 1972, SI 1972, No. 1758 apply only to aliens (foreign nationals): reg. 3: and see HC 394, paras. 65, 66; 122–124.

doctors and dentists; and private servants of diplomats.[8] Visitors, students, au-pairs, business and self-employed persons, persons of independent means, writers and artists, and husbands[9] will normally be required to register where leave is longer than six months. A wife or child under 18 (non-EEC foreign nationals) or a member of the family (EEC nationals) of a person who is required to register with the police,[10] will also normally be required to register. Any other foreign national may have a condition to register imposed 'exceptionally . . . where the immigration officer considers it necessary in order to ensure that (he) complies with terms of a limited leave to enter.[11]

If a condition is not imposed on entry but an extension of stay is later granted which permits the applicant to remain in the UK for employment (other than the permit free employment mentioned above) or for any other purpose for longer than six months reckoned from the date of arrival, a condition requiring registration is to be imposed unless the applicant is under 16.[12] A condition requiring registration lapses when a person is given indefinite leave to remain. It will not be revoked before then.[13] The police are required to keep a register of aliens.[14] A person must register at the police station nearest his address, or if in the Metropolitan Police area at the Aliens Registration Office.[15]

9.23 Registration must take place within seven days of the rules becoming applicable to the foreign national.[16] He must produce two identical recent photographs[17] and provide such information, documents and other particulars relating to him as are required for completing the register and issuing a certificate of registration.[18] The particulars to be entered in the register are as follows:[19]

---

[8] HC 394, para. 65(a).
[9] Ibid., para. 65(b).
[10] Ibid., para. 65(c).
[11] Ibid., para. 66.
[12] Ibid., para. 122.
[13] Ibid., para. 123.
[14] Immigration (Registration with the Police) Regulations 1972, reg. 4(2). The Chief Officer of Police for each police area is the registration officer for that area: ibid., reg. 4(1). He may authorise a police officer or other person to carry out his responsibilities under the Regulations; ibid., reg. 4(3).
[15] Ibid., reg. 4(1). The address of the Aliens Registration Office is 10 Lamb's Conduit Street, London WC1: tel. 01–725 2451.
[16] Ibid., reg. 5(1).
[17] Ibid. See also ibid., reg. 9(1).
[18] Ibid., reg. 5(1).
[19] Ibid., Sch.

(1) Name in full
(2) Sex
(3) Matrimonial status
(4) Date of birth; country of birth
(5) Present nationality; how and when acquired; previous nationality (if any)
(6) Particulars of passport or other document establishing nationality
(7) Business profession or occupation
(8) Residence in the UK (or address if no residence)
(9) Name and address of referee where applicable
(10) Last residence outside the UK
(11) Date, place and mode of arrival in UK
(12) Duration of limited leave and conditions attached thereto
(13) Restrictions or conditions, if applicable, for those travelling within the Common Travel Area
(14) Name and address of employer; address at which employed, if different (if employed in UK) or name under which business or profession is carried on; address at which business or profession is carried on
(15) Signature (or fingerprints if unable to write in the characters of the English language)
(16) Photograph.

9.24 The foreign national will then be issued with a certificate of registration.[20] This is in the form of a green booklet, although EEC nationals with a residence permit may have the registration endorsed in the permit.[1] There is a fee payable for the issue of the certificate to a non-EEC national.[2] A foreign national must notify the police of any change of address within seven days of his arrival at the new address.[3] He is also under a duty to inform the police if there is any change of name, marital

---

[20] Ibid., reg. 10(1).

[1] Ibid., reg. 10(2).

[2] The current fee for the issue of the certificate is £21.00 except that a £11.00 fee is payable for a certificate for a wife where a husband and wife are registering together, and for children under 18 where registering with a parent; for a non-EEC spouse or an EEC national where the spouses are registering together; and for a replacement certificate: the Immigration (Registration with Police) (Amendment) Regulations 1981, SI 1981, No. 534.

[3] Beginning with the date of arrival: Immigration (Registration with the Police) Regulations 1972, 7(2).

status, nationality, passport or employment, and to supply recent photographs, information, documents or further particulars required to complete the register.[4] Notification may be either in person at the appropriate police station, or in writing enclosing the registration certificate.[5]

There are also provisions for reporting to the police where a person is away from his residence for a continuous period of more than two months without adopting a new residence and where he has no residence in the UK for the time being.[6] In the latter case he may nominate a referee to provide the information to the police.[7] A person who has lawfully entered the UK on a local journey from a place in the common travel area who either (1) first arrived in the Islands or the Republic of Ireland from a place outside the common travel area; or (2) left the UK while having limited leave to enter or remain which has since expired, will be deemed to be admitted for a limited period and be subject to conditions restricting employment and reporting to the police.[8]

9.25 A person may be required to produce the registration certificate, (1) by a police officer, to make amendments to the certificate where there is an alteration to the register;[9] (2) by an immigration or police officer on demand. An explanation for failure to produce the certificate may be sought and this may be followed by a requirement to produce the certificate within 48 hours at a police station specified by the officer.[10] Failure to comply with any of the registration requirements is a criminal offence, the maximum punishment for which is a fine of £200 and/or six months' imprisonment.[11]

TRAVEL DOCUMENTS

9.26 A problem sometimes arises where a person finds that his Embassy or High Commission refuses to revalidate his passport or issue him with a

---

[4] Within eight days from the date of change; ibid., reg. 8.
[5] Ibid., reg. 9(2).
[6] Ibid., reg. 7(3)–(6).
[7] Ibid., reg. 7(6).
[8] Immigration Act 1971, s. 9(2).
[9] Immigration (Registration with the Police) Regulations 1972, reg. 11(1).
[10] Ibid., reg. 11(2).
[11] Immigration Act 1971, s. 26(1)(f). It is also an offence to give false information on regulation (s. 26(1)(c)) or to alter a certificate or to possess for immigration purposes a false certificate (s. 26(1)(d)).

new one. The Home Office may be prepared to issue a travel document in certain limited circumstances.[12]

9.27 A certificate of identity which is in book form and coloured brown may be issued to those who are settled here or who are in a category which leads to settlement. The applicant must show to the Home Office that he has been unable to obtain passport facilities from his own national authorities and that he has a need to travel abroad. A certificate of identity will be valid for a maximum period of one year for those whose stay is still subject to time conditions and two years for those who are settled in the UK. A certificate of identity in sheet form and coloured cream may be issued as an emergency travel document for persons who have an urgent compassionate or other compelling reason to travel,[13] but for whose documentation the Home Office are not yet prepared to accept general responsibility. The Home Office state that a typical case would involve insufficient evidence of formal refusal of passport facilities. The certificate in sheet form is normally valid for one year and for one return journey, and is impounded on the holder's return to the UK. A certificate of identity in whatever form effectively guarantees, within the period of its validity and without the need for a re-entry visa, the holder's readmission to the UK.

9.28 Refugees and stateless persons who have been recognised as such by the Home Office will also be issued with travel documents: the circumstances in which they are issued are discussed in Chapter 15.[14]

9.29 A declaration of identity which is in sheet form and coloured white may be issued by the Home Office to facilitate deportation or repatriation when alternative national documentation is not readily available. The declaration of identity is a one-way document and should not be confused with a certificate of identity.

[12] Letter, Home Office to Sir Leslie Kirklees, Chairman, Standing Conference on Refugees, 4 November 1980, from which source the information contained in the remainder of the text is taken.

[13] The Home Office has arrangements for the issue of travel documents in urgent circumstances. Although applications are normally considered in the order of receipt, applications for priority treatment are dealt with on their merits. The Home Office advises those seeking priority to produce evidence of urgency; for example, an employer's letter or medical certificate where appropriate.

[14] See paras. 15.20 and 15.24, post.

TEN

Criminal Offences

INTRODUCTION

10.1 There are a number of criminal sanctions arising from the enforcement of immigration control. The types of offences which are most likely to arise in practice can be summarised as follows:

(1) disregarding the requirements of immigration control (s. 24);
(2) assisting illegal entry and harbouring (s. 25);
(3) failing to co-operate with or misleading the immigration authorities (s. 26).[1]

Although most provisions of the Act came into force on 1 January 1973 the offence of assisting illegal entry[2] operated from 28 November 1971.[3] The offences are not retrospective and a person cannot therefore be convicted under the Act as a result of anything done before the Act came into force.[4] The offences can only be tried in a magistrates' court with the exception of assisting illegal entry under s. 25(1) which can be dealt with either in the magistrates' or Crown Court.

10.2 There is no time limit for bringing proceedings in the Crown Court, but magistrates must try on information laid within six months from the time when the offence is committed.[5] The Act, however, extends

---

[1] A fourth group of offences provides penalties for those connected with ships, aircraft and ports who fail to comply with requirements of the Act relating to the embarkation and disembarkation of passengers: Immigration Act 1971, s. 27.

[2] Ibid., s. 25(1).

[3] As did the other subsections of s. 25(3)–(8). This date was one month after the passing of the Act (28 October 1971). The offences of harbouring came into effect on 1 January 1973. Similar offences existed under previous legislation. For the full provisions of the date of operation of criminal sanctions, see s. 35(2), (3).

[4] *Waddington* v *Miah* [1974] 2 All ER 377 HL.

[5] Magistrates' Courts Act 1980, s. 127(1).

the time limit for the prosecution of most immigration offences in magistrates' courts. A prosecution can be brought if the information is laid (1) within six months after the commission of the offence; or (2) within three years after the commission of the offence and not more than two months after the date certified by a chief officer of police to be the date on which evidence sufficient to justify proceedings came to the notice of an officer of his police force.[6] The extended prosecution period applies to the offences of illegal entry, overstaying, (including overstaying by seamen and aircrew),[7] all offences involving assisting illegal entry and harbouring,[8] making false representations to an immigration officer and falsifying documents.[9] It is not necessary for the prosecution to know where the alleged offender was at the time the offence was committed. He is deemed to have committed the offence at any place at which he may be.[10] The starting of criminal proceedings does not preclude the immigration authorities from exercising their powers under the Act[11] (e.g. by serving notice of intention to deport).

DISREGARDING THE REQUIREMENTS OF IMMIGRATION CONTROL

10.3 The following offences apply to non-patrials only, and are dealt with in the magistrates' court; the maximum penalty on conviction is a fine not exceeding £200 or six months' imprisonment or both.

Illegal Entry

10.4 The offence of illegal entry is committed by knowingly entering the UK in breach of a deportation order, or without leave, contrary to s. 24(1)(a) of the Act. The burden of proving that the accused was an illegal entrant normally lies with the prosecution, but the Act requires the accused to prove he was given leave to enter if the prosecution is brought within six months of the date of entry.[12] The onus is also on the

---

[6] Immigration Act 1971, s. 28(1)(a). There are similar provisions relating to Scotland and Northern Ireland; ibid., s. 28(1)(b)(c), (2).

[7] Ibid., s. 24(1)(a), (b)(i), (c).

[8] Ibid., s. 25.

[9] Ibid., s. 26(1)(c), (d). See also ibid., ss. 24(3); 25(4), 26(2). If a conviction is obtained notwithstanding the time limits have expired, *certiorari* will be granted to quash the conviction: *R v Eastbourne Justices, ex parte Bassoum* (1979) CLY 488.

[10] Immigration Act 1971, s. 28(3).

[11] Ibid., s. 28(4).

[12] Ibid., s. 24(4)(b).

accused where he challenges the date of the stamp endorsed in the passport.[13] Proof by the accused is on a balance of probabilities. The offence must be committed 'knowingly'.

Overstaying

10.5 A person overstays if, having only limited leave to enter or remain in the UK, he knowingly remains beyond the time limited by the leave.[14] The accused must 'knowingly' have committed the offence. This must be proved by the prosecution. 'Knowingly' includes the state of mind of the accused who suspects the truth but deliberately avoids finding out.[15] In *R* v *Bello*,[16] the defence that the accused was so upset by his mother's death that at the particular time he did not know he had overstayed was rejected by the Court of Appeal on the basis that a person must have 'known' of something if he had the capacity for reviving it from his memory. The offence is not a continuing one,[17] but the indictment will not be defective if it charges the accused of remaining unlawfully on a day between two specific dates.[18] Where a person appeals under the Act against a refusal of an extension of stay,[19] he remains lawfully in the UK pending the hearing of the appeal, but if he withdraws the appeal he commits the offence of overstaying from the date of the withdrawal.[20] A person who has overstayed will not usually be detained on departure by the immigration authorities for prosecution, nor generally will he be questioned. A lengthy period of overstaying is, however, likely to result in a report being forwarded by the immigration officer to the Home Office, and difficulties may arise should that person wish to seek entry to the UK on a future occasion.

Failing to Observe a Condition of Leave

10.6 A person who, having only limited leave to enter or remain in the UK, knowingly fails to observe a condition of the leave commits an offence.[1] There are only two conditions which may be attached to a

[13] Ibid., s. 24(4)(a).
[14] Ibid., s. 24(1)(b)(i).
[15] *Roper* v *Taylor Garages Ltd* (1951) 2 TLR 284 at 288. For a more detailed discussion of the meaning of the word see Smith and Hogan, *Criminal Law* (4th Edn.), pp. 102–103.
[16] [1978] Crim LR 551 CA.
[17] *Singh (Gurdev)* v *R* [1974] 1 All ER 26.
[18] *R* v *Tzanatos* (1978) CLY 523, CA.
[19] See para. 9.9, ante.
[20] *Horne* v *Gaygusuz* [1979] Crim LR 594.
[1] Immigration Act 1971, s. 24(1)(b)(ii).

leave to enter or remain: (1) a restriction on taking employment or carrying out an occupation, and (2) a requirement to register with the police.[2] The condition attached to the grant of leave only continues to apply while the leave is in force. Once the leave expires, the condition expires with it and the offence of infringing a condition of limited leave is 'merged' in the offence of overstaying.[3] Thus, an overstayer originally prohibited from taking employment is not committing an offence by working after his leave has expired.[4] There is no obligation under the Immigration Act on a prospective employer to make enquiries to establish whether the applicant is subject to employment restrictions.[5] It is now, however, an offence to aid, abet, counsel or procure the offence.[6] The prosecution must prove that the employer desired the offence to be committed or was recklessly indifferent as to whether it was committed or not.[7]

Overstaying Seamen and Aircrew

10.7 Seamen and aircrew who, having lawfully entered the UK without leave because, for example, they are to depart on the same ship or aircraft,[8] commit an offence[9] if they remain without leave beyond the time allowed.

Miscellaneous Offences

10.8 A person who, without reasonable excuse, fails to comply with a requirement to report to, or attend or submit to an examination by a medical officer commits an offence.[10] The requirement is under Schedule 2 to the Act and relates to those seeking entry into the UK.[11] In addition

[2] Ibid., s. 3 (1)(c).
[3] *Singh (Gurdev)* v *R* cited, note 17 supra.
[4] See para. 9.11, ante.
[5] The Home Office accepts that this is the position. Letter, Timothy Raison, Minister of State at the Home Office to Eric Deakins MP, 15 June 1981.
[6] Magistrates' Courts Act 1980, s. 44 which extends the offence of aiding, abetting, counselling or procuring to summary offences in so far as they were not covered by earlier legislation.
[7] An offence may be committed if a person deliberately refrains from making enquiries, the result of which he does not care to have, but not if he merely neglects to make reasonable enquiries: *Roper* v *Taylor's Central Garages (Exeter) Ltd* (1951) 2 TLR 284.
[8] See Immigration Act 1971, s. 8.
[9] Ibid., s. 24(1)(c).
[10] Ibid., s. 24(1)(d).
[11] Ibid., Sch. 2, para. 2; those who may be examined on entry are set out in para. 2(1). See para. 5.31, ante.

it is an offence for a person, without reasonable excuse, to fail to observe a condition of residence or to fail to report to the police or an immigration officer.[12] These conditions may be imposed where a person, liable to be detained by an immigration officer, is given temporary admission or release by such officer,[13] or a person liable to deportation is similarly released by the Home Secretary.[14] They do not arise in any other circumstances.

10.8 It is an offence to disembark in the UK from a ship or aircraft after being placed on a ship with a view to removal.[15]

'Hostage Orders'

10.9 Where UK citizens are restricted when leaving or trying to leave another country, the Act enables retaliatory measures to be taken against non-patrial nationals of that country who are in the UK. An Order in Council may be made prohibiting the nationals from leaving the UK or restricting their departure to a specific port and imposing restrictions and conditions on their departure. This has aptly been described as a 'hostage order'.[16] It is an offence to contravene the requirements of such an order.[17]

POWERS OF POLICE AND IMMIGRATION OFFICERS

10.10 A police or immigration officer may arrest without warrant anyone (1) who has, or (2) whom he had reasonable cause to suspect to have, committed or attempted to commit any of these offences, except that of failing to report to a medical officer.[18]

There has been widespread complaint that the police regularly ask immigration questions of people with whom they come into contact for other reasons; e.g. on a person being stopped on suspicion of committing a driving offence or on the police visiting a house where there has been a disturbance on one floor and asking questions of an occupier of premises on another floor. Those questioned are often black but not

---

[12] Ibid., s. 24(1)(e).
[13] Ibid., Sch. 2, para. 21.
[14] Ibid., Sch. 3, para. 2(5).
[15] Ibid., s. 24(1)(f).
[16] See I. MacDonald, *The New Immigration Law* (1972) Butterworths, p. 82. No Orders in Council have been made under s. 3(7).
[17] Immigration Act 1971, s. 24(1)(g).
[18] Ibid., s. 24(2).

necessarily subject to immigration control.[19] The problem has become so serious as to warrant the Home Secretary issuing guidelines to Chief Officers of Police advising them to avoid any action which might be construed as harassment of immigrants 'such as request to inspect the passport of someone who comes to notice in connection with a minor offence but whom there is no reason to suspect of being in this country illegally'.[20] A similar instruction has been issued by the Metropolitan Commissioner of Police.[1]

The Home Secretary has since initiated a review of procedures adopted in joint operations by the police and the immigration service against illegal entrants and overstayers. He announced results of the review in a written statement in the House of Commons.

'The issues which gave rise to the greatest concern in recent operations, most of which took place in the Metropolitan Police District, were the arrest of people who were subsequently found not to have committed an immigration offence and the length of time for which some people were detained. Following discussions with the Metropolitan Police and the Association of Chief Police Officers, it has been agreed that every effort should be made before an operation takes place to identify those people who are suspected of committing immigration offences, in order to minimise the risk of arresting innocent people. A Metropolitan Police Order describing the procedures that will in future be adopted in such operations in the Metropolitan Police District has been issued by the Commissioner of Police of the Metropolis. This emphasises the sensitivity of immigration inquiries, and joint operations in particular, and the care which is needed to avoid any action likely to cause justifiable complaint. The Order states that in all cases the appropriate community liaison officer is to be consulted. It makes clear that where persons are questioned and can be immediately eliminated from suspicion they should be subjected to no further inconvenience, and that if their innocence can be established within a very short time, for example by calling at an address reasonably close to the place where the enquiry is being undertaken, this course of action should always be considered. The Order also stresses that where persons are taken to a police station all enquiries must be con-

[19] For a more detailed examination see I. MacDonald, 'Police Raids and Searches for Immigrant Offenders', *New Law Journal* (1981) July.

[20] 977 H. of C. Official Report, 29 January 1980, Written Answers, col. 552.

[1] 'When a person comes to notice for some minor offence or other reasons, he should not normally be asked to produce his passport unless there is reason to suspect an offence against the (Immigration) Act' – Metropolitan Police Instruction Book.

ducted as a matter of urgency, to reduce to a minimum any period of detention. . . . A Home Office Circular (No. 131–1980) has been sent to chief officers of police informing them of the outcome of the review in terms similar to those of this statement.'[2]

There will still be fears, however, that 'fishing' expeditions will continue. Those questioned may be taken into custody, but they will have no effective means to prevent or challenge police action at the time it occurs.[3] They are thus left with making a formal complaint against the police after the event or commencing civil proceedings for damages for wrongful arrest or false imprisonment.

ASSISTING ILLEGAL ENTRY AND HARBOURING

Assisting Illegal Entry

10.11 It is an offence for patrials or non-patrials to be 'knowingly concerned in making or carrying out arrangements for securing or facilitating the entry' of illegal entrants. This is the most serious offence under the Act. If tried by magistrates the maximum penalty is six months' imprisonment and a fine of £1,000 (or both); in the Crown Court the maximum is seven years and an unlimited fine.[4] The Court also has wide powers to order the forfeiture of ships, aircraft and other vehicles used for illegal entry if those convicted of the offence are the owners, or captain of such craft.[5] Assisting illegal entry is widely defined. In *R* v *Singh*,[6] the Court of Appeal rejected the submission that the offence could not be committed once the illegal entrants had left the part of the port under immigration authority control, entry into the UK having been effected. The court held that plans for getting the entrant away as quickly as possible from the point of disembarkation were facilitating entry. The offence may be committed overseas by British subjects who are not citizens of independent Commonwealth countries and by British protected persons. A police or immigration officer can arrest without warrant anyone who (1)

[2] 996 H. of C. Official Report, 12 December 1980, Written Answers, col. 844.
[3] There are serious problems, both practical and legal, in suggesting to an officer that he is acting outside his powers, and see the offence of obstructing an officer in the execution of the Act. See paras. 10.14, 10.15, post.
[4] Immigration Act 1971, s. 25(1) as amended by the Criminal Law Act 1977, s. 28(2).
[5] Ibid., s. 25(6)–(8).
[6] [1973] 1 All ER 122, CA.

has or (2) with reasonable cause he suspects to have committed the offence of assisting illegal entry.[7]

Harbouring

10.12 The Act makes it an offence for a person knowingly to harbour anyone whom he knows or has reasonable cause to believe is, (1) an illegal entrant; (2) an overstayer, or (3) in breach of his conditions of stay (i.e. working without permission or failing to register with the police).[8] The offence can only be tried in the magistrates' court. The maximum penalty is six months' imprisonment or a £400 fine (or both).[9] In *R v Mistry; R v Asare*[10] the Court of Appeal held that 'harbouring' means giving shelter: there is no necessity to prove an intention to protect the illegal entrant from the authorities or that the accused had a right or title to the premises in question provided he knew or had reasonable cause to believe he was sheltering an illegal entrant. The Court took the view that there was no reason in principle why a husband could not harbour his wife even though he would need an order under the Matrimonial Homes Act 1967 to evict her. This, however, is open to serious doubt.[11] An immigration officer has no power to arrest for this offence. A police officer needs a warrant before an arrest can be made.[12] The extended time limit for prosecutions applies to both assisting illegal entry and harbouring.[13]

FAILING TO CO-OPERATE WITH OR MISLEADING THE IMMIGRATION AUTHORITIES

10.13 The following offences also apply both to patrials (where appropriate) and non-patrials. They can only be dealt with in the magistrates' court. The maximum penalty is six months' imprisonment or a £200 fine (or both).

---

[7] Immigration Act 1971, s. 25(2).
[8] Ibid., s. 25(2).
[9] Ibid., as amended by the Criminal Law Act 1977, s. 28(2). See also *R v Mehet* [1980] Crim LR 374.
[10] [1980] Crim LR 177.
[11] See the commentary on the decision in [1980] Crim LR pp. 177–178.
[12] Immigration Act 1971, s. 25(3) limits arrest without warrant to offences under s. 25(1).
[13] Ibid., ss. 25(4), 28

(a) Failing to submit to an examination under Schedule 2.[14]
(b) Failing to provide the documentation required on a Schedule 2 examination.[15]
(c) Making false statements to an immigration officer or other person lawfully acting in the execution of the Act.[16] The extent to which other persons may lawfully act in the execution of the Act is considered in para. 10.14. The false statement may be made during the course of a Schedule 2 examination 'or otherwise'.[17] It is difficult to envisage in what other situations this can apply as these words must be *ejusdem generis* to the examination.[18] In *R v Gill*,[19] a police officer while investigating a disturbance involving the appellant was told that he was an illegal entrant. The officer investigated by asking the appellant to produce his passport. He said he had lost it but later made a written statement that he had entered illegally and lost his passport to avoid detection. He was convicted of making a false statement. On appeal the Court of Appeal held that no offence had been committed, because at the time the appellant made the original statement to the officer the officer was merely making an investigation. The fact that the purpose of the investigation was to establish whether there were grounds for suspecting the appellant was an illegal entrant did not make the officer a person 'acting in the execution of the Act'.
(d) Altering or possessing altered immigration documents.[20] The documents are any certificate of patriality, entry clearance, work permit or 'other document issued or made under or for the purpose of the Act', e.g. police registration document. It is also an offence to possess for use a false passport[1] or a genuine passport with false entries.[2]

---

[14] Ibid., s. 26(1)(a). For the requirements of a Sch. 2 examination, see para. 5.31, ante.
[15] Ibid., s. 26(1)(b).
[16] Ibid., s. 26(1)(c); Sch. 2, para. 1(1). Customs officers may be appointed to act as immigration officers: ibid; see para. 5.29, post.
[17] Immigration Act 1971, s. 26(1)(c).
[18] See the observations of James LJ in *R v Gill* [1976] 2 All ER 893 at 896, CA.
[19] [1976] 2 All ER 893.
[20] Ibid., s. 26(1)(d).
[1] Ibid.
[2] *R v Zaman* [1975] Crim LR 710, CA. The defence that the passport was being used only for the purpose of the British Nationality Act 1948 (to confirm citizenship) was rejected. On the facts it was impossible to say that the passport was not also being used for purposes under the Immigration Act.

(e) Failing to complete and produce a landing or embarkation card.[3]
(f) Failing to comply with regulations relating to registration with the police and keeping hotel records.[4]
(g) Obstructing an immigration officer or other person lawfully acting in the execution of the Act.[5]

10.14 'Other persons' who may lawfully act in the execution of the Act are:
   (1) police officers exercising powers in connection with,
       (a) criminal immigration offences,[6]
       (b) registration of foreign nationals with the police,[7]
       (c) the keeping of hotel records,[8]
   (2) medical inspectors or a qualified person carrying out a test or examination required by a medical inspector[9] or a medical officer of environmental health,[10]
   (3) those authorised by the Home Secretary to inspect hotel records.[11]

No other person has any powers under the Act. It has been suggested[12] that it may be an offence to obstruct employees of Securicor Ltd who staff detention accommodation.[13] It is submitted this is not the case. They have no powers of examination, arrest or detention. Although a person in detention may be committing an offence, where, for example, he refuses to obey an instruction of Securicor staff to submit himself to further examination by an immigration officer, the offence is one of obstructing the immigration officer alone. A person in detention is under no obligation to carry out instructions given by private security staff if those instructions do not arise out of the lawful requirements of other officers acting in the execution of the Act.

10.15 If the law relating to the obstruction of a police constable acting

---

[3] Immigration Act 1971, s. 26(1)(e), Sch. 2 para. 5 and the Immigration (Landing and Embarkation Cards) Order 1975, SI 1975, No. 65; see para. 4.10, ante.
[4] Immigration Act 1971, s. 26(1)(f), and see Immigration (Registration with Police) Regulations 1972, SI 1972 No. 1758, as amended, and Immigration (Hotel Records) Order 1972, SI 1972 No. 1689 made under powers conferred by ss. 4(3), (4) repectively.
[5] Immigration Act 1971, s. 26(1)(g).
[6] Ibid., ss. 24(2), 25(3).
[7] Ibid., s. 26(1)(f) and see note 4 supra.
[8] Ibid.
[9] Ibid., s. 26(1)(a), Sch. 2, para 1(2). Sch. 2, para. 2(2). See paras. 5.20, 5.36, ante.
[10] Ibid., s. 26(1)(a), Sch. 2, para. 2(2). See para. 5.22, ante.
[11] See note 20 supra.
[12] MacDonald op. cit., pp. 97–98.
[13] See para. 13.2, post.

in the execution of his duty is followed in cases under this subsection, then it is no defence that the accused did not know that the person was an immigration or other officer[14] or that he mistakenly but genuinely believed that the officer was not acting in the execution of his duty.[15] However by far the most serious problem will be the inability of the person to challenge at the time the legality of the action.

ILLEGAL ENTRANTS AND THE CRIMINAL LAW

10.16 It is rare for a prosecution to be brought charging a person with being an illegal entrant as there is an alternative, and from the authorities' viewpoint, a more effective course of action: namely to detain and remove a person who they suspect to be an illegal entrant by the administrative powers conferred on them by the Act.[16] For the same reasons, prosecutions are unusual for those offences arising from failure to co-operate with or misleading the immigration authorities as in most cases the offender will be regarded as an illegal entrant. There is no effective right of appeal against this procedure and such appeal that does exist can only take place after the person has left the UK.[17]

The most immediate effect of by-passing the prosecution process is that the provisions relating to bail in criminal cases do not apply to administrative detention, and release from custody is at the discretion of an immigration officer.[18] Other advantages to the immigration authorities are that they do not have to show that the person knowingly entered illegally[19] and the burden of proof will rest with the entrant to show that he did not so enter.[20] Thus, those who are removed by the administrative process might well have been acquitted had they been tried for the offence of illegal entry.[1]

[14] This issue now seems to be settled following *McBride* v *Turnock* [1964] Crim LR 456.
[15] *R* v *Fennell* [1970] 3 All ER 215.
[16] Ibid., Sch. 2 paras. 16, 17 (detention); para. 9 (removal). See paras. 12.1 et seq.; 13.13 et seq., post. The initial arrest is made under this subsection but the continued detention is justified by the Sch. 2 provisions.
[17] Ibid., s. 16.
[18] Ibid., Sch. 2, para. 21.
[19] E.g. the applicant in *Khan* v *Secretary of State for the Home Department* [1977] 3 All ER 538, CA, para. 12.5, post, could not have been convicted for illegal entry on the facts: illiterate woman obtained entry on false passport produced by her husband, but she was nevertheless removed as an illegal entrant.
[20] Cf., this with the provisions of s. 24(4).
[1] See, e.g. *Mohammed Anwar* (1978) 19 January 448/77 DC (unreported).

ELEVEN

Deportation

GENERAL RULES

11.1 All non-patrials (with a small number of exceptions) are liable to be deported from the UK if any of the following circumstances arise: (1) they have failed to comply with a condition of admission or have remained beyond the time limit on their stay; (2) the Home Secretary deems their deportation to be conducive to the public good; (3) another member of their family is to be deported; (4) they have been convicted of a criminal offence and the court recommends deportation.[1]

Right of Appeal

11.2 There is no right of appeal under the immigration appeals procedure following a recommendation for deportation by a court although a convicted person can appeal against sentence through the usual criminal appeals system.[2] In the first three categories of deportation, there is a right of appeal against the decision of the Home Secretary, either to an adjudicator at first instance, or directly to the Tribunal.[3] Where the appeal is against deportation based on security or political grounds,[4] there is no statutory right of appeal but there is provision to make representations to a three-man security advisory panel appointed by the Home Secretary.[5] A deportation order can be revoked on an application to the Home Office, and revocation may be granted if a sufficient period of time has elapsed since the making of the order or if there has been a change in the deportee's circumstances. In most cases

---

[1] See generally, Immigration Act 1971 ss. 3(5), (6), 5, 6, 7, 15, 16, 17; HC 394, paras. 133–156.
[2] See para. 11.38, post.
[3] Immigration Act 1971, s. 15.
[4] Ibid., s. 15(3).
[5] See para. 11.26, post.

there is again a right of appeal against a refusal to revoke a deportation order.[6]

Exemptions

11.3 The only non-patrials who are exempt from deportation are certain Commonwealth and Irish citizens. To qualify for exemption the person must show that:

(1) he was a Commonwealth citizen or citizen of the Republic of Ireland on date of decision; and
(2) he was a Commonwealth citizen or a citizen of the Republic of Ireland on 1 January 1973; and
(3) he was ordinarily resident in the UK on 1 January 1973, and
(4) he has been ordinarily resident in the UK for five years preceding the Home Secretary's decision, or in case of a recommendation following conviction, for five years prior to the conviction.[7]

The onus is on the deportee to show that he is entitled to the exemption.[8]

11.4 The general meaning of ordinary residence has already been discussed.[9] It must be lawful residence and thus illegal residents cannot qualify. However, for the purpose of this exemption only, once an initial lawful residence has been established, further residence in breach of the immigration laws will be accepted as ordinary residence and will count towards making up the five year period;[10] for example, a person who is given leave to enter and overstays can take into account the time here after the expiry of his leave. Periods spent in prison or detention in the UK do not count towards lawful residence if the accused was sentenced to at least six months.[11] Consecutive sentences are regarded as one sentence for this purpose. The period in prison includes absences from prison during escapes and, more unfortunately, remands in custody before trial and sentence.[12] The five years is calculated from the date on

---

[6] Ibid., s. 15(4), (5).

[7] Ibid., s. 7(1). In addition, those who are liable for deportation on grounds conducive to the public good are exempt, irrespective of the length of time they have been ordinarily resident here, provided they have been so resident at all times since 1 January 1973. This provision has become superfluous since 1 January 1978.

[8] Ibid., s. 3(8).

[9] See para. 8.3, ante.

[10] Ibid., s. 7(2).

[11] Ibid., s. 7(3).   [12] Ibid., s. 7(4).

which the decision to deport was made and not from the date of the signing of the deportation order.[13] The date on which the decision is taken is a question of fact and is not necessarily the same date as that of the *notice* of decision served on the deportee.[14] It should be noted that Irish and Commonwealth citizens are only exempt where they were such citizens both on 1 January 1973 and on the date of the decision. Thus, for example, citizens of Pakistan therefore no longer qualify for exemption.[15]

Finally, exemption from deportation does not confer a right of abode, nor even a right to settlement, although in most cases the Home Office will be prepared to regularise the position by granting indefinite leave to remain. Until his positions has been regularised the entrant is 'trapped' in the country, in that he is safe in remaining here but if he were to leave, he would have to qualify for re-admission in the same manner as any other entrant.

11.5 In practice, the making of a deportation order against a non-patrial citizen of the UK and Colonies is unlikely unless the person has a connection with a colony or has another nationality. Further, the immigration rules provide that a deportation order will not be made against a person if the only country to which he can be removed is one to which he is unwilling to go owing to a well-founded fear of being persecuted for reasons of race, religion, nationality, membership of a particular group or political opinion.[17] A person marrying a patrial will not thereby be exempt from deportation except that a woman who is a Commonwealth citizen will obtain patriality on marriage.[18] A foreign national woman or a man, although they may be permitted to settle here after marriage,[19] are still subject to the deportation provisions until they acquire a right of abode through naturalisation or registration as a UK

---

[13] *R v Secretary of State for the Home Department, ex parte A D Mehmet* [1977] Imm AR 68, CA.

[14] *Rehman* [1978] Imm AR 80.

[15] Citizens of Pakistan ceased to be Commonwealth citizens from 1 September 1973; see para. 2.27, ante. It is normally Home Office practice where deportation is in question to treat citizens of Pakistan as though they are still Commonwealth citizens, but this concession has not been granted in some cases where criminal offences have been committed in addition to overstaying.

[16] See the comments in *Din (Moh'd)* [1978] Imm AR 56.

[17] HC 394, para. 150, see para. 15.3, post.

[18] See para. 2.41, ante.

[19] HC 394, para. 117, see para. 8.56, ante.

citizen. There have been a number of cases where a husband who had become settled has been deported on the ground that he has contracted a marriage of convenience, the Tribunal emphasising that there was no right to remain by virtue of marriage and holding that deportation was justified on the ground that it was conducive to public good.[20]

PROCEDURE ON DEPORTATION

Making of Deportation Order

11.6 In those cases where there is a right of appeal under the immigration appeals procedure, once a decision to make a deportation order has been made by the Home Secretary, the person will be served with a notice of an intention to deport and be advised of the right to, and facilities for, appeal. The regulations require the notice to be sent by registered letter or recorded delivery to the 'last known or usual place of abode' of the proposed deportee;[1] if the notice is delivered but the deportee is away, it is nevertheless good service.[2] Service of the notice can be dispensed with altogether if the Home Secretary has 'no knowledge of the whereabouts of abode' of the deportee.[3] This may cause hardship, as a deportation order may be signed before the deportee has actual notice of the decision to deport.

Particulars of Notice of Decision to Deport

11.7 The notice must specify or it must be made clear to the proposed deportee on which ground the Home Secretary has decided to deport but there appears to be nothing to prevent the Home Secretary from deciding to deport on more than one ground.[4] However, the notice of intention to deport cannot be amended so as to change the grounds for

---

[20] See *Butt* 10750/76 (862) (unreported); *El Wahab* 11907/77 (981) (unreported); *Mohsen* 14412/77 (994) (unreported).

[1] Immigration Appeals (Notices) Regulations 1972, SI 1972, No. 1683, reg. 6.

[2] Immigration Appeals (Procedure) Rules 1972, SI 1972, No. 1684, r. 44, and see *Oni* 5539/74 (395) (unreported).

[3] Immigration Appeals (Notices) Regulations 1972, reg. 3(4) and see *Rhemtulla v Immigration Appeal Tribunal* [1979–80] Imm AR 168. The regulation is not *ultra vires* the powers conferred on the Home Secretary under the Act: *R v Secretary of State, ex parte Makhan Singh* (1978) 14 December 20, 21/76 CA (unreported) referred to in *R v Immigration Appeal Tribunal, ex parte Mehmet* [1977] 2 All ER 602.

[4] *R v Immigration Appeal Tribunal, ex parte Ahluwalia* [1979–80] Imm AR 1, per Widgery J at 8.

deporting a person. The Divisional Court so held in *R v Immigration Appeal Tribunal, ex parte Ekrem Mehmet*,[5] where the Home Office unsuccessfully sought to amend a notice specifying 'family' grounds to those of 'overstaying' in the case of a wife and child of a man whose deportation order had been quashed.

Notice of Appeal

11.8 The proposed deportee must give notice of appeal, usually within 14 days of the date of the decision of the Home Secretary. If notice of appeal is then given, the appellant will receive an explanatory statement from the Home Office setting out the basis upon which the decision was taken.[6] Where no appeal is lodged and the appeal period has expired or where an appeal is subsequently dismissed, the order for deportation will be submitted to the Home Secretary for his signature.[7] The order is not effective until signed but it will not be signed while there is a right of appeal or where there is an appeal pending. Although there is a right to apply to appeal out of time, it cannot be exercised if the deportation order is in force.[8] According to the rules, before any deportation order is signed, the Home Secretary will receive a summary of the facts of the case and 'a note of any other relevant information, whether or not it was available to the courts or appellate authorities.' Where deportation is on security or political grounds, the opinions of the advisers will be submitted to the Home Secretary for his consideration, and in cases where the court has recommended deportation, a summary of the case will similarly be submitted.[9]

Practitioners should note that representations against the signing of a deportation order can be made to the Home Secretary even where there has been an appeal of whatever nature which has been dismissed. Although it is likely that a deportation order will nevertheless be signed, there have been instances of successful representations, particularly where new circumstances have arisen which were not previously before the appellate authority or the Home Office. Moreover, representations are essential in cases where there has been a recommendation for deportation because there are only a limited number of issues which a court regards as relevant in deciding whether to make a recommendation: the

[5] [1978] Imm AR 46.
[6] HC 394, para. 151.
[7] Ibid., para. 152.
[8] Immigration Appeals (Procedure) Rules 1972 r. 11(4).
[9] HC 394, para. 152.

Directions to Remove Deportee

11.9 At the same time as the decision to make the deportation order, or at the time an order is signed following a recommendation by a court, notice will be given of directions to secure the deportee's removal from the UK.[10] The immigration rules state that this power should be exercised to secure the person's return to the country of which he is a national or which has recently provided him with a travel document, unless the deportee can show that another country will take him notwithstanding the deportation order.[11] The rules further limit departing from the normal arrangements for removal in that 'regard should be had to the public interest generally, and to any additional expenses that may fall on public funds'.[12]

There is a right of appeal, whatever the circumstances giving rise to the deportation, against being removed (if at all) to the specified destination named in the directions for removal.[13] In cases where there is a right of appeal against deportation to the immigration appellate authority, the two appeals will be heard together.[14] It should be noted that unless the appellant is unable to produce documentary evidence at the hearing that there is an alternative country which is willing to accept him, there is no point in appealing against destination.[15] The Tribunal may be prepared to give some time to investigate the possibility of removal to another country if it can be shown that the enquiries are realistic, but when considering an adjournment a relevant factor will be the additional expense

---

[10] Immigration Act 1971, s. 5(5), Sch. 3.

[11] HC 394, para. 154. If the appeal is against destination only – for example, where a deportation order has been made following a recommendation by a court – it is not possible to argue that the deportation itself is unreasonable: *Ali* v *Immigration Appeal Tribunal* [1973] Imm AR 33, see para. 11.13, post; *Mustafa* [1979–80] Imm AR 32.

[12] Ibid.

[13] Immigration Act 1971, s. 17; HC 394, para. 137. There is no right of appeal against the validity of making the directions except in the most limited circumstances: Immigration Act 1971, s. 16.

[14] Ibid., s. 15(3). If an objection to being removed to a specific destination is not made at the hearing or is not sustained, the deportee cannot later appeal against any directions subsequently made; ibid., s. 15(4).

[15] *Kelzani* [1978] Imm AR 193. The appellant, a stateless person, was removed to Egypt where he had no right to reside permanently but where he had obtained a travel document.

to public funds that the appellant's detention in custody would entail.[16]

Detention and Bail

11.10 Once a decision to make a deportation order has been taken, the Home Secretary has power to make a detention order pending appeal,[17] subject to a right of appeal to the appellate authority to grant bail, if an appeal against the deportation order itself can be and has been lodged.[18] If the court has recommended deportation and passes a suspended or other non-custodial sentence, the offender will be detained unless the court or the Home Secretary otherwise directs.[19] This subject is considered more fully in Chapter 13.

EFFECT OF DEPORTATION ORDER

11.11 A deportation order invalidates leave to enter or remain in the UK while it is in force,[20] although it ceases to have effect if the deportee becomes a patrial.[1] If he should try to enter while the order is current he will be refused admission and advised that after his departure he can apply for revocation from outside the country.[2] If he should manage to enter, he almost certainly will be deported under the original order, although the immigration rules state that 'every such case is to be considered in the light of all the relevant circumstances before the intention to enforce the order is notified to the person'.[3] A deportee has no right of appeal against removal except on the (highly unlikely) ground that there is no power to remove him.[4]

---

[16] *Kroohs* [1978] Imm AR 75, where the appellant had already been detained for nine months.

[17] Immigration Act 1977, Sch. 3, para. 2(2). He can also release a deportee subject to restrictions on the residence and a requirement to report to the police: ibid., para. 2(5).

[18] Ibid., Sch. 2, para. 29(1).

[19] Ibid., Sch. 3, para. 2(1).

[20] Ibid., s. 5(1).

[1] Ibid., s. 5(2).

[2] HC 394, para. 75.

[3] Ibid., para. 153. There is no right of appeal against a refusal to revoke the order if the deportee has not complied with the requirement to leave or if he has contravened a prohibition on re-entering: Immigration Act 1971, s. 15(5).

[4] Ibid., s. 16(1)(a), s. 16(2). Even in this situation he must appeal from outside the UK unless the ground of appeal is that he is not the person named in the order. He cannot dispute the validity of the original order; ibid., s. 16(3).

CONSIDERATIONS IN MAKING A DEPORTATION ORDER

11.12 Before examining the criteria applicable to each of the grounds on which a person is liable to deportation, mention must be made of the general considerations relevant to all cases of deportation. The immigration rules state that in considering whether deportation is the right course on the merits, the public interest is to be balanced against any compassionate circumstances. Although each case is considered in the light of its particular circumstances, the aim is said to be an exercise of power that is consistent and fair as between one person and another. It is nevertheless conceded that 'one case will rarely be identical with another in all material respects'.[5] A further guideline is to be found in the rules relating to deportation following a conviction, which are applicable to cases of deportation on other grounds.[6] The Home Secretary will take into account 'every relevant factor' known to him including (1) age; (2) length of residence in the UK; (3) strength of connections with the UK; (4) personal history, including character, conduct and employment; (5) domestic circumstances; (6) the nature of the offence of which the person was convicted; (7) previous criminal record; (8) compassionate circumstances; and (9) any representations received on the person's behalf.

In *Yuskel*,[7] the Tribunal rejected the decision of the adjudicator, that where there are no compassionate circumstances an appeal against deportation should nevertheless be allowed because 'the current political situation in Cyprus made (the appellants') present return there inappropriate'. The adjudicator held this to be 'a relevant factor'. The Tribunal took the view that while compassionate circumstances may in some cases spring from the political situation in the country to which a person is to be returned, there were in this particular case 'no circumstances flowing from the political situation in Cyprus which outweighed the public interest'. The Tribunal has held that it is a matter for the Home Secretary to determine the appropriate time to implement his decision to deport.[8]

11.13 As a deportation order cannot be made if the only country to which a person can be removed is one to which he is unwilling to go for

---

[5] HC 394, para. 139.
[6] Ibid., paras. 141, 143, 144.
[7] [1977] Imm AR 91.
[8] See *Yuskel*, cited supra., *Ahmed Mustafaj* 10039/75 (unreported) referred to in *Yuskel*, and also *Ali (MMH)* [1978] Imm AR 126.

fear of persecution, and representations to the Home Secretary can be made not to make a deportation order. This is a claim to political asylum. The applicant will have to show that the fear is well-founded and that the persecution is for reasons of race, religion, nationality, political opinion or membership of a particular group.[9] Representations are particularly important where deportation is being considered following a recommendation by a court, because political asylum cannot be raised as the sole issue on appeal against directions for removal. In *Ali* v *Immigration Appeal Tribunal*,[10] the Court of Appeal held that the only issue open to the appellate authority was simply whether or not the appellant should be removed to the country named in the directions: consideration of a claim for political asylum is a matter for the Home Secretary on representations made to him, and his decision on the matter is final. Political asylum can, however, be claimed where there is an appeal against a decision to make the deportation order itself, irrespective of whether the Home Secretary has considered the matter in deciding to make a deportation order. Political asylum is considered in detail in Chapter 15.

Breach of Conditions

11.14 Where leave to enter is granted for a limited period it may be subject to conditions. There are only two conditions, i.e. restricting or prohibiting employment and, in the case of certain foreign nationals, registering with the police. Overstaying the time limit or failing to comply with these conditions is a criminal offence punishable by imprisonment, and thus makes the offender liable to a recommendation for deportation by the court. It is also a ground for deportation under the Act, irrespective of whether there has been a prosecution or conviction.[11] The immigration rules state that deportation will normally be the proper course where a person has failed to comply with or has contravened a condition or has remained without authorisation, but 'full account is to be taken of all the relevant circumstances known to the Home Secretary before a decision is reached'.[12]

An appeal will be allowed if it can be shown that 'certain relevant circumstances have been ignored or improperly rejected',[13] and account is

---

[9] HC 394, para. 150.
[10] [1973] Imm AR 33, CA.
[11] See para. 11.9, ante.
[12] HC 394, para. 143.
[13] *Akpan* 955/72 (39) (unreported) but the Tribunal gave no examples.

to be taken of the same factors considered by the Home Secretary in deciding whether to give effect to a recommendation for deportation by a court.[14]

11.15 The Tribunal has been reluctant to overrule Home Office decisions even in cases which appear to be borderline. In *Jordan*,[15] the Tribunal held that compassionate circumstances were insufficient to outweigh the public interest where two brothers from India, whose parents were of English and Scottish descent, overstayed because they wished to remain with one of a number of relatives in this country. Despite findings of fact that the family had close connections with this country, that the brothers had been virtually adopted by a relative here and that their employment prospects in India were poor, the Tribunal concluded that were they to be permitted to remain here such action would hardly be 'consistent and fair' as between them and many others who were in a similar predicament. There have been few cases where compassionate circumstances have succeeded. The appellant's exemplary character and length of time that he has been here will not prevent deportation if he has ignored immigration requirements from shortly after arriving, nor will difficulties which are only temporary. In *Sherifali*[16] the Tribunal overruled an adjudicator's decision against deportation where the appellant's wife was expecting a child, while in *D'Souza*,[17] where there were very strong compassionate circumstances (genuine and happy marriage to a UK citizen born here and almost all close relatives resident in UK), the Tribunal nevertheless dismissed the appeal because of the appellant's long history of breach of immigration control (five years' overstaying, working in breach of conditions and evidence of some deception of the immigration authorities).

11.16 Examples of successful applications under this sub-paragraph include *Najam Anwar*,[18] where the appellants, a mother and child aged 13, entered the UK as visitors and overstayed. The mother was divorced from the child's father, remarried and divorced her second husband who was deported from the UK following a shoplifting conviction, and was thereby left destitute. The child was subsequently made a ward of court because of attempts by the father to reclaim the child and take him to Pakistan. The Home Secretary's decision to deport was not upheld:

[14] HC 394, para. 143.
[15] [1972] Imm AR 201.
[16] 2968/73 (245) (unreported).
[17] 15022/77 (1659) (unreported).
[18] 15563/77 (1173) (unreported).

although the appellants were in breach of the immigration conditions and had no right to remain under the immigration rules the following factors were taken into account: (1) the effect of the deportation would be to separate mother and child, which was wrong; (2) the mother had brought up the child in very difficult circumstances, there was a loving relationship and the child was doing well at school; and (3) the representations at the hearing of the Official Solicitor who was extremely anxious that the child should not be returned to Pakistan. In *Narseen Akhtar*,[19] the appellant entered the UK to marry and subsequently did so. As the Home Office had evidence that her purported husband was married at the time of the ceremony with the appellant, she was refused leave to remain and on her failure to leave the UK a decision to deport was made. The appeal was allowed because it would be oppressive to require her to leave for the following reasons: (1) the marriage had not been impugned in a court of law and the marriage certificate was *prima facie* evidence of a valid marriage; (2) the appellant was only 21 years of age; and (3) the appellant had a child by her purported husband and was expecting another by him.

In *Murderris*,[20] the appellant had arrived in the UK from Cyprus in 1973 with his parents. They had no claim to remain in the UK and after a number of unsuccessful appeals the parents were removed to Cyprus in 1979. As the appellant had not left with them, a decision to deport was made in his case. On appeal, the adjudicator took into account a section of the rules dealing with deportation of a member of a family,[1] *viz.* that deportation of children over 17 would not normally be contemplated if they had spent some years in the UK, and that the disruptive effect of the removal on the child's education and plans for his care and maintenance be taken into account. He allowed the appeal because the appellant, (1) was just 13 when he came to the UK, could not speak English and was not a free agent in the decisions made on his behalf; (2) was in the middle of a course of study at a technical college and was likely to benefit from the course; and (3) had grandparents settled in this country who were willing to look after him. The Tribunal upheld the adjudicator's decision stating that he was entitled to consider the age of the appellant, his length of residence in, and connection with, the UK and his general conduct.

In *Bano*[2] the Tribunal allowed the appeal of a 36-year-old Indian

[19] 50229/79 (1786) (unreported).
[20] 43694/79 (1690) (unreported).
[1] See para. 11.32, post.
[2] 61659/80 (1949) (unreported).

woman who was suffering from schizophrenia and depression despite deception practised by her relatives to secure her entry. Most of the family were in the UK and those in India were unable to care for her. The Tribunal held that '. . . the serious mental illness from which she is suffering is such that to remove her to India would involve inhumanity of such an order as to amount to grave compassionate circumstances outweighing the considerations of public interest which undoubtedly exist in this case'.

Administrative Deportation or Prosecution?

11.17 There is no certainty which course of action the authorities are likely to take in any given case of overstaying. As has been mentioned earlier,[3] stronger measures have now been adopted where a person who is refused an extension has no right of appeal, and the information and advice given in Chapter 9 should be carefully borne in mind. Prosecution is more likely to arise where the overstayer has few or no connections with the UK, and students are particularly at risk. There may be circumstances where a person has a strong case for an extension of stay but has lost the right of appeal against a refusal of extension. If there are factors which might otherwise have influenced the appellate authorities, it may be justified to encourage the Home Office to commence deportation proceedings by indicating to them that the case is not a proper one to be referred to the police with a view to prosecution. If deportation proceedings are commenced, it may be possible on appeal to argue the relevant matters. Care must be taken, as the adviser may be accused of encouraging a person to remain in the UK in breach of conditions.

There is, however, some judicial authority in support of this approach. In *R v Immigration Appeal Tribunal, ex parte Subramaniam*.[4] Lord Denning MR referred to an appeal against a decision to deport as a 'safeguard' provided for those who apply late for an extension of stay:

'On that appeal the merits of his case will be considered just as fully as if he had made his application (in time) and had been refused. So no injustice at all will be done to him.'

Conducive to the Public Good

11.18 This phrase is nowhere defined and gives the Home Secretary almost unlimited power. In the years prior to the introduction of an im-

---
[3] See para. 9.18, ante.   [4] [1976] 3 All ER 604, CA, at 608.

migration appeals procedure, the courts made it clear that they would not interfere with a deportation order made on this ground,[5] although they have hinted that they might intervene if the Home Secretary was abusing his powers.[6] The only indication of the exercise of these powers is contained in the immigration rules which state:

'General rules cannot be laid down and each case will be considered in the light of the relevant circumstances known to the Secretary of State including those listed in paragraph 141' (deportation following conviction).[7]

There is a right of appeal direct to the Tribunal from the decision of the Home Secretary to deport, unless the decision is made on 'security' or 'political' grounds, where no appeal is permitted but there is, however, a non-statutory advisory procedure.[8]

General Principles

11.19 The cases considered by the Tribunal offer little assistance in ascertaining the circumstances which make a deportation order appropriate. A number of general principles emerge, but caution must be exercised in comparing cases. The same approach is to be adopted as in other categories of deportation. Public interest will be balanced against compassionate circumstances and account is to be taken of the same factors considered by the Home Secretary in deciding whether to give effect to a recommendation for deportation. In all cases other than those relating to security, the deportee had either engaged in proven criminal activity or had entered into a 'marriage of convenience' for the purpose of settlement.

Criminal Activity

11.20 The most common situation in which a decision to deport arises is where a person has been convicted of a criminal offence but the court has not made a recommendation for deportation. However, in one case

[5] See *R v Governor of Brixton, ex parte Soblen* [1962] 3 All ER 641.
[6] Ibid., although the court emphatically precluded any supervisory role.
[7] HC 394, para. 144, see para. 11.39, post. Compare the wording of the former rules which began: 'The cases in which deportation is justified ... are likely to be few in number. Judging from past experience most of the cases in this category will be cases in which a court has convicted the person but had decided to leave the question of deportation to the Appeal Tribunal and the Secretary of State: HC 80, para. 43; HC 82, para. 50.
[8] See para. 11.26, post.

an order was made following a Home Office discovery that the deportee had previous convictions abroad.[9] A decision to deport may be made although the proposed deportee may be an illegal entrant or have been refused leave to enter.[10]

Marriage of Convenience

11.21 The Tribunal has consistently held that deportation is justified where the appellant has entered into a marriage primarily to obtain settlement in the UK with no intention that the parties will live together as man and wife. In *Patel (SVBA)*[11] the Tribunal confirmed that the burden of proof in a strict sense, is on the Home Secretary: what he is required to show is valid reasons for believing that the marriage is one of convenience. The burden then shifts to the proposed deportee to show that on a balance of probability that the marriage is not one of convenience.

Public Interest

11.22 Until recently the Tribunal has rarely explained its reasons for upholding decisions to deport. In *Munk-Hansen*,[12] it was argued that the decision should set out, as far as practicable, what part of the public good is being safeguarded, but the Tribunal refused to adopt that approach. However, a rationale now appears to be developing and the following factors have emerged as matters pertaining to the public interest:

(a) in many cases it is the propensity to commit offences which is a foundation of a finding that considerations of the public interest require the removal of a non-patrial;[13]

---

[9] *Long* 1883/72 (37) (unreported).

[10] See *Butt* [1979–80] Imm AR 82 (illegal entrant); and *Villone* [1979–80] Imm AR 23 (leave to enter refused).

[11] 63611/80 (1845) (unreported). For earlier cases see *Butt* 10750/76 (862) (unreported); *El Wahab* 11907/77 (981) (unreported); *Mohsen* 14412/77 (994) (unreported); and *Tasci* 22307/77 (1170) (unreported) which referred to unreported decisions of the Divisional Court (*Goma* (1977) 345/77 DC 1 November and *Shaw* (1978) 288/71 DC 19 January) approving the approach. In appropriate circumstances a woman may be deported on this ground: *Sijarn Kaur* 58392/80 (1752) (unreported). For an example of a successful appeal see *Asghar* 57739/80 (1722) (unreported).

[12] 880/73 (210) (unreported) which was a decision to exclude on conducive grounds, see para. 5.27, ante.

[13] *Akhtar M R* 49631/79 (1602) (unreported); *Mohd Ashraf* 43998/79 (1714) (unreported); and *McIntosh* 59267/80 (1782) (unreported). In *Akhtar* and *McIntosh* the appeal was nevertheless allowed.

(b) such considerations may nevertheless arise where a single offence has been committed.[14] Conviction of a serious offence is likely to lead to deportation, '... when an alien ... seriously misconducts himself by committing a grave crime, he should be sent out of the country;[15]
(c) this is particularly likely where the offender has slight connections with the UK[16] and conviction of an extremely serious offence will usually outweigh normal considerations in favour of allowing him to remain;[17]
(d) the nature of the offence must also be considered. The offender's conduct may cause such deep public revulsion that public policy may properly be considered to require his departure even though he is a first offender;[18]
(e) a risk that the public will be exposed if the appellant commits further offences is also a relevant consideration.[19]

Compassionate Circumstances

11.23 The relevant factors have already been referred to.[20] Youth, length of residence in the UK, family connections in the UK, few relatives overseas and an exemplary character before committing the offence may be important factors. There will be occasions when one factor in itself is insufficient, but a combination of factors may justify a decision permitting the appellant to remain.

The Tribunal has rejected the following arguments as grounds in themselves justifying the appellant's remaining in the UK: (1) the appellant is likely to be doubly punished by being retried for the same offence in his own country;[1] (2) deportation will affect his right to enter another country and thereby preclude him from visiting relatives[2] or getting a job;[3] (3) the appellant has an illegitimate child here and intends

---

[14] See, e.g. *Mohad Ashraf*, cited. supra.
[15] *Shing* 2293/73 (169). (Manslaughter: 12 months' imprisonment).
[16] *Shing*, supra, and see *Sweiden* 2598/73 (183) (unreported).
[17] *Trinca* 2996/72 (78) (unreported). (Malicious wounding of wife; 18 months' imprisonment. Italian lived here for 22 years. Deported. This decision was prior to the entry of the UK into the EEC).
[18] See *Akhtar*, supra (unlawful sexual intercourse with girl aged 10); and *Mohd Ashraf* supra (buggery of boy aged seven; two years' imprisonment).
[19] *Caleira* 1327/73 (148) (unreported).
[20] See para. 11.12, ante; HC 394, para. 141.
[1] *Sassi* 2581/73 (188) (unreported).
[2] *Eckstein* 2500/71 (unreported).
[3] *Curtis* 1575/72 (7) (unreported).

to marry the mother[4] or is living with the mother and child;[5] (4) his wife and children are citizens of the Republic of Ireland and his wife has lived here for almost all her life.[6] The Tribunal has, however, held that in the case of a genuine marriage, a decision to deport will not be upheld if the result of returning to his own country would be the termination of the marriage, or it seems, if he were to be prosecuted for living with his wife. Thus in *Bosch*,[7] the appellant was not deported where his marriage fell foul of the South African Immorality Act. In *Caleira*,[8] a Portuguese national, resident in the UK for 10 years, but convicted of causing death by dangerous driving and obtaining drugs by deception, was allowed to remain because his wife and children were settled here and there was a risk of a break-up of the family if he were to be removed. Again in *Akhtar M R*,[9] where the appellant had committed unlawful sexual intercourse with a 10-year-old girl, the same course was taken: it was accepted that the future of the appellant's marriage might be in jeopardy and that his young daughter would have little opportunity of seeing him if he were removed. The effect on the wife and child settled in the UK, particularly where the child is established in school, will be an important factor to be taken into account.[10] It would also seem that some mitigating factors proved at the trial cannot be relied upon at the Tribunal unless they are proved afresh. In *Stofile*,[11] where a charge of murder was reduced to manslaughter, the Tribunal held that if the appellant's condition were to be put forward as constituting compassionate circumstances, it must be shown to be continuing at the time of the appeal.

Examples of the Tribunal's Approach

11.24 Two cases give some useful indication of the Tribunal's approach. In *Al Ghoben*,[12] the appellant was convicted of causing grievous bodily harm and other offences of violence and sentenced to 12 months' imprisonment but no recommendation for deportation was made. The Tribunal allowed the appeal because (1) the violence of which the

[4] *Derrick* [1972] Imm AR 109.
[5] *Ghazanfar Khan* 3249/74 (394) (unreported).
[6] *Long* 1883/72 (37) (unreported).
[7] 2722/71 (unreported).
[8] 1327/73 (148) (unreported).
[9] 49631/79 (1602) (unreported).
[10] *Chand* 49904/79 (1609) (unreported).
[11] 122/72 (unreported).
[12] 25499/78 (1155) (unreported).

appellant was found guilty was occasioned entirely by his domestic circumstances which appeared to be 'now a matter of history'; (2) he had been in the UK for 10 years during which time he had proved himself to be a serious student; (3) it was extremely unlikely that he would commit any further offences in the country; and (4) the Tribunal heard character evidence from a close friend of the appellant and his probation officer which, if produced to the Home Secretary, would have resulted in his exercising his discretion differently. In *Arif*,[13] the Home Secretary's decision to deport was upheld. The appellant, aged 27, came to the UK in 1966 when aged 15 and had remained in the UK thereafter, apart from a visit to Pakistan in 1971 when he married there, returning with his wife. He was convicted with a total of four and a half years' imprisonment for offences of wounding with intent to occasion actual bodily harm, possessing an offensive weapon and breach of a suspended sentence. Previous offences included offences of violence. The Tribunal affirmed its comments in *S K Shing*,[14] stating that there were no compassionate or family circumstances to weigh in the balance since (1) the appellant's wife, parents and brother were in Pakistan; (2) although he had been in the UK for 11 years, three years were spent in prison and he would not be uprooted if he were to return to Pakistan; (3) although accommodation and employment were available and he wished to bring his wife to the UK, he had not brought her here after his return from Pakistan in 1971 although he had at the time planned to do so.

Criminal Courts and the Tribunal

11.25 The Tribunal does not appear to attach much importance to the decision of a court not to recommend deportation. Frequently, the Tribunal is unaware of the reasoning of the court in not making a recommendation. In few cases will the Tribunal have the transcript of the sentencing by the trial judge or of any subsequent appeal. In a number of cases the court may have wrongly not considered deportation; in others the court may have specifically left the matter for the Home Secretary to consider as the immigration rules envisage. But in others the court will have deliberately concluded that a recommendation is not appropriate because the offence is not sufficiently serious or there are other mitigating factors. Yet this in no way fetters the Home Secretary's power to make a deportation order on conducive grounds. This clearly can lead to some strange results.

[13] 22223/77 (1161) (unreported).
[14] See para. 11.22, ante.

In *Helies*,[15] the appellant was convicted of theft and not recommended for deportation, but the Home Secretary subsequently made an order. The Tribunal accepted the argument that he might commit further offences, although this was a factor undoubtedly considered by the Court of Appeal, which stated specifically that the offences were not serious enough to warrant a recommendation. There are cases where it is nevertheless appropriate for the Home Secretary to deport, but it is submitted that his power should be used only where there are additional factors not known to the trial judge or where there are policy considerations which were not appropriate for consideration by the court. In all cases these factors should be clearly set out by the Home Secretary. In several cases, a decision to deport has been made where there were no considerations not already known to the trial judge. In *Eckstein*,[16] a 23-year-old first offender was sentenced to two years' imprisonment for attempting to import drugs. He was not recommended for deportation, apparently because of his youth and previous good character. Yet the Tribunal upheld a deportation order, without giving any reasons.

Security Cases

11.26 Where the decision to deport is made on conducive grounds as being 'in the interests of national security or of the relations between the UK and any other country or for other reasons of a political nature', no right of appeal exists.[17] There is, however, a non-statutory three man panel of advisers which will hear representations,[18] but the deportee will have no right to subpoena witnesses and no opportunity of hearing or cross-examining Home Office or security witnesses. The advisers report to the Home Secretary but he is not bound by the advice he receives. This system was adopted following the fiasco in December 1970 in *Rudi Dutschke*,[19] where the former German student leader was refused an extension of stay because he was alleged to have constituted a security

[15] 3539/73 (208) (unreported).
[16] 2500/71 (unreported).
[17] Immigration Act 1971, s. 15(3).
[18] HC 394, para. 135. The original advisers appointed were Sir Derek Hilton (the first President of the Immigration Appeal Tribunal), Sir Richard Hayward and Sir Clifford Jarrett: *The Times*, 21 December 1972 and 23 January 1975. This panel heard representations in the *Agee* and *Hosenball* cases. There has been no change in the composition of the panel: 983 H. of C. Official Report 22 April 1980, Written Answers, col. 97.
[19] 381/70 (unreported) and see Hepple *Alias and Administrative Justice: the Dutschke Case* (1971) 34 MLR 501.

risk. The Tribunal, at the request of the Home Secretary, permitted evidence to be heard without the appellant or his lawyer being present and without the nature of this evidence being made known to them. Following the furore over the case, the Immigration Act removed from the Tribunal the power to hear appeals where an extension of stay was refused or a deportation order made for security or political reasons.

11.27 The procedure to be adopted was set out by the then Home Secretary in a statement to the House of Commons on 15 June 1971.

'All these proceedings start with a personal decision by the Home Secretary on national security grounds. The person concerned is notified of the decision and he will be given by the Home Office such particulars of allegations as will not entail disclosure of sources of evidence. At the same time the person will be notified that he can make representations to the three advisers and will be given time to decide whether or not to do so. The advisers will then take account of any representations made by the person concerned. They will allow him to appear before them, if he wishes. He will not be entitled to legal representation, but he may be assisted by a friend to such extent as the advisers sanction. As well as speaking for himself, he may arrange for a third party to testify on his behalf. Neither the sources of evidence, nor evidence that might lead to disclosure of sources can be revealed to the person concerned, but the advisers will ensure that the person is able to make his points effectively and the procedure will give him the best possible opportunity to make the points he wishes to bring to their notice . . . Since the evidence against a person necessarily has to be received in his absence, the advisers in assessing the case will bear in mind that it had not been tested by cross-examination and that the person has not had the opportunity to rebut it . . . On receiving the advice of advisers the Secretary of State will reconsider his original decision, but the advice given to him will not be revealed.'[20]

The panel was first invoked in January 1975 in the case of Franco Caprino, where the Home Secretary had made a deportation order against an Italian Marxist on security grounds, but revoked the order shortly before he was due to appear before the security panel.[1]

11.28 The total inadequacy of the procedure was highlighted by the

---

[20] 819 H. of C. Official Report 15 June 1971, Written Answers, col. 376.
[1] *The Times*, 23 and 25 January 1975.

only cases to be heard under the system, namely those of US citizens Philip Agee, the former CIA agent, and Mark Hosenball, a journalist, in February 1977. Mr Agee's notice informed him that he had (1) maintained regular contacts with foreign intelligence officers; (2) been involved in disseminating information; and (3) aided and counselled others to obtain information for publication. In the first two cases this was said to be harmful to UK security and in the third, 'could be harmful'.[2] In Mr Hosenball's case the allegation was that he had obtained information harmful to state security and 'prejudicial to the servants of the Crown'. In neither case was the Home Secretary prepared to give particulars of the allegations including the dates on which these matters were alleged to have occurred. The result was that Agee and Hosenball 'made representations' to the advisers about allegations of supposedly unlawful activity, the details of which were unknown to them. The Court of Appeal in *R v Secretary of State for the Home Department, ex parte Hosenball*[3] held that the refusal of the Home Secretary to give further particulars[4] was not a matter for the courts. The Home Secretary was only answerable to Parliament in these matters. The public interest in security of the realm was so great that the rules of natural justice were liable to be modified. The court appeared to have placed some importance on the fact that the Home Secretary personally reconsidered the request for further particulars and a majority expressed the view that if the Home Secretary or his advisers had 'acted unfairly' the courts would intervene to ensure that justice is done.[5]

Family Deportation

11.29 The 1971 Act introduced a new concept into the deportation system by giving the Home Secretary statutory powers to deport members of a family belonging to a person against whom a deportation order is to be, or has been made,[6] subject to a right of appeal direct to the Tribunal.[7] Only the immediate members of the family are liable to be deported: in the case of a male deportee, his wife and his or her children

---

[2] For a summary of the facts see the decision of the European Commission for Human Rights (7729/76) which declared inadmissible the application of Mr. Agee.

[3] [1977] 3 All ER 452.

[4] The issue of whether any particulars had been given at all does not seem to have been argued.

[5] [1977] 3 All ER at 461.

[6] Immigration Act 1971, s. 3(5)(c).

[7] Ibid., s. 15(1).

under 18;[8] in the case of a female deportee only her children under 18.[9]

Limitations on Deportation

11.30 A person cannot be deported if (1) the principal deportee has actually left the country and eight weeks have elapsed since his departure. This concession is meaningless as the Home Secretary will usually consider family deportation at the same time he examines the case of the principal deportee, and in calculating the eight week period there has to be disregarded any period during which an appeal is pending against the deportation decision;[10] (2) he/she ceases to 'belong to the family'. A wife whose marriage to the deportee is dissolved is not at risk as she will have ceased to 'belong' to his family.[11] Children, however, do not become protected until they reach the age of 18;[12] or (3) the deportation order against the principal deportee ceases to have effect.[13]

Procedure

11.31 As in all cases where deportation is proposed, members of the family must be informed separately of the Home Secretary's decision.[14] They must also be notified that it is open to them to leave voluntarily if they do not wish to appeal, or if they do and the appeal fails. The most sensible procedure to adopt therefore is to appeal where appropriate and then leave voluntarily if required, as this at least avoids the stigma of deportation.[15] There are severe limitations as to what can be challenged on appeal. It is not possible to dispute the truth of any statement made with a view to obtaining leave, unless it can be shown that the statement was not made by the appellants or anyone acting on their behalf, and that

[8] Ibid., s. 5(4)(a). 'Wife' includes each of two or more wives.
[9] Ibid., s. 5(4)(b). A legally adopted child will be treated as the child only of the adopter. If there is no legal adoption, it may so be treated. An illegitimate child (subject to the adoption rule) is treated as the child of the mother.
[10] Ibid., s. 15(2).
[11] Ibid., s. 5(3).
[12] Ibid; HC 394, para. 18.
[13] R v Immigration Appeal Tribunal, ex parte Mehmet (No. 2) [1978] Imm AR 46.
[14] HC 394, para. 145. An order cannot be made where there is a right of appeal against a decision to make it, nor while the appeal is pending: Immigration Act 1971, s. 15(2). Notice of the appeal must be given within 14 days – Immigration Appeals (Procedure) Rules, 1972, r. 4(7). Thus if the decision to deport is made more than six weeks after the principal deportee has left, it is advisable not to give notice of the appeal, otherwise the eight week period will stop running.
[15] Probably the most important consideration is whether to accept Home Office funds to assist in departure.

when they entered the UK they did not know about the statement, or if they did, they were under 18.[16]

11.32 The immigration rules provide that where a wife has qualified for settlement in her own right, for example following four years in approved employment, she will have a valid claim to remain here and deportation will not 'normally' be contemplated.[17] Similarly, if the wife has been living apart from her husband, it will not 'normally' be right to deport her or her children.[18] It is difficult to assess the meaning of 'normal' in this context. Possibly the Home Secretary wishes to keep open his options in cases where the couple have separated for only a short period before the order is made. There is certainly no justification for deporting a wife who has qualified for settlement independently of her husband.

Some attempt has been made to mitigate hardship to children. Deportation will not normally be contemplated if they have spent some years here or are nearing 18. Where the children are of school age, account is to be taken, on the one hand of the disruptive effect of removal on their education, and on the other hand, whether plans for their care and maintenance here if one or both parents were deported are realistic and likely to be effective.[19] The Tribunal will not easily accept that children should be permitted to remain in the UK if this results in their being separated from their parents.[20] Similarly, deportation will not normally be appropriate if the child has left home, taken employment and established himself on an independent basis; or if he married before a deportation order was contemplated.

General Considerations

11.33 The immigration rules set out the factors to be taken into account by the Home Secretary in considering whether to require a wife or children to leave:[1] these include length of residence here, any ties the family have, other than being the dependants of the principal deportee, the ability of the wife to maintain herself and the children without being a charge on public funds for the foreseeable future, any compassionate or other special circumstances, and any representations made on their behalf. There have been few cases of family deportation before the Tribunal.

---

[16] Immigration Act 1971, s. 15(6) and similarly where they appeal against a revocation of the deportation order.
[17] HC 394, para. 147.   [18] Ibid.   [19] HC 394, para. 148.
[20] *Ozter* [1978] Imm AR 137.   [1] HC 394, para. 146.

The Tribunal, as in other deportation cases, will balance the 'public interest' against 'compassionate circumstances' but will have little sympathy where the deportee has a bad history of breaches of immigration control as in *Anand*,[2] where the appellant had entered by deception, lived in the UK unlawfully for four years and had worked in breach of conditions of entry.

RECOMMENDATION BY THE COURT[3]

11.34 Any non-patrial aged 17 and over who has been convicted of a criminal offence punishable by imprisonment may be recommended for deportation by the court which sentences him for the offence.[4] Any court which has the power to sentence the offender for the offence may recommend deportation, except a court which commits him for sentence, or to be further dealt with by another court.[5] An appeal court may make a recommendation.[6] The conviction must arise after the accused has reached the age of 17.[7] A person is deemed to be 17 on conviction if on consideration of all the available evidence he appears to the court to have become 17.[8] Where a magistrates' court commits to the Crown Court for sentence, the date of the conviction is the date of the sentence.[9]

Offences Punishable by Imprisonment

11.35 The offender need not have received a sentence of imprisonment. It is sufficient that the offence is one which might carry such a sentence. A recommendation can be made notwithstanding that the accused is a first or young offender and consequently cannot be imprisoned because of legislation which prevents imprisonment:[10] it is the

---

[2] [1978] Imm AR 36.
[3] For a full account and criticism of the procedure see Zellick, *The Power of the Court to Recommend Deportation* [1973] Crim LR 612.
[4] Immigration Act 1971, s. 3(6).
[5] Ibid., s. 6(1).
[6] Criminal Appeal Act 1968 s. 50(2); Courts Act 1971 s. 9(2); *R v Kruger* [1973] Crim LR 133.
[7] A person became 17 at the start of his 17th birthday: Family Law Reform Act 1969, s. 9.
[8] Immigration Act 1971, s. 6(3)(a).
[9] See *R v Sweeney* [1964] Crim LR 37, a decision under the Commonwealth Immigrants Act 1962, s. 7(2) which used the same phrase.
[10] Immigration Act 1971, s. 6(3)(b).

offence which is the deciding factor and not the offender. A recommendation can follow a sentence of life imprisonment.[11] The accused is to be treated as convicted even where the sentence is not one which is treated as a 'conviction' in law,[12] for example where he he is given an absolute discharge or a probation order is made. The courts have, however, frowned upon the making of a recommendation where borstal training is given, although there may be exceptions.[13]

Procedure

11.36 The court may not make a recommendation unless the offender has received a written notice at least seven days before the recommendation is made.[14] The notice must state (1) that the offender is not liable to recommendation if a patrial (and it must describe who are patrials); (2) those who are exempt; and (3) that the burden of proving that a person is not liable lies on the offender.[15] In practice the notice is served on the accused some time before the trial, but the court in any event may adjourn after conviction to allow the notice to be served or to allow the seven day period to expire.[16]

The offender should be given an opportunity to address the court specifically on the question of deportation before any recommendation is made and should normally be provided with legal aid.[17] In *R v Nazari*,[18] the Court of Appeal made it clear that the Act required that a proper and full enquiry should take place before a recommendation was made and stated that it would be advisable for judges specifically to invite submissions on the question of deportation where there was a possibility that a recommendation would be made. It is not enough for a judge to add a sentence to his judgment 'as a sort of afterthought'. It is still often the case that magistrates do not properly understand the deportation system and where this appears to be the case it is important to explain that if a recommendation were not made the Home Secretary has a 'second bite at the cherry' by making a decision to deport on 'conducive' grounds if in his opinion deportation is warranted. A recommendation is a 'sentence' for the purposes of an appeal.[19]

---

[11] Ibid., s. 6(4).   [12] Ibid., s. 6(3).
[13] *R v Bisset* [1973] Crim LR 132.
[14] Ibid., s. 6(2).
[15] Ibid.
[16] Ibid.
[17] *R v Edgehill* [1963] IQB 593; *R v Antypas* (1972) 57 Cr App R 207.
[18] [1980] 3 All ER 880.
[19] Immigration Act 1971, s. 6(5)(a); Criminal Appeal Act 1968, s. 50(1).

Principles in Making a Recommendation

11.37 The correct approach is for the court first to consider the appropriate sentence for the offence, and only after that sentence or penalty has been dealt with, should the question of recommendation be considered.[20] In *R v Kamara*,[1] the Court of Appeal held that it was the wrong approach to impose a shorter sentence of imprisonment than would otherwise have been justified coupled with a recommendation so that the offender would be deported more quickly, thereby saving public funds. In *R v Nazari*,[2] the Court of Appeal set out guidelines as to what should be kept in mind by a court when considering whether to make a recommendation. The Court stressed that they were guidelines and not rigid rules and that there might be considerations which take a particular case outside them. As a result of this and other cases, the following principles emerge:

(a) the court must consider whether the continued presence of the offender in the UK is to its detriment. The court confirmed the general principle laid down in *R v Caird*:[3]

'. . . the question for the court is whether the potential detriment in this country of (the offender) remaining here has been shown to be such as to justify the recommendation; (the court) desires to emphasise that the courts when considering a recommendation for deportation are normally concerned simply with the crime concerned and the individual's past record and the question as to what is their effect on the question of potential detriment just mentioned.'[4]

(b) the more serious the offence, the more likely the recommendation will be made. An isolated minor offence should not justify the making of a recommendation. However, a crime which results in a sentence of imprisonment and involves some degree of deliberation

---

[20] *R v Edgehill*, cited, note 17 supra. For a further discussion on the issues see Thomas *Principles of Sentencing* (2nd Edn.) pp. 355 et seq.
[1] (1976) 16 January, CA referred to in *Thomas* op. cit.
[2] [1980] 3 All ER 880.
[3] (1970) Cr App R 499.
[4] Ibid., per Sachs LJC at 510. In *R v Secretary of State for the Home Department ex parte Santillo*, [1981] 2 All ER 897, at 916 Donaldson LJ stated that the existence of a previous criminal conviction was not in itself a basis for making a recommendation. It may, however, be relevant in considering the possibility of offending again, which is an important factor in deciding whether to make a recommendation. This was a case involving an EEC national but it appears that the court was making observations which were applicable in all cases.

is likely to attract a recommendation, and similarly where a person had been convicted of a series of relatively minor offences;[5]
(c) the courts are not concerned with the political systems of other countries and it would be wrong for them to express views about foreign regimes. It is for the Home Secretary to decide in each case whether an offender's return to his country of origin would have harsh consequences. In the case of a short sentence, however, the court might have to make up its mind whether to make a recommendation, and if it were satisfied, on the evidence, that it would be unduly harsh to return an offender to his country of origin, then the court might feel impelled, in fairness to the accused, not to recommend deportation.[6]
(d) it is proper for the court to consider the effect of a recommendation upon others not before the court. The court had no wish to break up families or to impose hardships upon those innocent of crimes. In *Nazari*, the court stated that this principle was illustrated clearly by the case of one of the offenders. His wife was a 'credit to herself and a good citizen of this country'. If her husband was deported, she would have a heart-rending choice to make; the court would therefore not make a recommendation;[7]
(e) the argument that the offender intends to return to his homeland voluntarily is not impressive: assertions of this sort were often subsequently forgotten;
(f) evidence of mental instability connected with or resulting in the commission of an offence is a good reason for making a recommendation;
(g) a recommendation should not normally be made in the case of an illegal entrant;
(h) the fact that a dependant is living on social security is not a factor the courts should consider if the offence[8] is of a minor nature.

---

[5] The court in *Nazari* compared an isolated offence of shoplifting with an offence committed by a member of a gang carrying out a planned raid on a store.

[6] The court stressed that this would depend on the evidence and circumstances and repeated that in general political considerations were inappropriate considerations for the court.

[7] See also *Brooks v Waldren* [1963] Crim LR 864; *R v Stewart* [1963] Crim LR 446: a court should be hesitant to recommend deportation where an offender has the whole of his family in the UK.

[8] *R v Serry* (1980) *The Times*, 31 October, CA.

Appeals

11.38 A recommendation is a sentence of the court and as such is always appealable.[9] An appeal can be brought against the recommendation alone: it is not necessary also to appeal against the remainder of the sentence. The Home Secretary cannot make a deportation order while an appeal against the recommendation or against the conviction is pending or until the time limit for bringing an appeal has expired.[10]

If the court does not recommend deportation, the battle may still not be won. The Home Secretary has the power to decide to deport on the ground that it is conducive to the public good, although there is a right of appeal against the decision.[11]

Considering the Recommendation

11.39 The immigration rules state that 'in considering whether to give effect to a recommendation, the Home Secretary will take into account every relevant factor known to him including, (1) age; (2) length of residence in the UK; (3) strength of connections with the UK; (4) personal history, including character, conduct and employment record; (5) domestic circumstances; (6) the nature of the offence of which the person was convicted; (7) previous criminal record; (8) compassionate circumstances; (9) any representations received in a person's behalf.[12]

The importance of making representations in appropriate cases cannot be overstressed. There may be a number of factors which are not known to the Home Secretary and which would not appear in the papers before him. In some cases representations through an MP may be desirable, in others information setting out compassionate circumstances can be sent directly to the Home Office. If representations are to be made by a number of people, it is often advisable for the efforts to be co-ordinated by arranging for the information to be sent through one agency, e.g.

---

[9] See para. 11.36, ante, note 17.

[10] Immigration Act 1971, s. 6(6). An appeal can be brought within 21 days in the case of a magistrates' court; 28 days for a Crown Court in England and Wales; and 28 days for all courts in Scotland.

[11] Ibid., s. 3(5)(b), and see para. 11.18, ante. The possibility of serving a notice of intention to deport under this subsection on a convicted person is considered 'as soon as possible during the sentence'. The stage at which this begins 'varies from case to case': 984 H. of C. Official Report, 23 April 1980, Written Answers, col. 137.

[12] HC 394, para. 141. The Home Secretary, in deciding whether to make an order, is under no obligation to have regard to the provisions of the European Convention of Human Rights: *R v Secretary of State for the Home Department, ex parte Fernandez* (1980), *The Times*, 21 November, CA.

solicitor or advice organisation. If an order is made there is no further right of appeal.

11.40 The stage at which the Home Office will give consideration to the recommendation where a custodial sentence has been imposed depends on the length of sentence. If the sentence is 12 months or less, consideration begins (once the period for appeal has expired or if an appeal has been lodged after the appeal has been heard) as soon as the court certificate and police report on the convictions are received by the Home Office. The decision is notified to the prison authorities as soon as it has been taken. If the sentence is longer than 12 months, the recommendation is considered on receipt of the certificate and report and a preliminary decision taken. A decision not to deport is notified to the authorities 'without further delay'. If deportation appears to be merited, the recommendation is reconsidered several months before the earliest date on which the person could be released, whether on parole or otherwise. The decision to deport is notified to the prison authorities as soon as the deportation order has been made.[13]

THE SIGNING OF A DEPORTATION ORDER

11.41 The order is usually signed by the Home Secretary although on some occasions another Secretary of State has signed an order. The order will be signed by the Secretary of State personally. The order requires the deportee to leave and prohibits him from entering the UK.[14] It is not the Home Secretary's practice to sign an order where he has knowledge that the proposed deportee has left the UK and Islands.[15]

REVOCATION OF DEPORTATION ORDER

11.42 The immigration rules set out the procedure and considerations

[13] 984 H. of C. Official Report, 23 April 1980, Written Answers, col. 136.

[14] Immigration Act 1971, s. 5(1).

[15] 983 H. of C. Official Report, 22 April 1980, Written Answers, col. 97. A deportation order is probably invalid if signed after the 'deportee' has left the UK: *Lazari* 10147/76 (1017) (unreported). The Tribunal now appear to have some doubts, see *Altiparmak* 35422/78 (1570) (unreported) and *Abiodun* 42792/79 (1627) (unreported) where the Tribunal held *obiter* that an order could be signed if the appellant was out of the country. The practical consequences are that where no order is made, there is no need to apply for revocation, and the applicant may qualify for entry in the same manner as any other person.

in revoking a deportation order.[16] An application will be considered in the light of (1) the grounds for making the original order; and (2) the case made in support of the application to revoke. The interest of the community (including the maintenance of an effective immigration control) will be balanced against compassionate circumstances. Where the applicant has been convicted of a serious criminal offence 'exclusion for a long period of time will normally be the proper course'. In other cases, the applicant will have to show either a change in circumstances or new information not available when the original order was made. An application can be made either to an entry clearance officer or direct to the Home Office.

The passage of time can itself be a sufficient ground to justify revocation. The rules do not set out any general principles as each case is to be judged on its own particular facts but the rules now state that 'save in the most exceptional circumstances the (Home Secretary) will not revoke a deportation order which has been in force for less than three years'.[17] There is a right of appeal against a refusal to revoke an order provided that the applicant has left the country, unless the Home Secretary personally deems that continued exclusion is conducive to the public good.[18] Revocation of the order does not entitle a person to re-enter: it merely makes him eligible to qualify for admission under the immigration rules.[19]

11.43 A deportation order remains in force in the case of a wife until it is revoked against her or her husband, but she will automatically cease to be the subject of the order if the marriage comes to an end; in the case of children, the deportation order ceases on their reaching 18.[20] When the order comes to an end, there is no right to re-enter: it will be necessary to requalify for admission under the immigration rules.

11.44 The cases before the Tribunal have been few, were decided under the earlier rules and have all involved the appropriate period of time which should elapse before revocation. In *Udoh*,[1] the Home Office set out the considerations which have now been incorporated into the present rules, and argued that in principle one year was too short a period to revoke. The Tribunal rejected the argument, holding that although

---

[16] HC 394, paras. 155, 156.
[17] Ibid., para. 156.
[18] Immigration Act 1971, s. 15(3).
[19] HC 394, para. 155.
[20] HC 394, para. 149.
[1] [1972] Imm AR 89.

the appellant had acted misguidedly and foolishly in taking employment in breach of his conditions of stay, his motive was to tide himself over an anticipated short period of financial difficulty caused by the Biafran war. In *Dervish*,[2] the Tribunal dismissed an application made 17 months after the making of a deportation order because the appellant had entered the country by deceit and had remained here on two occasions in breach of his conditions. Similarly in *Sanusi*,[3] an application to revoke in a little after a year was rejected because the appellant's conduct 'showed a studied disregard of immigration control'. In all these cases, by the date of the Tribunal hearing, a longer period had elapsed since the making of the original order, and in the latter two cases the Tribunal recommended that the Home Office give fresh consideration to the applications.

OTHER FORMS OF DEPARTURE

Supervised Departure

11.45 The rules provide that in certain circumstances where a court has recommended deportation, supervised departure with a prohibition on entry may be arranged provided that the person is willing to leave the country.[4] This may be particularly appropriate in the case of young or first offenders. In *Cseyni*,[5] the Tribunal held that this procedure was not a proper alternative in circumstances where the appellant had come here to obtain work and shortly after his arrival embarked on a course of dishonesty. The Home Office is reluctant to use supervised departure where a person has offended against immigration control (i.e. overstayed or worked in breach of conditions). Although such an offence is not in itself to be regarded as a bar to supervised departure, this is considered inappropriate where there has been persistent and determined breaches of the control.[6]

Curtailment or a Refusal to Extend Stay with Re-entry Prohibition

11.46 Where a court has not recommended deportation, the rules state that there may nevertheless be grounds 'in the light of all the relevant information' for either, (1) curtailment of stay, or (2) a refusal to extend

[2] [1972] Imm AR 48.
[3] [1975] Imm AR 114. See also *Ayoola* 151/72(16) (unreported).
[4] HC 394, para. 141.
[5] [1975] Imm AR 92.
[6] Letter, Home Office to JCWI, 31 August 1978. There are about 60 removals by supervised departures each year. 983 H. of C. Official Report, 21 April 1980, Written Answers, col. 9.

stay, followed after departure, by a prohibition on re-entry.[7] If this course of action is taken, there is a right of appeal against the decision under the immigration appeals procedure.[8] Although there are no available statistics, the powers of curtailment are used comparatively rarely.[9]

Voluntary Departure

11.47 The Act provides for those whose are the subjects of a family deportation order, or recommended for deportation by the court, to leave without an order being made against them if they agree 'to live permanently abroad'.[10] Payment can then be made for travelling and other expenses not only of the deportee but his family.[11] The disadvantage of this concession is the difficulty of ever being permitted to re-enter the UK. In the case of family deportations, the Home Secretary will give an opportunity for the family to leave the UK voluntarily if there is no appeal or if there is an appeal and the appeal is dismissed.[12] In other cases, while no opportunity to leave voluntarily will necessarily be given before the signing of a deportation order, an order will not be signed if it is known that the individual has left the UK.[13]

Departure by Bind-over

11.48 A Crown Court (but not a magistrates' court)[14] has power, if the offender consents to leave the country voluntarily, to bind him over to come up for judgment when directed by the court. He will be told that if he leaves the country within a specified time he will not be sentenced for the original offence. This procedure is frowned upon by the Divisional Court which has suggested that it may be unlawful.[15]

Removal of Mental Patients

11.49 The Home Secretary (or possibly the Secretary of State for

[7] HC 394, para. 142.
[8] Immigration Act 1971, s. 14(1).
[9] 983 H. of C. Official Report, 21 April 1980, Written Answers, col. 7. In *Grewal* [1979–80] Imm AR 119 the Tribunal upheld the Home Secretary's decision to curtail leave to remain where the appellant ceased to be a spouse of an EEC national on divorce and had no other claim to remain in the UK.
[10] Immigration Act 1971, s. 5(6).
[11] Ibid.
[12] HC 394, para. 145.
[13] But see para. 11.41, note 15, ante.
[14] See, e.g. *R v McCartan* [1958] 3 All ER 140.
[15] See *R v East Grinstead JJ, ex parte Doeve* [1969] 1 QB 136.

Health and Social Security) may order the removal of those receiving treatment for mental illness as in-patients. Authorisation is only to be given if 'it is in the interests of the patient to remove him' and proper arrangements have been made for his care and treatment outside the UK.[16] Removal by the Home Secretary will be made in consultation with the Department of Health and Social Security but will not generally arise if the patient, whether or not accompanied by an escort, is able and willing to travel without powers of detention and suitable arrangements have been made to effect his departure.[17] There is no right of appeal against such an order.

Removal of Illegal Entrants and Deserting Seamen and Aircrew

11.50 It is not necessary to make a deportation order in these cases. The Act gives power of removal by order of the Home Secretary without right of appeal.[18]

EXCLUSION AND DEPORTATION OF EEC NATIONALS

11.51 The immigration rules do not make any reference to the special position of EEC nationals in relation to exclusion and deportation. Community law has, however, provided certain safeguards for EEC workers from the rigours of the immigration rules. Despite their omission from the rules, Community law prevails. As has been shown the immigration rules provide that a non-patrial, whether settled in the UK or not, is liable to be excluded if (1) he has been convicted in any country, including the UK, of an extraditable offence (unless there are strong compassionate grounds justifying admission); or (2) exclusion is conducive to the public good, either on the personal direction of the Home Secretary

---

[16] Mental Health Act 1959, s. 90; Mental Health (Scotland) Act 1960, s. 82; Immigration Act 1971, s. 30. There have been 53 removals between when the Act came into force and 31 December 1979 (20 Commonwealth; 4 Irish Republic and 29 foreign nationals) 983 H. of C. Official Report, 21 April 1980, Written Answers, col. 8.

[17] DHSS Memorandum of Guidance (1960) to local health authorities, hospital authorities and general practitioners on the provisions of the Mental Health Act 1959, para. 277. The DHSS has recommended that compulsory removal should be limited to those detained under the Mental Health Act 1959, ss. 26 or 60 (i.e. long term powers) and that there should be an automatic review by a Mental Health Reviewal Tribunal following a decision to remove (DHSS Review of Mental Health Act 1959, Cmnd. 7320, para. 8.27).

[18] See para. 12.1, post.

or where from information available to an immigration officer 'it seems right to refuse leave to enter on that ground if, for example, in the light of the passenger's character, conduct or associations it is undesirable to give him leave to enter'.[19] A non-patrial is liable to be deported if (1) following conviction for a criminal offence punishable by imprisonment, the court recommends deportation; or (2) the Home Secretary deems the deportation to be conducive to the public good.[20]

11.52 The EEC Treaty, art. 48(3), provides that freedom of movement is subject to limitations justified by reasons of public order, public safety and public health. The circumstances in which these restrictions operate are set out in (Council) Directive (EEC) 64/221 which states, *inter alia*, that (1) measures taken on the grounds of public order, safety and health are not to be invoked to service economic ends; (2) measures taken on the grounds of public order or safety are to be based exclusively on the personal conduct of the individual concerned; (3) previous criminal convictions are not in themselves to constitute grounds for the taking of such measures.

'Personal Conduct'

11.53 In *Rutili*,[1] the European Court held that restrictions justifying refusal of entry and residence could not be imposed unless the applicant's 'presence or conduct constitutes a genuine or sufficiently serious threat to public policy'. Thus 'public policy' is not in itself a ground to refuse entry: the applicant must represent a real threat to the aspect of public policy which requires protection. This principle was considered further in *Van Duyn* v *The Home Office*,[2] when a Dutch woman was refused leave to enter the UK to take up employment with the Church of Scientology on the ground that her exclusion was 'conducive to the public good' in that the activities of that organisation, according to the stated policy of the UK Government, were considered socially harmful. The Court, while reiterating that past association itself cannot justify refusal to allow freedom of movement, accepted that present associations may be relevant in determining personal conduct. '... present association which reflects participation in the activities of the body or the organisation as well as identification with its aims and designs, may be considered

---

[19] HC 394, paras. 74, 76. See para. 5.27, ante.
[20] Immigration Act 1971, ss. 3(6), 5(5). See para. 11.18, ante. There are two other grounds: overstaying (s. 3(5)(a)) and family deportation (s. 3(5)(c)) which will not normally apply to EEC national workers.
[1] Case 36/75: [1976] 1 CMLR 140.   [2] Case 41/74: [1975] 3 All ER 190, ECJ.

a voluntary act of the person concerned and, consequently, as part of his personal conduct. . . .' A member state was justified in excluding EEC nationals on this ground even if the organisation was not unlawful in that state and even if no restrictions were placed on its own nationals on membership of the organisation.

Previous Criminal Convictions

11.54 Criminal convictions may be relevant but they cannot automatically justify restricting freedom of movement. In *Bonsignore*,[3] the Court held, following the conviction of an Italian worker in Germany for illegal possession of firearms, that expulsion on the ground of public security cannot be used as a general preventative measure to dissuade other foreign nationals from the Community from committing similar offences or from committing offences against public policy. The Court further held that expulsion cannot be used unless there is a likelihood that the offender will commit further offences or in some way infringe public security or policy. Thus the mere fact that a sentence has been passed does not in itself justify expulsion, nor do factors extraneous to the personal and individual case. 'Personal conduct . . . is strictly, the only determining criterion.'

Directive 64/221 was further considered by the court in *R v Bouchereau*,[4] in the context of the power to make recommendations for deportation. The Court directed that an EEC national may not be deported as a preventative measure alone. Before a recommendation is made there must be a likelihood that his continued presence constitutes a serious threat to 'the fundamental interest of society'. While such a threat may be inferred from the previous convictions of the offender, the court must be satisfied that it exists and a recommendation is not to be made simply to punish the offender or because he is regarded as a nuisance. In *R v Secretary of State for the Home Department, ex parte Santillo*[5] the Divisional Court confirmed that no court should make an order recommending deportation without enquiring into the full circumstances, and the court should give reasons for its decision to make a recommendation. Those reasons should indicate the extent to which the current and previous criminal convictions of the accused had been taken into account, and in so far as that had been done, the light which, in the view of the court, such conviction or convictions threw on the likely nature of the accused's personal conduct in the future.

[3] Case 67/74: [1975] 1 CMLR 472.
[4] [1978] 2 WLR 251.   [5] [1981] 2 All ER 897.

Failure to Comply with Immigration Control

11.55 The mere failure by an EEC national to comply with the formalities concerning entry, movement and residence of non-patrials is not of such a nature as to constitute in itself conduct threatening public policy and public security, and cannot therefore by itself justify deportation or even temporary imprisonment for that reason.[6] Further the judgment of the court in *R v Pieck*[7] indicates that the imposition of any time limit on the stay of an EEC national is inconsistent with the provisions of the Treaty. This must call into question whether an EEC national can commit the offence of 'overstaying'. The Court made it clear that failure to comply with requirements to obtain a residence permit may not be punished by a recommendation for deportation or by measures which go as far as imprisonment.

Omissions from the Immigration Rules

11.56 The effect of these decisions is that the immigration rules do not reflect the true position under EEC law. On exclusion, the rule that an entrant with a criminal conviction must be refused unless there are strong compassionate circumstances is misleading and the criteria stated above must be applied in deciding whether entry is to be given. Refusal on the ground that exclusion is conducive to the public good must also be considered in the light of these criteria. Similarly, deportation following conviction or on conducive grounds is only justified if these principles are observed.

Appeals

11.57 Directive 64/221 requires that where there is no right of appeal, an opinion must be obtained from a 'competent authority', i.e. a court or Tribunal, on the merits of the issue from a decision (1) to refuse entry to a person holding a residence permit; or (2) to refuse to grant a permit, to curtail the stay or to deport the applicant; or (3) to refuse to renew a permit, curtail the stay or deport the applicant.

It seems that there is no requirement for a right of appeal against an initial exclusion.[8] The immigration laws fall short of these requirements in two respects: (1) there is no right of appeal against exclusion arising from a refusal to revoke a deportation order where the Home Secretary personally decides it is conducive to the public good,[9] and (2) there is no

---

[6] Case 48/75: *Royer* [1976] 2 CMLR 619.
[7] Case 159/79: [1981] 3 All ER 46.
[8] Article 9.
[9] Immigration Act 1971, s. 15(5), see para. 14.3, post.

right of appeal against either a refusal to vary leave to remain or against deportation where the Home Secretary states that the person's departure is conducive to the public good as being in the interests of national security or the relations between the UK and any other country or for other reasons of a political nature.[10]

11.58 It is submitted that in each of these situations Community law requires there to be a hearing at least at the level of the immigration appellate authority. It is true that in the case of refusals of variation and deportation for 'security' reasons, there is the right to make representations to a panel of three advisers[11] but this almost certainly would not constitute a 'competent authority' as envisaged by the directive, as it has no power to reverse the Home Secretary's decision, there is no right for the applicant to be legally represented before it or to receive evidence in support of the allegations, nor is there a right to examine or cross-examine witnesses.[12] There is a further area where the right to an appeal is inadequate, viz. where an EEC national is given a lengthy sentence of imprisonment with a recommendation for deportation. In *Santillo*,[13] an Italian national was sentenced to a total of eight years' imprisonment and recommended for deportation for offences of buggery, rape and assault. A deportation order was made by the Home Secretary four and a half years after the recommendation. On a reference to the European Court it was held that a recommendation for deportation made by a criminal court at the time of conviction may constitute an opinion of a competent authority. The opinion must, however, be sufficiently proximate in time to the decision ordering expulsion to ensure that there are no new factors to be taken into consideration: a lapse of time amounting to several years between the recommendation for deportation and the decision by the administration is liable to deprive the recommendation of its function as an opinion within the meaning of the directive. It is essential that the social danger resulting from a foreigner's presence should be assessed at the very time when the decision ordering expulsion is made against him as the factors to be taken into account, particularly those concerning his conduct, are likely to change in the course of time.

11.59 Under the present procedure the Home Secretary does not give consideration whether to give effect to the sentence until towards its conclusion.[14] This procedure is no longer adequate, and the matter is now

---

[10] Ibid., s. 14(3), see para. 14.3, post.
[11] See para. 11.26, ante.
[12] A contrary view is taken by Hartley, op. cit., p. 239.
[13] [1981] 2 All ER 897.   [14] See para. 11.40, ante.

'receiving active consideration' by the Home Office.[15] Unless new legislation is introduced, it is likely that the Home Secretary will not give effect to a recommendation where a lengthy sentence has been imposed, but use his powers to make a decision to deport on the the ground that he deems the deportation to be conducive to the public good. The convicted person may appeal against this decision to the Immigration Appeal Tribunal. It should be borne in mind that it is the duty of the appellate authority to hear and take into account evidence which has occurred between sentence and the appeal hearing.

A NOTE ON REPATRIATION

11.60 The term 'repatriation' is used to describe the return to their country of origin of those who have come to the UK from overseas. It has been proposed by a number of politicians that the Government should use a policy of repatriation based on financial inducements as a means of substantially reducing the black population of the UK.

One scheme is operated by the Department of Health and Social Security (DHSS), the other by the International Social Service of Great Britain (ISS). Although the conditions attached to payment of repatriation grants under each scheme are different (e.g. the ISS scheme is only available to non-patrials whereas the DHSS scheme is available to anyone who has emigrated to the UK) there are some people who are eligible to apply under both schemes. Those in receipt of supplementary benefit are expected to apply first to the DHSS scheme, but this would not preclude them from applying to the ISS scheme if their former application was refused.

DHSS

11.61 The DHSS may use its discretionary power[16] in certain very limited circumstances 'to enable a claimant born outside Great Britain to return with his family to his country of birth – or some other country with which he has close or longstanding connections – for permanent residence.[17] The following provisions apply to those who intend to leave the common travel area.[18] Assistance is only available to those per-

[15] *R v Secretary of State for the Home Department, ex parte Santillo* [1981] 2 All ER 897.
[16] Supplementary Benefits Act 1976, s. 3.
[17] Supplementary Benefits Handbook (1981) (HMSO) prepared by the Department of Health and Social Security, para. 8.25.
[18] Ibid. There are separate provisions for those who wish to settle outside Great Britain but within the common travel area: paras. 8.28, 8.29.

manently resident here who have failed to settle down. A single payment will be made to a claimant if a number of conditions are satisfied, the main ones being: (1) he has not been able to settle in Great Britain nor is there any prospect of him doing so; (2) he has no prospect of employment in Great Britain in the foreseeable future, e.g. because of a physical or mental disability or because he has the sole care of dependent children, or is within five years of pensionable age; (3) he intends to take his partner and dependent children with him; (4) he has suitable accommodation and proposals for support in the country he is going to; (5) he and his family have insufficient capital – including the sale of any property owned by him – to meet the cost of the fares (only the first £50 of such capital is ignored) and the cost is not available from any other source; and (6) within two years of departure the saving in social security benefits will be greater than the single payments. The amount of payment will be a single fare by the cheapest means for each member of the family together with an additional sum to cover incidental expenses on the journey. No payment will be made for removal expenses or for resettlement in the other country.[19]

The International Social Service Scheme

11.62 The Immigration Act 1971, s. 29, enables the Home Secretary to 'make payments of such amount as may be so determined to meet or provide for expenses of persons who are not patrial in leaving the UK for a country or territory where they intend to reside permanently, including travelling expenses for members of their families or households'. The ISS has agreed to administer this scheme based on these repatriation provisions. The ISS stress that the scheme is based on voluntary repatriation. It is not publicised.[20] Local authorities have been advised that they should not draw attention to the existence of the scheme and only to give information about it in response to a specific enquiry. Assistance under the scheme is discretionary. The conditions set out below must be met before consideration will be given to an application, but there is no guarantee that a person who satisfies these conditions will receive a grant.

An applicant must satisfy the ISS that:

(a) the head of the family or household (but not necessarily other members of the family or household) is not a patrial;

[19] Ibid.; paras. 8.26, 8.27.
[20] The information on the scheme has been supplied to the authors by the International Social Service through the National Association of Citizens' Advice Bureaux.

(b) the current average weekly income of the family unit does not exceed the appropriate supplementary benefit level by more than £5 and there is no reasonable likelihood of the applicant earning more than this amount. In calculating the net income of a family unit, due allowance will be made for necessary and unavoidable expenses (e.g. the cost of fares to work). Families whose income is higher than that mentioned above and whose cases present exceptional welfare need may be given special consideration;
(c) those families having sufficient realisable capital to finance their own departure will not be eligible for assistance. The first £500 of any realisable capital will be disregarded, so families with less than this amount will not be expected to contribute to their expenses of travel, and families with more than this amount – but insufficient to be capable of meeting their own travel expenses – will be expected to make an appropriate contribution;
(d) the applicant (or head of the family) has a poor employment record and/or prospects – i.e. he is unemployed or has had, or is likely to have, significant periods of unemployment or frequent changes of low-paid work;
(e) the applicant has failed to settle satisfactorily in this country and wishes to go to a country or territory outside Europe. (Generally this would mean that people who have been here for an extremely long or extremely short time would not be able to obtain a grant);
(f) the departure of the applicant (and, if applicable, his family) from the UK would be in his (or their) interests.

If a grant is given it will cover, wholly or in part, the travel expenses and certain necessary incidental costs incurred by the applicant and his family in leaving the UK. The grant will not provide for help with resettlement within the country to which the applicant has travelled. ISS[1] will entertain applications only direct from the individuals concerned, and not by referral from other agencies.

[1] For address, see Appendix 5.

TWELVE

Removal of Illegal Entrants

ILLEGAL ENTRY BY DECEPTION

12.1 The Act defines an 'illegal entrant' as 'a person unlawfully entering or seeking to enter in breach of a deportation order or of the immigration laws, and includes also a person who has so entered'.[1] It had been assumed for the first three years during which the Act was in operation that, with the exception of those who entered in breach of a deportation order, illegal entrants were confined to those who entered the UK without submitting themselves to the immigration authorities on arrival. However, the courts in a number of cases from May 1976 onwards have made it clear that illegal entry will also arise where an entrant has submitted himself to immigration control but has gained entry by some form of deception of the authorities. The question of whether a person is an illegal entrant is not one of mere academic interest. It is of great importance, as those who are classified by the authorities as illegal entrants may be detained and removed without an opportunity of appeal before removal under the immigration appeals system, and indeed as will be seen, without any other effective remedy under the law.[2]

12.2 It should be emphasised that the wide interpretation by the courts took by surprise not only those advising immigrants but legislators and the Home Office ministers alike.[3] The question of illegal entry by decep-

[1] Immigration Act 1971, s. 33(1). An entrant is defined as 'a person entering or seeking to enter the United Kingdom': ibid.

[2] See para. 13.13, post. For a critical analysis of these developments, see A. Nicol, *Illegal Entrants* (1981) (JCWI and Runnymede Trust).

[3] There was no suggestion during the passing of the Act that those who entered by deception were 'illegal entrants', nor was this the Home Office understanding after the Act came into effect. E.g., in a letter to UKIAS dated 29 August the then

tion was not considered by the House of Lords until July 1980 in *R v Secretary of State for the Home Department, ex parte Zamir*.[4] The court had no hesitation in holding that a distinction between clandestine entrants and those exercising deception when coming in through ports of entry would be illogical and was unsupported by the statutory language. It thus affirmed the decisions of the lower courts that an apparent leave to enter which had been obtained by deception is vitiated, as not being 'leave given in accordance with this Act'.[5]

The Lords went on to consider in *Zamir* the question of the nature of the duty owed by persons arriving in the UK and seeking leave to enter. The appellant had applied in Pakistan when aged 15 for entry clearance as the dependant of his father, who was settled in Britain. Entry clearance was not issued until he was over 18, and after it was issued, but before travelling to the UK, he married. He was not asked by the immigration officer whether he was still unmarried, and was admitted with indefinite leave. Over two years later his wife and baby son applied for entry clearance to join him and he was detained as an illegal entrant. The court rejected the submission that the appellant's only duty was to answer if asked, and that he was under no duty to volunteer information. It held that deception may arise from conduct, or from conduct accompanied by silence as to a material fact. More than this, any alien seeking entry owes a positive duty of candour on all material facts, including those which denote a change of circumstances since the issue of the entry clearance. It is insufficient to set as the standard of disclosure that which applies in the law of contract; the relation of an intending entrant and the immigration authorities requires a higher and more exacting standard. On this basis, it is doubtful that the Court of Appeal in *R v Secretary of State for the Home Department, ex parte Mangoo Khan*[6] was right in allowing the appeal, on similar facts, but involving a son over 21 at the time of admission. The House of Lords in *Zamir* set no limits on the extent of illegal entry by deception, other than that the deception must relate to a material fact. The

---

Minister of State at the Home Office, Mr Alex Lyon, stated that 'bogus children and persons with forged documents who are admitted with leave are not illegal entrants' and that they were eligible to apply for registration. This advice was subsequently passed on by advisory agencies. Some applicants no doubt were accordingly registered as UK citizens.

[4] [1980] 2 All ER 768, HL.

[5] As to leave to enter, see generally Immigration Act 1971, s. 3(1), (3). The earlier decisions are discussed later in the text.

[6] [1980] 2 All ER 337, CA.

test appears to be whether the immigration officer is deceived into giving entry or whether he had authority to give leave to enter.[7]

Fraud as to Identity or Status

12.3 The earlier decisions in the lower courts involved fraud as to identity. In *R v Secretary of State for the Home Department, ex parte Maqbool Hussain*,[8] the entrant had been granted indefinite leave to enter after presenting, as it was later discovered, a passport which did not belong to him. In *R v Bangoo*,[9] the Court of Appeal took the same view when holding that an entry was void *ab initio* if it were obtained by producing to the immigration authorities a false passport. In *Dawood Shah*,[10] and *R v Secretary of State for the Home Department, ex parte Choudhary*,[11] the court held that the applicants were illegal entrants and removal was justified where they had been readmitted as returning residents after having overstayed in the UK and obtained fresh passports. In *Mohammed Anwar*,[12] the entrant was held liable to removal as a bogus dependant son (notwithstanding the fact that a criminal prosecution on this basis had been abandoned). In *Satwant Kaur*,[13] a daughter was held to have entered as a dependant illegally because she was already married. In *Zafar Iqbal and Arif Hussain*,[14] two sons were held to be illegal entrants because they failed to disclose the death of their father, which occurred after they applied for entry clearance but before it was issued to them as dependants.

False Information on Obtaining Work Permits

12.4 One of the most extreme interpretations of illegal entry involves those who originally entered on work permits. In *Claveria*,[15] a woman was held to have entered illegally because the existence of children had been concealed when she obtained a work permit as a resident domestic, one of the conditions for which was that the holder should have no dependent children. Other work permit holders have been removed

[7] Per Wilberforce LJ at 773.
[8] [1976] 1 WLR 97.
[9] [1976] *The Times* 28 July, [1976] Crim LR 746.
[10] (1977) 5 October 284A/77 (unreported).
[11] [1978] 3 All ER 790, CA.
[12] (1978) 19 January 448/77 (unreported).
[13] (1977) 13 October 331/77 (unreported).
[14] (1980) 7 February 251/79 (unreported).
[15] (1979) 22 November 37, 38/79 DC (unreported).

when the references provided to the Department of Employment have been discovered to have been false.

Further Examples

12.5 It is not only those who have obtained indefinite leave who may be regarded as illegal entrants. In *Sadiq Masih*,[16] a fiancé was held to be an illegal entrant because he knew that the girl he had purportedly come to marry within three months would still be under 16. In *R v Secretary of State for the Home Department, ex parte Ibrahim*,[17] a fiancée was held to be an illegal entrant because before her arrival her uncle who had arranged the marriage had been told by her stated fiancé that he did not in fact intend to marry her. In *Nuzrat Shah*[18] and *Khalid Mehmud*,[19] people who had been given leave to enter as visitors were held to be illegal entrants because they had concealed their immigration history and their true intentions.

False Information Given by Third Parties

Lack of knowledge by the entrant that a deception had been practised is of no help. In *Khan v Secretary of State for the Home Department*,[20] a false passport produced by the entrant's husband was sufficient for the Court of Appeal to hold that a false document obtained by an agent made the entry illegal, despite the entrant being illiterate. In *Ibrahim*,[1] it was also accepted that no deception was knowingly practised by the entrant herself. The Home Office has, however, stated that 'such cases are always examined with great care to ensure that innocent victims of such deception are not removed if there are strong compassionate reasons for allowing them to remain'.[2]

Grant of Citizenship

12.6 A subsequent grant of citizenship may be of no protection to the immigrant if the initial entry was obtained by fraud. In *R v Secretary of State for the Home Department, ex parte Sultan Mahmood*[3] the facts were that

---

[16] (1980) 5 March 513/79 DC (unreported).
[17] (1980) *The Times* 29 March.
[18] (1979) 22 November 467/79 DC (unreported).
[19] (1979) 26 July 90/79 DC (unreported).
[20] [1977] 3 All ER 538, CA.
[1] (1980) *The Times* 29 March.
[2] Memorandum by the Home Office to the Home Affairs Committee: Race Relations and Immigration Sub-committee: HC (1980–81) 89, para. 15.
[3] [1980] 3 WLR 312, CA.

the applicant had entered the UK in 1973 on the passport of a cousin who had died in 1972: subsequently he purported to obtain registration as a UK citizen (under section 5A of the British Nationality Act 1948)[4] by the fraudulent use of that passport. The Court of Appeal took the view that his detention under Schedule 2 of the Act was lawful as he was subject to immigration control: the registration was a nullity. In *R v Secretary of State for the Home Department, ex parte Akhtar*,[5] the Court of Appeal held that an immigration officer had reasonable grounds to believe that a person refused entry was a bogus son and not the person on whose behalf the bogus father had applied for registration. In order to rely on the grant of citizenship, the appellant would have to show that he was indeed the person registered and the son of the father. The court rejected the argument that the British Nationality Act 1948, s. 20, which provides for an inquiry where the Secretary of State proposes to deprive a person of citizenship because his registration was obtained by fraud, prevented the appellant from being treated as an illegal entrant. The Court held that section 20 applies to an admitted or proven citizen, and there is ample scope for its operation where fraud is involved without including fraud which in fact failed to procure the registration of the appellant as a citizen: the court gave by way of example fraud as to the period of residence.

Home Office View

12.7 The Home Office has set out the approach it adopts in deciding whether a person is an illegal entrant by deception:

'. . . since such deception has to involve an element of guilty mind, the Home Office would not consider the person an illegal entrant unless satisfied that he realised or should have realised that the facts he failed to disclose were material'.[6]

On a number of occasions the Home Office has made submissions to the Tribunal that for a person's leave to be vitiated, the deception practised must have been of such a nature that, had the full facts been known to the immigration officer, those facts would have rendered the person seeking entry ineligible for admission under the immigration laws. The Tribunal has, however, sometimes disposed of appeals by holding that persons

[4] See para. 2.13, ante.
[5] [1980] 2 All ER 735.
[6] Memorandum by the Home Office, cited note 2 supra., para. 14.

who practised deception as to their intentions are illegal entrants even in circumstances which on the basis of the Home Office's submission would have resulted in entry being lawful.[7]

Leave to Enter Given by Mistake

12.8 It is, however, established that where the immigration officer gives leave to enter by mistake, in the absence of fraud or dishonesty on the part of the entrant, the entry is valid.[8] But in most cases the courts have accepted uncritically Home Office submissions that a mistake must have been induced by deception even where there is no evidence that this was the case.

THE 'AMNESTIES' FOR ILLEGAL ENTRANTS

12.9 On 11 April 1974 the then Home Secretary announced[9] that he did not propose to exercise the power of removal held in *R v Governor of Pentonville Prison, ex parte Azam*[10] to apply retrospectively to illegal entrants who were exempt from removal before the coming into effect of the Immigration Act 1971. His decision applied to Commonwealth citizens and citizens of Pakistan who entered illegally on or after 9 March 1968 and before 1 January 1973, or who entered illegally before 9 March 1968 after having been earlier refused admission by an immigration officer. It did not apply to those who were not affected by the retrospective provisions, including aliens (other than citizens of Pakistan), seamen, stowaways or those who had overstayed or entered in breach of a deportation order.

On 29 November 1977, the succeeding Home Secretary announced[11] the extension of the so-called amnesty to bring the treatment of Commonwealth citizens and citizens of Pakistan who entered illegally by deception into line with that of clandestine entrants. The effect of this announcement was severely limited by the fact that it did not apply to those who first entered by deception before 1973, but subsequently left the

---

[7] See *Shazad* 32163/78 (1626) (unreported), and para. 14.28, post.
[8] *R v Secretary of State for the Home Department, ex parte Ram* [1979] 1 All ER 687. See also *R v Secretary of State for the Home Department, ex parte Badaike* (1977) *The Times* 4 May. See also the observations of Donaldson LJ in *Shahnaz Noreen* (1980) 26 November 261/80.
[9] 872 H. of C. Official Report cols. 637–646. The text is set out in *LAG Bulletin*, 1976 (April) pp. 85–86.
[10] [1973] 2 All ER 765.
[11] Details of the announcement are set out in *LAG Bulletin*, 1978 (March) p. 7.

country and re-entered after 1 January 1973 as returning residents. The final date for applications under both announcements was set at 31 December 1978. No applications under the amnesties can now be made. It was promised that when the amnesty arrangements had ended, those who would have qualified under them, had they applied in time, will be removed only on the personal authorisation of a Minister.[12] Such removals have now begun to take place, although others who made late application have been allowed to remain exceptionally.

The Court of Appeal in *Birdi*,[13] held that the amnesty conferred no right on the applicant: it was simply an expression of an intention to mitigate the rigours of the Act under certain circumstances, and gave the applicant an expectation that the facts of his case would be examined administratively and if he satisfied the burden of proof which lay upon him, the Secretary of State might exercise his discretion to give him leave to remain. Neither the courts nor the immigration appellate authorities have therefore reviewed the decisions reached by the Home Office on applications made under the amnesties.

12.10 When a grant of indefinite leave under the amnesties has been obtained by deception, the Home Office is not bound by it. In *Mohammed Munawar Moghal*,[14] a person given leave as a pre-1973 clandestine entrant was held, on the basis of subsequent informer evidence that he had in fact been an overstayer, to have obtained indefinite leave by deception.

PRE-1968 ENTRANTS

12.11 A person who entered as a Commonwealth citizen before 9 March 1968 without presenting himself to an immigration officer, and without having previously done so and been refused, committed no offence and is not an illegal entrant. The Home Office takes the view that entry obtained by deception by a Commonwealth citizen before 9 March 1968 does not constitute illegal entry and does not therefore nullify subsequent leave to re-enter founded on the previous residence even if the re-entry is in the original false identity.[15]

The Home Office reasoning is that 'the Commonwealth Immigrants Act 1962 did not require a Commonwealth citizen to seek leave to enter

[12] 940 H. of C. Official Report 29 November 1977, Written Answers, Col. 125.
[13] (1975) *The Times*, 12 February, CA.
[14] 223/79 (1980) 1 February, CA (unreported).
[15] Letter, Timothy Raison, Minister of State at the Home Office, to Sheila Wright, MP, 18 January 1981.

the UK from an immigration officer and those Commonwealth citizens who had not previously been refused admission and who entered without being examined by an immigration officer became irremovable after remaining for 24 hours'.[16] The Commonwealth Immigrants Act 1968 which came into force on 9 March 1968 made it an offence to enter without examination by an immigration officer.

[16] Ibid.

THIRTEEN

Detention and Release

This chapter deals with all situations where a person may be detained and sets out the ways in which release from detention may be sought.

ON SEEKING LEAVE TO ENTER

Provisions for Detention

13.1 A passenger examined at a port or airport may be detained under the authority of an immigration officer pending further examination and a decision to give or refuse him leave to enter.[1] If leave to enter is refused he may be detained under the authority of an immigration officer pending his removal.[2] The places at which a person may be detained are set out in the Act and in the Immigration (Places of Detention) Direction 1972.[3] They are as follows:

(a) on board the ship or aircraft in which the person arrived, but only if he has been refused leave to enter;
(b) any place used by the immigration officer for the purpose of his functions at the port at which the person is seeking leave to enter, or has been refused leave to enter;
(c) any place specially provided for the purpose of detention at any port or at Government Buildings, Harmondsworth;
(d) any premises at which appeals are heard, or any place provided for detention in the vicinity of such premises;

[1] Immigration Act 1971, Sch. 2 para. 16(1).
[2] Ibid., para. 16(2).
[3] Made on 7 November 1972 by the Home Secretary in exercise of powers under Immigration Act 1971, Sch. 2, para. 18(1). The Direction has never been officially published. It came into operation on 1 January 1973.

(e) any police station, prison or remand centre, or in the case of a person under the age of 17, any place of safety.[4]

Normally detention is arranged in port detention accommodation, if available, or on board ships, or in police cells. The Immigration (Places of Detention) Direction, however, sets limits on detention at ports and in police cells. A detained person must, once five days have elapsed, be removed to the detention centre at Harmondsworth or to a prison (if aged over 21) or to a remand centre (if aged over 17 and under 21) or to a place of safety (if under 17). The only exceptions to this rule are (1) a person may be detained for up to a further two days if it is proposed to remove him from the UK within that time, in accordance with directions which have been given, and (2) a person who has been held in detention for five days at a port or in police cells, removed to prison, remand centre or place of safety, and is then brought back to the port for removal from the UK may be held for a further two days at the port if, e.g., the departure of his flight or ship is delayed. There is no limit on the time for which a person may be detained at Harmondsworth or in prison, a remand centre or place of safety.

The Home Office has indicated that the aim is to use the accommodation at Harmondsworth for the great majority of cases where detention has to exceed five days, and 'only where there are special circumstances (pointing, e.g. to a determination to abscond or a risk of violence) would detention in prison be authorised'.[5]

13.2 Harmondsworth and other immigration service detention accommodation are staffed by employees of Securicor Ltd. The Home Office has confirmed that these employees 'have no powers of arrest or detention and work under the authority of the Immigration Service'.[6] The official explanation for the use by the Home Office of a private security company is that,

'before 1970 the carrying companies employed private security firms to enable them to fulfil their statutory obligations for the detention and

---

[4] A 'place of safety' is defined as 'a community home provided by a local authority or a controlled community home, any police station or any hospital, surgery or other suitable place, the occupier of which is willing temporarily to receive a child or young person'. Children and Young Persons Act 1933, s. 107, as amended by the Children and Young Persons Act 1969, Sch. 5.

[5] Evidence to Expenditure Committee (Education Arts and Home Office Sub-Committee) HC (1977–78) no. 56, p. 482.

[6] Ibid., p. 483; see para. 10.14, ante.

removal of passengers refused leave to land. In July 1970 carrying companies at major airports were relieved of their responsibility for the detention of passengers and the Home Office entered into a contract with Securicor for the provision of staff for the manning of Immigration Service detention centres and for escorting persons in detention to and from prisons, appeal centres and other places where they are required to attend.'[7]

Releasing from Detention

13.3 The Act provides a machinery for the release of those who, on seeking admission to the UK, are being detained by the immigration authorities. As will be seen the possibilities for release are somewhat restricted. There is a right to apply for bail in certain circumstances and also the Act gives an immigration officer the power to give temporary admission. The table below sets out the position.

Action by Immigration Officer	*Circumstances*	*Possibilities for Release*
No decision on entry yet made	Less than 7 days elapsed	Temporary admission
	7 days elapsed	Temporary admission
		Bail
Refusal of leave to enter	No right of appeal until outside UK	Temporary admission
	Right of appeal while in UK	Temporary admission
		Bail

Bail

13.4 A right of appeal against refusal does not normally arise until the individual has been removed from the UK,[8] but a passenger has a right of

[7] Ibid.
[8] Immigration Act 1971, s. 13(1), (3); para. 14.9, post.

appeal while in the UK if at the time he was refused leave he holds a current entry clearance or a current work permit in his name.[9] In these circumstances, once notice of appeal has been given, bail can be granted by a chief immigration officer or police inspector on the appellate entering into his own recognizance to appear before the appellant authorities at a specified time.[10] If bail is not forthcoming there is a right to apply to an adjudicator, or in appropriate cases the Tribunal.[11] As in bail applications in criminal proceedings, conditions designed to secure the appellant's attendance at the appeal hearing may be attached and also sureties may be taken.[12] If bail is granted and the conditions fixed, the appellate authority may specify some other person (e.g. the police) to take the bail. This may be appropriate when the sureties are not available to attend the hearing.[13]

There are provisions for the forfeiture of recognizances and for the arrest of appellants released on bail where there is reason to believe bail conditions are likely to be or have been broken.[14]

Restrictions on Granting Bail

13.5 Once the remedies under the immigration appeals system have been exhausted, bail cannot continue without the consent of the Home Secretary. There are also a number of other restrictions on the granting of bail: the Act gives the appellate authorities a discretion to refuse bail if the appellant (1) has been in breach of bail conditions previously in an immigration case; (2) is likely to commit an offence; (3) is likely to cause a danger to public health if released; (4) is suffering from a mental disorder and should be detained for his protection or for that of others; (5) is under 17 and no satisfactory arrangements exist for his care.[15] It is submitted that, subject to these restrictions, an identical approach should be adopted in bail applications in immigration cases as those in criminal proceedings.[16] It must be right that as there is a presumption of bail for those who are alleged to have committed criminal offences, the same presumption should apply where no such allegation is being made.

[9] Ibid., s. 13(3).
[10] Ibid., Sch. 2, para. 29(1), (2).
[11] Ibid., para. 29(3), (4).
[12] Ibid., para. 29(5).
[13] Ibid., para. 29(6).
[14] Ibid., paras. 31, 32.
[15] Ibid., para. 30(2).
[16] See the Bail Act 1976.

Attitude of the Immigration Authorities towards Bail

13.6 The factors which the immigration officer will take into account in deciding whether to oppose an application for bail are (1) the likelihood of the appellant, if released, failing to appear when required; (2) the facilities available for detention, considered in relation to the appellant's age, sex and state of health; (3) the period of time likely to elapse before the appeal is disposed of; (4) any special reason such as those set out in the Act giving the appellate authorities a discretion to refuse bail; (5) the reliability and standing of the sureties.

The authorities regard certain circumstances or behaviour on the part of the appellant as presenting a special risk of absconding. They include (1) an attempt by the appellant to avoid examination on arrival, or to escape from custody; (2) a statement by him or his sponsor (e.g. in correspondence which he is carrying) indicating an intention to go to ground if admitted; (3) any fact demonstrating conclusively that the appellant has deliberately set out to obtain admission by fraudulent means; (4) refusal by the appellant's apparent sponsor to stand surety for him, even if other sureties are produced; (5) an association or link between the appellant and any other person known to have entered the country illegally or to be concerned with facilitating evasion of immigration controls; (6) terrorist connections or other considerations in which the public interest is involved.

13.7 An immigration officer will consult the Home Office before making a decision. If bail is opposed, particular stress will be laid on these factors which apply on an application for bail before the appellate authorities. Immigration officers have been given instructions which emphasise that

'there will be many cases in which the immigration service would not willingly release the applicant because he belongs to a class of immigrant which has strong economic or other incentives to obtain entry to this country and because of the frequency with which other immigrants of that class have evaded or attempted to evade immigration controls. Applications for bail from appellants in this category should normally be left to the appellate authorities. . . .'

At the hearing of a bail application in these circumstances immigration officers are instructed to,

'. . . refer to the incentives which the appellant has to obtain entry to the country, the temptation he will have to go to ground if released on bail, and (if applicable) the difficulty the police would have in tracing him in an existing immigrant community. But references to the tendency of immigrants of particular national origins to evade immigration control should be avoided.'

If, however, there are adequate sureties, bail on application is to be granted where refusal would entail transferring the appellant to a prison, remand centre or place of safety; or the accommodation is otherwise unsuitable because of the appellant's state of health or other special circumstances.

Procedure on Making a Bail Application

13.8
1. Advisers should first, check to see whether the immigration officer will give the passenger temporary admission without going through the bail procedure. If he is prepared to do so, conditions, limited to residence and reporting to the police, can be attached.
2. If temporary admission is refused an application for bail to an immigration or police officer should be made orally.[17]
3. If the officer is not prepared to grant temporary admission or bail, an application should be made to the adjudicator's office at the port of entry for a hearing date for a bail application.
4. A hearing date can be given by telephone. An application can be made, either orally or in writing,[18] but an oral hearing is desirable as the case will only have proceeded to this stage if the immigration authorities are objecting to bail.
5. The application form for bail is set out in the schedule to the Procedure Rules.[19] It is strictly only necessary to complete this form if a written application is being made but the appellate authorities usually request the form to be submitted before a hearing. It is sensible to do so, where practicable, but submitting of the form should not hold up the fixing of a hearing date.
6. The hearing of a bail application should commence with the immigration authorities setting out their objections to bail, if any. Those representing the applicant should then deal with the objections and proceed in the same way as if they were making an application in a magistrates' court. Sureties should be present and give evidence as to their ability to stand surety wherever possible.

[17] Immigration Appeals (Procedure) Rules 1972, SI 1972, No. 1684, r. 23(1)(a).
[18] Ibid., r. 23(1)(b).
[19] Ibid., Sch. Forms 3–7 inclusive.

7. If an adjudicator refuses bail, there is no right of appeal against that decision. There is nothing, however, to prevent a further application to the adjudicator. Moreover, if the appeal against refusal of leave to enter is dismissed, the appellant has an automatic right of appeal to the Tribunal, and once an appeal to the Tribunal has been lodged, a bail application can be considered by the Tribunal.
8. Those detaining the applicant must release him once they are satisfied that he has entered into his own recognizance and where sureties have been required, their recognizances have also been taken.[20]

Bail after Seven Days without a Decision Being Made

13.9 In the unlikely event of seven days elapsing without a decision having been made as to whether to grant leave to enter, an application for bail may be made to an adjudicator. An immigration or police officer has no power to give bail in these circumstances, but an immigration officer may nevertheless grant temporary admission. In practice the same rules apply as in other circumstances where bail may be given.

Temporary Admission

13.10 Anyone detained by an immigration officer either pending a decision to admit or, if refused entry, pending his departure, may be granted temporary admission by an immigration officer.[2] The authority to admit must be in writing. It may be subject to restrictions decided by the immigration officer as to (1) residence; and (2) reporting to the police or the immigration service.[3]

In almost all cases where temporary admission is granted, a restriction on residence will be applied, but a requirement to report to the police is rare, and will only be imposed when the immigration officer believes it appropriate to retain strict control over the passenger's movements. During the period of temporary admission the passport is usually retained by the immigration officer. There is no authority in law for this practice.[4] Temporary admission will usually be granted where the im-

---

[20] Ibid., r. 23(4): (for Scotland see r. 23(5)).
[1] Immigration Act 1971, Sch. 2, paras. 21–25.
[2] Ibid., para. 21(1).
[3] Ibid., para. 21(2).
[4] An immigration officer has power to detain certain types of documents (Sch. 2 para. 4(4)), viz. those decribed in Sch. 2 para. 4(2)(b), but a passport is not included in the description, and is specifically referred to elsewhere in the sub-paragraph (4(2)(a)). The Home Office has issued a note reminding the Immigration Service that a passenger should be given back his passport if he asks for it. See para. 5.34, ante.

migration officer is satisfied that the passenger can be trusted to comply with its terms. It is frequently granted in the case of women, young children and elderly or infirm persons, and where the passenger has close relatives in the UK or there are other compassionate circumstances making detention unnecessary or inappropriate. There is a reluctance to grant admission in other cases, particularly to (1) men of working age; (2) those whose refusal of entry is obligatory (e.g. because of the absence of an entry clearance for settlement); and (3) those who have used false documents or have deliberately deceived the immigration officer to obtain entry. However, the authorities may be persuaded to grant admission in these cases if it can be shown that there are strong compassionate features.

13.11 Temporary admission may be withdrawn and the passenger taken into detention at any time.[5] Normally, however, it will not be curtailed nor will there be a refusal to extend it prior to the completion of enquiries unless the passenger fails to observe residential or reporting restrictions.

Advice on the Obtaining of Temporary Admission

13.12
1. It should be made absolutely clear to the immigration authorities from the earliest possible moment where the passenger is going to reside.
2. The authorities will always take into account the reliability of the sponsors involved. It is essential that the person with whom the appellant is to reside has (if applicable) a good immigration record and he should also be a person of good character. The immigration authorities may make enquiries of the police to establish that the person is 'suitable'.
3. It will be appropriate to grant temporary admission where representations are being made which involve the immigration authorities in further enquiries and which will take some time to complete. If an MP is involved, he may be able to persuade the authorities to admit on this basis.
4. Where entry has been refused the immigration authorities may be more easily persuaded to grant admission if they can be informed of circumstances which were not apparent to them at the time they made the decision to refuse.
5. The weakness of the temporary admission system is that there is no provision for sureties. Nevertheless, it may be of help to show the

[5] Ibid., Sch. 2, para. 21(1).

authorities that there are persons of substance who have a connection with the passenger and who are prepared to 'back' him by coming forward and offering assistance, e.g., as to residence and financial support.

ILLEGAL ENTRANTS

13.13 The definition of an illegal entrant has already been discussed.[6] An immigration or police officer may arrest without warrant anyone suspected of being an illegal entrant.[7] It is rare for a person to be subsequently charged for the criminal offence of illegal entry but once the immigration authorities are satisfied that the arrested person is an illegal entrant further detention by an immigration officer is provided for under the Act.[8] The individual should be given a form stating that he is being so detained. An immigration officer may give directions for removal of the illegal entrant.[9]

Temporary Release

13.14 Temporary release may be granted.[10] The procedure is identical to that where temporary admission is granted after refusal of entry, and the advice given earlier[11] applies equally to cases of alleged illegal entry. In many cases the entrant may well have established a home in the UK, his family may be with him and he is likely to be in employment. These points should be stressed to the immigration officer responsible, to emphasise that there is little or no likelihood of the entrant disappearing were he to be released. There is no system of bail so that sureties as such cannot be offered or taken.

The granting of temporary release only provides temporary relief for the detainee. It does not assist in establishing that he is not an illegal entrant. If after a further examination of the information made available to him, an immigration officer concludes that the person is an illegal entrant, arrangements will be made for his removal. In practice, the only effective method to secure the right to remain in the UK is for successful representations to be made to the Home Secretary through a Member of Parliament.

[6] See para. 12.1, ante.
[7] Ibid., s. 24(2).
[8] Ibid., Sch. 2, para. 16(1) (detention of those liable to examination under para. 2); ibid., Sch. 2, para. 16(2) (detention of those liable to removal).
[9] Ibid., para. 9.
[10] Ibid., para. 21.   [11] See para. 13.12, ante.

Habeas Corpus

13.15 Where a detained person disputes that he is an illegal entrant, the only other course of action open to him to secure his release, if temporary admission is refused, is to apply for a writ of *habeas corpus*.[12] This is a writ issued out of the High Court addressed to the detainer who will usually be the Governor of the prison if the immigration officer has handed over the person; otherwise it will be the immigration officer who signed the detention notice handed to the detainee. The writ demands that the detainer produces the detainee before the court and give the reasons for the detention. When produced the court considers the reasons given and decides whether detention should continue.[13] This procedure, if successful, could not only secure release but also establish that the applicant has a right to remain in the UK. The courts have been extremely reluctant to grant *habeas corpus* in illegal entry cases and there is every reason to believe that they have severely eroded the principles upon which *habeas corpus* is based.[14]

Guide Lines

13.16 The following guidelines, however, can be deduced from a series of confusing decisions:

The applicant must first show that there is a *prima facie* case. In *R v Governor of Pentonville Prison, ex parte Azam*, Lord Denning MR explained the procedure thus:

> 'If a *prima facie* case is shown that a man is unlawfully detained it is for the one who detains him to make a return justifying it. In my opinion, therefore, if any of these men can raise a *prima facie* case that he is not an illegal entrant, he is entitled to have a writ of *habeas corpus* to have the matter determined.'[15]

---

[12] For a summary of the history see de Smith *Constitutional and Administrative Law* (4th Edn.) pp. 584 et seq. Also *R v Secretary of State, ex parte Greene* [1941] 3 All ER 388, per Lord Wright at 399.

[13] The procedure is set out in RSC, Ord. 54, and the Administration of Justice Act 1960, s. 14. An excellent practical guide to the procedure can be found in *LAG Bulletin*, 1979, (August) p. 182.

[14] For a critical review see A. Nicol, *Illegal Entrants* (1981) (JCWI and Runnymede Trust); D. Lloyd Jones, *The Role of Habeas Corpus in Immigration Cases* 95 LQR 171.

[15] [1973] 2 All ER 741, at 751. See also *Re Wajid Hassan* [1976] 2 All ER 123, per Widgery LCJ at 129–130.

This will give him a right to a hearing. There are, however, a number of serious obstacles to overcome before he can be sure of release from detention.

13.17 The courts have placed the burden on the detainee to prove that he is not an illegal entrant: there is no requirement that immigration authorities must justify the detention. In *R v Secretary of State for the Home Department, ex parte Choudhary*,[16] the Court of Appeal stated:

'The return, on the face of it, affords sufficient justification for his detention and removal from the United Kingdom. It is *prima facie* good. If that return is to be challenged, it is for him to challenge it. The burden is upon him to show that he is being unlawfully detained.'[17]

The effect is that the detainee is left with the formidable, if not impossible, task of proving a negative. In the event of his being able to show the immigration authorities that he is in the UK lawfully, he will almost certainly be released without the need to proceed to *habeas corpus*. In the cases which do proceed, there is therefore no conclusive evidence which can be produced.

13.18 The task is made more difficult for the detainee in that the court requires him to prove that the Home Secretary or immigration officer did not have reasonable grounds to believe that he was an illegal entrant: the decision to detain and remove 'can only be attacked if it can be shown that there were no grounds upon which the Secretary of State, through his officers, could have acted, or that no reasonable person could have decided as he did'.[18]

The court is prepared to conduct a limited investigation into whether the Home Secretary, or those acting under him, are correct in their belief.[19] It considers the case on affidavit evidence, as to which cross-examination, although allowable, does not take place in practice. It is not possible to find out the truth between conflicting statements, nor

[16] [1978] 3 All ER 790, CA.
[17] Per Lord Denning MR at 792.
[18] *Zamir v Secretary of State for the Home Department* [1980] 2 All ER 768, per Wilberforce LJ at 772. This confirms the approach of Geoffrey Lane LJ in *R v Secretary of State, ex parte Hussain* [1978] 2 All ER 427 at 429: 'If, on the evidence taken as a whole, the Secretary of State has grounds, and reasonable grounds for coming to the conclusion that the applicant is here illegally, in contravention of the terms of the 1971 Act, the court will not interfere.'
[19] 'We have to examine afresh the respondent's decision in the light of the . . . submissions . . . put before us as to the sufficiency of the material before him' per Stephenson LJ in *Mohammed Munawar Moghal* 223/79 (1980) 1 February, CA.

'. . . to weigh the materiality of personal or other factors, present or not present, or partially present, to the mind of the immigration authorities'. It cannot act as a court of appeal as to the facts on which the immigration officer decided. The court will not make any further enquiry once it has satisfied itself that the authorities had reasonable grounds to believe the facts upon which the decision is made are true.[20]

13.19 The courts have indicated that as a matter of practice (1) if the Home Secretary is relying on informer evidence (which he often is) he should depose whether the informer is known to him or is anonymous; and (2) where interviews between the immigration authorities and the applicant are quoted by the authorities in affidavits before the court, then the transcript of the whole interview should be annexed to the affidavit.[1]

Where the alleged illegal entrant puts forward an explanation of his entry which is consistent with his being lawfully here, the burden shifts to the immigration authorities and the courts will enquire to see what 'the overall situation is'.[2]

The effect of these decisions is that while the Act gives power to remove an illegal entrant, a person so removed may be no more than one whom the Home Secretary 'reasonably believes to be an illegal entrant'. There is no evidence to suggest that this was the intention of Parliament from the debates during the course of the passing of the legislation, but the House of Lords in *Zamir* concluded that the framework of the Act offered no other approach.[3]

CRIMINAL OFFENCES

Before Sentence

13.20 There is no distinction between patrials and non-patrials and the normal rules relating to those charged with criminal offences apply. An application for bail may be made, as appropriate, to a magistrate, a judge of the Crown Court or a judge in chambers.[4]

Problems may arise if the accused has only a limited connection with

---

[20] *Zamir v Secretary of State for the Home Department* [1980] 2 All ER 768.

[1] *Moghal*, see note 19, supra.

[2] *R v Secretary of State, ex parte Ram*, [1979] 1 All ER 687 per May J at 692. (Immigration officer was mistaken, and gave indefinite leave without any fraud or misrepresentation by the applicant.)

[3] Per Wilberforce LJ at 774.

[4] See generally B. Raymond *Bail: A Practical Guide* (1979) Oyez.

this country (e.g. where he is here as a visitor or student). Particular care should be taken in presenting applications for bail in these cases: wherever possible, sureties should be offered, and, if necessary, the accused should be prepared to agree to conditions being attached to the granting of bail. Often the difficulty will not be that the prosecution fear the accused will leave the country, but that he will disappear inside the country, and applications should deal with this aspect where relevant. If the prosecution fears that the accused will leave the UK, it should be borne in mind that the Bail Act 1976 provides for a surety to pay money into court by way of security.[5]

After Sentence

13.21 There are three situations following a sentence by a criminal court which require consideration: (1) a sentence short of immediate imprisonment but with a recommendation for deportation; (2) an immediate custodial sentence with a recommendation for deportation; (3) an immediate custodial sentence without a recommendation for deportation. In each of these situations a person may appeal against conviction and/or sentence. Appeal against sentence may be limited, where appropriate, to appeal against recommendation for deportation. An application for bail may be made if an appeal is pending.[6]

No Custodial Sentence: Recommendation for Deportation

13.22 The courts have power to recommend for deportation, subject to certain minor exceptions, non-patrials aged 17 or over who have been convicted of a criminal offence, punishable by imprisonment, irrespective of whether a custodial sentence is imposed.[7]

It is important to remember that detention is automatic unless there is a specific decision to the contrary by the court or subsequently by the Home Secretary.[8] The court which must release the convicted person is the court which passed sentence, or, where there is an appeal against conviction or sentence, any court which has the power to grant bail pending appeal. Where a person is convicted by a magistrates' court and unsuccessfully appeals to the Crown Court against a recommendation for

---

[5] Bail Act 1976, s. 3(5).

[6] If the appeal is from a magistrates' court to a Crown Court, application for bail may be made to either court (Magistrates' Courts Act 1980, s. 113; Courts Act 1971, s. 13(4)). In the case of an appeal from a Crown Court, application may be made to the Court of Appeal only (Criminal Appeal Act 1968, s. 19).

[7] Immigration Act 1971, ss. 3(6), 9(1). See para. 11.34, ante.

[8] Ibid., Sch. 3, para. 2(1).

deportation, the Crown Court has power to grant release notwithstanding the dismissal of the appeal.[9] The effect of these provisions appears to be that if the prisoner has not been immediately released after sentence and no appeal is pending, only the Home Secretary or those acting under him can authorise his release. The wording of the Act does, however, admit the possibility that the Court making the recommendation for deportation has the power to direct release at any time between sentence and the making of a deportation order, and therefore it may be possible to return to the court and apply for release.

13.23 Concern has been expressed as to the numbers being detained in custody in these circumstances, and following a deputation to the Home Office by representatives of the Joint Council for the Welfare of Immigrants and the National Council for Civil Liberties, the Home Office agreed to issue a circular to the courts advising them of the possible consequences of recommending a person for deportation.

The circular is set out in full, as practitioners may find it necessary to remind both magistrates' and Crown Court judges of its contents in appropriate cases.

Home Office Circular No. 113/1978 12 July 1978

Immigration Act 1971: Detention Pending Deportation

'I am directed by the Secretary of State to refer to the Home Office Circular No. 216/1972 (215/1972 in the case of the Clerk to the Justices) which described the provisions of the Immigration Act 1971 relating to deportation. Paragraph 12 of that circular (paragraph 23 of 215/1972) describes the effect of paragraph 2(1) of Schedule 3 to the Immigration Act 1971. This provides that a person who is recommended for deportation by a court will be detained pending the making of a deportation order unless the court directs otherwise, or unless the Secretary of State subsequently directs his release pending further consideration of his case.
2. The number of persons detained in prisons pending deportation has been rising steadily in recent years. Under section 6(6) of the 1971 Act the Secretary of State is precluded from making a deportation order against a person recommended for deportation by a court until the expiration of the time for bringing an appeal against the conviction or recommendation. This is 21 days in the case of a recommendation made by a magistrates' court and 28 days where the recommendation is made by a higher court. Where the Secretary of State decides to make an

[9] *R v Inner London Crown Court, ex parte Obajuwana* (1979) 69 Cr. App. R 125.

order, the deportee has a further fortnight in which to appeal against the destination specified in the removal directions. Thus a detainee who fully exercises his appeal rights will spend at least 5 weeks in detention even where there are no additional factors (for example, the absence of a valid travel document) to delay the implementation of the court's recommendation.

3. It should not be assumed that the Secretary of State will be in full or immediate possession of the facts which will enable him to consider whether the case is an appropriate one for the exercise of his own powers of release under paragraph 2(1) of Schedule 3 to the Immigration Act 1971. Accordingly, the Secretary of State would be grateful if, in the light of the factors described above, courts would give the most careful consideration to all cases where they make a recommendation for deportation and the question of detention or release arises. Although the provisions of the Bail Act 1976 do not apply to the grant or refusal of bail under the Immigration Act 1971, the Secretary of State suggests that courts may wish to bear in mind, when deciding whether or not to order release in these circumstances, the principal grounds for withholding bail in criminal proceedings: in particular, it may be thought that detention would not be appropriate unless there were good reasons to suppose that the person would abscond or commit further criminal offences, if released on bail (courts are reminded that there is no power to impose restrictions or conditions on the release of a person recommended for deportation).

4. In all cases it is essential that the court's certificate that a recommendation for deportation has been made be sent to the Home Office without delay (paragraph 12 of Home Office Circular 216/72 (15 of 125/72 refers). The envelope containing the certificates should be clearly marked "For the attention of the Deportation Machinery Group, Home Office, Lunar House, 40 Wellesley Road, Croydon CR9 2BY".'

Custodial Sentence: Recommendation for Deportation

13.24 There is no provision for bail once the convicted person has exhausted his remedies under the criminal appeals system. After a person has completed his sentence, he will remain in custody unless the Home Secretary otherwise directs.[10] The Home Office begins its consideration whether to make a deportation order before the end of the sentence[11] and

---

[10] Ibid. If released 'pending further consideration of his case' there appears to be no provision for imposing conditions as to residence and reporting to the police.

[11] See para. 11.40, ante.

advisers should ensure that representations are sent to the Home Office before the sentence is completed to avoid further unnecessary imprisonment.

Custodial Sentence: No Recommendation for Deportation

13.25 At the completion of his sentence the prisoner will be released unless the Home Secretary has (1) served on him a notice of intention to deport under the Act;[12] and (2) made a direction authorising his detention pending the making of the deportation order.[13] If the Home Secretary has served notice and agrees to release, he may impose conditions as to residence and reporting to the police.[14] Where detention has been authorised there is a right to apply for bail once notice of appeal against the decision to deport has been lodged.[15] The application is normally made to an adjudicator[16] and the procedure is as outlined earlier in this chapter.[17]

FOLLOWING A DECISION TO DEPORT

13.26 A person need not have committed a criminal offence before the Home Secretary may make a decision to deport under the Act. Indeed, in most cases where a decision is made the person will not be in any form of custody. However, once the decision has been made, the Home Secretary may authorise detention pending the making of the deportation order.[18] There are the same provisions for release subject to conditions[19] and the right to apply for bail after notice of appeal has been given.[20] The situation where the Home Secretary is most likely to

---

[12] Immigration Act 1971, s. 3(5)(a)–(c). See para. 11.6, ante. If, however, the prisoner was never granted leave to enter (this may arise in cases where there has been a conviction for possession or importation of drugs) he will remain in prison at the end of his sentence and directions will be given for his removal in the same manner as any other person refused leave to enter; see para. 5.40, ante.

[13] Ibid., Sch. 3 para. 2(2).

[14] Ibid., para. 2(5).

[15] Ibid., Sch. 3 para. 3; Sch. 2 para. 29(1).

[16] Ibid., Sch. 3 para. 3; Sch. 2 para. 29(3). The Tribunal may also grant bail where cases go to it at first instance ('conducive' and 'family deportations') and also where it has given leave to appeal in 'breach of conditions' cases (Sch. 2 para. 29(4)). In theory officers of the rank of at least chief immigration officer and police inspectors can grant bail (para. 29(2)) but this is hardly likely to occur if the Secretary of State has authorised detention.

[17] See para. 13.8, ante.

[18] Ibid., Sch. 3 para. 2(2). There are powers to arrest without warrant and take necessary steps to identify and ascertain nationality (para. 2(4)).

[19] Ibid., Sch. 3 para. 2(5).

[20] Ibid., Sch. 3 para. 3; Sch. 2 para. 29(1).

authorise detention is where a notice of appeal against the decision to deport has not been lodged. This usually arises where the person has not had actual notice of the decision until after the appeal period has expired because, as the rules permit, notice of the decision was sent to an old address, or not sent at all.[1] It is possible to apply for leave to appeal out of time, provided the deportation order has not been signed,[2] and in such cases, an application for bail may be made at the same time.

FOLLOWING THE MAKING OF A DEPORTATION ORDER

13.27 Once a deportation order has been signed the Home Secretary may authorise a person's detention pending removal or departure from the UK.[3] If he is already in detention by the authority of the Home Secretary, the detention order will continue unless the Home Secretary otherwise directs. If the Home Secretary agrees to a release it may be made subject to conditions as to residence and reporting to the police.[4]

There are other situations where the question of release may arise after a deportation order has been made. In the event of a person appealing against his removal on the ground that he objects to being sent to the destination specified by the Home Secretary, such an objection must be dealt with on the substantive appeal against refusal of entry or deportation. There is however one situation where there is no substantive right of appeal, viz. where the Home Secretary makes a deportation order following a recommendation by the court. Although an appeal against destination may be lodged in these circumstances and a right to bail arises[5] the Act states that 'if directions for the removal of the appellant from the UK are for the time being in force, or the power to give such directions is for the time being exercisable', the appellant shall not be released without the consent of the Home Secretary.[6] The appellate

---

[1] Immigration Appeals (Notices) Regulations 1972, SI 1972, No. 1683 regs. 2(4), 6; see para. 14.7, post.

[2] Immigration Appeals (Procedure) Rules 1972 SI 1972, No. 1684; notice of appeal must be given within 14 days of the decision (r. 4(7)); the Home Office may object to the appeals proceeding out of time (r. 8(3)(6)); the appellate authority may nevertheless allow the appeal to proceed (r. 11(4)). See generally para. 14.15 et seq., post.

[3] Ibid., Sch. 3 para. 2(3). A person may be arrested without warrant and steps may be taken to identify him and ascertain his nationality (para. 2(4)).

[4] Ibid., Sch. 3 para. 2(5).

[5] Ibid., s. 17(1)(b), Sch. 2 para. 29(1).

[6] Ibid., Sch. 2 para. 30(1).

authorities have held that they therefore have no power to grant bail[7] but the correctness of their decision must be doubtful.

SEAMEN AND AIRCREW

13.28 Those who are given permission to enter for the purpose of joining a ship or aircraft as a member of the crew or who have been admitted for a short period as seamen or members of aircrew may be detained and removed should they overstay.[8] They are in a similar position to illegal entrants. There is no right of appeal while they are in the UK[9] and therefore the question of bail does not arise. Temporary admission may, however, be granted.[10]

---

[7] See *Yusuf* 2863/73; *Gowreesunker* 4177/74 and *Jhureea* 1065/75 (unreported adjudicators' decisions).
[8] Ibid., Sch. 2 paras. 12–15; para. 16(2).
[9] The right to appeal from outside the UK is limited (s. 16(1)(b)).
[10] Ibid., Sch. 2 para. 21.

FOURTEEN

Appeals

WHAT DECISIONS CAN BE APPEALED AGAINST

14.1 There has been a statutory right of appeal since 1969 against certain decisions of immigration officers, entry clearance officers and the Home Secretary.[1] There is a right of appeal in most situations following:

(1) refusal of leave to enter at the port of entry;[2]
(2) refusal of entry clearance;[3]
(3) refusal of certificate of patriality;[4]
(4) conditions imposed on admission, variation of length of stay and refusal to vary;[5]
(5) a decision to make a deportation order;[6]
(6) refusal to revoke a deportation order.[7]

LIMITED RIGHT OF APPEAL

14.2 There is a right of appeal on limited grounds only against:

(1) removal to a particular destination;[8]
(2) removal of illegal entrants;[9]

---

[1] Immigration Appeals Act 1969, repeated and largely re-enacted by the Immigration Act 1971. A number of aspects of the appeals system are under review. See Home Office discussion document: Review of Appeals under the Immigration Act 1971.
[2] Immigration Act 1971, s. 13(1).
[3] Ibid., s. 13(2).
[4] Ibid.
[5] Ibid., s. 14.
[6] Ibid., s. 15(1)(a).
[7] Ibid., s. 15(1)(b).
[8] Ibid., s. 17.
[9] Ibid., s. 16(1)(a).

(3) removal of seamen and aircrew;[10]
(4) removal on the ground that the direction for removal is invalid.[11]

NO RIGHT OF APPEAL

14.3 There is no right of appeal in the following situations:

(1) a decision to deport on the ground that it is conducive to the public good as being in the interests of national security (although some form of representations can be made to an advisory panel);[12]
(2) a decision by the Home Secretary personally to exclude on the ground that it is conducive to the public good, or to refuse to revoke a deportation order on the ground that it is conducive to the public good as being in the interests of national security;[13]
(3) in certain cases, a decision to refuse a certificate of patriality;[14]
(4) the refusal or delay in the issuing of or the method of allocating a special voucher to a citizen of the UK and Colonies;[15]
(5) the refusal of the Department of Employment to issue a work permit or to approve training schemes or of the Home Office to refer applicants to the Department of Employment;[16]
(6) the making of a 'hostage order.'[17]

The Appellate Authorities

14.4 There is a two-tier system of appeal. Appeals are normally heard by an adjudicator at first instance, with leave to appeal in certain limited circumstances to the Tribunal.[18] Adjudicators are appointed by the Home Secretary, and members of the Immigration Appeal Tribunal by the Lord Chancellor.[19] At the time of writing there are 16 full time and 68 part-time adjudicators. The number to be appointed is decided by the Home Secretary. One of them is appointed chief adjudicator and he is required to allocate duties among the adjudicators. He does not,

[10] Ibid., s. 16(1)(b).
[11] Ibid., s. 16.
[12] Ibid., s. 15(3).
[13] Ibid., s. 15(4).
[14] Ibid., s. 13(3).
[15] See *R v Entry Clearance Officer Bombay, ex parte Amin* (1980) *The Times*, 1 May.
[16] *Pearson v Immigration Appeal Tribunal* [1978] Imm AR 212, CA.
[17] Ibid., s. 14(4). See s. 3(7) for the nature of such an order.
[18] Ibid., ss. 19–21.
[19] Ibid. Sch. 5.

however, have any powers to compel adjudicators to take a particular course of action. Adjudicators sit at most of the large cities and at the ports of entry.[20]

The number of Immigration Appeal Tribunal members is determined by the Lord Chancellor. He also appoints a president who must be a lawyer of seven years standing. At present there are two vice presidents who are similarly qualified. Other members of the Tribunal are not necessarily lawyers. They may sit in more than one division, there must be a minimum of three members sitting and the chairman must be a lawyer of at least seven years standing. The Tribunal is not known ever to have sat with more than three members. It may reach decisions by a majority vote. The Tribunal only sits in London.

STARTING AN APPEAL

14.5 All appeals are made at first instance to an adjudicator with the exceptions of appeals (1) against a decision to deport on conducive grounds; (2) a decision to deport as a member of a family or a refusal to revoke such a deportation order; and (3) where there is pending another appeal related to a family member deportation.[1]

Notification of Right of Appeal

14.6 The Immigration Act empowers the Home Secretary to make regulations providing for written notice to be given where a person has a right of appeal from a decision taken (or would have had such a right but for the ground on which it was taken).[2] This he has done by the Immigration Appeals (Notices) Regulations 1972.[3] We have already seen that when immigration officials reach a decision as to whether a person is to be given leave to enter or remain, written notice of the decision must be given.[4] It is not necessary for two sets of notices to be served if leave is refused:[5] it will be sufficient if the applicant receives a notice which complies with these Regulations; and similarly where a notice of refusal to revoke or vary conditions is served notification about the right of appeal will be contained in the same notice.

[20] I.e. Birmingham, Bristol, Dover, Gatwick, Glasgow, Harmondsworth, Leeds, Manchester and Southampton.
[1] Ibid., s. 15(7).
[2] Ibid., s. 18.
[3] SI 1972, No. 1683.
[4] See paras. 5.40–5.41, ante.
[5] Ibid., reg. 5(1).

Service

14.7 Notices will be served by an immigration officer or an entry clearance officer in the case of those seeking entry to the UK and by the Home Secretary in all other cases.[6] The notice is to be served on the person making the application or anyone who has made an application on his behalf.[7] It may be served personally or sent by post (registered or recorded delivery) to the applicant's last known or usual place of abode.[8] It is not necessary for any notice to be given if the whereabouts or place of abode of the applicant is unknown to the authorities.[9]

Contents

14.8 The notice must contain (1) a statement of the reasons for the decision; (2) information about the right of appeal (if any), how the appeal can be made and where the notice of appeal is to be sent, the time limit for appealing, and facilities for advice on appeal; (3) where the decision gives directions for removal, the country to which the person is to be removed.[10] The notice may be amended at the hearing if the amendment is necessary to arrive at the real question in issue.[11] The amendment must be 'in the nature of an amplification, correction or clarification'; but it must not alter the basis of the proceedings.[12]

LIMITATIONS ON RIGHT OF APPEAL

Appeals against Exclusion

Refusal at Ports of Entry

14.9 A person refused leave to enter at a port of entry is not allowed to

---

[6] Ibid., reg. 3(2). Written notice is to be given 'as soon as practicable' after the decision; ibid., para. 3(1).

[7] Ibid., reg. 3(3).   [8] Ibid., reg. 5(2).

[9] Ibid., reg. 3(4). This regulation is not *ultra vires* the Act: *R v Secretary of State for the Home Department, ex parte Mukhan Singh* (1976) 14 December 20, 21/76, CA (unreported); *R v Immigration Appeal Tribunal, ex parte Mehmet* [1977] 2 All ER 602; *R v Immigration Appeal Tribunal, ex parte Jaspal Singh* [1977] Imm AR 105.

[10] Ibid., reg. 4(1).

[11] *Cooray* [1974] Imm AR 38. The Tribunal held that refusal of leave was essentially a civil matter, and in civil matters the court would allow an amendment if no injustice was done to the other side: *Baker (GL) Ltd v Medway Building and Supplies Ltd* [1958] 2 All ER 532 applied.

[12] *Tambimuttu* [1979–80] Imm AR 91. See also *Rinta Dutta* 40028/79 (1455) (unreported). For a substantive amendment which would not be permitted see *R v Immigration Appeal Tribunal, ex parte Mehmet*, para. 11.7, ante.

appeal from within the UK unless he holds a current entry clearance or a current work permit in his name.[13] These limitations were contrary to the recommendations of the Report of the Committee on Immigration Appeals, which proposed a system of immediate appeals for those refused entry.[14] Those without such documentation must therefore serve their notice of appeal from overseas. It is unlikely that there will be sufficient time for advice to be taken before sending the notice for officially there is no right to seek legal advice before departure.[15] Although the passenger will be advised in the notice of refusal that he can consult the United Kingdom Immigrants Advisory Service (UKIAS), consultation will be by correspondence as the UKIAS is generally advised only of those refusals from which there is an immediate right of appeal. The most serious difficulty is that the passenger will not be permitted to enter the UK at a later date for the hearing of the appeal which may not take place for as long as 18 months. The passenger would be well advised to write out in detail everything which took place between the immigration authorities and himself from the moment of arrival. This should be signed with the date and time indicated and forwarded to his advisors with a view to the notes being used as evidence at the hearing. Where there is a right of appeal exercisable from within the UK, the hearing is likely to take place within a few days after giving notice of appeal.

No right of appeal lies if the Home Secretary certifies that he has personally given directions that entry is to be refused on the ground that it is conducive to the public good or if leave to enter was refused in obedience to such directions.[16]

In *Chandra*[17] the Tribunal finally resolved that a person who is in possession of an entry clearance has a right of appeal from within the UK against a refusal to admit him on the ground that he did not qualify under the immigration rules, notwithstanding that the entry clearance has become ineffective because it was obtained, for example, by the use of a false representation or the concealment of material facts.

Refusal of Entry Clearance

14.10 Similar problems of delays, obtaining advice and presentation of

[13] Immigration Act 1971, s. 13(3).

[14] Cmnd 3387 (Wilson Committee).

[15] A passenger should, however, be given the opportunity to telephone friends or relatives here, or his High Commissioner or Consul; HC 394, para. 78.

[16] Ibid., s. 13(5).

[17] 75343/81 (2043). The Tribunal reversed its earlier decisions in *Kent Tak Lok* 68500/80 (1911) (unreported) and *Ngen Chung Kwan* 70577/80 (1929) (unreported).

evidence arise where a person is refused entry clearance. An appeal against refusal of clearance must be dismissed if the adjudicator is satisfied that at the time of refusal a deportation order was in force.[18] There is no right of appeal where the Home Secretary personally directs that exclusion is conducive to the public good.[19]

Refusal of Certificate of Patriality

14.11 If an application is made overseas, there is a right of appeal under the immigration appeals system in all cases against refusal.[20] The Act does not give any power to immigration officers to refuse entry to those holding certificates of patriality but those who arrive in the UK without a certificate claiming to be patrial and therefore not to require leave to enter, have no right of appeal against a decision that leave to enter is required if they fall into one of the following categories: (1) UK citizens who claim patriality by settlement and five years' residence in the UK; (2 Commonwealth citizens whose only claim to patriality is through their mother having been born in the UK or Islands; and (3) women who are Commonwealth citizens claiming to be patrial by marriage to a person in categories (1) and (2) above.[1]

Appeals against Variation, Refusal to Vary and Conditions

14.12 The regulations provide that the Home Secretary is not required to serve a notice setting out the decision and the right of appeal where, on application to vary the limited leave to enter or remain in the UK, the decision was not less favourable than that which was requested.[2] The right of appeal against variation or conditions imposed nevertheless still remains. It may still be necessary to exercise the right if, e.g., there was a disagreement between the Home Office and the applicant as to whether the decision was more favourable than that requested.

There is no right of appeal against a variation which shortens the stay or against a refusal to extend the stay or alter the conditions if the Home Secretary personally decides that the applicant's departure is conducive to the public good, as being in the interests of national security or the relations between the UK and any other country, or for other reasons of a political nature.[3] Nor can an appeal be brought against any variation

[18] Ibid., s. 13(4).
[19] Ibid., s. 13(5).
[20] Ibid., s. 13(1).
[1] Ibid., s. 13(3).
[2] Immigration Appeals (Notices) Regulations 1972, reg. 4(2).
[3] Immigration Act 1971, s. 13(3).

made by statutory instrument or against any refusal by the Home Secretary to make a statutory instrument.[4] Finally, as has been discussed earlier there is no right of appeal where the application for variation is made after the previous leave has expired.[5] If on the refusal of an application the Home Office permits a person to remain for the purpose of making arrangements to leave the country, no right of appeal arises from that permission as he has not been given a further right to remain, but merely an 'indulgence' on the part of the Home Office.[6]

Appeals against Deportation

14.13 These are considered in Chapter 11.

TIME LIMIT FOR APPEALING

14.14 The period within which notice of appeal must be given differs according to the type of decision appealed against. The time limits set out below refer to the most common cases. For a full list see Appendix 4.

(1) Those refused entry at the port have 28 days after departure.[8] They cannot give notice of appeal until after they have left the UK unless they hold a current entry clearance or work permit. Those holding such documents who choose to appeal before departure have 28 days after departure of the ship or aircraft on which they would have otherwise been removed;[9]

(2) Those refused entry clearance have three months after the date of refusal;[10]

---

[4] Ibid., s. 14(4). Variation may be in respect of any class of person by order made by statutory instrument (ibid., s. 4(1)). The only statutory instrument made under this section is the Immigration (Variation of Leave) Order 1976, SI 1976, No. 1572.

[5] *Suthendran* and *Subramaniam*, see para. 9.9, ante.

[6] *R v Immigration Appeal Adjudicator, ex parte Bhanji* [1977] Imm AR 89, CA. See para. 9.16, ante. No doctrine of estoppel operates if the Home Office mistakenly explains that there is a right of appeal. *Balbir Singh v Secretary of State* [1978] Imm AR 204, CA.

[7] Paras. 14.14–14.36 apply to appeals both to the adjudicator and to the Tribunal at first instance: Immigration Act 1971, s. 19(4): Immigration Appeals (Procedure) Rules 1972, SI No. 1684 rr. 3(a).

[8] Immigration Appeals (Procedure) Rules 1972, SI 1972, No. 1684 r. 4(1)(a).

[9] Ibid., r. 4(1)(b).

[10] Ibid., r. 4(4).

(3) those in the UK wishing to appeal against a Home Office decision (e.g. refusal to vary leave, refusal to issue a certificate of patriality, the making of a deportation order) have 14 days after the date of the decision.[11]

We have already seen that the decision is given in writing. For the purpose of calculating the period in which notice of appeal must be given, the decision is deemed to have been taken, if sent by post, on the date on which it was sent by the immigration authorities, and if served personally, on the date on which it was served.[12]

Appealing Out of Time

14.15 Where an appellant is out of time in giving notice of appeal against a decision of the immigration authorities, there are two methods of applying for an extension. He may petition the adjudicator in writing for a further opportunity to appeal.[13] Alternatively he may simply proceed with the appeal, and when the immigration authorities allege that the time limit has expired, the adjudicator will consider the matter as a 'preliminary issue'.[14] In the latter case the adjudicator will usually require a written submission from the appellant and will decide whether or not to grant an extension without a hearing. The only difference between the two methods is that if the adjudicator rejects a petition there is no right of appeal to the Tribunal against the decision, whereas if the adjudicator rejects an application as a preliminary issue, there is a right of appeal subject to leave being granted. There is therefore no advantage whatsoever in petitioning the adjudicator: applicants should always proceed with the hearing and let the matter be dealt with as a preliminary issue. The same principles apply where the appeal is to the Tribunal at the first instance.

In *R v Immigration Appeal Tribunal, ex parte Bahadur Singh*[15] the Divisional Court confirmed that there was no right of appeal if the applicant went by way of petition, but nevertheless ordered the Tribunal to hear the appeal, holding that where there were two methods of approach the authorities should not be able to choose that which was less favourable to the appellant unless there were special reasons for doing so.

[11] Ibid., r. 4(5)–(7).
[12] Ibid., r. 4(11).
[13] Ibid., r. 5.
[14] Ibid., r. 8(3)(b), unless there is a deportation order in force, ibid., r. 11(4).
[15] Noted at [1976] Imm AR 143.

One reason will be where the appellant insists on a particular course of action. In *R v Secretary of State for the Home Department, ex parte Rai*[16] the appellant's solicitors wrote on his instructions, 'It is not our intention that our client's request for the appeal should proceed under Rule 8(3)'(b)' i.e. by way of preliminary issue. The Divisional Court held that the appellant must stand by his decision.

In practice if an applicant or his representative purports to proceed by way of petition, he will be informed by the appellate authorities of the alternative method and its advantage, and asked to make a decision as to how he wishes to proceed.

Considerations in the Granting of Leave to Appeal out of Time

14.16 The procedure rules provide that appellate authorities may allow the appeal to proceed 'if the authority is of the opinion that, by reason of special circumstances, it is just and right so to do'.[17] There is only one exception: leave to appeal out of time cannot be given if a deportation order against the appellant has been signed.[18]

14.17 What therefore amounts to special circumstances? Two important factors are the merits of the case and the reasons for the delay. The Court of Appeal in *R v Immigration Appeal Tribunal, ex parte R P Mehta*[19] and *R v Immigration Appeal Tribunal, ex parte V M Mehta*[20] has set out the approach which should be adopted. The adjudicator must look at all the material before him in order to decide whether there are special circumstances which would make it right and just to allow the appeal. The material might include material which could be said to relate to the substantive merits, i.e. 'a provisional assessment of the chances of success of the appeal, if the appeal were allowed to proceed despite the lateness of the notice'. The material should be 'looked at' with a view to seeing whether it includes evidence of a factor which, in the opinion of the adjudicator, would weigh in the balance in deciding (after taking into account all the relevant factors) whether the required 'special circumstances' exist. The adjudicator must look at the material in order to make the assessment but the weight, if any, to be given to that factor, is a matter for his discretion.

In *R P Mehta* Lord Denning MR suggested that the appellate

[16] [1976] Imm AR 140.
[17] Immigration Appeals (Procedure) Rules 1972, r. 11(4).
[18] Ibid., *Morgan* 46014/5/79 (1586) (unreported).
[19] [1975] 2 All ER 1084, CA.
[20] [1976] Imm. AR 174, CA.

authorities 'might well follow' the practice of the Court of Appeal in deciding what weight should be given to the substantive merits of the case in making an assessment. He stated,

'We often like to know the outline of the case. If it appears to be a case which is strong on the merits and which ought to be heard, in fairness to the parties, we may think it proper that the case should be allowed to proceed, and we extend the time accordingly. If it appears to be a flimsy case and weak on the merits, we may not extend the time.'[1]

The Court of Appeal rejected the argument that an error by the appellant's solicitors could not amount to special circumstances. Lord Denning MR, in dealing with that argument, stated:

'In applying Rule 11, I should have thought that the appellate authority might well adopt the practice which we adopt in the Court of Appeal here. We are often asked to extend the time for giving notice of appeal. We never let a party suffer because his solicitors make a mistake and are a day or two late in giving notice of appeal. We always treat it as a ground for extending time see *Gatti* v *Shoosmith* [1939] 3 All ER 916. All the more so in a case like the present where Miss Mehta would have no remedy against her solicitor for any negligence. If she were out of time for appeal, she will be removed from this country and it would be of little consolation to her to say that she has a remedy against her solicitor.'[2]

The period of delay in *R P Mehta* was seven days, but leave to appeal out of time has been granted when the delay has been for a longer period.

The Notice of Appeal

14.18 When a person is notified of an adverse decision by the immigration authorities, he will receive at the same time a form to be completed if he wishes to appeal.[3] This is the notice of appeal. Where the applicant is already in the UK he will receive an additional form asking for information about the number of witnesses likely to be called, whether an in-

---

[1] At 1088. These principles were applied in *R* v *Immigration Appeal Tribunal, ex parte Mehmet* [1977] 2 All ER 602.
[2] Ibid.
[3] See generally Immigration Appeals (Procedure) Rules 1972, r. 6. A person who has been refused entry who has a right of appeal from within the UK may give oral notice to the immigration officer, ibid., r. 6(1).

terpreter is required and, if so, in what language, and the name and address of his representatives.

Completing the Forms

14.19 The notice of appeal is a simple form to complete.[4] The only difficulty may arise in setting out the grounds of appeal. Although the applicant will have been informed in general terms of the reasons for the decision, he will not have received a detailed explanation. This will be only given after he has given notice of appeal. There may therefore be occasions when it is better to wait until this statement is received before giving the grounds, and simply to state on the form 'grounds to follow'. Some adjudicators may comment adversely if no grounds of appeal are lodged before the hearing, while others are less concerned about receiving detailed grounds.

In the many cases where the decision involves an exercise of discretion it may be easier to state 'the discretion should have been exercised differently', and in other cases the words 'the decision is not in accordance with the law and immigration rules applicable to the case' will suffice.[5]

The grounds may be varied or amplified at any time during the course of the appeal.[6] In *Francis*,[7] the Tribunal held that the grounds could be varied slightly provided they did not amount to a material alteration which should form the basis of a new application.[8] There is generally no obligation to provide any additional information in support of the appellant's case at this stage. The only exception is that on an appeal against removal on objection to destination, the appellant is required to submit with the notice of appeal a written statement of the matters which support his objection.[9] The applicant is also required to specify on the notice of appeal whether a hearing is required, as there is provision for the appellate authorities to decide cases based on written submissions. Normally a hearing will be required. The form makes no reference to the place where the appeal is to be heard. Where an appellant has a preference he should state this in a covering letter and ask that the appeal

---

[4] The form is set out in the Immigration Appeals (Procedure) Rules 1972, Sch., Form 1.

[5] See the wording of Immigration Act, 1971, s. 19(1)(a).

[6] Immigration Appeals (Procedure) Rules 1972, r. 6(3).

[7] [1972] Imm AR 162.

[8] See *Muthulakshmi* [1972] Imm AR 231, where an application to enter as a student of dentistry was refused because of the appellant's deficiency in English. An amendment of the grounds of appeal to change to an English course was a material alteration.

[9] Immigration Appeals (Procedure) Rules 1972, r. 9.

should take place at a particular centre. He should give reasons, e.g. ease of travelling for himself, witnesses, or his representative. The form is to be signed by the appellant or any person he authorises to act on his behalf, or in the case of a child or someone who is incapable of acting, it may be signed by any person acting on their behalf.[10] It is sensible to complete the form which accompanies the notice of appeal, but often it may not be possible immediately to provide all the information requested. The form should be completed as far as possible and an indication given that further information will follow.

Serving the Notice of Appeal

14.20 Service is on the immigration authorities and it is they who inform the adjudicator or Tribunal that an appeal has been lodged.[11] When an applicant receives the decision of the authorities and notification of the right of appeal he will also be informed where to forward the notice of appeal. Normally service is on either the officer who made the decision, viz. the immigration officer or entry clearance officer; or the Home Secretary. Whoever is served with the notice will become the party to the appeal although the Home Secretary has the power to designate another officer or himself where it is impracticable or impossible for an immigration or entry clearance officer to act.[12] There is also provision for the Representative of the United Nations High Commissioner for Refugees to become a party in refugee cases if he so desires.[13]

REASONS FOR THE DECISION: EXPLANATORY STATEMENT OF IMMIGRATION AUTHORITIES

14.21 The immigration authorities are required to provide the appellant with a written statement of the facts relating to the decision and also the reasons for the decision. This is referred to as an 'explanatory statement' and is to be prepared 'as soon as practicable' and given to both the appellate authorities and the appellant.[14]

The effect of a procedure which requires notice of appeal to be given to the 'opposition' rather than an independent authority is that the order

[10] Ibid., r. 6(4).
[11] Ibid., r. 6(5)–6(7).
[12] Ibid., rr. 6(2), 7.
[13] Ibid., r. 7(3).
[14] Ibid., r. 8(1).

in which appeals are heard is determined by the Home Office and not by those responsible for the administration of the appeals system. Under the procedure rules the latter are merely a post-box and are not in a position to take any steps until the immigration authorities notify them. An immigration officer is not required to produce an 'explanatory statement' if he takes the view that to do so is impracticable because there is insufficient time before the hearing. If this situation arises he must inform both the appeallate authorities and the appellant of this and confirm that an oral statement will be given at the hearing.[15] In practice, this is rare and a written statement will usually be prepared in advance of the hearing.

The 'explanatory statement' will often have documents annexed in support. Experience has shown that the documents are often incomplete and may not give a true picture of the appellant's immigration history or his relationship with the authorities e.g., an application for citizenship or correspondence between a Home Office minister and an MP following representations may be omitted. Moreover, interviews with the immigration authorities may be referred to in the 'statement' but the notes of these interviews will rarely be annexed.[16] The 'explanatory statement' usually represents the whole of the immigration authorities' case, as it is most unusual for the statement to be supported at the hearing by calling witnesses.

FIXING A DATE FOR THE APPEAL

14.22 The usual practice where the appellant is appealing from within the UK is for the appellate authorities to inform him of the date of the hearing at the same time as the explanatory statement is sent to him. In overseas appeals, a date is not fixed when the explanatory statement is sent out. The appellant or his representative is told that the appeal will not be listed for hearing until notification is received that he is ready to proceed but that if no request is received within a fixed period, usually six months, it will be assumed that the appellant is content for the appeal to be determined on the basis of the documents alone without a hearing.

---

[15] Ibid., r. 8(2).
[16] As to the means of obtaining additional information see para. 14.52, post.

OBJECTIONS BY THE IMMIGRATION AUTHORITIES TO HEARING: DECIDING PRELIMINARY ISSUES

14.23 The procedure rules set out three circumstances in which the immigration authorities may object to a hearing taking place, where they allege (1) the appellant has no right of appeal because the Immigration Act prohibits him from doing so; or (2) the appellant has no right of appeal because the passport, travel document, certificate of patriality, entry clearance or work permit is forged in some way; or (3) the notice of appeal was given outside the permitted time limit.[17] If any of these allegations are made, the adjudicator or Tribunal may, and at the request of the immigration authorities, must decide as a preliminary issue whether the claim is valid.[18] The immigration authorities must provide a statement setting out the basis for their allegation but are entitled to restrict the statement to that issue alone.[19] If the allegation is rejected by the adjudicator, they are then required to produce an 'explanatory statement' on the substantive issue.[20] In the meantime the hearing will be adjourned.

Prohibited from Appealing by the Act

14.24 The immigration authorities are required to specify the section of the Act which prohibits a right of appeal and to prove the allegation.[1]

Prohibited from Appealing because of Forged Documents

14.25 The Act does not specifically prohibit a person from appealing because of forged documents, and the provisions in the procedure rules for a preliminary hearing are therefore somewhat confusing. The one reference in the Act to forgery[2] specifies that if there is an allegation of forgery of any of the documents already mentioned and that disclosure of the appellant of matters relating to the method of detection would be contrary to the public interests, then the appellant and his representatives will be excluded from the hearing while the appellate authority examines the issue of disclosure. If the decision is that disclosure will be

---

[17] Ibid., r. 8(3).
[18] Ibid., r. 11(1).
[19] Ibid., r. 8(3).
[20] Ibid., r. 11(2).
[1] Ibid., r. 8(3)(a)(i).
[2] Immigration Act 1971, s. 22(4).

'directly or indirectly' contrary to the public interest, the appellant and his representatives can be kept out for further periods while the evidence is presented to the adjudicator.

Notice of Appeal out of Time

14.26 This has been discussed earlier at para. 14.15.

Appealing against Determination of Preliminary Issue

14.27 As will be seen there is a general right of appeal from any determination of an adjudicator to the Tribunal, subject to the obtaining of leave in certain circumstances.[3]

Allegation that the Appellant is an Illegal Entrant

14.28 This may be raised prior to or at any time during the appeal by the Home Office or at the appeal by the adjudicator. If the appellant is found to be an illegal entrant the appeal will not proceed and the appellant will face administrative removal.[4]

DETERMINATION OF APPEAL WITHOUT HEARING

14.29 An adjudicator may determine an appeal without a hearing in any of the following circumstances:[5]

(1) No party to the appeal has requested a hearing.
(2) Having received written representations from or on behalf of the appellant and given the immigration authorities an opportunity to reply, he decides to allow the appeal.
(3) He is satisfied that the appellant is outside the UK, or it is impracticable to give him notice of the hearing and no person is authorised to represent him at a hearing.
(4) He is satisfied that the only issue on appeal is an objection by the appellant to removal to a particular destination or to a claim that he

---

[3] See para. 12.7, ante.

[4] See paras. 12.1, 13.3, ante. *Shazad* 32163/78 (1626) (unreported); *Tareen* 55850/79 (1745) (unreported). If during the course of an appeal against deportation under the Immigration Act 1971, s. 3(5)(a) (breach of conditions of leave) it emerges that the applicant is an illegal entrant, the appeal should be allowed. The Home Secretary has no power to deport on this ground as the appellant never had leave: *Sikayenah* 20263/77 (1738) (unreported). The appellant is of course liable to administrative removal. See para. 12.1, ante.   [5] Immigration Appeals (Procedure) Rules 1972, r. 12.

ought to be removed (if at all) elsewhere, and that the appeal does not warrant a hearing.

(5) A preliminary issue has been raised by the immigration authorities and the appellant has been given an opportunity to submit a written statement rebutting the matters raised, and the appellant has not submitted a statement, or has done so, but the adjudicator is of the opinion that the matters put forward do not justify a hearing.

An adjudicator must hear an appeal if none of these circumstances apply,[6] whatever the apparent merits.[7]

POWERS AND DUTIES OF ADJUDICATORS

Determination of Appeals

14.30 An adjudicator must allow an appeal if he considers (1) that the decision or action against which the appeal is brought is not in accordance with the law or the immigration rules applicable to the case;[8] or (2) where the decision or action involved the exercise of the Home Secretary's discretion, that the discretion should have been exercised differently.[9] The adjudicator must dismiss an appeal in all other cases.[10] If the adjudicator allows an appeal, he is required to give such directions as are necessary to give effect to his decision. He may also make recommendations with respect to any other action he considers should be taken under the Act. The directions (but not the recommendations) must be complied with by the immigration authorities, subject to any right of appeal which they may choose to pursue.[11]

14.31 In *Thabet*,[12] the Tribunal disapproved of adjudicators who specify time limits when giving directions on allowing appeals against refusal of entry clearance. It took the view that it was for the immigration authorities to decide what time limit should be imposed. In this par-

---

[6] *Bahmanpour* 45131/79 (1753) (unreported) but note the procedure for second identical appeals, para. 14.58, post.

[7] *Lawyer* 49561/79 (1755) (unreported).

[8] Immigration Act 1971, s. 19(1)(a)(i).

[9] Ibid., s. 19(1)(a)(ii).

[10] Ibid., s. 19(1)(b). He has no power to defer a decision once he is satisfied that it was made in accordance with the law and immigration rules. He cannot therefore require a deportation order not to be implemented until a particular date; *Ojikutu* 8110/76 (1029) (unreported).

[11] Ibid., ss. 19(3), 20(2).   [12] [1977] Imm AR 75.

ticular case it further disapproved of the adjudicator's setting out a series of stringent conditions which the appellant was required to comply with on arrival, holding that there was no power to impose conditions as to residence or to stop the appellant applying for a change of status.

An adjudicator is entitled to take into account all relevant immigration regulations in deciding an appeal, and he is not limited to those relied upon by the immigration authorities. If, however, an adjudicator is intending to base his determination on an immigration rule which has not been so relied upon, he should indicate his intention to the appellant or his representative, to afford them an opportunity of addressing him upon the matter and in some cases this may involve granting an adjournment.[13]

Reviewing the Evidence

14.32 The adjudicator may review any determination of a question of fact on which the decision or action is based. But a serious restraint is placed by the Act on an adjudicator in that where a decision or action is in accordance with the immigration rules, he must dismiss the appeal if the only ground of appeal is that the immigration authorities should have made a decision or taken action outside the rules.[14] Thus an appeal must fail if the adjudicator is asked to accept a man as an au pair or a foreign national as a working holiday maker. He therefore cannot depart from the rules because he believes that it is in the interest of natural justice.[15]

The adjudicator is required to make a complete review of all the material before him in order to decide a question of fact. He has to take into account all matters pertaining to the decision appealed against[16] and not merely those set out in the grounds of refusal.[17] He should apply his mind afresh to the problem presented by the facts, and determine what is the correct exercise of discretion: it is wrong for the adjudicator to approach a case on the basis that he will not upset a decision unless it could be shown that an officer had taken into account some matter which

[13] *Oberoi* [1979–80] Imm AR 175.

[14] Immigration Act 1971, s. 19(2).

[15] See *Glean* [1972] Imm AR 84 decided under earlier legislation identical in this respect.

[16] See generally *Purushothaman* [1972] Imm AR 176 and *Abdullah* [1973] Imm AR 57. Also note *R v Immigration Appeal Tribunal, ex parte S G H Khan* [1975] Imm AR 26 where the Divisional Court held that the adjudicator had the power to make a complete review of the material in order to decide a question of fact. As to the issue of 'fresh' evidence: see paras. 14.33, 14.34, post.

[17] *Cooray* [1974] Imm AR 38.

he ought to have excluded or he had failed to take into account something which ought to have been included.[18]

The Nature of the Evidence

14.33 The Immigration Appeals (Procedure) Rules 1972 provide that

'an appellate authority may receive oral, documentary or other evidence of any fact which appears to the authority to be relevant to the appeal, notwithstanding that such evidence would be inadmissible in a court of law'.[19]

Thus hearsay evidence is admissible although the weight attached to it may be less than that given to direct evidence. In *Altaf*[20] the Tribunal allowed evidence obtained from villages which arose from a trip made by the entry clearance officer to the sponsor's village.

In *R v Immigration Appeal Tribunal, ex parte Abdul Rashid*[1] the Divisional Court indicated that this rule should be regarded as authorising the reception by an adjudicator of any relevant and admissible evidence which is put before him for his consideration at the time he determines the matter. In *Hassan Mohammed*,[2] the Tribunal confirmed its approach in earlier cases in holding that fresh evidence tendered on appeal should always be received by adjudicators, provided (1) it related to facts already in existence when the immigration authorities made the decision appealed against; and (2) it was relevant. In the case of documentary evidence, it did not matter that the document was not in existence at the time of the immigration authorities' making a decision provided it related to facts which were in existence at that time.

Facts Already in Existence at the Date of the Decision

14.34 In *Abdullah*[3] the Tribunal held that evidence of facts subsequent

---

[18] *R v Peterkin (Adjudicator), ex parte Soni* [1972] Imm AR 253. Similarly if the notice of refusal or explanatory statement omit matters, thereby indicating that consideration had not been given by the immigration authorities to relevant matters, an adjudicator should use his power under s. 19(2) to consider these matters: *Moussa* [1976] Imm AR 78.

[19] Immigration (Appeals) Procedure Rules, r. 29(1).

[20] [1979–80] Imm AR 141. Following *Mohammed Ejaz v Secretary of State for the Home Department* (1978) 21 December, CA (unreported) cited at [1979–80] Imm AR 141 where it was held in *habeas corpus* proceedings that the Home Secretary was entitled to take into account information supplied by 'informers', provided he acted fairly.

[1] [1978] Imm AR 71.   [2] [1978] Imm AR 168.   [3] [1973] Imm AR 57.

to the date of the decision appealed against which, if they had been before the officer, might have influenced his decision by indicating some change in the applicant's original circumstances should normally form the basis of a fresh application. In that case the entry clearance officer refused the application of the appellant father on the ground that he was not dependent on his son. The adjudicator allowed the appeal making a finding that since the refusal of his application the appellant had become 'mainly dependent' on his son and thereby qualified for entry under the then rules. The Tribunal allowed the appeal by the entry clearance officer on the ground *inter alia* that the finding was based on fresh evidence.[4]

The circumstances in which the Tribunal is prepared to depart from the general principle are not clear. There appears to be no hard and fast rule and a pragmatic approach seems to have been adopted. Nevertheless the Tribunal has tended to allow new evidence, where, because of the delay which would result, it would be unduly onerous to require a fresh application to be made[5] or where external factors beyond the control of the applicant have occurred,[6] e.g. subsequent political events. In *Huda*,[7] where the adjudicator dismissed an appeal mainly because he erroneously believed the appellant had come from a poor family, evidence of the appellant's employment record subsequent to the decision was admitted as it was regarded as not 'self-serving' i.e. designed to bolster his claim to enter as a visitor.

Relevant Evidence

14.35 An adjudicator must consider all evidence which relates to the issues before him. He may decline to receive evidence the relevance of which is limited to whether he should give consideration to a recommendation to the Home Secretary that a favourable decision should be made outside the immigration rules.[8] He is not required to consider incidental facts and law which cannot affect the correctness of the decision, e.g. determination of the appellant's nationality.[9]

---

[4] Examples of cases where the Tribunal has followed this approach are *Ashraf* [1979–80] Imm AR 45, *Yosef* [1979–80] Imm AR 72, *Mauraj Begum* 23765/78 (1502) (unreported), *Shahid Ali* 30807/78 (1553) (unreported), *Heng* 27726/78 (1575) (unreported) and *Leong* 55181/79 (1846) (unreported).

[5] See *Thaker* [1976] Imm AR 116. [6] *Thakerar* [1974] Imm AR 60.

[7] [1976] Imm AR 109. [8] *Wadia* [1977] Imm AR 92.

[9] *Fazil* 7523/76 (1027) (unreported). The Tribunal has jurisdiction to determine issues of nationality where they are relevant; *Deva* 62141/80 (1975) (unreported), reversing *Mohamedy* 29097/78 (1435) (unreported).

Precedent

14.36 Adjudicators are not bound to follow the decisions of the other adjudicators and sometimes do not. They are bound by Tribunal decisions where the facts are indistinguishable.[10] The Tribunal generally follows its previous decisions although there are a number of conflicting decisions, due in part to the Tribunal not having had drawn to its attention earlier cases. In *Bhambra*[11] it was said that, '... the Tribunal, although it takes due note of matters of principle laid down by it in previous decisions, considers the testimony of particular facts in each case'.

APPEALS TO THE TRIBUNAL FROM AN ADJUDICATOR

The Right to an Appeal

14.37 The Act allows appeal from an adjudicator to the Tribunal by any party 'dissatisfied with (the) determination'.[12] Thus an appeal may be brought not only by the appellant but also by the immigration authorities. In almost all cases leave to appeal is required.[13] Leave may be obtained either from the adjudicator or from the Tribunal.

14.38 There is a right of appeal without leave arising from (1) a decision that the appellant required leave to enter where he had at the time of the decision a certificate of patriality;[14] (2) a refusal to give leave where the entrant had, at the time of the decision, an entry clearance;[15] (3) a decision imposing a limited leave to remain on members of diplomatic missions and military personnel previously exempt;[16] (4) a determination of a preliminary issue under the Immigration (Appeals)

---

[10] *Sylvester* [1972] Imm AR 104.
[11] [1973] Imm AR 14.
[12] Immigration Act 1971, s. 20(1).
[13] See generally Immigration Appeals (Procedure) Rules 1972, r. 14. The rules are not *ultra vires* the Act: *R v Immigration Appeal Tribunal, ex parte Jeyaveerasingham* [1976] Imm AR 137 DC.
[14] Ibid., s. 22(5)(a).
[15] Provided he was not an illegal entrant or subject to a deportation order, ibid., s. 22(5)(b).
[16] Immigration Appeals (Procedure) Rules 1972, r. 14(1)(a), (c); Immigration Act 1971, ss. 14(2), 8(2)–(4).

Procedure Rules, r. 11, dismissing the application other than one made under s. 14 of the Act.[17]

14.39 Leave is required in all other situations but must be granted:

(1) if the appellate authority is satisfied that the determination of the appeal turns on an arguable point of law;[18]
(2) where the appellant is in the UK, if the adjudicator has dismissed the appeal but the appellate authority is satisfied that he is to be removed to a country which he is unwilling to go to for reasons qualifying him for political asylum.[19]

14.40 There is no right of appeal against the decision of an adjudicator on any incidental or interlocutory decision arising during the course of the hearing. In *R v Immigration Appeal Tribunal, ex parte Lila*[20] the Divisional Court held that the Tribunal was right in not interfering with an adjudicator's decision to refuse to admit certain evidence. The Tribunal had declined to entertain the application on the ground that it had no jurisdiction to review a decision by an adjudicator which did not amount to a 'determination' under s. 20(1) of the Act. The Tribunal thus have power only to review a decision which either allowed or dismissed the original appeal.

Powers of the Tribunal

14.41 The Tribunal may affirm the determination of the adjudicator or make any other determination which the adjudicator could have made.[1] If they agree with the adjudicator who allowed an appeal, they may alter or add to his directions and recommendations or replace them with their own directions.[2] If they disagree with the adjudicator who dismissed an appeal, they have the same powers to make directions and recommendations as an adjudicator.[3] While the appeal period remains, or if an

---

[17] Immigration Appeals (Procedure) Rules 1972, r. 14(1)(b). These are appeals against variations of conditions and the imposition of conditions on those previously exempt from control.

[18] Ibid., r. 14(2)(a). See also *Harmail Singh v Immigration Appeal Tribunal* [1978] Imm AR 140 where the Court of Appeal upheld the Tribunal which had decided on the particular facts that there was no arguable point of law. Interpretation of the immigration rules is considered a point of law.

[19] Ibid., r. 14(2)(b).

[20] [1978] Imm AR 50.

[1] Immigration Act 1971, s. 20(1).

[2] Ibid., s. 20(2).

[3] Ibid., s. 20(3).

appeal is brought during that time, the adjudicator's directions need not be complied with. The Tribunal will not upset a decision of the adjudicator where it disagrees with the reasons of the adjudicator if the decision was in accordance with the law and rules applicable.[4] The approach adopted by the Tribunal was further explained in *Khanma Jan*,[5] when it was said,

'The Tribunal will not lightly overturn adjudicators' findings of fact, particularly where the adjudicators have the advantage of observing witnesses which the Tribunal has not. . . . We apply the test of whether a reasonable adjudicator properly directing himself and applying his mind to the evidence before him, could have come to the conclusion reached by the adjudicator in this case.'

This approach must now be modified in the light of the recent decision of the Court of Appeal in *R* v *Immigration Appeal Tribunal, ex parte Alam Bi*.[6] The Court held that the Tribunal when hearing appeals from an adjudicator is not limited to considering points, but can hear appeals on the facts, and if after reviewing an adjudicator's decisions on the facts it comes to the conclusion that they are wrong, it has the power and the duty to review and reverse those decisions and the determination based on them. There was no doubt that the Tribunal would be sparing in reversing an adjudicator's decisions on the credibility of witnesses whom he had seen and heard. The Tribunal would act only if there were compelling reasons and the cases in which it can do so must be rare.

Procedure on Appeal

Notices

14.42 Notice of appeal must be given even where leave is not required. Where leave is required, application for leave should be made to an adjudicator 'forthwith' after the determination. The Tribunal has accepted that this word does not have to be read literally but the application should be made speedily.[7] Sometimes a short delay in making an application will arise because time will be needed to consider the

---

[4] *Sampson* [1974] Imm AR 27.
[5] 11541/77 (1183) (unreported).
[6] [1979–80] Imm AR 146, CA.
[7] In *Kaur* 7810/76 (968) (unreported), it was held that an application made within 24 hours complies with the rule but that a longer period may be justified.

adjudicator's decision. An application can be pursued before the Tribunal if rejected by an adjudicator. Alternatively, the applicant may by-pass the adjudicator and apply direct to the Tribunal. An application can be made to the adjudicator orally after the hearing but the rules provide for applications to be heard by both the adjudicator and the Tribunal without a hearing unless the appellate authority 'considers that special circumstances render a hearing desirable'.[8] An application for leave to the Tribunal[9] or a notice of appeal must be made not later than 14 days after the determination if the applicant appeals from inside the UK;[10] otherwise 42 days are available.[11] The determination takes place either when given to the appellant or his representative at the hearing; when delivered to the appellant if there has been a hearing and the determination has been reserved; and in any other case when sent to him by post.[12]

There is no provision in the rules for extending the time limits for making applications to the Tribunal for leave to appeal from the determination of the adjudicator.[13] There is a simple form to complete where application for leave to appeal is made or notice of appeal is given.[14] In cases where an application is made to an adjudicator immediately following the hearing, the appeal forms are to be completed after leave is granted and notice of appeal served on the adjudicator. The forms are to be sent to the clerk, to the adjudicator or to the Tribunal as appropriate.

Grounds of Appeal

14.43 The form requires 'grounds of appeal' to be set out. Where an application for leave is to be made, and these grounds have not been

---

[8] Immigration Appeals (Procedure) Rules, 1972, r. 16(4). It is incumbent on the appellant to request an oral hearing and set out in his grounds of appeal the 'special circumstances' which must be circumstances relevant to some ground on which the appeal was sought to be based: *Mehta (B K D) v Immigration Appeal Tribunal* [1979–80] Imm AR 16.

[9] The application can be dealt with by the President or the Chairman acting alone. Ibid., r. 42.

[10] Ibid., r. 15(1).

[11] Ibid., r. 15(2).

[12] Ibid., rr. 15(4), 39(2). Time runs from the day on which the appellant or his representative first learnt or could have learnt of the decision: *R v Immigration Appeal Tribunal, ex parte Suleman* [1976] Imm AR 147. See also *Shams* 59327/80 (1977) (unreported) where the Home Office was held to be out of time.

[13] See *R v Immigration Appeal Tribunal, ex parte Armstrong* [1977] Imm AR 80 DC.

[14] Immigration Appeals (Procedure) Rules 1972, r. 16(1), (2). The form is set out in the Schedule, Form 2.

properly formulated by the expiry date for the application, it may be desirable to state that 'grounds will follow'. The grounds should be sent as soon as possible thereafter. The grounds may be amplified or varied during the course of the appeal or application.[15]

Parties

14.44 The rules concerning parties to the appeal are similar to those where the adjudicator acts at first instance.[16]

Evidence

14.45 The Tribunal will have received before the hearing a copy of the record of proceedings[17] kept by the adjudicator and copies will be supplied to the parties.[18] The clerk to the Tribunal will normally supply as a numbered bundle the complete set of documents before the adjudicator together with the record of proceedings and his determination.

New evidence may be submitted to the Tribunal provided notice is given indicating its nature but the Tribunal has a discretion as to whether to receive the evidence.[19] The Tribunal may of its own motion call for further evidence.[20] If the Tribunal decides to receive the evidence, they may take it orally or in writing or may remit the appeal to an adjudicator solely for the purpose of taking the evidence.[1]

Remittal to an Adjudicator

14.46 An appeal may be remitted by the Tribunal to the original or another adjudicator if it thinks it appropriate.[2]

Determination without a Hearing

14.47 The Tribunal may dispose of the appeal without a hearing if (1) no party has requested a hearing; or (2) the Tribunal is satisfied the appellant is outside the UK or that it is impracticable to give him notice and no person is authorised to represent him at the hearing.[3]

---

[15] Ibid., r. 16(3).
[16] Ibid., r. 17. See para. 14.20, note 12, ante.
[17] Ibid., r. 18(1). A record in the form of a summary of the proceedings is to be kept (ibid., r. 40), but failure to do so will not invalidate the proceedings: *Sidique* [1976] Imm AR 69. Adjudicators usually make their own notes.
[18] Ibid., r. 19.
[19] Ibid., rr. 18(2), (3)(a).
[20] Ibid., r. 18(3)(b).
[1] Ibid., r. 18(3)(c).   [2] Ibid., r. 21.   [3] Ibid., r. 20.

REFERENCES BY THE HOME SECRETARY

14.48 The Act provides that the Home Secretary may refer either to an adjudicator or Tribunal for their consideration 'any matter relating to the case' which was not before the appellate authority.[4] A reference can be made where (1) a case was dismissed at first instance by an adjudicator or the Tribunal; or (2) on appeal to the Tribunal, the decision went against the immigrant. The Divisional Court held in *R v Immigration Appeal Tribunal, ex parte Nathwani*[5] that this power to refer was entirely a matter within the Home Secretary's discretion and was not subject to judicial review.

GENERAL RULES OF PROCEDURE: ADJUDICATOR AND TRIBUNAL

Notification of Hearing

14.49 The appellate authority will give notification of the time and place of any hearing.[6] These are provisions in the case of port appeals for notification to be given to an immigration officer who is then required to inform any other party,[7] but this practice is rarely adopted. If representatives find a particular date unsatisfactory (e.g. because of difficulty with witnesses) the clerk to the adjudicator or Tribunal should be informed immediately. On some occasions it may be advisable to telephone in advance of putting the problem in writing.

Representation

14.50 The appellant may be represented by the following as of right: (1) solicitor or counsel; (2) a consular officer or a person performing a corresponding function; (3) a representative of the United Kingdom Immigrants Advisory Service. Any other person appearing to the appellate authority to be acting on behalf of the appellant may appear with its permission.[8]

---

[4] Immigration Act, 1971, s. 21. The appellate authority is to consider the matter in whatever manner it thinks appropriate: Immigration Appeals (Procedure) Rules 1972, r. 41. There do not appear to have been any references under this section: 983 H. of C. Official Report, 22 April 1980, Written Answers, col. 96.

[5] [1979–80] Imm AR 9.   [6] Ibid., r. 24(1).

[7] Ibid., r. 24(2).   [8] Ibid., r. 26(1)(a).

The issue of unqualified practitioners appearing before the appellate authorities was considered by the Chief Adjudicator in *Neharun Nessa Khatun*[9] where he held that he could not give a representative blanket leave to appear in future cases: leave to appear was a matter of discretion for each individual adjudicator. The Chief Adjudicator stated that when deciding whether to exercise discretion in favour of an unqualified representative, an adjudicator had to bear certain factors in mind. He noted that 'the corpus of immigration law had become much more complex' in recent years and that there had been a growth in unqualified practitioners for profit who were, in many cases, more danger than help to appellants: adjudicators had to consider whether or not assistance could be rendered by such representatives.

The Home Secretary, immigration or entry clearance officer may be represented by counsel, solicitor or any officer of the Home Office.[10] In practice, representation at port appeals is generally by an immigration officer and at other appeals by a Home Office official known as a presenting officer. In cases involving refugees, the UK Representative of the United Nations High Commissioner for Refugees may be represented by any person appointed by him for that purpose.[11]

A representative may take any action open to an appellant under the Procedure Rules.[12]

Burden of Proof

14.51 The burden of proof lies with the appellant only where he asserts a fact which by virtue of the Act or rules it would be for him to satisfy the immigration authorities is true. In such circumstances, the burden is on the appellant to prove the assertion.[13] The standard is on a balance of probabilities: in *R v Secretary of State for the Home Department, ex parte S B Hussain*[14] Widgery LCJ approved the Tribunal's approach and remarked:

'I can see no possible reason for requiring a higher standard of proof . . . it would be quite unreasonable to assume that (the immigration rules)

---

[9] 54541/79 (unreported).
[10] Ibid., r. 26(1)(c).
[11] Ibid., r. 21(1)(c).
[12] Ibid., r. 26(2).
[13] Ibid., r. 31(2). See also r. 31(1) where there is a similar burden if the appellant maintains that he is not a person to whom the provisions apply.
[14] (1972) 226/72 19 September (unreported). Referred to in *Diljar Begum* 682/73 (461) (unreported).

contemplate proof beyond dispute, or even proof beyond reasonable doubt'.[15]

In all other cases the burden of proof (with the same standard) is on the immigration authorities, e.g. where facts are asserted in support of a refusal of an extension of stay on the grounds of character, conduct or association, or in support of exclusion or deportation on the grounds that it is conducive to the public good.

Pre-Trial Procedures

14.52 The appellate authority may at any time require a party to provide further particulars if they are necessary to decide the appeal.[16] An opportunity to inspect and to be supplied with copies of any documentary evidence relevant to the appeal must be given to the parties[17] unless (1) the document is one which has been used to obtain entry and is a forgery; and (2) disclosure is contrary to the public interest in that it would reveal matters relating to detection methods.[18]

More use should be made of these procedures as the immigration authorities frequently do not supply full information in the explanatory statement or at the hearing.[19] It should be borne in mind that the representative of the immigration authorities at the hearing may have received additional points of detail from those who conducted the interview or prepared the explanatory statement. He may also have the advantage of possessing unpublished instructions to immigration officers, entry clearance officers and other interviewers, and internal documents, for example, memoranda, telexes and immigration officers' reports. There may be grounds for seeking further particulars or inspecting or requiring the production of additional documents if it can be shown that they are relevant to the appeal; for example, it is only rarely that notes of interviews with the appellant or others are attached to explanatory statements, although the immigration authorities' case may rest largely on what was said at the interviews and the appellant may be cross-examined about them. Where it becomes clear before the hearing that further information is required, it may be advisable initially to make the request to the immigration authorities in writing and if the response is unsatisfactory, then to make application to the appellate authorities.

[15] See also the decision in *Lai* [1974] Imm AR 98; *Patel (AD)* [1975] Imm AR 95; *Channo Bi* [1978] Imm AR 182 and *Kalsoom Begum* [1978] Imm AR 206.
[16] Immigration Appeals (Procedure) Rules 1972, r. 25.
[17] Ibid., r. 30(1).   [18] Ibid., r. 30(2).   [19] See para. 14.21, ante.

Summoning of Witnesses

14.53 An appellate authority has the power to summon witnesses to attend the hearing to answer questions or produce documents in their custody or control relating to the matter under appeal.[20] Conduct money covering the return fare from his home to the hearing must be tendered if the witness is being asked to travel more than 10 miles from his home. It is submitted that any adjudicator (and not necessarily the adjudicator hearing the case) may issue a summons. Similarly the President or Chairman of the Tribunal acting alone may do so.[1] Although serving a witness summons may sometimes be useful, the appellate authority has no jurisdiction to compel the attendance of the witness. Failure to comply with the summons without reasonable excuse is an offence carrying a maximum fine of £100,[2] but this will be of little help to the appellant if the witness fails to appear. There is no power to compel anyone to give evidence or to produce any document if such compulsion would not be possible in a civil action.[3] Witnesses may be required to give evidence on oath or affirmation.[4] Some adjudicators require this but the Tribunal rarely does.

The Conduct of the Hearing

14.54 The rules provide that each party to an appeal shall have an opportunity to give evidence, call witnesses, cross-examine and address the authority, including an opportunity to address on the evidence on its completion.[5] Subject to this, the rules leave it open to the authority to conduct proceedings in such a manner as it considers appropriate.

Procedure at the Hearing

At Adjudicators' Hearings

14.55
(1) The immigration authorities will first be given an opportunity to expand on the explanatory statement. They rarely do. If matters are

---

[20] Ibid., r. 27(1).
[1] Ibid., r. 42.   [2] Immigration Act 1971, s. 22(6).
[3] Ibid., r. 29(2).   [4] Ibid., r. 29(3).
[5] Ibid., r. 28. In *Mannah* 3546/76 (1141) (unreported) although the adjudicator had failed to comply with rules in not allowing the appellant's representative to address him at the close of the evidence, the Tribunal refused to remit the case to an adjudicator under r. 21, because *inter alia* the Tribunal was prepared to hear the appellant's evidence afresh.

not clear, the presenting officer should be persuaded to explain any ambiguity before the appellant commences his case. Consideration should be given to asking for additional documentary evidence and for the supplying of further information by the immigration authorities.

(2) The appellant then has an opportunity to address the adjudicator by outlining his case. The adjudicator will usually have read the papers and it is therefore not necessary to take him through all the documents. It is, however, useful to give some indication as to how the appellant's case is to be put and to give some indication of the nature of the evidence to be presented.

(3) The appellant is called first. Other witnesses will normally be required to wait outside the hearing room until they are called to give evidence.

(4) The representative of the immigration authorities will cross-examine the appellant and his witnesses. The adjudicator can and usually does put questions.

(5) It is rare for the immigration authorities to call any witnesses and its representative will usually seek to attack the appellant's case by challenging the credibility of witnesses and by highlighting inconsistencies between the evidence given at the hearing and the statements previously made to immigration officials.

(6) It will not generally be possible to secure the attendance of the immigration official who dealt with the case initially. In *Padmore*,[6] the Tribunal held that when an immigration officer was the respondent, it was desirable whenever practicable that he should be present at the appeal but it was not obligatory under the rules. In practice this never occurs and the Tribunal has made no attempt to implement their decision in later cases.

(7) At the close of the evidence, the respondent will address the adjudicator, followed by the appellant. Some adjudicators follow the practice, where no witnesses are called, of requiring the appellant to make the address first, followed by the respondent, with the opportunity for the appellant to address the adjudicator further.

(8) The practice is for 'approved' interpreters only to be used. The authority will provide the interpreter on request. This procedure according to the Tribunal has 'a great deal to commend it'. But where

[6] [1972] Imm AR 1. See also *Kassam* [1976] Imm AR 20 where the Tribunal took the view that there were circumstances when the immigration authorities should be prepared to produce evidence in rebuttal by affidavit at least.

some unusual or rare language or dialect is encountered the appellate authority will use any available person to translate.[7]

At Tribunal Hearings

14.56 At first instance the same procedure is adopted as in hearings before the adjudicator. On appeal, the appellant opens his case followed by the respondent and the appellant has a further opportunity to address the Tribunal.

Public Hearings

14.57 All hearings are public with the following exceptions.[8]

(1) The appellant and his representatives together with the public must be excluded from cases involving forgery of documents where the appellate authority is asked to arrange a private hearing.[9]
(2) The public or any member of the public may be excluded, (a) at the request of one of the parties; (b) if there is an interference with the conduct of the proceedings; (c) if evidence is given relating to a person not a party to the proceedings which should not be given in public and no party has asked for a public hearing.[10]

Second 'Identical Appeals'

14.58 Second or further appeals before an adjudicator or Tribunal involving the same appellant which do not materially differ from the original appeal may be dismissed without a hearing provided that the parties have been given an opportunity to make representations against the operation of this procedure. It is difficult to indicate clearly how this rule operates, but some help may be obtained from comparing *Ahmed*[11] (child of sponsor refused entry: only new evidence on second appeal new affidavits from sources rejected as fraudulent on first appeal) with *Taj Bibi*[12] (wife of sponsor refused entry: new evidence – birth of child which sponsor claimed as his). The adjudicator may invoke this rule at any stage up to and including the beginning of the hearing.[13]

[7] *Rafique* 12374/77 (1206) (unreported).
[8] Immigration Appeals (Procedure) Rules 1972, r. 32(1). Members of the Council on Tribunals or its Scottish Committee cannot be excluded in any circumstances: r. 32(4).
[9] Ibid., r. 32(2).
[10] Ibid., r. 32(3).
[11] [1977] Imm AR 25.
[12] [1977] Imm AR 25.
[13] *Ramzan* [1978] Imm AR 111. As to the procedure see also *Rahman* 17209/77 (1203) (unreported).

Withdrawal of Appeals

14.59 An appeal may be withdrawn by a party probably at any time before the appellate authority makes its decision.[14] Once the appeal is withdrawn there is no method of re-instating it.[15]

Hearing Appeals in the Absence of the Parties

14.60 The appellate authority may hear an appeal in the appellant's absence if they think it is proper to do so where it is satisfied that he is (1) not in the UK; or (2) suffering from a communicable disease or from mental disorder; or (3) unable to attend because of accident or illness.[16] The authority may also proceed if satisfied that the appellant has been given notice of the hearing unless he provides a reasonable explanation for his absence.[17] In these circumstances the case may be decided on the evidence available to the appellate authority.[18]

General Powers

14.61 The rules provide for (1) transferring proceedings from one adjudicator to another;[19] (2) combining two or more hearings by agreement of the parties where the issues are similar or the appellants are part of the same family;[20] (3) postponing and adjourning appeals and related matters subject to which the appallate authorities may regulate their own procedure;[1] (4) remedying minor irregularities to prevent the proceedings being rendered void.[2]

The Decision

14.62 The authority shall either at the conclusion of the hearing or at a later date make a decision and give reasons for it. A document setting this out must be produced and a copy sent to all the parties to the appeal.[3] If the determination is given orally at the conclusion of the hearing, reasons for the decision must be stated.[4]

---

[14] *Saleh* [1975] Imm AR 154.
[15] *Ancharaz* [1976] Imm AR 49.
[16] Immigration Appeals (Procedure) Rules 1972, r. 34(1).
[17] Ibid., r. 34(2), (3).
[18] Ibid., r. 34(4).
[19] Ibid., r. 33.
[20] Ibid., r. 36.
[1] Ibid., r. 37.
[2] Ibid., r. 38. See *Akhtar Jan* [1977] Imm AR 107.
[3] Immigration Appeals (Procedure) Rules 1972, r. 39.
[4] Ibid., r. 39(1).

Time Limits

14.63 The rules provide that where time for doing any act under the rules expires on a Sunday or public holiday and for that reason it cannot be done on that day, the act will be in time if done on the next working day.[5] If acts are to be done 'not later' than a specified period after any event, the period is to be calculated from the expiry of the day on which the event occurred.[6]

Service of Notices and Documents

14.64 The rules set out on whom and where notice and documents should be served.[7] Any party may, by giving notice to the appellate authority, change his address for service. It should be noted that documents to be forwarded to the appellant may be sent to 'his last known or usual place of abode' if he has not given notice of any other address; and that it is good service if a document is sent to a person who is representing a party to an appeal.

APPLICATIONS FOR JUDICIAL REVIEW

14.65 The High Court has power to review decision of adjudicators and the Tribunal by means of judicial review.[8] The substantive law concerning prerogative writs is not discussed here but can be found in the standard texts.[9] The following information may, however, be of some help to practitioners.[10]

(1) An applicant may apply for any of the prerogative orders, either jointly or in the alternative without having to select any particular one.

(2) Applications for leave to apply for judicial review must be made as soon as possible after the date of the decision but in any event within three months. The court can extend the time limit, but will only do so where it is satisfied there are very good reasons.

(3) Leave of the court is required before an application may be made.

---

[5] Ibid., r. 43(1).   [6] Ibid., r. 43(2).   [7] Ibid., r. 44.

[8] See generally RSC Ord. 53; *Halsburys Laws* (4th Edn.) *Crown Proceedings and Practice*, Vol. 11, paras. 521 et seq.

[9] *Halsburys Laws* (4th Edn.), *Administrative Law*, Vol. 1; de Smith *Judicial Review of Administrative Action* (4th Edn), Chapter 12. See also de Smith *Constitutional and Administrative Law* (3rd Edn.), Chapters 26 and 27.

[10] RSC Ord. 53 has recently been amended by SI 1980, No. 2000 to which reference should be made in order to ascertain the complete procedure on an application for judicial review. The amendments came into operation on 12 January 1981.

Applications will be considered in one of two ways: (a) unless the applicant otherwise requests in his notice of application, the papers in the case will be placed before a judge who will decide whether to grant leave without hearing any oral submissions. The purpose of this procedure is said to be to ensure that applications may be dealt with speedily and without unnecessary expense. If leave is refused, an applicant may renew the application to a single judge sitting in open court; (b) if at the outset an applicant requests an oral hearing, the application will go directly to a judge either in chambers or in open court.

(4) If leave is refused by a single judge, the application cannot be renewed to the Divisional Court but application may be made to the Court of Appeal.

(5) Applications for leave must be made on a form (form 86A) obtainable from the Crown Office at the Royal Courts of Justice and be supported by an affidavit verifying the facts. At an oral hearing an applicant may appear in person or be represented by counsel.

(6) Where leave is granted the applicant or his solicitor must, within 14 days from the grant of leave, serve notice of motion on all persons directly affected and enter a copy in the Crown Office together with an affidavit of service.

(7) A party upon whom a notice of motion is served may, if he wishes, file an affidavit in reply, but must inform the Crown Office of his intention of doing so as soon as practicable and must file it as soon as practicable and in any event within 21 days after service, having given notice thereof to the applicant. He may be represented at the hearing and all parties who file affidavits will be informed of the date fixed for hearing.

(8) When an application is ready to be heard it will be entered in the warned list and the applicant or his solicitor informed. Cases will be heard by a single judge sitting in open court unless the court otherwise directs.

(9) It is a general rule that the party which loses is ordered to pay the costs of the other side.

(10) There may be some delay in a hearing taking place but the Divisional Court is speeding up its backlog. There are provisions for expedited hearings where justified.[11]

(11) There is a right of appeal from a decision of the Divisional Court without leave to the Court of Appeal;[12] and from the Court of Appeal to the House of Lords, subject to the granting of leave.[13]

---

[11] See Practice Direction [1974] 3 All ER 528 for the procedure.
[12] RSC Ord. 53(1)14/36.   [13] RSC Ord. 59(1)18.

(12) An application to the Divisional Court cannot be made from a decision of an adjudicator where there is an alternative form of appeal available. The correct procedure is to apply to the Tribunal.[14]

(13) Care should be taken in making applications to the Divisional Court. A large number of unmeritorious cases appear to be brought and there is the danger that decisions will be handed down which will have far-reaching implications in other cases.

THE EUROPEAN COURT OF JUSTICE[15]

14.66 The EEC Treaty provides for national courts and tribunals to refer to the European Court of Justice questions of community law which arise during proceedings.[16] Issues involving exclusion and deportation are the most likely to give rise to a reference. The European Court will give the national court a 'preliminary ruling'. A court is not required to refer all issues involving community law to the European Court but it may ask for a ruling where it considers that a decision on the interpretation of the Treaty is necessary to enable it to give judgement.[17] If the national court is one of last instance, it must refer the case in these circumstances to the European Court, otherwise the reference is discretionary.[18] An immigration appeals adjudicator or the Immigration Appeal Tribunal constitutes a court tribunal for the purpose of a reference. There are no provisions in the Treaty for an individual to appeal to the European Court of Justice from a decision of a national court or tribunal.

14.67 Legal aid may be granted by the European Court but proceedings before the European Court following a reference are proceedings for which domestic legal aid is available.[19]

---

[14] *R v Peterkin (Adjudicator), ex parte Soni* [1972] Imm AR 253.
[15] For a useful explanation as to the jurisdiction and procedure of the European Court of Justice, see L. N. Brown and F. E. Jacobs (Sweet & Maxwell 1977), *Court of Justice of the European Communities*.
[16] EEC Treaty, art. 177.
[17] Ibid. An example of a reference on an immigration matter is *Van Duyn v The Home Office* [1974] 3 All ER 178.
[18] EEC Treaty, art. 177.
[19] *R v Bouchereau* [1978] 2 WLR 251.

THE EUROPEAN COMMISSION OF HUMAN RIGHTS AND THE EUROPEAN COURT OF HUMAN RIGHTS

14.68 The UK is a signatory to and has ratified the European Convention for the Protection of Human Rights and Fundamental Freedoms.[20] The Convention sets out a number of basic human rights. It also provides for the legal protection of those rights by enabling an individual, whatever his nationality, to petition the European Commission of Human Rights complaining of a breach of the Convention by a government provided that government has recognised the right to petition. The UK has recognised this right. There are in addition to the Convention four protocols: the UK has not ratified the fourth protocol which deals in part with citizenship and immigration.

The rights under the Convention which are most likely to be relevant to immigration law and practice are freedom from degrading treatment (Article 3); the right to liberty and security of person (Article 5); the right to a fair and public hearing within a reasonable time by an independent and impartial tribunal established by law (Article 6); the right to respect for private and family life (Article 8); the right to marry and found a family (Article 12); the right to the enjoyment of the rights and freedoms in the Convention without discrimination on ground of sex, race or colour (Article 14).[1]

Complaints are dealt with first by the European Commission of Human Rights, and may later be sent either to the Court of Human Rights or the Committee of Ministers of the Council of Europe. The Commission and Court each consist of one person from each country who is a member of the council. The Committee of Ministers is a political body, consisting of government representatives from each country.

The procedure for making a complaint is outside the scope of this book and is well documented elsewhere.[2] Practitioners should, however, bear in mind that the jurisprudence of the Commission has severely limited the extent of many of the rights granted under the Convention, that the procedure for handling of complaints is cumbersome and that there can

---

[20] For the main text of the Convention, see Cmd. 8969.

[1] For an examination of UK immigration cases under the Convention, see C. Palmer, *Rights without Remedies: the European Convention of Human Rights and UK Immigration Law* 1981 (Runnymede Trust).

[2] See for example F. G. Jacobs *The European Convention on Human Rights* (1975) (OUP).

be delays of several years before a final decision is reached. Where there is a complaint involving the deportation or removal of an individual, there is no obligation on the government to postpone his departure pending the outcome of the petition to the Commission,[3] although the government may be persuaded to allow the individual to remain. Legal aid from the Commission is available if it considers the case has merit.

[3] *R v Secretary of State for the Home Department, ex parte Fernandez* (1980) *The Times* 21 November, CA.

FIFTEEN

Refugee Status and Political Asylum

REFUGEE STATUS IN INTERNATIONAL LAW

15.1 A refugee is a person who,

'owing to a well-founded fear of being persecuted for reasons of race, religion, nationality, membership of a particular social group or political opinion, is outside the country of his nationality and is unable or, owing to such fear, is unwilling to avail himself of the protection of that country; or who not having a nationality and being outside the country of his former habitual residence as a result of such events, is unable or, owing to such fear, is unwilling to return to it.'

This definition is to be found in the 1951 Convention Relating to the Status of Refugees[1] which together with the 1967 Protocol to the Convention[2] is the main international instrument relating to refugees. The Convention sets out the minimum obligations which signatory

---

[1] Cmd 9171.
[2] Cmd 3906. At the time of the 1951 Convention (which came into force on 22 April 1954) the refugee problem was seen as confined to those who had become refugees because of the Second World War. The definition of a refugee and the rights of refugees were therefore confined to: '(i) events occurring in Europe before 1 January 1951; or (ii) events occurring in Europe or elsewhere before 1 January 1951 . . .' However, the next 10 to 15 years saw changes which led to many 'new' refugees appearing, who did not fall within this definition because of the cut-off date (e.g. Hungary in 1956 and Czechoslovakia in 1968). As a result of these changes a Protocol was added to the Convention in 1967 which widened the Convention to include any person who fell within the definition at any time.

states are to accord refugees in their country of asylum. The main right of a person recognised as a refugee and granted asylum is the protection against return to the country in which he fears persecution. This is known as 'non-refoulement'. Other rights set out in the Convention cover areas which facilitate the settlement of a refugee in the country of asylum, including the right to travel documentation, employment, housing, education, public relief and freedom of movement and religion.

REFUGEE STATUS AND POLITICAL ASYLUM

15.2 Any person who is deemed to be entitled to refugee status, by the authorities of the country in which he is seeking asylum or the United Nations High Commissioner for Refugees, cannot be returned to the country in which he fears persecution.

It is the right of the individual to be recognised as a refugee but it remains the decision of the host country to grant asylum. Refugee status and asylum are therefore two separate issues. It is, however, unusual for a government to refuse asylum to a recognised refugee who has arrived directly from a country where he fears persecution, but it can occur, e.g. where there is serious concern that the refugee's presence would be a danger to public security. In these circumstances the refugee would not be returned to his country of origin but efforts would be made to find an alternative country of asylum through the United Nations High Commissioner for Refugees.

THE STATUS OF REFUGEES UNDER UNITED KINGDOM LAW

15.3 The UK is a party to both the 1951 Convention and the 1967 Protocol. The UK therefore has international obligations to act in accordance with these instruments. However, the UK, unlike many other countries, has not incorporated the provisions of the Convention and the Protocol into its domestic law.[3]

There is no reference to refugees or asylum in the Immigration Act but there are a number of short statements in the immigration rules, viz.:

---
[3] The provisions of the Convention and Protocol have been incorporated into the domestic law of most countries in Western Europe, North America and the Mediterranean.

(a) where a person is a refugee full account is to be taken of the Convention and Protocol. Nothing in any section of the rules is to be construed as requiring action contrary to the United Kingdom's obligations under these instruments;[4]
(b) leave to enter will not be refused if removal would be contrary to the provisions of the Convention and Protocol;[5]
(c) a person may apply for asylum in the United Kingdom on the ground that, if he were required to leave, he would have to go to a country to which he is unwilling to go owing to a well-founded fear of being persecuted for reasons of race, religion, nationality, membership of a particular social group or political opinion;[6]
(d) a deportation order will not be made against a person if the only country to which he can be removed is one to which he is unwilling to go for the reasons set out in the previous paragraph. This provision is said to be 'in accordance with the provisions of the Convention and Protocol.'[7]

The rules do not, however, provide for a procedure for establishing refugee status. Moreover, those who meet the requirements of the Convention may not necessarily be granted asylum. The Convention defines a refugee as a person who cannot return to his country of nationality or, in the case of a stateless person, to his country of former habitual residence. Under the rules, however, a grant of asylum is to be made where the only country to which the applicant can be removed[8] is one which he is unwilling to go for fear of persecution. Thus in *Two Citizens of Chile*,[9] the Tribunal upheld a Home Office refusal to grant extensions of stay on the ground that the appellants had failed to show that they would have to return to Chile: Rumania had accepted them for asylum initially but there was no evidence that they could return there. The Tribunal held that the fact that they had no legal right of entry to any country other than Chile did not mean that they would have to return there. The same approach was adopted in *K*,[10] where it was accepted that

[4] HC 394 paras. 16, 87, 138.   [5] Ibid., and para. 64.
[6] Ibid., para, 120.   [7] Ibid., para. 150.
[8] Ibid., paras. 64, 150; para. 120 is worded slightly differently but the effect is the same.
[9] [1977] Imm AR 36.
[10] 34539/78 (1732) (unreported). Both these decisions were under the old rules which were less clear on the granting of asylum, but there is no reason to believe that the Tribunal would come to a different decision if the same situation arose under the present rules.

the appellant could not return to South Africa (her country of nationality) or Swaziland (the country which first recognised her as a refugee), for fear of persecution there. There was, however, evidence that she had visited other African countries subsequent to her arriving in the UK and applying for asylum there, and as a result the Tribunal held that she would be able to enter those countries if she desired.[11]

15.4 There is no statement in the rules or elsewhere as to the procedure which is adopted in the consideration of refugee cases, other than that in the case of a potential refugee at a port of entry, an immigration officer must refer the matter to the Home Office for decision.[12] The rules are also silent as to the circumstances in which extensions of stay may be given and settlement obtained. The result is that all these matters are a question of Home Office practice which may be altered at any time without the changes becoming public knowledge. The current Home Office practice, as far as it is known, is set out in this chapter.

DETERMINING WHO IS A REFUGEE

15.5 It is often not an easy task to establish whether a person seeking asylum falls within the definition of a refugee. The following guidelines may be of some assistance.

(1) The key phrase in the Convention definition of a refugee is 'well-founded fear of persecution'. This involves both a subjective and objective test: the element of fear must be a state of mind and therefore a subjective condition; that the fear must be well-founded involves consideration of objective criteria.
(2) A person may well have a fear without it being well-founded. In other cases a fear may be exaggerated but nevertheless be 'well-founded'.
(3) Persecution is not defined in the Convention but there is an inference that a threat to life or freedom on account of race, religion, nationality, political opinion or membership of a particular social group is always persecution.[13] There may be many reasons for a

---

[11] It should be noted that the *Two Citizens* were subsequently given permission to remain. In *K* an application to the Divisional Court for judicial review was withdrawn following a Home Office decision to grant her indefinite leave to remain.
[12] HC 394, para. 64.
[13] 1951 Convention, art. 33.

person not wishing to return to his country of origin. Discrimination against the individual in itself may not be sufficient to amount to persecution, nor normally is escape from prosecution or punishmeent for offences against the general criminal law of a country.[14] Those who seek asylum on the ground that they do not wish to undertake military service or that they will not be able to earn a living may have compelling reasons for not wishing to return to their country, but these reasons may not in themselves constitute a well-founded fear of persecution.[15]

(4) Although persecution is normally associated with activities of agencies of the government of a country, actions committed by groups which the government are not prepared to or are unable to control may justify a claim of persecution.[16]

(5) The fact that a person holds a passport from his country of origin is not conclusive evidence that those who issued the passport do not intend to persecute the holder. In some cases it may be evidence that he is not at risk; in others it may have arisen because he has not told the issuing authorities of his political opinions, or because the authorities themselves issued his passport for the sole purpose of securing his departure.[17]

(6) The Convention limits refugees to those who are outside their country of nationality or, in the case of stateless persons, those who are outside their place of habitual residence. It therefore follows that the question of asylum cannot arise where a person is within the territorial jurisdiction of his own country.[18] Nationality is often a complex issue, and although the issuing of a passport is not conclusive evidence that the holder is a citizen of the issuing country, it is bound to be highly persuasive.

(7) The requirement that a person must be outside his country to be a refugee does not necessarily mean that he must have left that country for fear of persecution. Events subsequent to his departure may justify his claiming refugee status even where he has lived overseas

---

[14] Some countries impose heavy penalties for remaining overseas without permission but this will not itself make a person a refugee; see, e.g. *Kus* 31628/78 (1470) (unreported).

[15] The requirement to undertake military service may in some cases be evidence of persecution, but other evidence of persecution would have to be produced if the applicant were to succeed in claiming he was a refugee.

[16] An example of a situation where this may occur can be found in *Hussein* 898/74 (unreported adjudicator's decision).

[17] As to use of passport after asylum granted see para. 15.23, post.

[18] See '*X*' (*A Chilean Citizen*) [1978] Imm AR 73.

for some time. A person who was not a refugee when he left his country, but who becomes one at a later date is known as a *refugee sur place*.

(8) Those interviewing potential refugees will have to take into account these considerations and make an assessment based on the following factors: (a) the individual, including his personal and family background, his personal experiences, his membership of a particular racial, religious, national, social or political group and his own interpretation of his situation; (b) the situation in his own country; (c) a determination based on information gained from (a) and (b) as to whether the person's life or freedom would be in danger if he returned to his country of origin, or whether he may face other forms of persecution.

APPLICATIONS FOR POLITICAL ASYLUM

At the Port of Entry

15.6 Refugees rarely make applications for asylum at the port of entry unless it appears that there is no other way of gaining entry. There is a simple explanation for this: a person who is fleeing from the authorities of his own country is often unlikely to have much confidence in the authorities of another, and his first aim will be to ensure that he is securely inside the country to which he has fled. The main fear of those who arrive at the port is that they might be returned immediately to their own country. Entry may be therefore sought as visitors or students by those who are refugees.

Although the rules do not provide specifically for entry as a refugee, the rules specify under the heading 'asylum' that 'special considerations arise where the only country to which a person can be removed is one to which he is unwilling to go owing to a well-founded fear of being persecuted for reasons of race, religion, nationality, membership of a particular social group or political opinion'.[19] Leave to enter is not to be refused if removal would be contrary to the provisions of the Convention and Protocol.[20] Any case in which it appears to the immigration officer as a result of a claim or information given by the person seeking entry at a port that he might fall within the terms of the asylum rule is to be referred to the Home Office for decision regardless of any circumstances which might otherwise justify refusal of entry.[1]

[19] HC 394, para. 64.   [20] Ibid.
[1] Ibid.

15.7 A person applying for asylum at the port of entry will normally be informed that he may seek assistance from the UK Representative of the United Nations High Commissioner for Refugees (UNHCR) or from the United Kingdom Immigrants Advisory Service Refugee Unit.[2] However, this information will not be given until the Home Office has completed its enquiries; that is, in effect, in the event of a decision which is unfavourable to the applicant. Assistance from the UNHCR or UKIAS may be given even where there is no right of appeal against refusal of entry from within the United Kingdom. In some cases representations have resulted in the applicant being admitted and granted asylum.

After Entry

15.8 It often happens that refugees will remain in the UK by any means, sometimes illegally, without claiming asylum until such time as they feel that they have no alternative to making a claim. An applicant therefore may be in the UK in a temporary or permanent capacity or have overstayed or entered illegally.

The immigration rules provide that a person may apply for asylum on the ground that if he were required to leave, he would have to go to a country to which he is unwilling to go owing to a well-founded fear of being persecuted for the reasons of race, religion, nationality, membership of a particular social group or political opinion. The rules state that 'any such claim is to be carefully considered in the light of all the relevant circumstances'.[3] An application should be made in writing to the Home Office explaining the history of the person seeking asylum and setting out precisely why the applicant fears persecution in his country of origin. Wherever possible the application should be supported by documentary evidence. Although there is frequently no information available to support the applicant's claim other than his own evidence, he should give a satisfactory explanation for the lack of evidence. National and international organisations may be able to give some support. Amnesty International has in the past provided documentary evidence of the situation in the country of origin. The British Section of Amnesty International has a refugee co-ordinator and approaches should first be made to that section. There may also be academics specialising in the history or politics of the applicant's country of origin who may be able to provide additional background material or indicate where information might be obtained. Newspaper cuttings in-

[2] See para. 15.25, post.   [3] HC 394, para. 120.

dicating the political situation in the applicant's country should be supplied if they can support the application. The London office of the UNHCR may be able to provide advice. If, however, their assistance is sought in support of the application, the result of their enquiries, whether favourable to the applicant or not, will be made available to the Home Office, if so requested by the Home Office. It is often therefore preferable only to make a formal approach to the UNHCR where the Home Office has refused the application and there is a right of appeal against that decision or, where there is no such right, further representations are to be made to the Home Office.

15.9 It is advisable for representatives to make written representations to the Home Office even in cases where the Home Office is already aware a person is seeking asylum, and may have already interviewed the applicant. There may be additional information which the representative can supply to the Home Office, but even if there is not, an application ensures that the Home Office is aware that the applicant is represented and often makes the applicant more confident in the knowledge that he is not dealing alone with the Home Office.

15.10 The Home Office, which has a special section handling applications for asylum, will usually arrange for the applicant to be interviewed some two or three months after the application has been made. If the applicant is in the south-east of England he will be asked to attend the Home Office's immigration headquarters at Lunar House, Croydon; if he lives elsewhere a local police officer will interview him at the request of the Home Office unless the applicant specifies that he wishes to attend at Croydon. The quality of police interviewing has often proved to be poor and whenever possible an applicant should be encouraged to specify Croydon as the place of interview. It is always desirable for a representative to attend at the interview and to take a full note of the questions and answers. Although the representative will not be permitted to participate, he can ask the interviewer to put to the applicant questions on specific issues if he feels the interviewer has omitted or not fully covered particular areas of importance. The Home Office will provide an interpreter, if required. Advance notice of the need for an interpreter should be given. The applicant will not usually be permitted to have his own interpreter present at the interview. The Home Office will make its own enquiries in order to assess the claim and will rely heavily on information supplied by the Foreign and Commonwealth Office and by the Embassy or High Commission in the applicant's country of origin.

15.11 An applicant for asylum is in the same position as any other person applying for leave to remain. He is not accorded any special treatment under the rules while the application is under consideration. An applicant may have to wait for many months from the date of application before a decision is reached.

In the event of an unfavourable decision from the Home Office, the notice of refusal will simply state that the applicant has failed to show that he qualifies for asylum. He will not receive a detailed explanation as to why he has been refused. It is not therefore known at this stage whether the Home Office disagrees with the facts as presented or whether the Home Office officials have come to a different conclusion from the applicant and his representative on facts which are not disputed. If the applicant has a right of appeal[4] which is exercised, he may discover more detailed reasons when the Home Office delivers its explanatory statement for the appeal, but the statements often lack detail. The existence of a pending appeal should not prevent further representations to the Home Office, where appropriate. Often the advantage of knowing the information contained in the Home Office statement before making further representations is off-set by the delay which results between the lodging of the notice of appeal and the receipt of the statement. Where there is no right of appeal, the making of further representations is the only course of action which remains open.

15.12 Further representations should always be made in the following circumstances: (1) where further information has come to light; (2) where the situation in the applicant's country has changed since the date on which information was last supplied to the Home Office by the applicant: in some cases the situation may have deteriorated and it may be possible to provide documentary evidence in support; (3) where the case appears to be meritorious, and would thus justify representations being made by an MP to the Home Office Minister.

The benefits arising from the application being successful are discussed later in this chapter.[5]

APPEALS

15.13 There appears to be no right of appeal under the Immigration Act against a refusal to confer refugee status when leave to enter or

[4] See para. 15.13, post, and Appendix 4.   [5] See para. 15.15 et seq, post.

[6] The right of appeal arises from decisions to vary a refusal to vary conditions of stay. Immigration Act 1971, s. 14(1). 'Conditions' appear to be limited to time, employment, or registration with the police: ibid., s. 3(1)(c).

remain is granted.[6] However, the issue of asylum may arise on appeal not only against a refusal by the Home Office to grant leave to remain but also where there has been a decision to deport. The rules provide that a deportation order will not be made where the only country the deportee can be removed to is one to which he is unwilling to go for fear of persecution for the reasons set out in the Convention.[7]

There will be occasions when an appeal has been lodged against a refusal to grant leave to remain where the Home Office is unaware that the appellant will claim that he is a refugee and entitled to asylum. Similarly the Home Office may have no knowledge of such claim on an appeal against a decision to deport. In these circumstances it is advisable to make an application to the Home Office as early as possible prior to the appeal, providing documentary evidence, where available, in support of the application. There is nothing to be lost by this approach, for if the Home Office refuse to grant asylum, the arguments can be restated at the hearing of the appeal. If the adviser has only been given short notice that political asylum is to be an issue it may be appropriate to make an application to the Home Office and to seek an adjournment of the hearing. A claim to asylum cannot be considered by the appellate authorities if the appeal is solely against the directions for removal.[8]

15.14 There is provision in the appeals procedure rules for the UK representative of the UNHCR to be treated as a party to an appeal where a person is or claims to be a refugee under the Convention.[9] The representative must, however, give written notice to the appellate authority either before or during the appeal that he desires to be treated as a party.[10] The practice of the UNHCR has been to provide advice and assistance if requested by either the appellant or the Home Office,[11] including providing evidence for use at the appeal, but not to appear as a party. There have, however, been occasions when the UNHCR has asked that it be treated as a party to an appeal.[12]

There have been few successful appeals. This is in part due to problems relating to proof. The burden lies on the person submitting the claim to prove on a balance of probabilities that he has a well-founded fear of being persecuted. The problem is that the appellate authorities often fail

[7] HC 394, para. 138.
[8] *Ali* v *Immigration Appeal Tribunal* [1973] Imm AR 33, CA.
[9] The Immigration Appeals (Procedure) Rules 1972, SI 1972, No. 1684 para. 7(3).
[10] Ibid.
[11] The Home Office rarely avails itself of the services of the UNHCR.
[12] See, e.g. *Acharya* 2246/71 (60) (unreported).

to appreciate that there are serious difficulties in providing evidence, and that a person may have discharged the burden of proof although there may be gaps in the evidence which would have justified dismissal of any other type of appeal.[13] It is submitted that the Tribunal's approach is wrong and that there is no absolute standard of proof which is applicable to all cases. The degree of probability will depend on the subject matter and will vary from case to case.[14] It is nevertheless important to stress that, if the appellant's account appears credible, considerable weight should be attached to his evidence and, even where there is no other evidence in support other than background information about his country, he should nevertheless be regarded as having discharged the burden of proof on the balance of probabilities unless there are compelling reasons for concluding otherwise. The appellate authorities should be reminded that,

(a) documentary or other proof in support of the appellant will be the exception rather than the rule because (i) when a person flees from persecution he may leave behind personal and other documents which might have justified his claim but would have put him in danger if found on his departure; and (ii) other people who are in the UK who might be expected to give evidence on behalf of the appellant may be unwilling to come forward because of fear of the authorities in their country of origin;

(b) although unsupported statements must not necessarily be accepted as true if they conflict with the general account put forward by the appellant, a person may because of his own experiences fear his own authorities and distrust others, so that he is afraid to speak freely and give a full and accurate account of his case;

(c) untrue statements are not in themselves grounds for dismissing the appeal, and such statements have to be assessed in the light of the circumstances of the case;

[13] See, for example, *Hailu* 3926/76 (923) (unreported); *Kus* 31628/78 (1470) (unreported). The issue of standard of proof was raised by the refugee's representative in the *Two Citizens of Chile* [1977] Imm AR 36 but the Tribunal failed to comment on the submissions.

[14] *Bater* v *Bater* [1951] P 35, at 37 per Denning LJ when he referred to 'a degree of probability commensurate with the occasion.' There is also a strong argument to suggest that the balance of probabilities test is inappropriate (see *Hailu*, and *Two Citizens of Chile*, supra), and that the reasoning of the House of Lords in *Fernandez* v *Government of Singapore* [1971] 2 All ER 691, HL, should be applied in asylum cases. The court held that the balance of probabilities test was inappropriate where the court is called on to prophesy what might happen in the future.

(d) it may be misleading to take isolated incidents out of context and the cumulative effect of the appellant's experience must be taken into account; there may be circumstances where no single incident stands out above others and it may be something which appears to be quite insignificant which turns out to be 'the last straw'.

THE GRANTING OF ASYLUM

Convention Refugees

15.15 Although the immigration rules are silent on the matter, a person granted asylum who is accepted as a refugee under the Convention is usually given permission initially to remain for 12 months without restriction on employment. Thereafter, an extension will be granted on application for a further period of three years. At the end of this period the refugee may apply for and will be granted indefinite leave to remain in the UK. The granting of the three year extension is a new arrangement which was introduced on 1 July 1980.[15] The Home Office has, however, made it clear that there will be some cases where only 12 months' extensions will be granted. The circumstances 'will depend on the individual case and cannot be specified'. Moreover, the Home Office will not give reasons why an extension is of a particular length. On the granting of asylum, the refugee will be entitled to a Convention Travel Document which is issued by the UK Government.

Refugees rarely face problems under the immigration laws once asylum is granted and the rights set out in the Convention relating to employment and welfare are in the main complied with.

De Facto Refugees

15.16 There are those who cannot return to their country of nationality but do not qualify as refugees under the Convention and Protocol. They are sometimes known as *de facto* refugees. The Home Office recognises this category of refugee by granting the applicant asylum without refugee status.

As with Convention refugees economic motives alone will be insufficient to make a person a *de facto* refugee. An example of an applicant who might qualify in this category is a person from Eritrea who has not been actively involved in the armed struggle or faced any problem when last in the country sometime ago, but who because of the upheaval

---

[15] 512 H. of L. Official Report, 1 August 1980, cols. 1244–1245.

caused by the war can be expected to face grave problems and indiscriminate persecution if he were to return home. Those granted asylum without refugee status are given permission to remain without restriction on employment in the same manner as Convention refugees. They may apply annually for extensions of stay and after four years may apply for and will usually be granted indefinite leave. A *de facto* refugee has no entitlement to a Convention Travel Document but they may be supplied with a Home Office Certificate of Identity.[16]

Exceptional Leave to Remain

15.17 The Home Office has recently in a number of cases granted extensions of stay to persons who would normally be regarded as *de facto* refugees 'exceptionally outside the immigration rules'. Although in practice the applicants are treated in the same manner as *de facto* refugees, there is no recognition by the Home Office that the applicants are refugees. This will not make any difference in terms of their immigration status: unless there is a significant change of circumstances extensions of stay will be granted annually and indefinite leave granted after four years.

15.18 In some cases, however, it may be important to press for refugee status. As in practice a person granted leave 'exceptionally' is in the same position as a *de facto* refugee, it would usually only be worthwhile pursuing an application with the Home Office if Convention refugee status was being sought, for example, because the application required a Convention Travel Document.

Letters of Status

15.19 The Home Office now makes clear under which category a person has been given permission to remain. After a person has been granted leave to remain, he will receive a letter explaining that he has been recognised as a Convention refugee, or that he has qualified for asylum without refugee status, or that he has been allowed to remain in the UK despite not qualifying for asylum or for recognition as a refugee.

TRAVEL DOCUMENTS

Convention Travel Document

15.20 After a person has been granted asylum with refugee status, his

[16] As to travel documents, see para. 15.20, post.

passport is not stamped with permission to remain. The stamp will be endorsed on the letter of status.

A refugee granted asylum is not expected to use his national passport to travel. If he does so there is a serious risk that he will lose his refugee status. If he wishes to travel he should apply for a Convention Travel Document (CTD) which is issued through the Home Office. The document is in book form and coloured blue. The CTD is issued by the UK Government to recognised refugees on its territories and is valid for all countries except the refugee's country of origin. In the UK the CTD is valid until the end of the current extension of stay when it must be renewed. Where indefinite leave to remain has been granted the CTD will be issued for a five year period.[17] There is an agreement between a number of European countries permitting travel for up to three months without visas in any of those countries by persons holding CTDs issued by the governments party to the agreement.

Certificates of Identity

15.21 A *de facto* refugee who is unable to use or obtain a national travel document may be issued with a certificate of identity on application to the Home Office. A *de facto* refugee will have his passport stamped unless he applies for a certificate of identity in which case the endorsement will be made in the certificate. The certificate is issued in book form and coloured brown. A certificate of identity does not confer any status on the holder, and may be issued in circumstances which have no connection with refugees, e.g. to a person who is returning to his own country on a journey requiring him to be in transit where his own government has refused or delayed in issuing him with a passport.[18]

TRANSFER OF ASYLUM

15.22 Asylum will not normally be granted where a person has obtained asylum elsewhere. Many countries, including the UK, adopt the practice that a person should seek asylum in the country to which he first flees. This 'doctrine' of country of first asylum may result in an applicant being refused leave to enter or remain on the ground that he is able to obtain the protection of the original country where he retained asylum. There are no rules which set out the circumstances in which this operates. The length of time the applicant remained in the country to

---

[17] Letter, Home Office to Sir Leslie Kirklees, Chairman, Standing Conference on Refugees, 4 November 1980.   [18] See para. 9.27, post.

which he fled will be a relevant factor (a period of stay of two to three months may justify a claim that the country had given asylum) as will be the quality of the stay in that country (a nine month period in conditions which were clearly transitory may not amount to that country having granted asylum). Asylum may be transferred to the UK if the applicant has close ties with the UK, e.g. many of his family are in the UK or he has spent most of his life or has been educated there; or as part of a Government programme, e.g. admission of Vietnamese boat people who had been granted asylum in Hong Kong.

LOSS OF REFUGEE STATUS

15.23 There are only a limited number of circumstances where a Convention refugee may lose his status.[19] They are:

(1) *Voluntary Re-establishment in the Country where Persecution was Feared*

This applies both to refugees who have no nationality and to stateless persons. It implies intention of residence on a permanent basis: a temporary visit by a refugee to his former country of residence may not itself result in loss of status.

(2) *Voluntary Re-availment of National Protection*

The act must be voluntary, the refugee must intend to avail himself of protection and actually obtain the protection. This may arise where a refugee either returns to his country of origin or where he applies for and obtains a national passport or its renewal. In both cases there is a presumption of re-availment but this may be negatived. Travel on a national document to another country will be a presumption of re-availment which will be almost impossible to negative.

(3) *Voluntary Re-acquisition of Nationality where that Nationality has been Lost*

(4) *Acquisition of a New Nationality and Protection of Country of New Nationality*

(5) *The Reason for Becoming a Refugee has ceased to Exist*

This applies where there has been a fundamental change of cir-

[19] 1951 Convention, art. 1(c). It is submitted that these categories are exclusive.

cumstances in the country, and not simply a change of events which might be transitory. Moreover refugees should not lose their status and be required to return if reasons relating to previous persecution exist for their refusing to return. A change in regime may not produce a change in the attitude of the population or in the mind of the refugee.

STATELESS PERSONS

15.24 The 1954 Convention Relating to the Status of Stateless Persons[20] defines a stateless person as 'someone who is not considered a national by any state under the operation of its law'. It should be borne in mind that a stateless person is not necessarily someone who has a fear of persecution, although if he does he may at the same time be a refugee The UK is a party to this Convention. However, the Convention is not incorporated into UK law, nor is there any mention of stateless persons in the immigration rules. Any stateless person in the UK must have had an acceptable travel document when he was given leave to enter the UK. On entry any person who later claims to be stateless would have been either accepted as a national of another country or accepted by another country as a stateless person and provided with the relevant documentation. The Home Office does not therefore readily accept claims that after arrival a person has become stateless. If a person cannot obtain a national passport or renewal of a Stateless Persons Travel Document from the issuing state, the Home Office should be informed in writing of the problem to ensure that no action is taken against him for overstaying while the matter is being resolved. Thereafter all efforts must be aimed towards renewing the document on which the person arrived in the country and approaching any other country with which the person has close ties. This should be done in the form of recorded delivery letters by either the individual or his representative. It frequently happens that no reply is received. A formal application for consideration as a stateless person should be made to the Home Office, outlining (and proving) that action has been taken by the individuals or their representatives to acquire a renewed travel document. It is likely that prior to consideration of this request the UK authorities will approach the authority who issued the document on which the person entered the UK even where there is a formal reply refusing facilities. The Convention requires the Government to provide stateless persons with identity documents. In appropriate cases, the Home Office will issue a

[20] Cmnd. 1098.

stateless person with a travel document. The document is in book form and coloured pink. The maximum period of validity of the document is the same as that for recognised refugees, but almost without exception, holders are long residents who are issued with five-year documents.

If a person is offered a one-way document back to his own country he is not stateless. This often happens with persons from the Middle East who are required to return to undergo military service obligations. If the only document offered is a one-way document and the person is reluctant to accept this, the reasons for this reluctance need to be explored and if the applicant has a claim as a refugee, an application for asylum should be made.[1]

REFUGEE AGENCIES

15.25 The United Nations High Commissioner for Refugees (UNHCR) has a United Kingdom Representative who will give advice and assistance in the circumstances which are set out in the text. In 1976 the UNHCR established jointly with the United Kingdom Immigrants Advisory Service (UKIAS) the UKIAS Refugee Unit, whose terms of reference are explained in Appendix 5.

---

[1] See note 17, supra.

SIXTEEN

The Prevention of Terrorism Act

16.1 The Prevention of Terrorism (Temporary Provisions) Act 1976 is based on earlier legislation which was speedily introduced following the 1974 Birmingham pub bombings.[1] The Act applies throughout the UK.[2] The Act gives wide powers of arrest and questioning, detention and search of those suspected of being involved in terrorism, and enables the Home Secretary to exclude people from parts of the UK and to ban terrorist organisations. There are a number of provisions which are relevant to immigration control, namely (1) the making of exclusion orders; (2) controls at the port of entry.

EXCLUSION ORDERS

16.2 It should be remembered that the UK comprises Great Britain and Northern Ireland; Great Britain comprises England, Scotland and Wales. A Secretary of State (usually the Home Secretary or in Northern Ireland the Secretary of State for Northern Ireland)[3] may make an order excluding a person from the whole or part of the United Kingdom if (1) it appears to him expedient to prevent acts of terrorism (whether in the UK or elsewhere) designed to influence public opinion or Government

---

[1] Prevention of Terrorism (Temporary Provisions) Act 1974, which was repealed by the 1976 Act. For a detailed analysis of the operation of the Act see C. Scorer and P. Hewitt: *The Prevention of Terrorism Act: The case for repeal* (1981) (NCCL).

[2] The 1976 Act is reviewed annually and remains in force until 25 March 1982 when it may be extended for a further 12 months: s. 17(1). There is power to extend the Act by Order in Council to the Channel Islands and the Isle of Man: s. 16(1). This has been done by SI 1976, Nos. 772 (Guernsey); 895 (Isle of Man); 896 (Jersey).

[3] For convenience, the phrase 'Home Secretary' is used throughout.

policy with respect to affairs in Northern Ireland;[4] and (2) he is satisfied that the person, (a) is or has been concerned anywhere in the world in the commission, preparation or instigation of acts of terrorism;[5] or (b) is attempting or may attempt to enter either Great Britain or Northern Ireland with a view to being concerned in the commission, preparation or instigation of acts of terrorism.[6] Terrorism is defined as 'the use of violence for political ends, and includes any use of violence for the purpose of putting any section of the public in fear'.[7]

16.3 The Act requires the Home Secretary, before making an order against a person who is ordinarily resident in Great Britain or ordinarily resident in Northern Ireland, to have regard to the question whether that person's connection with any other territory is such to make it appropriate to make an order.[8] Thus there may be powerful arguments against making an exclusion order if a person has strong connections with either Great Britain or Northern Ireland.

Limitations on the Extent of Exclusion Orders

16.4 There are a number of constraints on the making of an exclusion order[9] which depend on the nationality of the person against whom an order may be made.

Citizens of the United Kingdom and Colonies

16.5 A person cannot be excluded from the whole of the UK as the Act prohibits the removal from Great Britain to Northern Ireland of those who are already excluded from Northern Ireland, and there is a similar prohibition on the removal from Northern Ireland of those who are subject to a Great Britain exclusion order.[10] The Act provides that a person may be excluded from Great Britain and sent to Northern Ireland unless (1) he is at the time ordinarily resident in Great Britain and has been ordinarily resident there throughout the last 20 years;[11] or (2) he was born in Great Britain and has been ordinarily resident there throughout his life.[12] Similarly a person can be excluded from Northern Ireland and sent to Great Britain unless (1) he is at the time ordinarily resident in Northern Ireland and has been ordinarily resident there throughout the last 20 years;[13] or (2) he was born in Northern Ireland

[4] Prevention of Terrorism (Temporary Provisions) Act 1976, s. 3(1).
[5] Ibid., s. 4(1)(a).   [6] Ibid., s. 4(1)(b).   [7] Ibid., s. 14(1).
[8] Ibid., s. 4(2); s. 5(2), s. 6(2).
[9] The term exclusion order is taken from ibid., s. 3(2).
[10] Ibid., s. 4(3)(c), s. 5(3)(c).
[11] Ibid., s. 4(3)(a).   [12] Ibid., s. 4(3)(b).   [13] Ibid., s. 5(3)(a).

and has been ordinarily resident there throughout his life.[14] A person is not to be treated as ordinarily resident at a time when he is in a territory in breach of an exclusion order or of any immigration legislation;[15] nor during time spent in prison in the UK or Islands following conviction for an offence where the sentence was six months or over.[16]

Making Representations against an Exclusion Order

16.6 There is no right of appeal against the making of an exclusion order. A person on whom an exclusion order has been served may, however, make representations to the Home Secretary against the order provided he does so within 96 hours of the notice being served on him. He may also request an oral hearing before a Government-appointed adviser.[17] If the representations are not considered frivolous, or the applicant has not left the territory voluntarily, they will be referred to an adviser.[18] An interview will be arranged with the adviser but its value is limited as the person subject to the order has no right to know the evidence on which the order was made, or to cross-examine witnesses or to call witnesses in support of his case. There is no provision for legal representation but a representative will be allowed to attend the hearing on application. It usually takes two weeks to obtain a hearing date during which period the applicant will be detained in prison. There is no formal or public hearing of the representations. A decision is usually made within one week of the hearing of the representations. A transcript of the hearing will be provided if requested. Although the making of representations will delay removal, the chances of success are very limited.

Powers of Removal

16.7 A person who has been served with an exclusion order may be removed if (1) he consents; or (2) at least 96 hours have elapsed since service of the notice and no representations have been made; or (3) representations have been made and turned down.[19]

Criminal Offences Relating to Exclusion Orders

16.8 It is a criminal offence for a person (1) not to obey an exclusion

[14] Ibid., s. 5(3)(b).
[15] Ibid., Sch. 2 para. 1(1).
[16] Ibid., para. 1(2).
[17] See generally ibid., s. 7.
[18] Ibid., s. 7(4).
[19] Ibid., s. 8.

order once he is liable to be removed;[20] (2) to be knowingly concerned in arrangements for securing or facilitating the entry into the UK[1] of anyone or to knowingly harbour[2] anyone whom he knows or has reasonable cause to believe to be subject to an exclusion order. The consent of the Attorney General is required before a prosecution may be brought.[3] The maximum penalty is a fine of £1000 and/or six months' imprisonment, in the magistrates' court,[4] or an unlimited fine and/or five years' imprisonment in the Crown Court.[5] A police officer may arrest without warrant anyone he reasonably suspects to be guilty of an offence.[6]

Revocation of Exclusion Orders

16.9 There is no procedure set out in the Act for the revocation of an exclusion order. The Home Secretary announced in 1979 that he will automatically review an order after three years but conceded that there were difficulties if the Home Office were not aware of the whereabouts of the persons excluded.[7] The Home Office will write to the person subject to the exclusion order at his last known address informing him of the review. Where a person wishes to make an application he should write to the Home Office (Police Department), Queen Anne's Gate, London SW1, supplying name, date of birth, present address and previous address in the UK, name and address of current employer and previous employers and setting out any information which he believes the Home Secretary should consider in making a review of the order. Those who are made subject to an order are now informed at the time it is served of the three year review. Representations may of course be made at any time for the revocation of an order. Change in family circumstances or other compassionate grounds may warrant a review even if there has been no change in the applicant's own political viewpoint. An application for an early review will not affect the three year review which will take place in any event.

---

[20] Ibid., s. 9(1).
[1] Ibid., s. 9(2)(a).
[2] Ibid., s. 9(2)(b).
[3] Ibid., Sch. 3 para. 3. If the offence is committed in Northern Ireland, the consent of the Attorney General of Northern Ireland is required.
[4] Ibid., s. 9(3)(a) as amended by the Criminal Law Act 1977, s. 28(1), (7).
[5] Prevention of Terrorism (Temporary Provisions) Act 1976, s. 9(3)(b).
[6] Ibid., s. 12(1).
[7] 968 H. of C. Official Report, 18 June 1979, Written Answers, col. 380.

CONTROLS AT THE PORT OF ENTRY

16.10 There are provisions for stringent controls at the port of entry to deal with those suspected of committing offences under the Act.[8] There are a number of designated ports and control areas and embarkation and disembarkation is limited to those places.[9]

Examination

16.11 The powers at the ports are exercised by 'examining officers'. An examining officer may either be a police officer, immigration officer or officer of customs and excise who is the subject of arrangements under the Immigration Act 1971 for his employment as an immigration officer.[10] In Northern Ireland only, a member of the forces on duty may perform any function of an examining officer.[11] An examining officer may examine anyone who has arrived in or is seeking to leave Great Britain or Northern Ireland[12] by ship or aircraft for the purpose of determining[13] (1) whether the person appears to be one who is or has been concerned in the commission, preparation or instigation of acts of terrorism; or (2) whether the person is subject to an exclusion order; or (3) whether there are grounds for suspecting a person has committed an offence relating to exclusion orders or the offence of failing to provide information about acts of terrorism.[14]

---

[8] These are set out in the Prevention of Terrorism (Supplemental Temporary Provisions) Order 1976, SI 1976, No. 465 as amended by SI 1979, No. 169 which applies to Great Britain, and the Prevention of Terrorism (Supplementary Temporary Provisions) (Northern Ireland) Order 1976, SI 1976, No. 466 as amended by SI 1979, No. 168, which applies to Northern Ireland. The orders are almost identical.

[9] SI No. 465, para. 12; SI No. 466, para. 13. The orders also impose requirements regarding embarkation and disembarkation on captains of craft (SI No. 465, para. 13; SI No. 466, para. 14).

[10] SI Nos. 465, 466, paras. 4(1), 4(2).

[11] Ibid., para. 4(3).

[12] There are provisions for examining those who are travelling to and from the Republic and Northern Ireland: ibid., paras. 5(2)–(4).

[13] SI Nos. 465, 466, para. 5(1). A person may also be required in writing to submit to a further examination: ibid., paras. 5(2), 5(5).

[14] It is an offence for a person who has information which he knows or believes to be of material assistance (i) in preventing acts of terrorism . . .; or (ii) in securing the apprehension, prosecution or conviction of any person for an offence involving the commission, preparation, or instigation of an act of terrorism to fail without reasonable excuse to disclose that information as soon as reasonably practicable: Prevention of Terrorism (Temporary Provisions) Act 1976, s. 11.

Production of Documents and Supplying Information

16.12 It is the duty of a person being examined to furnish to the officer 'all such information as is in his possession' to enable the officer to carry out his functions.[15] Further, he must (1) produce, if required by the officer, a valid passport or travel document; and (2) declare whether or not he is carrying or conveying documents of any relevant description specified by the examining officer; and (3) produce such documents.[16]

Search

16.13 The powers of search may be carried out not only by an examining officer but also by any person he authorises to carry out a search on his behalf.[17] An examining officer may search any ship or aircraft or anything on board or anything taken off or about to be taken aboard for the purpose of satisfying himself whether there are persons he may wish to examine.[18] If the examining officer finds a person he wishes to examine he may search that person and any baggage belonging to him or any ship or aircraft and anything on board or anything taken off or about to be taken aboard a ship or aircraft.[19] In Northern Ireland vehicles which are not being taken on or off may also be searched in certain circumstances.[20] A woman may only be searched by another woman.[1]

Detention of Property

16.14 An examining officer may detain anything he finds during the course of his search for a period not exceeding seven days, unless he is of the opinion that the property may be needed (1) in connection with the Home Secretary's deciding on whether to make an exclusion order; or (2) for use as evidence in criminal proceedings; in which case he may detain it until satisfied that it is no longer needed.[2]

---

[15] SI Nos. 465, 466, para. 6(1).

[16] Ibid., para. 6(2). 'Relevant description' means any description appearing to the examining officer to be relevant for the purpose of the examination.

[17] SI No. 465, paras. 6, 7; SI No. 466, paras. 7, 8. In Scotland any person employed by a police authority for the assistance of the constables of a force under the Police (Scotland) Act 1967, s. 9, may perform any functions of examining officers: SI No. 465, para. 8.

[18] SI Nos. 465, 466, para. 7(1).

[19] Ibid., para. 7(2).

[20] SI No. 466, para. 7(3).

[1] SI No. 465, para. 7(4); SI No. 466, para. 7(5).

[2] SI No. 465, para. 7(4); SI No. 466, para. 7(3).

Completion of Landing and Embarkation Cards

16.15 There is provision for the completing of landing and embarkation cards on journeys between Great Britain and Northern Ireland, the Islands and the Republic of Ireland.[3]

Removal of Persons Subject to an Exclusion Order

16.16 A person who is found to be subject to an exclusion order may be removed by an examining officer, otherwise the Home Secretary must give removal directions.[4] The circumstances in which a person may be removed once the Home Secretary has signed an exclusion order are set out earlier in this chapter.[5] Directions will be given to remove the person to the country from which he embarked or to one of which he is a citizen or to one in which he obtained travel documents or to one where there is reason to believe he will be admitted.[6] No directions will be given which will have the effect of excluding a citizen of the UK and Colonies from the whole of the UK unless he is also a citizen of another country and indicates that he is willing to be removed to that country.[7]

Detention Pending Examination and Removal

16.17 There are provisions for lengthy detention of those who are required to submit to examination under the Act.[8] A person may be detained pending his examination on consideration of the question of whether to make an exclusion order against him (1) on the authority of an examining officer, for a period not exceeding 48 hours; and (2) on the direction of the Home Secretary, for a further period of five days after the 48 hour period is completed.[9] There are further powers to detain a person who is the subject of an exclusion order and against whom directions for removal may be given.[10]

---

[3] SI Nos. 465, 466, para. 8.

[4] Ibid., para. 9(1).

[5] See para. 16.7, ante.

[6] SI Nos. 465, 466, para. 9(4). As to removals from Northern Ireland to the Republic: No. 466, para. 10.

[7] SI Nos. 465, 466, para. 9(4).

[8] See generally SI No. 465, para. 10; SI No. 466, para. 11.

[9] SI No. 465, para. 10(1); SI No. 466, para. 11(1). (Provision for detention by Secretary of State for five days, and an order for a further five days after the expiry of the initial period.) As from 18 April 1979, these provisions have been amended: SI 1979, Nos., 169, 168, para. 2.

[10] SI No. 465, para. 10(2); SI No. 466, para. 11(2).

Arrest and Search of those Liable to Detention

16.18 A person liable to be detained may be arrested without warrant by an examining officer. A search warrant may be obtained authorising a police officer to enter premises if there is reasonable ground for suspecting that there is a person liable to be arrested in the premises.[11]

[11] SI No. 465, para. 11; SI No. 466, para. 12.

SEVENTEEN

Conclusion

'The Commission finds it established that the 1968 Act had racial motives and that it covered a racial group. . . . It further considers that the discriminatory provisions of the above Act should be seen in the context of two other laws, and of further regulations, in the field of citizenship and immigration which also gave preference to white people. . . . The Commission considers that the racial discrimination, to which the applicants have been publicly subjected by the application of the above immigration legislation, constitutes an interference with their human dignity which, in the special circumstances described above, amounted to "degrading treatment" in the sense of Article 3 of the Convention.'[1]

'Immigration law in this country has developed mainly as a series of responses to, and attempts to regulate, particular pressures, rather than as a positive means of achieving preconceived social or economic aims.'[2]

The immigration law and practice set out in the preceding chapters is racially discriminatory in its motivation and in its effect: it is in violation of the UK's international human rights obligations and of standards of natural justice and civil liberties generally claimed to be respected in Britain. Thus far we have (with some difficulty) restricted ourselves to describing the existing system and have refrained from commenting upon it. In this concluding chapter, we present from our own experience as practitioners and the wider involvement of the organisations for which we have worked, the Joint Council for the Welfare of Immigrants and the National Council for Civil Liberties, a brief statement of our objections to this system. To present a full critique and to illustrate it

[1] European Commission of Human Rights, report on the East African Asians Case, quoted in Proposed New Immigration Rules and the European Convention on Human Rights, First Report from the House of Commons Home Affairs Committee (1979–80) HC 434, 11 February 1980, pp. 52–55. The full report may be consulted by arrangement with JCWI.
[2] Home Office, evidence printed in Immigration, First Report from the Select Committee on Race Relations and Immigration (1977–78), HC 303, 13 March 1978, Vol. II, p. 1.

would require another book, but to end this one without a statement of our own position might seem to imply a weary acceptance of a situation to which we are in fact deeply opposed.

Racialism operates in the present system of immigration control in two ways. The first is the drawing of the definition of those subject to immigration control and those eligible for admission under the immigration rules in such a way as to favour white entrants while restricting as far as possible those who are not white. The second is the provision of arbitrary and oppressive powers and wide ranging administrative discretion, which apply in theory to all those subject to control but which in practice are levelled in their full severity at black entrants.

The most careful yet damning analysis of the way in which immigration legislation has been racially motivated in the definition of those subject to control is contained in the report of the European Commission of Human Rights on the East African Asian cases. The Commission found it established that the Commonwealth Immigrants Act 1968 had racial motives and that it covered a racial group, and referred to statements made in both Houses of Parliament during the debate on the Bill in February 1968: the Government, while claiming that the Act was based on geography, nevertheless admitted it had racial motives. The Commission noted that even before the 1968 Act, the British Nationality Act 1964 had introduced, as a condition for an entitlement to resume citizenship of the UK and Colonies, a 'qualifying connection' of ancestry which would normally be fulfilled by white settlers but not by members of the Asian communities in East Africa.[3]

By the time the Commission made its report, Parliament had replaced the Commonwealth Immigrants Act 1968 and its predecessor with the Immigration Act 1971. While the 1971 Act is generally referred to as a highly restrictive piece of legislation (as indeed it is in the powers of deportation and removal and the criminal sanctions it provides) its effect on the definition of those subject to immigration control was to restore free entry to millions of Commonwealth citizens, overwhelmingly white. It did this by defining as patrials with a right of abode Commonwealth citizens with a UK-born parent. The original Bill would have extended the right of abode to any Commonwealth citizen with a UK-born grandparent; this was defeated in Committee by an alliance of Enoch Powell and the Labour opposition, but draft immigration rules which would have left these white Commonwealth citizens subject to the new work permit requirement were rejected by a revolt of Conser-

[3] European Commission of Human Rights, op. cit., pp. 52–54.

vative MPs. The immigration rules have therefore since 1973 provided for the admission for settlement of any Commonwealth citizen with a UK-born grandparent, and this provision survived unscathed (and almost without comment) the latest Conservative Government's supposed assault on the remaining loopholes for primary immigration.[4] The Commission took account of both the 1971 Act and the 1973 rules in reaching its conclusion on the racially discriminatory nature of UK immigration control.

The immigration rules are prefaced with the injunction that immigration officers will carry out their duties without regard to the race, colour or religion of people seeking to enter the UK.[5] The latest revision of the rules has, however, seen the incorporation of the most overtly racially discriminatory provision yet to feature in UK immigration control. The right of British women and other women settled in the UK to have their husbands or fiancés admitted to live with them here, qualified as it is by supposed safeguards against marriages arranged for immigration purposes, is now denied to women who are not citizens of the UK and Colonies born or with one parent born in the UK.[6] The Government has thus divided patrial women into two categories in order to deny even women who are patrial UK and Colonies citizens, by registration or naturalisation (or by citizenship acquired overseas but followed by five years' residence and settlement here), the right to live with a non-patrial husband in this country. It has refused to offer any serious answer to the powerful case that the new rules are thus in breach of Article 3 (degrading treatment), and Article 14 (discrimination) linked with Articles 8 (respect for family life) and 12 (right to marry and found a family) of the European Convention on Human Rights.[7]

Apart from the 'exception on grounds of UK ancestry', the rules for husbands and fiancés, and the (now somewhat less generous) provision for working holidays for young Commonwealth citizens under which thousands of almost exclusively white Commonwealth citizens have in the past found Britain hospitable to their entry and employment,[8] there is little hint in the rules of the racial discrimination that exists in practice. The objections to be made are that they are so tightly drawn as to impede

[4] HC 79, para. 27; now HC 394, para. 29.
[5] HC 394, para. 2.
[6] HC 394, paras. 50, 52, 117; see paras. 8.56, 8.57, ante.
[7] Compare Home Office evidence with the evidence of Lord Scarman and Anthony Lester, QC, printed in Proposed New Immigration Rules and the European Convention on Human Rights, op. cit.
[8] HC 79, para. 28; now HC 394, para. 30, para. 7.23, ante.

the family life of those already settled here or the reasonable expectations of would-be entrants, and that they leave wide areas for the operation of highly subjective discretion.

There are now two definitions of the family contained in the immigration rules. For EEC workers, protected by EEC regulations, the family includes the spouse, children under 21, other children and grandchildren if dependent, and dependent parents and grandparents.[9] Although the rules omit to reflect it, EEC regulations also require member States to facilitate the admission of any other family member if dependent on the member or living under his roof in the country from which he comes.[10] For others, the admission of a husband is subject to the racially discriminatory birthplace test already discussed, and only children under 18 are readily admitted: the new rules have rendered the criteria for the admission of children over 18 and of parents so stringent that very few will now qualify.[11]

The wide areas left to the subjective discretion of very junior officials (a Chief Immigration Officer, who must authorise a refusal, is only a Higher Executive Officer) is best seen in the deceptively simple provisions for students and visitors. A student must satisfy the immigration officer that he intends to leave the country on completion of his course of study;[12] a visitor must satisfy the immigration officer that he is genuinely seeking entry for the period of the visit as stated by him.[13] The Act requires that a person refused entry must be given written notice including a statement of the reasons for the decision:[14] the most common statement among the set formulae provided to immigration officers for this purpose must surely be the statement without amplification that 'I am not satisfied that you intend to stay only for this limited period'. Immigration officers are trained to draft their explanatory statements for appeals in the form 'I was not satisfied', and to avoid assertions which would bring upon them an onus of proof that they lack the evidence to discharge.[15]

It is these areas of subjective discretion into which racial discrimination can so easily enter. Although the instructions to immigration officers are secret, it is not to be supposed that they prescribe overt racial discrimina-

[9] HC 394, para. 62, para. 7.49, ante.
[10] Council Regulation (EEC) 1612/68, art. 10, para. 7.45, ante.
[11] HC 394, paras. 47, 48, para. 8.40, ante.
[12] HC 394, para. 22, para. 6.17, ante.
[13] HC 394, para. 17, para. 6.5, ante.
[14] Immigration Act 1971, s. 18(1)(b).
[15] Secretary of State's instructions to immigration officers (unpublished).

tion. They do, however, make reference to a would-be entrant being subject to suspicion 'because he belongs to a class of immigrant which has strong economic or other incentives to obtain entry to this country and because of the frequency with which other immigrants of that class have evaded or have attempted to evade immigration controls'. Immigration officers are instructed that 'references to the tendency of immigrants of particular national origins to evade immigration control should be avoided' and that 'gratuitous opinions, generalisations, and expressions which might be construed as biased or prejudiced . . . can have a very damaging effect on our case at an appeal and must on no account be included in a report'. These injunctions seem aimed more at inhibiting the acknowledgement of prejudice in circumstances where it might result in a successful appeal than at preventing it from influencing decisions: a proper view of the public interest would surely prefer prejudice, if it operates, to be admitted and open to rectification.

The statistical chances of refusal of passengers of different nationalities can be calculated from the Control of Immigration Statistics.[16] In 1979, the top and bottom countries were as set out in the table overleaf.

The greatest single source of distress to the immigrant community has been the entry clearance queue allowed to develop in the Indian subcontinent, in clear contravention of assurances, when entry clearance was made mandatory for dependants in 1969, that it would not delay their admission. The length of the waiting period is the product of three factors: the rate of application, the time devoted to interview and consideration of each application, and the number of entry clearance officers in post. The growth of the queue in the early 1970s was not due to any increase in applications but to the increasing time devoted to each application as a result of the priority accorded to preventing the admission of non-entitled applicants. While staff were increased, especially in 1975–6, it is impossible to believe that the separation of white families for such periods of times as still exist for wives, children and husbands in Bangladesh and Pakistan and for husbands in India would be tolerated.

For years an equivalent distress was inflicted on the families of citizens of the UK and Colonies in East Africa, as a limited quota of special vouchers required heads of household to undergo periods of unemployment in East Africa before they received their vouchers. In 1975, the annual quota was increased to 5,000 and the queues in Africa were therefore soon eliminated. The announced quota is now an official

---

[16] Home Office, Control of Immigration Statistics 1979 (Cmnd. 7875).

Refusal Rates, 1979

(1) Country	(2) Admitted (all categories)	(3) Refused	(4) Refusals per 1,000 admitted	(5) Detained in Harmondsworth
Algeria	25,000	1,254	50.2	59
Morocco	16,000	470	29.4	32
Zimbabwe	5,600	154	27.5	20
Tunisia	9,900	231	23.3	8
Iran	170,000	3,776	22.2	1,400
Turkey	44,000	910	20.7	215
Ghana	28,000	535	19.1	270
Colombia	21,000	288	13.7	44
Pakistan	89,000	1,133	12.5	1,004
Sri Lanka	23,000	282	12.3	57
Cyprus	35,000	380	10.9	29
Bangladesh	22,000	237	10.8	247
Tanzania	11,000	97	8.8	46
Peru	7,100	62	8.7	1
Nigeria	120,000	952	7.9	321
India	180,000	1,206	6.7	1,074
Stateless	59,000	393	6.7	22
Hong Kong	36,000	223	6.2	147
Japan	280,000	174	0.6	24
Switzerland	270,000	132	0.5	7
USA	1,900,000	654	0.3	90
EEC	5,100,000	1,347	0.3	38
Norway	210,000	54	0.3	4
Sweden	360,000	78	0.2	7
Australia	340,000	73	0.2	16
Canada	400,000	85	0.2	14
All countries	11,600,000	20,252	1.7	6,391

Source: columns (2) and (3) are taken from the Control of Immigration Statistics 1979 op. cit., and (4) is derived from (2) and (3). Column (5) is taken from 971 H. of C. Official Report, 25 July 1979, Written Answers, col. 244; 977 H. of C. Official Report, 31 January 1980, Written Answers, col. 705.

deception, since the only remaining queue is of those who went temporarily to India from East Africa when vouchers were not promptly available there. Successive Governments have so far refused to increase the allocation to India within the quota, even though vouchers allocated

CONCLUSION

to Africa are not being taken up: thus applicants in India have now waited nearly six years, while only 1,390 special voucher holders were admitted in 1980 against a theoretical quota of 5,000.[17] (4,037 mainly white Commonwealth citizens with a UK-born grandparent were admitted or accepted for settlement in 1979, in addition to an unrecorded number of white patrial UK and Colonies and Commonwealth citizens).

Some of the worst treatment of black people and the most blatant disregard for their civil liberties result from the powers of detention, deportation and removal, and the criminal provisions of the Immigration Act 1971. An immigration officer at a port of entry can search a passenger and his baggage and detain documents,[18] can require him to be examined by a medical inspector[19] (with no restriction on the nature and purpose of the medical examination, so that the internal vaginal examinations formerly carried out on women seeking entry as fiancées supposedly to determine virginity were not precluded by law); and can detain him for further examination for up to seven days before he can even apply for bail.[20] An illegal entrant can be detained for any length of time without an opportunity to apply for bail, and irrespective of length of residence can be removed without prior right of appeal.[1] Anyone in either of these categories detained on the authority of an immigration officer can be moved around in the custody of a private security company, and his custodian 'may take all such steps as may be reasonably necessary for photographing, measuring and otherwise identifying him'.[2] These powers substantially exceed those of the police. A police officer, however, as well as an immigration officer, may arrest without warrant anyone he has reasonable cause to suspect is an illegal entrant or overstayer,[3] and this power is easily abused to allow small and sometimes large fishing expeditions in which the suspects are almost invariably black.

The Home Secretary has unlimited power to deport or exclude most non-patrials when he deems this 'conducive to the public good', with no right of appeal where he personally orders an exclusion or a deportation

[17] Home Office, Control of Immigration Statistics (1980) (Cmnd. 8199).
[18] Immigration Act 1971, Sch. 2, para. 4.
[19] Ibid., Sch. 2, para. 2.
[20] Ibid., Sch. 2, paras. 16(1), 22.
[1] Ibid., Sch. 2, paras. 16(2), 9; s. 16(2). The Home Office discussion document: 'Review of Appeals Under the Immigration Act 1971', contemplates changing this.
[2] Ibid., Sch. 2, para. 18.
[3] Ibid., s. 24(2).

as being 'in the interests of national security or of the relations between the UK and any other country or for other reasons of a political nature'.[4] This power of deportation is now used to terminate the right to settlement the settlement of people alleged to have obtained it by marriages of convenience. Most deportations, however, continue to be of overstayers or those convicted of criminal offences. Those recommended for deportation by a court are automatically detained unless the courts direct release, and only deportees with a pending appeal have an opportunity to apply for bail.[5] In 1979, 6,391 persons including 304 children under 17 were detained at the immigration service's Harmondsworth Detention Centre,[6] and 1,168 non-criminal prisoners were received into prison department establishments under Immigration Act powers.[7] 1,267 deportation orders were signed[8] and 885 persons were removed as illegal entrants.[9]

In addition to its racism and general disregard for civil liberties, the existing immigration system often discriminates on grounds of sex. The Immigration Act 1971 follows the sex discrimination in the British Nationality Act 1948 by providing for a Commonwealth citizen to be patrial by marriage to a UK and Colonies citizen husband but not wife.[10] The immigration rules for husbands and fiancés are discriminatory on grounds of sex as well as race, and even fiancés eligible for admission, unlike fiancées, require entry clearance.[11] Married women who are non-patrial UKPH are not usually regarded as heads of household eligible for special vouchers. Men working in approved employment or here as students may have their wives admitted: women are denied the equivalent rights.[12]

Some remedies for this situation might be thought to exist in the immigration appeals system and the supervisory role of the courts. From the start, however, the immigration appeals system has appeared more concerned at providing the appearance of an independent review of administrative decisions than a recognition of the necessity of an effective appeal: as the Wilson Committee put it:

[4] Ibid., s. 3(5)(b); s. 15(3).
[5] Ibid., Sch. 3, para. 2.
[6] 971 H. of C. Official Report, 31 January 1980, Written Answers, col. 244.
[7] Home Office, Prison Statistics England and Wales 1979 (Cmnd. 7978).
[8] 977 H. of C. Official Report, 31 January, Written Answers, col. 713.
[9] Home Office, Control of Immigration Statistics, 1979, op. cit.
[10] Immigration Act 1971, s. 2(2).
[11] HC 394, paras 52, 55.
[12] HC 394, paras. 25, 40.

'It is one thing for us, after a protracted inquiry, to express our confidence that the power of final decision entrusted to officers of the Immigration Service is being exercised fairly: it is another thing to expect a newly arrived immigrant, and his relatives and friends at the other side of the barrier, to feel the same confidence. They are not aware of the safeguards provided by the immigration officer's responsibility through his superiors to the Home Secretary, and the Home Secretary's responsibility to Parliament: all that seems evident to them is that an immediate and summary power to refuse admission rests with one or two officials at the port. In this situation it is understandable that an immigrant and his relatives or friends should feel themselves from the outset to be under a disadvantage, and so should be less willing than they might otherwise be to accept the eventual decision.'[13]

The majority of appeals take place in the absence of the appellant, who remains or has been removed overseas. Adjudicators place great weight on the explanatory statements prepared by entry clearance officers, immigration officers or the Home Office, with no facilities for cross-examining the interviewing official even when he is accessible in the UK. Home Office presenting officers adopt a highly adversarial approach. Adjudicators are appointed by the Home Office itself. The Act gives the adjudicators and the Tribunal no discretion to make favourable decisions outside the rules, and the approach of the appellate authorities has been to interpret the rules in a narrow fashion. An example of this is the interpretation of rules for the admission of the children of single parents.[14] The success rate in appeals is not surprisingly low: 15·6% in 1979.[15] The Immigration Appeal Tribunal is now the only tribunal from which there is no right of appeal to the courts on a point of law. It is not, however, to be supposed that such a right of appeal would have been of much avail to the immigrant given the attitudes the courts have displayed when immigration matters have come before them. There are few more glaring examples of judicial double standards than the contrast between recent attitudes of the House of Lords in the extension of administrative law and its destruction of *habeas corpus* in *Zamir*.[16]

[13] Home Office, Report of the Committee on Immigration Appeals, August 1967, p. 84 (Cmnd. 3387). The Home Office discussion document shows no change of attitude.
[14] See para. 8.36, ante.
[15] 405 H. of L. Official Report, 28 February 1980, Written Answers, col. 1670.
[16] See para. 13.18, ante, See also A. Nicol, *Illegal Entrants*, (1981) (JCWI and Runnymede Trust), J. Levin, Second Class Justice, in *LAG Bulletin*, (1980) August, and C. Blake, The Death of Habeas Corpus, in *New Law Journal* (1980) 28 August.

Ministers, immigration officials, the appellate authorities and the courts have all been acting in response to a climate of hostility to black immigration. The immigration system they have thus created is sometimes justified by the proposition that strict immigration control is the necessary pre-requisite for good race relations. We cannot too strongly express the opposite belief: that the racism of the existing immigration system undermines any attempts to create an equal multiracial society in Britain. At a time when changes in the immigration rules have rendered them yet more racially discriminatory, and when the new British Nationality Act entrenches injustices already done by immigration legislation, and when the political supervision of immigration control has never been less sensitive to justice and compassion, it is hard to be optimistic about achieving the necessary reform. Compelling this reform is, however, a moral duty incumbent on all those who in the meantime must practise within the existing system.

APPENDIX ONE

A Note on 'Recourse to Public Funds'

It is not within the scope of this book to attempt to define the circumstances in which immigration status is relevant to entitlement to social security payments, free National Health Service treatment, educational provisions or public housing. Access to such public provision is governed not by immigration law, but by social security legislation, NHS guidance and the discretionary policy of local authorities, and these may or may not make use of categories which correspond to those set out in the Immigration Act and rules.

It is necessary, however, for advisers to know what is likely to be regarded by the Home Office as having 'recourse to public funds', since having had or even anticipating such recourse may result in a refusal of admission or extension of stay. Under the old rules, a visitor was to be refused if he might 'become a charge on public funds';[1] self-employed persons, such as artists and writers, had to be able to support themselves and any dependants 'without recourse to public funds';[2] and the general provisions for dependants (other than the wife or child under 18 of a Commonwealth citizen who has the right of abode or was settled in the UK on 1 January 1973) required that the sponsor must be 'able and willing to support and accommodate his dependants without recourse to public funds'.[3]

Various statements of Home Office policy under the old rules were made in correspondence with voluntary organisations. In relation to work permit holders and their families, it was stated that 'Family Income Supplement, rent and rate rebate, welfare benefits and legal aid would

[1] HC 79, para. 15; HC 81, para. 13.
[2] HC 79, para. 36; HC 81, para. 32.
[3] HC 79, para. 39; HC 81, para. 34.

not be taken into account, nor would contributory National Insurance benefits. Payment of Supplementary Benefit is, however, material in considering the case of a work permit holder who is out of work.'[4] Similarly, with overseas students, the policy was that 'a student and his dependants in accommodation provided by the local authority under the Housing (Homeless Persons) Act or in receipt of rent allowances or rate rebates must be treated as having inadequate funds available and be refused an extension'; the same policy applied to long term visitors.[5] In *Klein*, the Home Office refused the applicant an extension of stay as a person of independent means because she suffered from a heart complaint and might not have sufficient means to pay for medical expenses. The Tribunal upheld the decision.[6]

In the new rules, references to 'recourse to public funds' are made in relation to visitors; students; young Commonwealth citizens on working holidays; businessmen and self-employed persons; persons of independent means; writers and artists; dependants both of persons with limited leave and of persons settled here (other than the wife and child under 18 of a Commonwealth citizen who has the right of abode or was settled in the UK on 1 January 1973); fiancés before marriage; and fiancées before and after marriage.[7] A new power is introduced to request an undertaking in writing that a person is 'able and willing to maintain and accommodate his dependants without recourse to public funds in accommodation of his own or which he occupies himself'.[8]

The intention to enforce such undertakings if those admitted as dependants apply for supplementary benefit is indicated by the corresponding provisions in the Social Security Act 1980. These impose a liability to maintain a person in respect of whom an undertaking has been given, enforceable in a magistrates' court and ultimately subject to criminal prosecution for failure to maintain.[9] The Supplementary Benefit regulations now make use of the references in the immigration rules to 'recourse to public funds' in restricting entitlement to benefit. There is no entitlement to benefit for persons who are not EEC nationals (or in certain circumstances, nationals of the Council of Europe states) who have limited

[4] Letter Home Office to London Council of Social Service 15 September 1978.
[5] Letter Mr. Brynmor John, MP, Minister of State, Home Office to JCWI 21 September 1978.
[6] *Klein* 34474/78 (1629) (unreported)
[7] HC 394, paras. 17, 21, 25, 30, 36, 37, 38, 39, 42, 52, and 55. These requirements applying on entry are maintained in the after entry rules.
[8] HC 394, para. 42.
[9] Social Security Act 1980, Schedule 2 (Amendments of Supplementary Benefits Act 1976), Part II (Provisions of the Act as Amended) ss. 17, 18, 25.

leave given in accordance with any provision of the rules 'which refers to there being, or there needing to be, recourse to public funds, or to there being no charge on public funds, during that limited leave.'[10] Overstayers, persons subject to deportation orders and illegal entrants are also excluded from entitlement. Urgent payments may be made for up to 42 days if resources are available but not readily available, and to persons with applications for variation pending or awaiting the determination of an appeal against a refusal to vary (but not against a decision to deport).[11]

Attempts to obtain from the Home Office a statement of intended policy in the application of the 'without recourse to public funds' requirement have so far been unsuccessful. Shortly after the new immigration rules came into effect the following statement was made by the Minister of State at the Home Office:

'Perhaps the first point I should make is that the requirement to avoid recourse to public funds is not new: the term was used in the old rules in relation to dependants. The requirement on visitors that they should not become "a charge on public funds" was also in the old rules and comes to much the same thing. We have only extended the range of persons to whom these considerations apply. If the Joint Council for the Welfare of Immigrants are asked to advise, they will be able to offer similar guidance to whatever they have said previously in similar circumstances.

'I appreciate that people would prefer to have a definitive list of those forms of recourse to public funds which would in our view reflect adversely on a person for the purposes of immigration control as opposed to those which might be disregarded. However, as I have explained in several answers, it is simply not possible to issue guidance covering all the possible circumstances of particular cases in this respect. As you know we have not followed a rigid line particularly in dealing with longer term residents. And in practice we tend to disregard benefits to which people have contributed, although I do not rule out an adverse view being taken of a case in which the contributions were made while a person was working illegally or was here in breach of the immigration laws or where the benefits greatly outweigh any contributions he made.

---

[10] Supplementary Benefit (Requirements) Regulations 1980 (SI 1980 No. 1299), as amended by Supplementary Benefit (Aggregation, Requirements and Resources) Amendment Regulations 1980 (SI 1980 No. 1774), regulation 10 (4A) and Sch. 2 (9A).
[11] Supplementary Benefit (Urgent Cases) Regulations 1980 (SI 1980 No. 1642), regulation 21.

'I believe that the objective of preventing a person with only a qualified claim to be here from becoming an unacceptable burden on the public purse is a proper one. Such a circumstance might arise from his demands for a particular benefit or a combination of benefits. Moreover, the degree of latitude we might be prepared to allow would depend on the category in which the person has entered or remained, and whether there are indications that the person has had it in mind all along to take advantage of our facilities and services, or has been unfortunate. I do not believe that the practice so far followed of considering cases on their individual merits has given rise to any serious difficulty; there is clearly a strong case for the flexibility it provides.'[12]

Elsewhere, the Home Office has explained its approach as follows:

'A number of the changes in the immigration rules were essentially of a technical nature stemming from a need to clarify the wording of earlier editions in the light of experience at appeals rather than from a wish to extend the criteria to be met by a variety of entrants and seekers of extensions. There is, however, as you know, a general principle running through the rules that those who come here for temporary purposes are expected to be self-sufficient both as to maintenance and accommodation without calling for assistance or making use of services provided for what may loosely be called the permanent inhabitants.

'We appreciate, of course, that it is possible to distinguish among people temporarily here those who have reasonable expectations within the rules of eventually achieving settlement. The dependants of a work permit holder are a category in point, for whom it might well be right not to take too serious a view of, for example, their receipt of rent or rate rebates should the information ever come to our notice, whereas application for a subvention of this kind from public funds by a holiday visitor, if that were a possibility, could properly be regarded as an abuse. Within these extremes, there will be a variety of cases that can only be judged on their particular circumstances. A temporary financial setback experienced by an otherwise worthy applicant that forces him to seek short-term benefit is a different matter from the person determined from the outset to exploit the system, and we try to ensure as far as possible that people who find themselves in difficulty through no fault of their own receive sympathetic consideration.

[12] Letter Mr. Timothy Raison, MP, Minister of State, Home Office to Dr Shirley Summerskill, MP, 10 March 1980.

'From the above, it is clear that there are difficulties in laying down any hard and fast instructions. Certainly at this stage we would not think it right to attempt to do so. Instances where the receipt of public funds is a crucial factor are rare and the variety of possible circumstances is such that it would seem a pity to sacrifice flexibility in favour of a more rigid approach which would not be capable of giving proper weight to the special features of individual cases.'[13]

In relation to overseas students the Home Office has reaffirmed since the new rules came into effect that 'we would generally expect a student to have adequate funds of his own for his support and accommodation and where it came to our notice that application had been made for a rent allowance or rate rebate, account would necessarily have to be taken of subvention of this kind from public funds in considering any application for extension of stay.'[14]

A helpful distinction has been drawn in *R v Immigration Appeal Tribunal ex parte Ved* (1981).[15] Considering the case of a person applying as a person of independent means the adjudicator, in assessing the means of the family, had felt bound in law to treat the children, who were educated at state-aided schools, as if they were educated at fee-paying schools, and the Tribunal had refused leave to appeal on the ground that there was no arguable point of law. The application had been made under the old rules[16] in which the words 'without recourse to public funds' did not appear, but the Divisional Court found that the rule had in the past properly been interpreted as if they had been included and that it was therefore necessary to decide their true meaning. The Court held that there were two separate departments of state aid: on the one side were such matters as unemployment benefit, supplementary benefit and pensions, which were matters of recourse to public funds; on the other were the facilities provided by the state, such as state-aided education, a result of compulsory education, and the National Health Service. Taking advantage of these other facilities could not be regarded as 'recourse to public funds' in any fair sense. It is submitted that contributory benefits should not be included as recourse to public funds in this otherwise helpful distinction.

[13] Letter Home Office to JCWI, 1 September 1980.
[14] Letter Mr. Timothy Raison, MP, Minister of State, Home Office, to Mr. Gerald Kaufman, MP, 15 October 1980.
[15] *The Times*, 13 May, DC.
[16] HC 82, para. 27.

APPENDIX TWO

Immigration Certificates and Endorsements in Passports

CERTIFICATES AND ENDORSEMENTS

(A) Before Entry

(1) Entry Certificate

Issued by British representatives overseas to Commonwealth citizens. The certificate is evidence of the holder's eligibility to enter the UK. The issuing officer sets out the basis on which the certificate has been granted.

The entry certificate can only be used on one occasion and is valid for a limited period, usually six months. If not taken up, a fresh application will have to be made in those cases where clearance is mandatory.

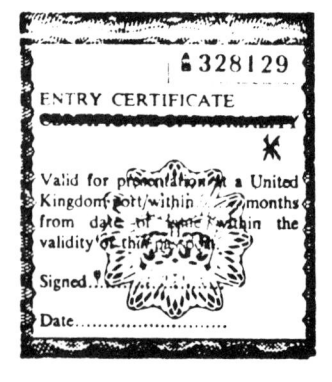

(2) Single Entry Visa

Issued by British representatives overseas to visa nationals, stateless persons and the holders of non-national identity documents. The visa is evidence of the holder's eligibility to enter the UK.
Valid for one entry only.

```
Seen at the British Embassy

            [Place]

Good for a single journey to .............
within three months of date hereof, if passport
remains valid.
                                    ✳
..............................................

(Signed).......................................
Date ..........................................
```

(3) Multiple Entry Visa

As (2), but valid for entry on more than one occasion.

```
Seen at the British Embassy

            [Place]

Good for journeys to the United Kingdom
within six months of date hereof, if
passport remains valid.
                                    ✳
..............................................

(Signed).......................................
Date ..........................................
```

(4) Home Office Letter of Consent

Issued by British representatives overseas to citizens of countries not belonging to the Commonwealth or EEC and not subject to visa arrangements. The letter is a separate document and no endorsement is made in the passport.

IMMIGRATION ACT 1971
LETTER OF CONSENT

Surname or family name
1. Brown
2. Brown (formerly Smith)
3. Brown

Forenames
1. Arthur
2. Mary
3. Jane

Sex
1. Male
2. Female
3. Female

Nationality
1. United States citizen
2. United States citizen
3. United States citizen

Date of birth
1. 18.9.1915
2. 18.8.1919
3. 20.3.1961

Place of birth
1. Buffalo, N.Y. United States of America
2. Paris, France
3. Las Vegas, New Mexico United States of America

Purpose of entry
1. Independent means
2. Accompanying husband
3. Accompanying father

Dear Mr Brown

You have applied for consent to the entry into the United Kingdom of the three persons described in the margin of this letter. I am pleased to inform you that the Secretary of State has agreed to this. The entry of the persons named will be facilitated if this letter is presented to an Immigration Officer on arrival at a United Kingdom port. The original must be presented and it is important that no alteration or amendment be made to it. A copy is not a valid entry clearance. In addition to this letter the persons named will require a valid passport or travel document.

On arrival in the United Kingdom the Immigration Officer will probably ask some questions and there are circumstances in which he may refuse leave to enter, but if he takes this exceptional course the reason will be given and there will be an entitlement to appeal immediately to an independent adjudicator.

This letter is valid if presented to an Immigration Officer within six months of its date. If it is not required for any reason it should be returned to this Office.

Yours sincerely

H Robinson
British Vice Consul

H.O. . . . .   EMBOSSING OR AUTHENTICATING STAMP

(B) On Entry

(5) Leave to enter

Where leave to enter is granted, the following rectangular stamp will be placed on the passport.

identifies the immigration officer who gave leave to enter →
identifies the date of entry →

indicates the port of entry →

```
IMMIGRATION OFFICER
    *   (369)   *
     22 JUL 1980
    HEATHROW (2)
```

The following endorsements may accompany the stamp.

(6) Limited leave to enter as a visitor (from 1 March 1980)

Endorsed if the immigration officer is satisfied that the passenger is a genuine visitor.

> LEAVE TO ENTER FOR SIX MONTHS
> EMPLOYMENT PROHIBITED

(7) Limited leave to enter as a visitor: EEC Nationals

This stamp is now used only for EEC nationals entering as visitors and will be endorsed if the immigration officer is satisfied that the passenger is a genuine visitor. It may also be found where leave was granted before 1 March 1980 in the passports of other nationals.

> GIVEN LEAVE TO ENTER THE
> UNITED KINGDOM FOR SIX MONTHS

(8) Limited leave to enter with a restriction on taking employment

(a) Endorsed in the case of students, work permit holders and businessmen and self-employed persons.

> Leave to enter the United Kingdom, on condition that the holder does not enter or change employment paid or unpaid without the consent of the Secretary of State for Employment, and does not engage in any business or profession without the consent of the Secretary of State for the Home Department, is hereby given for/~~until~~
> *TWELVE MONTHS*

(b) Foreign nationals may be required to register with the police.

> The holder is also required to register at once with the police.

(c) May also be endorsed with stamps (9) and (10). This is an indication to an immigration officer to 're-admit' the passenger for the same period and on the same conditions as the previous leave, unless there are any unusual circumstances.

> This will apply, unless superseded, to any subsequent leave the holder may obtain after an absence from the United Kingdom within the period limited as above.

(9) Limited leave to enter with a prohibition on taking employment

Endorsed in the case of persons of independent means and fiancés. Also for some students.

> Leave to enter the United Kingdom, on condition that the holder does not enter employment paid or unpaid and does not engage in any business or profession, is hereby given for/until

Foreign nationals may be required to register with the police.

> The holder is also required to register at once with the police.

(10) Limited leave to enter (straight time)

Endorsed in the case of working holidaymakers, certain permit free categories, and dependants of persons admitted on (3) above, for example, students' wives and children.

> Leave to enter the United Kingdom is hereby given for/until

(11) Further leave to enter within the period of the previous leave

Leave to enter granted to students, working holidaymakers, employed and self-employed persons, persons of independent means, and, where applicable, their wives and children, who have already obtained stamp 8(c).

> Given leave to enter—Section 3 [3] [b].

(12) Indefinite leave to enter

Endorsed in the case of passengers who qualify for settlement on arrival: for example, holders of 'settlement' entry clearances, such as wives and children of people already settled in the UK, parents, grandparents and relatives.

> Given leave to enter the United Kingdom for an indefinite period.

(13) Indefinite leave to enter under para 6(1) of Schedule 2

Endorsement in circumstances where more than 12 hours has elapsed after the conclusion of a passenger's examination without a decision to grant or refuse leave to enter. Has been endorsed where the following has occurred: (i) extension of stay without stamp 8 (c) and (ii) readmission with stamp 11 (which renders the endorsement meaningless).

> Given leave to enter the United Kingdom for an indefinite period. under the provisions of para 6(1) of Schedule 2.

Where there is no additional wording accompanying the stamp the immigration officer will have given leave to enter for an indefinite period, if the passenger is subject to immigration control. This is the usual practice in the case of returning residents. It is common practice for an immigration officer to date stamp the passport of those who are specifically exempted from control under the Act (for example, members of diplomatic missions): the stamp is simply evidence of the date of arrival and does not confer indefinite leave to remain.

Landing Cards

All passengers other than EEC nationals are required to complete landing cards on arrival and hand them to immigration with the passport. An endorsement will be made on the landing card identical to that contained in the passport. Passengers are required on departure to complete an embarkation card.

(14) Landing Card serial numbers

New style landing cards were introduced on 1 May 1980. The cards are printed with a serial number comprising two letters and six figures. The number is now copied by the immigration officer onto the passport below the stamp granting leave to enter.

The number is also inserted by the immigration officer on the embarkation card. The pairing of landing and embarking cards is now computerised. The Home Office states that the computer 'relies primarily on these numbers'. The present system provides 'a positive identification for record purposes and overcomes the difficulty of matching nominal records'. The number has 'no other significance, but it could indicate when and where the card was printed'.[1]

(C) After Entry

Where leave to remain is granted, similar endorsements to those made on entry are placed in the passport by the Home Office officials in the Immigration and Nationality Department at Croydon. A pentagonal stamp is used.

---

[1] H. of C. Official Report 17 July 1980, Written Answers, Cols. 658–659. Letters from Mr. Timothy Raison, Minister of State, Home Office to Lord Avebury, 22 August and 18 September 1980.

CERTIFICATES AND ENDORSEMENTS 369

(15) Limited leave to remain with a restriction on taking employment

See text to stamp (8).

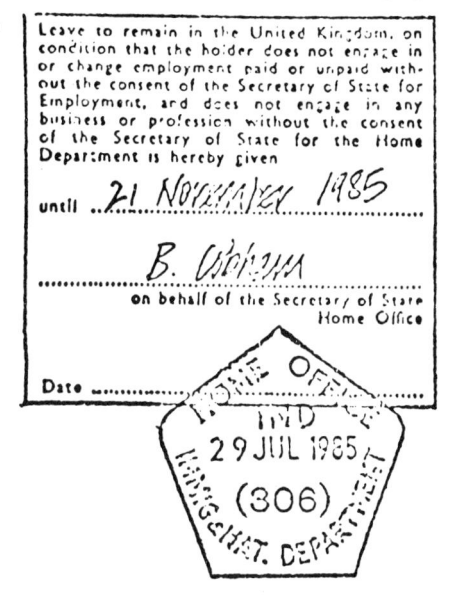

> Leave to remain in the United Kingdom, on condition that the holder does not engage in or change employment paid or unpaid without the consent of the Secretary of State for Employment, and does not engage in any business or profession without the consent of the Secretary of State for the Home Department is hereby given
>
> until 21 November 1985
>
> B. Oldham
> on behalf of the Secretary of State
> Home Office
>
> Date ....
>
> [HOME OFFICE I.N.D. 29 JUL 1985 (306) IMMIGRATION DEPARTMENT stamp]

(16) Limited leave to remain with a prohibition on taking employment

See text to stamp (9).

> Leave to remain in the United Kingdom, on condition that the holder does not engage in employment paid or unpaid and does not engage in any business or profession, is hereby given
>
> until 21 November 1985
>
> B. Oldham
> on behalf of the Secretary of State
> Home Office
>
> Date ....
>
> [HOME OFFICE I.N.D. 29 JUL 1985 (306) IMMIGRATION DEPARTMENT stamp]

(17) Limited leave to remain (straight time)

See text to stamp (10).

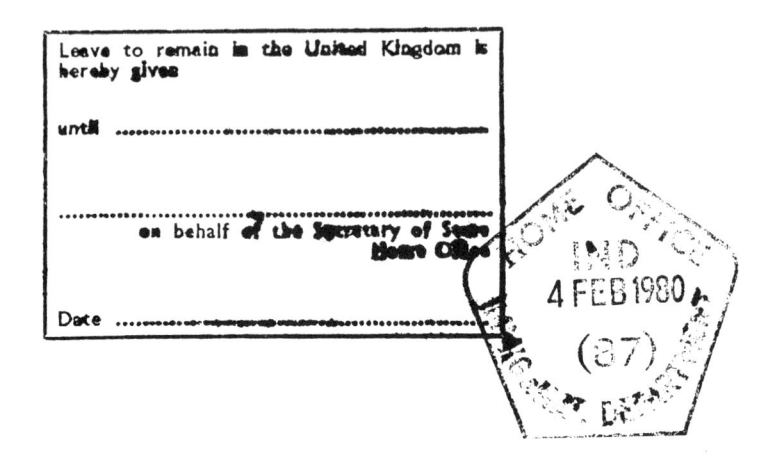

> Leave to remain in the United Kingdom is hereby given
>
> until ....
>
> ....
> on behalf of the Secretary of State
> Home Office
>
> Date ....

HOME OFFICE I.N.D. 4 FEB 1980 (87) IMMIGRATION DEPARTMENT

(18) Indefinite leave to remain

Endorsed in the case of those who qualify for settlement after having been given entry for a limited period, for example, husbands after 12 months and work permit holders after four years.

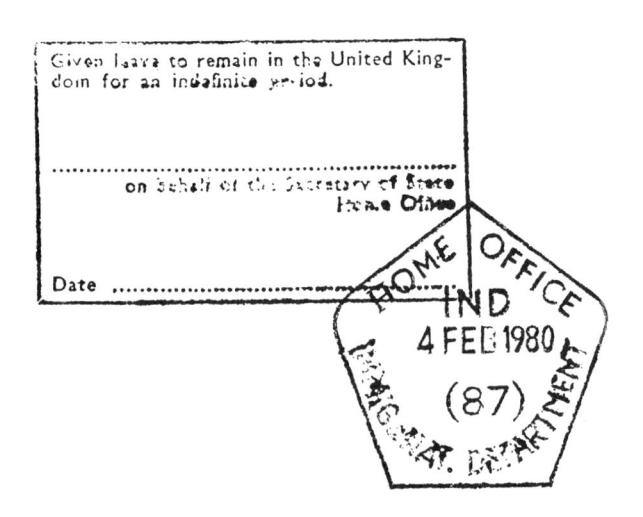

> Given leave to remain in the United Kingdom for an indefinite period.
>
> ....
> on behalf of the Secretary of State
> Home Office
>
> Date ....

HOME OFFICE I.N.D. 4 FEB 1980 (87) IMMIGRATION DEPARTMENT

(19)
See text to stamp 8 (c).

This will apply, unless superseded, to any subsequent leave the holder may obtain after an absence from the United Kingdom within the period limited above

(D) On Departure

(20)
The following triangular endorsement will be placed in the passport.

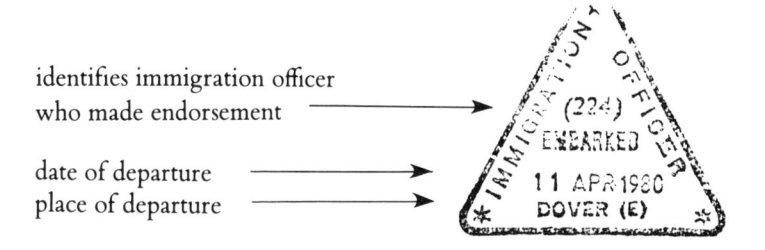

identifies immigration officer who made endorsement ⟶

date of departure ⟶
place of departure ⟶

```
*IMMIGRATION OFFICER*
(224)
EMBARKED
11 APR 1980
DOVER (E)
```

MARKINGS ON THE ENDORSEMENTS

These markings (which are made in pen) may be helpful in that they explain in greater detail the immigration history of the passport holder; and, more importantly, indicate the view taken of the holder by the immigration authorities.

(A) Before Entry

This indicates that the passenger applied for an entry certificate but clearance could not immediately be issued.

E.C. Applied for
Bombay
17 April 1980

(2)
The underlining indicates that entry clearance was refused.

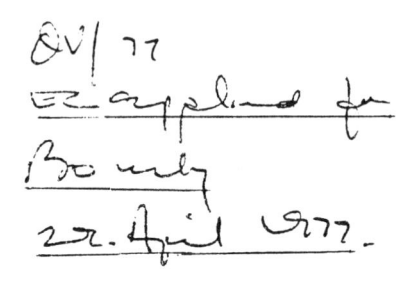

(3) and (4)
Identical markings operate in respect of visas.

(B) On Entry
(5)
Indicates that the passenger has been refused entry to the UK.

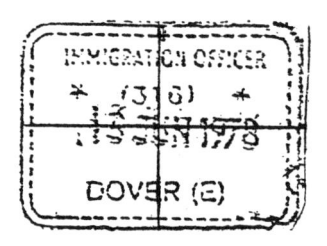

CERTIFICATES AND ENDORSEMENTS

(6)

This indicates that after an initial examination by an immigration officer, the passenger was issued with a form requiring him to submit to a further examination (Form IS81) and the passenger decided to return before a decision was made. The passenger has not been refused entry and therefore the right of appeal against refusal does not arise.

> *Issued with form IS81 at Heathrow on 6th Jan 1975*

(7)

Note that (1) appears between the words 'ONE' and 'MONTH' and compare the normal stamp on entry shown earlier. The (1) indicates that a report has been sent by the immigration service to the Home Office. If entry is given, e.g., for three months then (3) will appear between the lettering.

> Leave to enter the United Kingdom on condition that the holder does not enter employment paid or unpaid and does not engage in any business or profession, is hereby given for/until *ONE (1) MONTH*

> IMMIGRATION OFFICER
> ✳ (20) ✳
> 11 DEC 1978
> HEATHROW (1)

(8)

Certain non-EEC foreign nationals require entry clearance (in the form of a visa stamped in the passport) before they will be admitted to the United Kingdom even in a temporary capacity, e.g. a visit. This visa must be applied for before departure. However 'visa nationals' occasionally arrive without having obtained a visa and the immigration officer may admit them. The 'W' indicates that the passenger has been given leave to enter without a visa and has been warned that he must obtain a visa before departure on the next occasion.

(9)

The 'X' indicates that the passenger is a Commonwealth working holidaymaker.

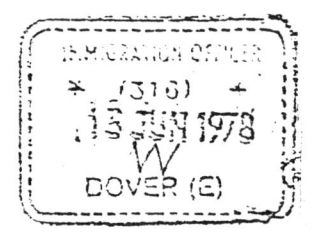

(C) After Entry

(10)

This is a Home Office file number endorsed on the inside back cover of the passport. This number should always be quoted in correspondence with the Home Office.

G 987654

(11)

If on a first application to the Home Office for an extension of stay the application is refused, the passport will be returned to the applicant with the date of expiry of the last leave to enter underlined; or

Leave to enter the United Kingdom, on condition that the holder does not enter employment paid or unpaid and does not engage in any business or profession, is hereby given for *until*

ONE MONTH

−1 JUN 1980
FOLKESTONE

(12)

the date when the leave was given underlined.

GIVEN LEAVE TO ENTER THE
UNITED KINGDOM FOR SIX MONTHS

IMMIGRATION
−4 OCT 1979
GATWICK

(13)

Similarly, if on a second or further application, the application is refused, the Home Office may return the passport underlining the date of expiry of the last extension.

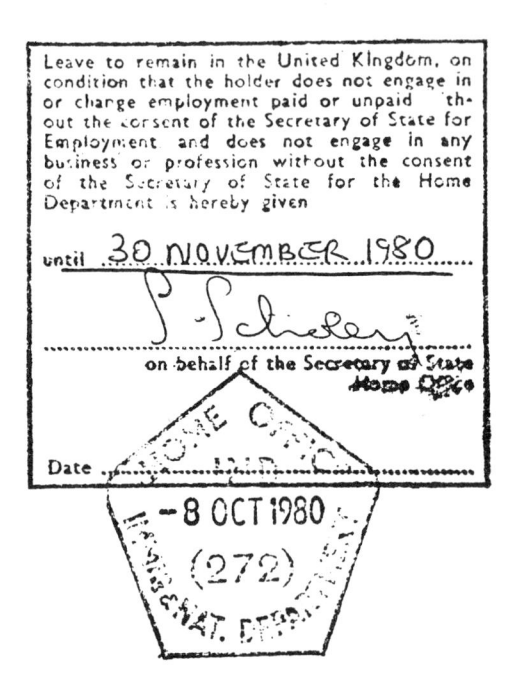

> Leave to remain in the United Kingdom, on condition that the holder does not engage in or change employment paid or unpaid thout the consent of the Secretary of State for Employment and does not engage in any business or profession without the consent of the Secretary of State for the Home Department is hereby given
>
> until 30 NOVEMBER 1980
>
> J. Schley
>
> on behalf of the Secretary of State Home Office
>
> Date ...
>
> −8 OCT 1980
> (272)

The underlinings of these stamps ((11)–(13) above) indicate to an immigration officer on any subsequent entry
either
  (i) the passenger had been told to leave because he no longer qualifies to remain in the UK; *or*
  (ii) the passenger has overstayed or contravened or attempted to contravene the conditions attached to his stay; *or*
  (iii) the Home Office know something against the passenger but this information would not necessarily justify refusal of leave to enter.

(14)

The Home Office may return a passport after an application with the letters 'EMB' written under the last admission stamp or extension. This indicates that the Home Office requires confirmation by the immigration office of departure. This marking may appear on the inside back cover of a new passport. It indicates the same information as in (2) – (4) above. (It is used because as the passport is new, there is no entry which can be underlined.)

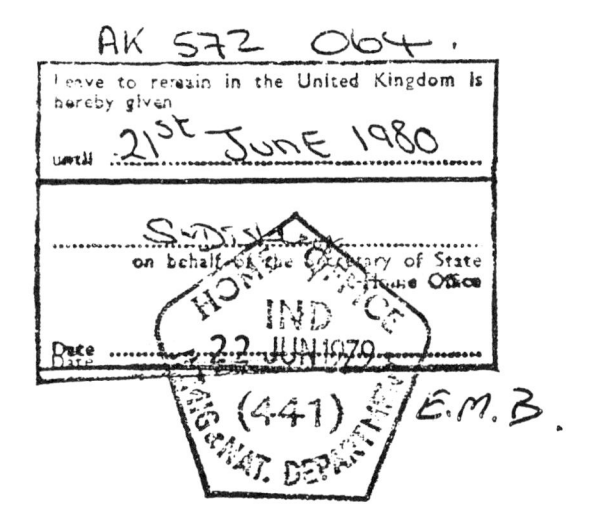

AK 572 064.

Leave to remain in the United Kingdom is hereby given

until 21st June 1980

on behalf of the Secretary of State Home Office

Date 22 JUN 1979

(441)   E.M.B.

(D) On Departure

(15)

The number on the stamp is underlined. This indicates that either

(1) the immigration officer believes the passport to be false: or
(2) the passenger has obtained a new passport in place of the first one and he is using the embarkation stamp as evidence of residence in the UK.

This stamp is only used where the immigration officer has information about the passenger on these matters which cannot be seen from an examination of the passport. A report will have been submitted to the Immigration Service Intelligence Unit. A copy of the report remains on the port files.

(16)

The date on the stamp is underlined. This indicates that the passenger is being deported or embarking under supervised departure arrangements.

CERTIFICATES AND ENDORSEMENTS 379

(17)

This endorsement appears only in Pakistani and Bangladesh passports and indicates who is embarking.

holder only / holder & wife /
holder w/ife and 3 children

APPENDIX THREE

Detention under Immigration Act 1971

Power	Authority	Circumstances	Length of detention	Release: Appeal against Detention – Bail	Other forms of Release
(1) *Liability to examination on entry* sch 2, para 2 — Sch 2 para 16(1)	Immigration Officer	All	pending decision to give or refuse leave to enter	To adjudicator if in custody seven days without decision sch 2, para 22 (1)	Temporary admission by Immigration Officer sch 2, para 21 (1)

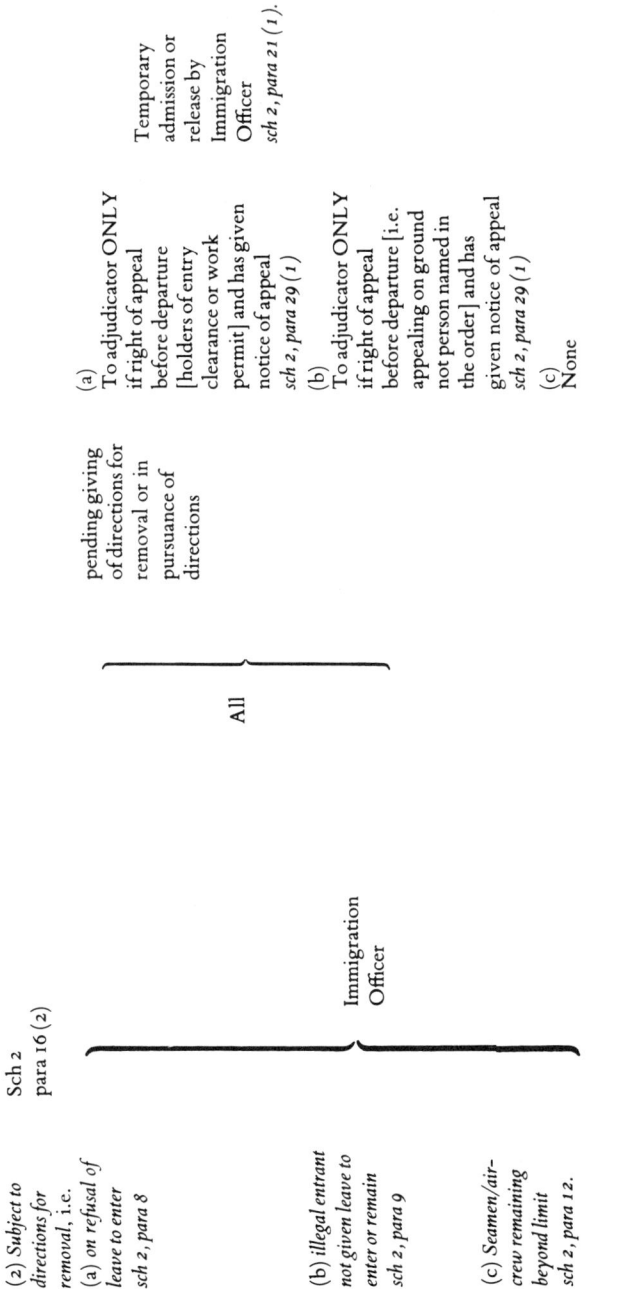

(2) *Subject to directions for removal*, i.e.	Sch 2 para 16 (2)		
(a) *on refusal of leave to enter* sch 2, para 8		pending giving of directions for removal or in pursuance of directions	(a) To adjudicator ONLY if right of appeal before departure [holders of entry clearance or work permit] and has given notice of appeal sch 2, para 29 (1)
(b) *illegal entrant not given leave to enter or remain* sch 2, para 9	Immigration Officer	All	(b) To adjudicator ONLY if right of appeal before departure [i.e. appealing on ground not person named in the order] and has given notice of appeal sch 2, para 29 (1)
(c) *Seamen/air-crew remaining beyond limit* sch 2, para 12.			(c) None
			Temporary admission or release by Immigration Officer sch 2, para 21 (1).

	Power	Authority	Circumstances	Length of detention	Appeal against Detention – Bail	Other forms of Release
(3) *Recommended for deportation by court*	Sch 3 para 2 (1)	Criminal Court (including appeal courts)	(i) No sentence of imprisonment by that or any other court subsists; *and* (ii) not on bail by any other Court. ONLY IF COURT DIRECTS RELEASE pending consideration of recommendation	pending making of deportation order	None	Appeal to Criminal Appeal Court but only if appeal against recommendation successful. By Secretary of State pending further consideration of case
(4) *Notice of decision to deport given*	Sch 3 para 2 (2)	Secretary of State	(i) Not under any prison sentence; *or* (ii) not on bail ONLY IF SECRETARY OF STATE DIRECTS	pending making of deportation order	To adjudicator once appeal lodged against decision *sch 3 para 3*	By Secretary of State

(5) Deportation order in force	Sch. 3 para 3	Secretary of State	(1) Where *not* in detention at time order made IF SECRETARY OF STATE DIRECTS; (ii) where in detention at time order made, DETENTION CONTINUES UNLESS SECRETARY OF STATE OTHERWISE DIRECTS	pending departure from UK	None	By Secretary of State
(6) Criminal offences illegal entry, overstaying working without permission and other offences concerning breach of control under s. 24	S. 24 (2)	Police Constable, Immigration Officer	Arrest without warrant anyone (1) who has; or (2) whom with reasonable cause is suspected of committing an offence (other than offence of of refusing to report to a medical officer)	pending charge and appearance in court or release	Police bail. Bail by court	

	Power	Authority	Circumstances	Length of detention	Release	
					Appeal against Detention – Bail	*Other forms of Release*
(7) Criminal offences assisting illegal entry and harbouring s. 25	S. 25 (3)	Police Constable, Immigration Officer	Arrest without warrant anyone (1) who has (2) who with reasonable cause is suspected of committing an offence	pending charge and appearance in court or release	Police bail. Bail by court	—

APPENDIX FOUR

Immigration Appeals Machinery

Decision appealed against	Limitations on right of appeal	To whom	From Inside UK	From Outside UK	Must be dismissed	Time limit for appealing following refusal
Refusal of Leave to Enter [by Immigration Officer at port of entry] S. 13 (1)	1. No appeal where Secretary of State certifies *personally* that entry not conducive to public good or leave to enter refused in obedience to such directions. 2. No appeal on ground that he is patrial if circumstances set out in S. 13 (3) apply. But note *Phansopkar* see para. 2.49	Adjudicator	1. If already given entry clearance. 2. If holding a current work permit	All other circumstances	If at time of refusal: 1. Illegal entrant. 2. Deportation order in force	If right of appeal from *outside UK only*: after departure and not later than 28 days thereafter. *In all other cases*: before or after departure but not later than 28 days thereafter
Refusal of Entry Clearance (by entry clearance	No appeal where Secretary of State certifies *personally* that entry not conducive to	Adjudicator	—	All circumstances	—	Three months

Decision appealed against	Limitations on right of appeal	To whom	From Inside UK	From Outside UK	Must be dismissed	Time limit for appealing following refusal
officer at place of departure or by Secretary of State if non-visa national applies in UK) S. 13 (3)	public good or entry clearance refused in obedience to such directions					
Refusal of Certificate of Patriality S. 13 (2)		Adjudicator	If application is made after entry from within UK	If application is made from outside UK	———	If refusal by ECO, three months. If refusal by Secretary of State, 14 days
Variation of stay (duration or conditions); or refusal to vary S. 14 (1)	No appeal if: 1. Secretary of State certifies departure from UK conducive to public good as being in interests of *national security*, etc., or decision appealed against was taken on that ground by *Secretary of State personally*. 2. Variation made by statutory instrument or refusal by Secretary of State to make statutory instrument. 3. Application made after leave has expired	Adjudicator	In all circumstances and appellant can remain until appeal heard		———	14 days

Decision to deport made by Secretary of State: Overstaying S. 3 (5) (a) and S. 15 (1) (a)		Adjudicator	In all circumstances. Can remain until appeal heard. Deportation order cannot be signed by Secretary of State while time for appealing; or if appealed, until heard	14 days
Decision to deport: conducive to the public good S. 3 (5) (b) and S. 15 (1) (a)	No appeal if Secretary of State certifies conducive to public good as being in interests of national security, etc. (except application can be made to Security Panel)	Tribunal	Ditto	14 days
Decision to deport: family deportation S. 3 (5) (c) and S. 15 (1) (a)		Tribunal	Ditto	14 days

Decision appealed against	Limitations on right of appeal	To whom	Inside UK	From Outside UK	Must be dismissed	Time limit for appealing following refusal
Recommendation for deportation made by Court	Right of appeal to criminal appeal court in normal way otherwise no right of appeal in any circumstances (except against destination)	—	—	—	—	—
Refusal to revoke deportation order S. 15 (1) (a)	No appeal if Secretary of State certifies conducive to public good or refusal by Secretary of State *personally* on that ground	Adjudicator	—	In all circumstances	If appellant still in UK because failed to comply with request to leave or because contravening prohibition on re-entering	28 days
Removal on ground illegal entrant having entered in breach of deportation order S. 16 (1) (a)	Right of appeal on ground that in law no power to give direction for removal. Cannot dispute validity of original order	Adjudicator	Only on ground not person named in order	In all other circumstances	—	If right of appeal from *outside UK only*: after departure and not later than 28 days thereafter. *In all other cases*: before or after departure but not later than 28 days thereafter

Removal on ground illegal entrant S. 16(1)(a)	Right of appeal on ground that in law no power to give directions for removal	Adjudicator	Only if deportation order made against him and appeals on ground not person named in order	Ditto	Ditto
Removal of Seamen/ Aircrew (coming to UK to join ship or aircraft and then absconds) S. 16(1)(b)	Right of appeal on ground that in law no power to give directions for removal	Adjudicator	Only on ground not person named in order	Ditto	Even if ground of appeal made out if there were power by Secretary of State to give directions for removal on ground that the appellant illegal entrant	*If right of appeal from outside UK only:* after departure and not later than 28 days thereafter. *In all other cases:* before or after departure but not later than 28 days thereafter
Removal on ground that direction for removal invalid	No right of appeal whatsoever except in circumstances under S. 16(1) above	—	—	—	—

Decision appealed against	Limitations on right of appeal	To whom	From Inside UK	From Outside UK	Must be dismissed	Time limit for appealing following refusal
Removal to a particular destination S. 17 (1)	Right of appeal in following circumstances only: 1. *Refusal of leave to enter but only if* (i) also appealing against refusal to give leave or decision that leave is required and (ii) has current clearance or work permit when refused.	Adjudicator	Yes	—	If cannot specify another country willing to accept him	Where directions given on being refused leave to enter: at any time before departure. In all other cases: not later than 14 days after giving directions
	2. *Deportation order made against him.* Objection must be made in both cases of appeal against deportation.	Adjudicator	Only if appealing on ground that he is not person named in deportation order	In all other circumstances		
	3. *Entry in breach of deportation order*	Adjudicator				
Refusal of or delay in issuing or method of allocating Special Vouchers to Citizens of UK and Colonies	No right of appeal	—	—	—	—	—

Refusal of Department of Employment (DE) to issue work permits to approve training schemes or of Home Office to refer applicants to DE	No right of appeal	—	—	—	—
Making of a hostage order under S. 3(8)	No right of appeal	—	—	—	—
Removal/Exclusion under Prevention of Terrorism Act 1976	No right of appeal (but representations to adviser)	—	—	—	—

APPEAL FROM ADJUDICATOR TO TRIBUNAL

[by 'Any party if dissatisfied': S. 20]

Without Leave

1. Refusal of leave to enter where appellant holds certificate of patriality. S. 22 (5) (a)
2. Refusal of leave to enter where appellant holds current entry clearance or work permit. S. 22 (5) (b)

With Leave

1. Appeal under any provision of Act except variation of *conditions* of stay or refusal to vary conditions.
   (Note there is a right of appeal against variation or refusal to vary *time limit* attached to stay.)
2. Leave is discretionary but must be granted
   (a) if appeal turns on arguable point of law,
   (b) if adjudicator has dismissed appeal but appellant cannot be removed to country specified for fear of persecution there

Time limit for appealing:
See Immigration Appeals (Procedure) Rules 1972
If to the adjudicator: forthwith after his determination
If to Tribunal: 14 days, but if outside UK and Islands 42 days after determination

Note limited power to grant extension of time to appeal – Rule 11 (4) and see *R v Secretary of State for Home Department ex parte Mehta (RP)* (1975). See para. 14.17.

APPENDIX FIVE

Agencies advising immigrants

Joint Council for the Welfare of Immigrants

44 Theobalds Road, London WC1X 8SP. Telephone 01-405 5527

JCWI is a national voluntary organisation established in 1967, whose policy is to retain full independence of government by not seeking government funding. It operates a single office in central London, and has a staff of ten. Its advice on the whole range of immigration and nationality law procedures is available to other voluntary organisations and direct to clients, who are seen by appointment: services are provided free of charge. It provides representation at immigration appeals in limited circumstances only. It is also a campaigning organisation, and in 1976 joined with the National Council for Civil Liberties and the National Association of Community Relations Councils to establish the Action Group on Immigration and Nationality (AGIN). Membership of JCWI is open to organisations and individuals, and these elect its Executive Committee.

United Kingdom Immigrants Advisory Service

Central Office: Brettenham House, 7th Floor, Savoy Street, Strand, London WC2E 7EN. Telephone 01-240 5176

UKIAS is a national voluntary organisation established in 1970 on the recommendation of a working party convened by the Home Office, and is funded by the Home Office under section 23 of the Immigration Act 1971. It maintains offices in London and at a number of ports in the UK. The notice of right of appeal given by the Home Office advises appellants of the availability of assistance from UKIAS and it represents a substantial proportion of all immigration appeals, as well as giving general immigration advice. No charge is made for its services. Organisations may become associate members, and these elect two representatives to the Executive Committee. (See also Refugee Unit, below.)

Other UKIAS offices

Thanet House
Room 004,
231 Strand,
London WC2R 1DA
(01–353 8060, Ext. 11)

Gatwick
Room 550, 5th Floor,
Terminal Office Block,
Gatwick Airport,
Horley, Surrey
(0293 33385)

Harmondsworth
Government Buildings,
Colnbrook By-Pass,
Harmondsworth,
Middx
(01–897 9167/1514)

Heathrow
Room 0001A, Queens Building,
Heathrow Airport,
Hounslow, Middx
(01–759 9234/7376)

Birmingham
Government Buildings,
Clay Lane,
Yardley,
Birmingham 26
(021–706 9765/4256)

Channel Ports
Platform One,
Folkestone Harbour,
Folkestone, Kent
(0303 57829)

Glasgow
2nd Floor,
115 Wellington Street
Glasgow G2
(041–227 6051)

Leeds
14 Eldon Terrace,
Woodhouse Lane,
Leeds LS2 9AB
(0532 42460)

Manchester
Elliot House,
2 Jackson's Row,
Deansgate,
Manchester M2
(061–834 9942/5370)

Southampton
Clifford House, 2nd Floor,
New Road,
Southampton,
Hants SO2 0AB
(0703 25126)

Other organisations giving general immigration advice

Immigration advice is available locally at some citizens advice bureaux, law centres, community relations councils, ethnic minority organisations and other community organisations: it is not possible to detail or assess the availability of competent advice in different local areas. *Citizens Advice Bureaux* have available to assist them in advising the written information and telephone advice of the National Association of Citizens Advice Bureaux. A directory of *legal advice and law centres* can be obtained from the Legal Action Group, 28A Highgate Road, London NW5. A list of *community relations councils* can be obtained from the Commission for Racial Equality, Elliot House, 10/12 Allington Street, London SW1E 5EH.

Some of the best assistance in local areas is provided by organisations which are not easily categorised. Examples of well-established local immigration advice services with advisers speaking appropriate languages are the Asian Resource Centre in *Birmingham* (101 Villa Road, Handsworth, Birmingham) and the Self-Help Neighbourhood Project in *Leicester* (65 Melton Road, Leicester).

International Social Service of Great Britain

Cranmer House, 39 Brixton Road, London SW9 6DD   Telephone 01-735 8941/4

ISS is an independent branch of the international organisation which has its headquarters in Geneva. It operates an inter-country casework service for social workers and others needing information, reports or the mobilising of social work help in countries abroad for the benefit of their clients. This can include providing supporting information on social condition for immigration appeals. It operates, on behalf of the Home Office, the repatriation provisions of the Immigration Act 1971 for immigrants wishing to return home. It also advises on the procedures for inter-country adoption but does not bring children to this country for adoptive placement.

Kent Committee for the Welfare of Migrants

39 Limes Road, Folkestone, CT19 4NU.   Telephone 0303 75920

The Committee was set up at the Channel ports in 1963 with the object of providing welfare assistance for migrants who face difficulty with immigration control. The Committee was responsible for setting up

welfare services in Calais (45 Quai du Rhin, telephone
010 33 21-34 36 62) and Ostend (12 Kerkstraat, telephone
010 32 59-80 30 45).

National Union of Students

3 Endsleigh Street, London WC1. Telephone 01-387 1277

NUS gives general advice on application for entry and stay to members of the union only.

United Kingdom Council for Overseas Student Affairs

60 Westbourne Grove, London W2. Telephone 01-229 9268/9

UKCOSA is a focal point for action and research in the field of overseas student affairs. Services to institutions and organisations include regular mailings of journal, UKCOSA NEWS, guidance leaflets for advisers on specialist topics and information sheets for students. Immigration issues make up an important part of all these activities, but UKCOSA also seeks to improve immigration practices and procedures affecting overseas students by representations to the Home Office.

REFUGEES

UKIAS Refugee Unit

Brettenham House, 8th Floor, Savoy Street, Strand, London WC2E 7EN. Telephone 01-379 7969

The Refugee Unit is funded by the United Nations High Commissioner for Refugees. The Unit gives general advice on refugee status and asylum, makes application to the Home Office for asylum, and represents those refused on appeal in appropriate cases. The Unit will give evidence on request about asylum in general but will only give opinions in individual cases after interview.

British Refugee Council

Bondway House, 3-9 Bondway, Vauxhall, London SW8 1SJ. Telephone 01-582 6922

The British Refugee Council offers counselling and assistance to all refugees in the UK. Help is given in finding accommodation; in applying for welfare benefits, if needed; in enrolment in English classes; in finding employment or training courses, and in providing for other needs.

APPENDIX SIX

Some Useful Addresses and Telephone Numbers

HOME OFFICE

Immigration and Nationality Department, Lunar House, Wellesley Road, Croydon, Surrey CR9 2BY.
 Immigration inquiries: 01–686 0688
 Nationality inquiries: 01–681 3421

PORTS OF ENTRY: *Immigration Service and Detention Areas*

London
 Heathrow Terminal 1: 01–759 7715/6
  Terminal 2: 01–759 7105 and 7911
  Terminal 3: 01–897 9631
   Queen's Building Detention: 01–759 9280 and 9372,
 Harmondsworth Detention Centre 01–897 2302
  Securicor: 01–897 8040
  Detainees: 01–759 1849
  Harmondsworth Intelligence Unit: 01–897 0771
  Isis House: 01–928 6824
Belfast: 0232 22547
   08494 52500 (weekends)
Birmingham
  Immigration: 021–743 4272
  Detention: 021–743 2813

Bristol: **027587 2843**
Cardiff: **0222 396127**
Dover East
  Immigration: **0304 204192**
  Detention: **0304 206260**
Dover West
  Immigration: **0304 201913**
  Detention: **0304 203203, ext. 3308**
Dover Hoverport: **0304 207513**
Edinburgh: **031–344 3330**
Folkestone
  Immigration: **0303 56541**
  Detention: **0303 54202**
Gatwick
  Immigration: **0293 28822**
  Detention: **0293 30731 and 24284**
Glasgow: **041–887 4115**
Gravesend: **0474 52308**
Harwich
  Immigration: **02555 4371**
  Detention: **02555 2141**
Hull: **0482 223017**
Leeds: **0532 603126**
Liverpool: **051–236 8974**
Luton: **0582 421891**
Manchester Ringway: **061–437 2402**
Newcastle: **0632 869469**
Prestwick: **029 78675**
Ramsgate: **0843 54716**
Sheerness: **07956 67733**
Southampton: **0703 26970**

IMMIGRATION APPEALS OFFICES

London
  Thanet House, 231 Strand, London WC2 1DA: **01–353 8060**
  Harmondsworth Government Buildings, Colnbrook By-Pass, Harmondsworth, West Drayton, Middlesex: **01–897 9641**
Birmingham
  Government Buildings, Clay Lane, Yardley, Birmingham, B26 1EA: **021–706 4382/3**

Dover
 2nd floor, 72/75 Maison Dieu Road, Dover, Kent CT16 1RE: **0304 206494**
Gatwick
 Roof Office Block, Terminal Building, Gatwick Airport, Horley, Surrey: **0293 32754**
Leeds
 1, Tranquility, Crossgates, Leeds, LS15 8QT: **0532 603126**
Manchester
 3rd Floor, Aldine House, New Bailey Street, Salford, Manchester: **061–832 9571**, ext. **338/339**
Southampton
 Clifford House, Six Dials, New Road, Southampton, Hants: **0703 26970**
Part Time Offices

Belfast: **0232 22547**
Bristol: **0272 823157**
Cardiff: **0222 396127**
Edinburgh: **031–344 3330**
Glasgow: **041–887 4115**

PASSPORT OFFICES

London
 Clive House, 70 Petty France, London SW1H 9HD
  surnames: A–D: **01–213 3344**
       E–K: **01–213 7272**
       L–Q: **01–213 6161**
       R–Z: **01–213 3434**
Belfast
 Foreign and Commonwealth Office Passport Agency, Marlborough House, 30 Victoria Street, Belfast, BT1 3LY: **0232 32371**
Glasgow
 1st Floor, Empire House, 131 West Nile Street, Glasgow G1 2RY: **041–332 0271**
Liverpool
 5th Floor, India Buildings, Water Street, Liverpool, L2 0QZ: **051–227 3070**
Newport
 Olympia House, Upper Dock Street, Newport, Gwent: **0633 52431**

Peterborough
55, Westfield Road, Peterborough, PE3 6TG: **0733 895555**

OTHER GOVERNMENT DEPARTMENTS

Aliens Registration Office, 10 Lamb's Conduit Street, London WC1 3MX: **01–725 2458**
(Deportation Section): **01–725 2196/7/8**

Department of Employment, Overseas Labour Section, Caxton House, Tothill Street, London SW1: **01–213 6055**

Department of Health and Social Security, Overseas Branch, Longbenton, Newcastle-upon-Tyne, NE98 1YX: **0632 793356**

Foreign and Commonwealth Office, Migration and Visa Department, Clive House, 70 Petty France, London SW1H 9HD: **01–213 6033**

Foreign and Commonwealth Office, Nationality and Treaty Department, Clive House, 70 Petty France, London SW1H 9HD: **01–213 3000**

Home Office (Ministers' Private Offices), Queen Anne's Gate, London SW1: **01–213 3000**

Manpower Services Commission, Employment Permits Branch, Netherleigh, Massey Avenue, Belfast BT4 2JP: **0232 63244**

OTHER USEFUL NUMBERS

Houses of Parliament: **01–219 3000**
Treasury Solicitor: **01–233 6975**
Home Office Presenting Officers, Africa House: **01–405 2716**
Immigration (Officers) Appeals Unit, Harmondsworth: **01–897 2919**

Index

accommodation and support 'without recourse to public funds', 357–61; for visitors, 93; for students and dependants, 100, 101; for workers etc., 118, 121, 123, 124, 125, 128, 129; for dependants of workers, etc., 131, 132; for dependants coming for settlement, 148
adjudicators, 287–8; appeals to, 292–305; powers and duties of, 301–5; *see also* appeals
adoption: acquisition of UK citizenship by, 18; and patriality, 28, 29; and entry for settlement, 163–4
Agee, Philip, 240
agricultural workers, *see* seasonal agricultural workers
aircrew, 51, 85, 119, 120; overstaying, 213, 285
airlines, responsibilities of, 75, 84, 86–7
'aliens', status of, 1–2, 14, 27, *et passim*
'amnesties' for illegal entrants, 265–6
Amnesty International, 328
appeals, 4–5, 286–321, 354–5; against refusal of leave to enter, 85–6, 88; against refusal to vary leave, 191–3; leaving UK while a. pending, 196–8; against deportation, 221–2, 225–6; against destination of removal, 226–7; against court's recommendation to deport, 247; of EEC nationals against deportation, 255–7; decisions appealable, 286–7; notice of right of a., 288–9; limitations on, 289–92; to the adjudicator, 287–8, 292–305; time-limits on, 292–5, 308, 317; notice of, 295–7, 307–8; explanatory statement and date for, 297–8; 'preliminary issues' at, 293, 299–300; grounds of, 296, 308–9; determined without hearing, 301–5, 306–7, 316–17; to Tribunal from adjudicator, 305–9; references by Home Secretary, 310; procedure at, 310–17; pre-trial procedures, 312; second, 'identical', 315; withdrawal of, 316; service of notices and documents for, 317
art students, 108
artists, 127–9; and settlement, 145
assisting illegal entry, 210, 216–17
asylum, *see* political asylum
'au pairs', 110–11; men as, 111; application to change category of, 188–9

bail: for passengers detained, 83, 270–74; for overstayers detained, 199; for deportees, 222, 280–85; for those charged with criminal offences, 279–83; *see also* detention
Bangladesh, queues for entry clearance in, 35
bind-over, departure by, 251
birth: UK citizenship by, 17–18; and patriality, 28, 29; and British Citizenship, 38
bone x-ray examinations, 78, 158
breach of conditions, *see* overstaying, limited leave
'British Citizenship' (1981 Nat. Act), 37, 38–40
British Dependent Territories citizenship, 37, 39
British Overseas Citizenship, 37–8, 40
British Protected Persons, 14, 27; naturalisation of, 22, 30–31; and patriality, 28, 30–31; and 1981 Nat. Act, 38, 39, 40; and special voucher scheme, 45

'British subject', definition of, 1, 25–7; and 1981 Nat. Act, 38
British Subjects without Citizenship, 27; and 1981 Nat. Act, 39, 40; and special voucher scheme, 45
burden of proof in appeals, 311–12
businessmen, 122–7; and 'old rules', 125, 126; EEC nationals as, 134–5, 136–8, 139, 140; and settlement, 145; application to change category of, 189

Caprino, Franco, 239–40
certificate of identity, 209, 334, 335
certificate of patriality, *see* patriality
certificate of registration with police, 207–8
Channel Islands, 16, 53–4; and EEC, 33–4
children: entry of as dependants, 155–64; 'sole responsibility' for, 158–9; and compassionate grounds, 160–61; aged over 18, 162–3; and 'old rules', 170; assisting sponsors of, 172; *see also* adoption, minors, wives and children
citizenship of the UK and colonies, 1, 3–4, 16–25; acquisition of, 17–23; loss of, 23–4; resumption of, 24–5; and exclusion orders, 340–41
'close relatives to turn to', 167
cohabitees, *see* 'permanent association'
collective passports, 51–2
colonies, 16–17
Commission for Racial Equality, 7 n. 19
common law: on 'subjects', 1; on 'aliens', 1–2
common travel area, 6, 44, 53–7; exclusion from provisions of, 55–7
Commonwealth citizenship, 1, 25–7; loss of, 26; countries of C., 26 n. 20; and patriality, 28, 32; and residents returning from Europe, 51–3
'Commonwealth citizens settled in UK at coming into force of Act': registration of, 19–20; exemption from deportation of, 142; wives and children of, 7, 143–4, 147; as returning residents, 180–81
'Commonwealth citizens with UK ancestry', 121

'compassionate grounds/circumstances': and children coming for settlement, 160; and other dependent relatives, 168–9; and deportation, 230–32, 235–6
'conducive to the public good', *see* deportation . . . conducive to the public good, exclusion conducive to the public good
consular officials, 50; private servants of, 119
Convention Relating to the Status of Refugees (1951), 322–7, 331, 333, 334–5, 337; 'Convention travel documents', 333, 334–5
Convention Relating to the Status of Stateless Persons (1954), 337–8
Court of Appeal, 318
court's recommendation to deport, 243–8; and bail, 280–83
crew members, *see*, airmen, seacrew
criminal convictions: as grounds for refusing entry, 71; and deportation conducive to public good, 233–4, 235, 236–8; and court's recommendation to deport, 243–8; and deportation of EEC nationals, 254
criminal offences connected with immigration, 210–20; time-limits for proceedings on, 210–11; illegal entry, 211–12; overstaying, 212, 213; failing to observe conditions of leave, 212–13; miscellaneous, 213–14; failing to co-operate with, or misleading, immigration authorities, 217–20; detention when charged with, 279–83; relating to exclusion orders, 341–2
curtailment of stay, 250–51

daughters aged 18–20, 156, 162
deception: and variation of leave, 189–90; and illegal entry, 260–65
declarations, *see* sponsorship declarations
declarations of identity, 209
dentists: as postgraduate students, 101; and employment, 107, 119, 191
dependants coming for settlement, 144, 147–73; of special-voucher holders, 46; general requirements

dependants coming for settlement—*cont.*
for, 148; wives, 148–55; children, 155–64; parents and grandparents, 164–7; other relatives, 167–9; and 'old rules', 170–71; assisting sponsors of, 171–3
deportation, 221–57, 353–4; of EEC nationals, 140, 252–7; exemptions from, 146, 222; of overstayers, 199–200; appeal against, 221–7; procedure on, 224–7; effect of d. order, 227; considerations on making d. order, 228–38; for breach of conditions, 229–32; conducive to the public good, 232–8; in 'security' cases, 238–40; family d., 240–43; on court's recommendation, 243–8; signing of d. order, 248; revocation of, 248–50; bail pending, 280–83; and political asylum, 324
deprivation of UK citizenship, 23–4
descent: acquisition of UK citizenship by, 18–19; and patriality, 28, 29–30; and acquisition of British Citizenship, 38
detention, 268–85, 353; of passengers arriving, 82–3, 268–76; of overstayers, 199; of deportees, 227; of illegal entrants, 276–9; when charged with criminal offences, 279–83; pending deportation, 280–85; under Prevention of Terrorism Act, 346
DHSS repatriation scheme, 257–9
diplomats, 48–50; private servants of, 119
'discrepancies' in entry-clearance applications: of wives, 149; of children 157–8
discretion in administration of rules, 350–51
'disguised employment', 123, 125, 127
'distressed relatives', *see* relatives
Divisional Court, 318–19
doctors: as postgraduate students, 101; and employment, 107, 119, 120, 191
domestic employment, 111, 114
'domicile' and polygamous marriages, 150–53

dual nationality, 22–3; and patriality, 28; and 1981 Nat. Act, 39
Dutch nationals, 43; *see also* EEC nationals
Dutschke, Rudi, 238–9

East African Asians, 3–4, 26, 38, 45, 47, 347, 348, 353–3; *see also* special voucher scheme, UK passport holders
EEC, patrials and, 33–4
EEC nationals: and immigration rules, 9, 136–40; special provisions for, 41–3; referral to medical inspector of, 70; as visitors, 99; as workers, 132–4, 135–9; as businessmen and self-employed, 134–5, 136–8, 139, 140; and 'provision of services', 135; families of, 135–6, 148; as persons of independent means, 136; and settlement, 145; and variation of leave, 187; exclusion and deportation of, 252–7
Eire, *see* Ireland
embarkation cards, 57, 345
employment: while a student, 107–8; of trainees, 109–110; with work permit, 112–18; permit-free, 118–20; extensions for, 117, 120, 121–2; of Commonwealth citizens with UK ancestry, 121, 348–9; of working holidaymakers, 121–2; under 'old rules', 122; EEC nationals coming for, 132–4, 135–9, 140; and settlement, 117, 120, 125, 128, 129, 139–40, 145; application to change category, 189; variation to allow e. after entry, 190–91; after leave has expired, 193–4
Employment, Department of, 107–8, 109–10, 113, 114–15, 116–17, 190–91
entry certificates, 60, 61; *see also* entry clearance
entry clearance, 59–65; validity of documents for, 63; false representations etc. in obtaining, 63–5; procedure for obtaining, 88–92; appeal against refusal of, 290–91; *see also* queues for entry clearance
entry clearance officers, 12, 59; powers and duties of, 91–2

INDEX

European Commission of Human Rights, 47, 175, 320–21, 347, 348
European Community, see EEC, EEC nationals
European Court of Human Rights, 320–21
European Court of Justice, 319
evidence at appeals, 302–4, 309, 312–13
examining officers (Prev. of Terrorism Act), 343–6
'exclusion conducive to the public good', 72–4
exclusion orders (Prev. of Terrorism Act), 339–43, 345; revocation of, 342
exit visas, 67
explanatory statements, 297–8
extensions of stay: for visitors, 94; for students, 108–9; for 'au pairs', 111; for work-permit holders, 117; for permit-free workers, 120; for 'working holidaymakers', 121–2; for businessmen and self-employed, 124–5; for writers and artists, 128, 129; see also variation of leave

families: of EEC nationals, 135–6, 137, 148; as defined in immigration rules, 350; see also dependants, wives and children
family deportations, 240–43
fiancées: coming for settlement, 144, 177; seeking limited leave, 178
fiancés: coming for settlement, 144, 173–4, 349; and 'old rules', 178–9; seeking limited leave, 177–8
'fishing expeditions', see raids
French nationals, 42–3; see also EEC nationals

Gibraltar: and EEC, 33; special provisions for, 42 n. 4
grandparents, see parents and grandparents
Greek nationals, 42 n. 10

habeas corpus, 82, 88, 227–9
harbouring illegal entrants or overstayers, 217
High Court, 317–19
Hosenball, Mark, 240

'hostage orders', 214
House of Lords, 318
husbands coming for settlement, 144, 173–7, 349; and 'old rules', 178–80; of EEC nationals, 135–6

illegal entrants: removal of, 85, 260–67; and criminal law, 220; detention of, 276–9
illegal entry: criminal offence of, 211–12; assisting, 210, 216–17; by deception, 260–65; pre-1968, 266–7
Immigration Appeal Tribunal, 12, 287, 288; appeals from adjudicator to, 305–9; powers of, 306–7; see also appeals
immigration officers, 12; powers and duties of, 74–7, 78–85, 214–16
immigration rules, 7–11, 349–50, *et passim*; 1973 rules, see 'old rules'
independence legislation and loss of UK citizenship, 23, 25–6
'independent means', persons of, 129–31; and 'old rules', 130–31; and settlement, 145; application to change category of, 189
India UK passport-holders in, 352–3
Indian law and dial nationality, 23
Indian sub-continent, queues for entry clearance in, 35, 88–90
International Social Service of Great Britain, 172, 395; repatriation scheme of, 258–9
Ireland, citizens of Republic of, 14, 25; registration of, 19–20; and patriality, 28; and 1981 Nat. Act, 38; entry into UK of, 44, 53–7
Ireland, Northern: and work-permits, 113 n. 5; see also common travel area, Prevention of Terrorism (Temporary Provisions) Act 1976
Islands, see Channels Islands, Isle of Man

Joint Council for the Welfare of Immigrants, 347, 359, 393
judicial review, 88, 317–19

Kenya, 3–4, 26

INDEX

landing cards, 57, 59, 345
language assistants, 119, 120
lawyers coming to UK for work, 124 n. 8
Legal Advice Scheme, 87
'letters of consent', Home-Office, 60, 61–2
limited leave, 186–209; *see also* extensions, variation of leave; leaving UK while with, 195–8; failure to observe conditions of, 212–13

maintenance 'without recourse to public funds', *see* accommodation and support . . .
Man, Isle of, 16, 53–4; and EEC, 33–4
'marriages of convenience', 173, 175, 178, 234
medical examinations, 78, 158, 213–14, 353
medical inspectors, 68–71; powers and duties of, 77–8
members of Parliament, *see* representations by MPs
mental patients, removal of, 251–2
midwives: students, 101; taking employment, 107
military personnel, 50–51
ministers of religion, 118
minors, registration of, 20–21
missionaries, *see* ministers of religion
MPs, *see* representations by MPs
multiple nationality, *see* dual nationality

National Council for Civil Liberties, 347
nationality, 14–40 *et passim*
naturalisation, 22–3, 147; by fraud etc., 23–4; and patriality, 28, 30–31; and British Citizenship, 39
non-patrial UK citizens, *see* UK passport-holders
non-patrials, special provisions for, 41–52
'notice of decision to deport', 224–5
nurses: student, 101, 102 n. 14; and employment, 107, 191

'old rules', 8–9, 348–9; and working holidaymakers, 122; and writers and artists, 128–9; and persons of independent means, 130–31; and workers' wives and children, 132; and dependants, 170–71; and husbands and fiancés, 178–80
'ordinarily resident', meaning of, 141–2; and returning residents, 182–4; and exemption from deportation, 222–4
out-of-time appeals, 293–5, 308, 317
overseas firms, representatives of, 118
overseas governments, representatives and employees of, 48–50, 119
overseas newspapers, representatives of, 119
overstayers, 199–202; and right of appeal, 192; taking employment, 193–4; applications for variation by, 195, 203; as criminal offenders, 212, 232; and deportation, 222, 229–32; of EEC nationals, 255

Pakistan: and 'old rules', 8; queues for entry clearance in, 35
Pakistani citizens, 26; and deportation, 223
'parent', meaning of for children's entry for settlement, 155–7
parents and grandparents coming for settlement, 164–7; 'dependency' of, 166–7; accommodation for, 167; and 'old rules', 171
passports: and entry into UK, 58–9; *see also* collective passports, travel documents, visitor's passports
patrial Commonwealth citizens, registration of, 20
'patrial wives', 32
patriality 6, 14–15, 28–37; patrial UK citizens, 29–31; loss of, 32; patrial Commonwealth citizens, 32; and the EEC, 33–4; certificates of, and entry into UK, 34–7; and 'certificates of entitlement' (1981 Nat. Act), 39–40; and settlement, 146–7; appeal against refusal of certificate of, 291
'permanent association' of man and woman, 153–4; and 'old rules', 170
permit-free employment, 66, 118–20; and settlement, 145

police: and service of refusal notices,
200–201; prosecuting overstayers,
201–2, 204; registration with, 205–8;
powers of, 214–16, 219–20
political asylum, 322–38; and restricted
returnability, 68; and deportation
orders, 223, 228–9; applications for,
327–33; granting of, 333–4; travel
documents and, 334–5; transfer of,
335–6; *see also* refugees
polygamous marriages, 150–53, 154
precedent in appeals, 305
'preliminary issues' at appeals, 293,
229–300
presenting officers, 311, 313–15
proxy marriages, 153

queues for entry clearance, 35, 88–90,
352
quota vouchers, *see* special voucher
scheme

racism in British immigration control,
347–56
raids, police/immigration, 214–15,
353
'recourse to public funds', *see*
accommodation and support . . .
re-entry visas, 196
refugees, 61, 145–6, 322–38; travel
documents for, 209; convention and
de facto, 333–4; loss of r. status,
336–7; agencies for, 338; *see also*
political asylum
refusal notices, 200–201
refusal of entry, 62–5; grounds for,
67–74; restricted returnability and,
67–8; medical reasons for, 68–71;
criminal convictions and, 71;
deportation order and, 72;
exclusions conducive to public
good, 72–4; general immigration
history and, 74; notification of
decision of, 80–81; to work-permit
holders, 116; limitations on appeal
against, 289–90; refusal rates,
351–2
refusal of variation of leave: general
principles, 188; right of appeal
against, 191–3; *see also* extensions,
variation of leave
'register of dependants', 13

registration as UK citizen, 19–21, 22–
3, 147; by entitlement, 19–20; of
minors, 20–21; of wives of UK
citizens, 21; of stateless persons, 21;
by fraud etc., 23; and patriality, 28,
30; and 1981 Nat. Act, 39
registration with police, 205–8
relatives as dependants for settlement,
167–9; and 'old rules', 171; assisting
sponsors of, 173
release from detention, *see* bail,
temporary admission, temporary
release
religious orders, members of, 118
removal from UK: of passengers
refused entry, 84–5, 87–8; of illegal
entrants, 85, 353; of deportees, 226;
under exclusion order, 341, 345; *see
also* deportation
renunciation of UK citizenship, 23
repatriation schemes, 257–9
representation at appeals, 310–11
representations by MPs: on
registration and naturalisation, 22; to
prevent removal of passengers, 87–
8; for those refused variation of
leave, 201–2, 203–4; against
deportation, 247–8; for temporary
release, 276; against exclusion
orders, 341
residence permits (for EEC nationals),
138–9
'resident', *see* 'ordinarily resident'
'restricted returnability', 67–8
resumption of UK citizenship, 24–5
returning residents, 180–85; and
'ordinary residence', 182–4; absent
longer than 2 years, 184–5
revocation: of deportation orders, 72,
221–2, 248–50; of exclusion orders,
342
'right of abode', 6, 14; and 1981 Nat.
Act, 40; and deportation, 223–4; *see
also* patriality

seamen, 51, 85, 119, 120; overstaying,
213, 285
seasonal agricultural workers, 119, 120
'Secretary of State', 11
'section 3(3)(b) endorsements', 196
Securicor Ltd, 82, 219, 269
security cases, and deportation, 238–40

self-employed persons, 122–7; and 'old rules', 125–6; EEC nationals as, 134–5, 136–8, 139, 140; and settlement, 145; application to change category of, 189
settlement, 141–85; or workers etc., 117, 120, 125, 128, 129; of EEC workers, 139–40; meaning of, 141–2, 146; in UK when Act came into force, 142–4; qualifying under rules for, 144–6; and patriality, 28, 31, 146–7; of dependants, 147–73; of husbands and fiancés, 173–7, 178–80; of fiancées and wives, 177–8
sex discrimination in immigration system, 354
shipping companies, responsibilities of, 75, 84, 86–7
'sole responsibility' for children, 158–9
South African citizens, 26
special voucher scheme, for UK passport-holders, 4, 44–7, 145, 352–3; and 1981 Nat. Act, 40
sponsorship declarations, 90–91, 171–2
stateless persons, 337–8; travel documents for, 209
students, 99–109; intention to leave of, 102–6, 108; and full-time study, 106; and 'adequate means', 106–7; and employment, 107–8, 191; extensions for, 108–9; extensions as trainees for, 109; applications to change category of, 188–9, 190
supervised departure, 250

Tanganyika, 3–4
tax-allowance claims, false, 157–8
teachers, 119, 120
temporary admission, 83–4, 274–6
temporary release, 276, 284
trainees, 109–10
transitional provisions in 1980 rules, 10
travel documents, 58–9, 67, 208–9; 'Convention travel documents', 333, 334–5; for stateless persons, 209, 338; *see also* passports, visitors' cards
Tribunal, *see* Immigration Appeals Tribunal

Uganda, 3–4, 26
UK citizenship, *see* citizenship of the UK and colonies
UK Council for Overseas Student Affairs, 99 n. 2, 396
UK Immigrants Advisory Service, 83, 85, 290, 310, 328, 393–4
UKIAS Refugee Unit, 338, 396
UK passport-holders (non-patrial), 3–4; acquisition of patriality by, 28, 31; and special voucher scheme, 44–7, 145, 352–3; in UK without voucher, 46–7; as visitors, 97; as students, 105; as returning residents, 182; and deportation, 223
'undesirable aliens', 2
United Nations High Commissioner for Refugees, 297, 311, 328, 329, 338

vaginal examinations, 77–8
variation of leave, 186–91, 202–4; general principles of, 187–8; changing category, 188–9; and deception, 189–90; permission to work after entry, 190, 191; appeals against refusals of v.o.l., 191–3, 291–2; successive applications, 194–5; abandoning application, 198–9; and 'old rules', 204–5; *see also* extensions
'visa nationals', 60–61, 66
visas, 59–61; *see also* entry clearance
visitors, 93–9; extensions for, 94; coming for medical treatment, 94–5; and intention to leave, 95–8; purpose of visit, 98–9; EEC nationals as, 99; extensions as trainees for, 109; applications to change category of, 188–9, 190
visitors' cards, 58–9
visitors' passports, 51
voluntary departure, 241, 251
voucher scheme, *see* special voucher scheme

Wilson Committee on Immigration Appeals, 5 n. 20, 290, 354–5
widow(er)s coming for settlement, 165–7
witnesses at appeals, 313, 314
wives; registration of, 21, 39; patrial, 31

wives and children: of students, 101–2, 191; of permit-free workers, 120, 131–2; of Commonwealth citizens with UK ancestry, 121, 131–2; of persons of independent means, 130, 131–2; of EEC nationals, 135–6, 137, 148; of Commonwealth citizens settled in UK on 1/1/73, 7, 143–4, 147; coming for settlement, 148–55 (wives), 155–64 (children), 171–2 (wives); applying for settlement while here temporarily (wives), 177; of returning residents, 181; and family deportations, 240–43
work permits, 65–6, 112–18; application for, 114–15; and entry into UK, 115–16; and settlement, 145
working holidaymakers, 121–2, 349
writers, 127–9; and settlement, 145; applications to change category, 189

x-ray examinations, 78, 158

Yellowlees Report on medical examinations, 78, 158

The Cobden Trust

The Cobden Trust is a registered charity, established in 1963 to undertake research and education work in the field of civil liberties. It seeks the protection and extension of civil liberties in the United Kingdom and has a two fold strategy to achieve this objective: research, into the causes of injustice, and education work, informing the public about their rights and responsibilities.

How you can help
While we are able to raise funds from charitable trusts and foundations, we depend also on generous public support. As a registered charity, the Trust can recover tax from the Inland Revenue on any covenanted donation. If you would like to help us in this way or would like further information, then please write for details to the Secretary, the Cobden Trust, 21 Tabard Street, London SE1 4LA.